Praise for *River in the Desert*

"Roberts' style is passionate, angry, and often very funny … the work of a writer in love with his subject." — ORIANA FALLACI

"Smart, energetic, hysterically funny … a worthy companion to the rich selection of English writers about Egypt." — THE LOS ANGELES TIMES

"… as intricate and vibrant as an Islamic carpet." — MACLEAN'S

"From its early pages, with quotes from such disparate sources as the ancient Greek historian Herodotus and the late mystic Gurdjieff, this travel book proves unconventional, highly entertaining, instructive and beautifully written. Roberts spent three months taking in the ambience of Egypt's great sites and cities, from the desert to Cairo and Alexandria and along the Nile to Luxor, Thebes and Aswan. His observations, punctuated by those of other writers who visited the country (such as Flaubert, Agatha Christie and Norman Mailer) reveal a well-stocked mind, a charming wit and sophisticated interest in people … The elegance and verve of his personalized and seductive account of this ancient culture's history, mythology and politics will likely prompt many readers to agree."
— PUBLISHERS WEEKLY

"Fine, quirky account of Roberts' recent travels through Egypt's teeming modern cities, Pharaonic monuments, ancient monasteries, and Edenic oases … In addition to visiting such sites as the temples of Luxor, Karnak, and Abu Simbel, the Monastery of St. Catherine in the Sinai desert, the burial chamber of the pyramid of Mycerinus (where he spends the night), and neon-and-Naugahyde Red Sea resorts, Roberts takes us to an eerie Sufi ceremony in the back streets of Cairo, to the crest of Mount Sinai (where bus loads of grumbling pilgrims await the dawn), and on a hot-air balloon flight over the Valley of the Kings … Roberts's knowledge of and affection for Egypt is palpable, but these qualities do not blind him to the inanities of the land. He traverses a desert on a camel called "Michael Jackson"; he wonders why a condom should have been named after Ramses, who reputedly sired 186 children; he speculates that the lack of conversational ability of a German mortician he meets may be "an occupational hazard." Informative and entertaining: Roberts is the sort of witty, knowledgeable, stimulating guide every armchair traveler hankers for but seldom finds." — KIRKUS REVIEWS

Praise for *Journey of the Magi*

"What a valuable book! At the very least, it is an engaging travelogue, and Roberts' account of his journey through Iran, Iraq, and Syria to retrace the steps of the Magi will easily hold an audience from beginning to end. But, more than a travelogue, it is a provocative invitation to reexamine the Zoroastrian background of Christianity, providing an occasion for serious reflection on the intersection of religion and politics in one of the most troubled regions on the planet."

— BOOKLIST

"An adventure story woven with strands of scholarship ... will miff the experts [and] delight general readers ... This is a laugh-out-loud travel book."

— MACLEAN'S

"Thought-provoking, laugh-provoking ... " — MARTIN AMIS

Praise for *A War Against Truth*

"I read Roberts's lacerating chronicle in a single night, couldn't stop. Despite the bitter humor and riveting eyewitness accounts of the Iraq tragedies, reading it is about as enjoyable as ripping off scabs, but it is so vivid and compelling that it is impossible to put down." — NOAM CHOMSKY

"A testament to the hideousness of modern warfare, and a sermon about 'a tragedy and a crime whose enormity in truth defies description or comprehension.'"

— THE GLOBE AND MAIL

"Roberts is a terrific writer and his account of being caught in the bombing ... is one of the most intense reading experiences imaginable." — OTTAWA CITIZEN

Paul William Roberts

RIVER
IN THE
DESERT

A MODERN TRAVELLER
IN ANCIENT EGYPT

RAINCOAST BOOKS

Vancouver

Copyright © 2006 by Paul William Roberts

Originally published in 1993 by Random House of Canada

Raincoast Books gratefully acknowledges the ongoing support of the Canada Council for the Arts, the British Columbia Arts Council and the Government of Canada through the Book Publishing Industry Development Program (BPIDP).

Front cover design by www.onethreefiveight.com
Interior design by Tannice Goddard

Library and Archives Canada Cataloguing in Publication

Roberts, Paul William
        River in the desert / Paul William Roberts.

ISBN 10 1-55192-963-5
ISBN 13 978-1-55192-963-7

        1. Roberts, Paul William—Travel—Egypt.   2. Egypt—Description and travel. I. Title.

DT56.2.R62 2006   916.204'55   C2005-906762-4

Raincoast Books
9050 Shaughnessy Street
Vancouver, British Columbia
Canada V6P 6E5
www.raincoast.com

Raincoast Books is committed to protecting the environment and to the responsible use of natural resources. We are working with suppliers and printers to phase out our use of paper produced from ancient forests. This book is printed with vegetable-based inks on 100% ancient-forest-free paper (100% post-consumer recycled), processed chlorine- and acid-free. For further information, visit our website at www.raincoast.com/publishing.

Printed in Canada by Friesens.

10 9 8 7 6 5 4 3 2 1

*For Constance and Dorothy, who put up with me for so long
and gave me so much. With love.*

ALSO BY PAUL WILLIAM ROBERTS

Empire of the Soul: Some Journeys in India

The Demonic Comedy: Some Detours in the Iraq of Saddam Hussein

Smokescreen: One Man Against the Underworld (with Norman Snider)

A War Against Truth: An Intimate Account of the Invasion of Iraq

Journey of the Magi: In Search of the Birth of Jesus

CONTENTS

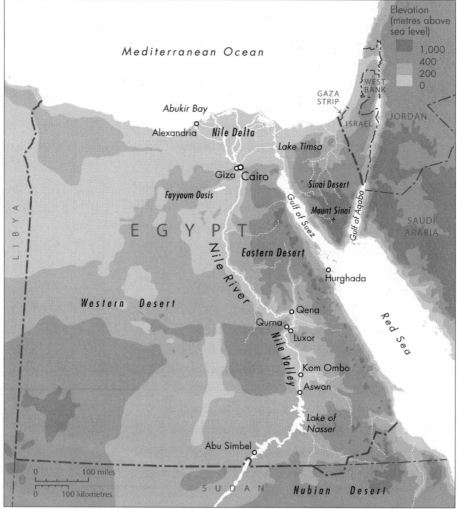

PREFACE

Concerning Egypt I will now speak at length, because nowhere are there so many marvellous things, nor in the whole world beside are there to be seen so many things of unspeakable greatness.

—HERODOTUS

Twenty-five hundred years after Herodotus visited Egypt, this statement is still true. Most of the monuments he gazed upon in wonder were as far away from his own time then as he is from ours now. The span of Egyptian history boggles the mind.

It clearly boggles the Western education system, too, for we learn little or nothing at school about the most potent and enduring civilization ever to have existed on this planet. When I first stood at the foot of the Great Pyramid, I realized with the shattering force of a revelation that I was back at The Beginning. The Greeks recognized ancient Egypt as the foundation of civilization. For some reason we want to give the Greeks this credit. It would have embarrassed them.

If this book encourages one reader to visit Egypt, it will have fulfilled its purpose entirely. The synthesis of several trips made over the last few years — although the trip is perfectly viable as a single visit — the following pages attempt to be also the book I wish I'd read before my first visit. It is a compilation of experiences, histories, anecdotes, feelings, and conversations. In visiting ancient Egypt, we also visit modern Egypt — a place more sinned against than sinning — and I have tried to correct many misconceptions about one of the most misunderstood countries on earth.

More than anything, the book is a gesture of gratitude, many kinds and levels of gratitude. There are very few places of which it can be said they are essential to visit. If I were to travel abroad only once in my life, Egypt would be my destination. Few fail to feel there still what Herodotus felt five hundred years before the Christian Era, that he had come home, returned to the beginning. In our beginnings are our ends.

ACKNOWLEDGEMENTS

This book could not have been written without the kindness and generosity of the Egyptian government and the Ontario Arts Council, both of which made impossibly expensive research possible. I owe a debt of gratitude also to Chris Wendland and Lufthansa German Airlines, whose service to Egypt and the Middle East is unrivalled in both quality and convenience. To Himo Mansour of Menatours I am greatly indebted for the efficiency and sophistication of his approach to tourism, and for that seemingly limitless fund of knowledge concerning the land of his ancestors that he is always willing to share generously with me and others. To John Anthony West, who became my friend during the writing, I owe all the understanding I may have gained regarding the real wonders of ancient Egypt; his erudition, insight, scholarship, and patience with fools are without equal. I also owe much to Douglas Pepper, not only for his faith, support, and friendship, but also for giving me an exceptional editor, Kathleen Richards, who made my words shape up or ship out. From my friend Nagui Ghali I received much input and was disabused of many romantic notions — even if the mountain had to come to Muhammad. Thanks to Marc Gabel, great friend and shaman of genius, I was able to see how much I was in Egypt compared to how much Egypt was in me. Thanks also to Frank Zingrone, dear friend and mentor, for some of the most illuminating conversations I've been privileged to enjoy. If it weren't for Marq de Villiers I might still be in Western Samoa; I thank him for his editorial prowess and his unfailing support over many years. Thanks also to John Fowles for gracious encouragement and resourceful introductions. The Royal Ontario Museum, the British Museum, the Metropolitan Museum of Art, the Field Museum, and the Egyptian Museum in Cairo all made a lonely job into a pleasure. And my wife, Tiziana, to whom I owe more than words can say, made a lonely life into something rich and full. Finally, I must thank my agent and dear friend, the late Peter Livingston. Without his tireless efforts none of this would exist. I wish he had lived to see it. I wish he had lived.

INTRODUCTION TO THE
NEW EDITION

Before the advent of American hegemony, Egypt was central to the Arab world. Apart from Israel, it now receives Washington's largest foreign "aid" handout, without which it simply could not survive. Though vast in area, it is largely desert with little arable land, nearly all of it along the banks of the Nile and in the Delta, where plantations that used to grow the world's finest cotton have now mostly been converted to grow food for a population that has doubled since 1993 when this book was first written. Surprisingly little else has changed. I reread this book, assuming I needed to update my picture of the contemporary social and political scene; I found, however — with the exception of a few personalities — that what I had originally written remained true, and if anything, more so now than it was then.

The regime of President Hosni Mubarak remains, with America's help, firmly in place. For those who oppose it — and their numbers have grown enormously — the system can be brutal in response. Human rights organizations have repeatedly decried the imprisonments without trial and the torture of dissidents, yet the Western media mostly ignore these reports, and the American media tend to regard Egypt as if it were a democracy. But hot winds of change are blowing across the Sahara. Thanks to the U.S.–British intervention in Iraq and the rhetoric of President George W. Bush on a theme of spreading "freedom" and "democracy" in the Middle East and West Asia, Egyptians are on the whole now determined that their next leader will be freely and fairly elected by popular vote.

The real test of President Bush's doctrine will come when and if Egypt elects a government dominated by the Islamist Muslim Brotherhood, whose influence among the professional classes, as well as over the rural poor and the millions of unemployed in Cairo's shantytowns, has grown exponentially in the past decade. Although Egyptians would not wish theocratic rule, a hard-line Islamist government would almost certainly incite alarm in Israel, with which Egypt shares a border. It would also challenge what Washington likes to call "America's legitimate foreign interests." The main U.S. interest in Egypt and the source of its strategic importance is of course the Suez Canal, without which the ceaseless flow of tankers bearing oil from the Gulf to Western industrial states and the U.S. would be obliged to make a long, expensive and somewhat perilous voyage around the Horn of Africa. When Egypt's first president, Nasser, closed the canal — an action largely designed to demonstrate for other newly independent Arab states the illusory nature of their hard-won independence — the skies over Port Said were almost instantly filled with British and French paratroopers spearheading the invasion force sent to wrest control of Egypt's canal away from Egypt.

For Arabs, Pax Americana is regarded as the culmination of the Crusades, their last stand. They are seen to be a beaten, humiliated, reviled people, presented by Hollywood, if at all, in the form of cruelly insulting stereotypes worthy of Der Stürmer. Like the Sharif in *Lawrence of Arabia*, they dream of the gardens in Cordoba, where there were three miles of street lighting when all of Europe lay in darkness. A millennium ago, Arab civilization was the glory of the world, its innovative triumphs in mathematics, chemistry, engineering, medicine, music, and architecture represented the summit of human achievement. Without them there would have been no Renaissance. Even Western classical music could not have developed as it did, since all the instruments in our orchestras owe their origin to Turkish and Arabic sources.

No other ethnic group has contributed so much to our own civilization as the Arabs, but the debt has been forgotten or ignored.

I make no secret of my deep, abiding love for the Arabs and their culture. I find them an extraordinary people, generous, graceful, intelligent, and patient. Nowhere is this profound grace more evident than at Al-Azhar in Cairo, the world's oldest university, where some of the finest Arab minds continue to be educated in a manner so gravely traditional it makes Oxford or Cambridge look like experimental schools. This is the heart of Sunni Muslim orthodoxy, the place to which all Arabs turn for determination of the start of Ramadan, the holy month. It is also where the future direction of Sunni Islam is, albeit slowly, determined. With the fall of Baghdad, which has historically shared with Cairo the title of "Intellectual Centre of the Arab World" (once it was the whole world), all eyes are turned toward Egypt — and Egyptians are conscious of this. Indeed, they view leadership of the Arabs as something of a natural right, and Cairo as the obvious capital of a future United States of Arabia. While unlikely, for reasons Boutros Boutros-Ghali explains in this book, the dream of pan-Arabism is still very much alive in Egypt, perhaps because it offers the only viable Arab solution to Egypt's chronic problems of poverty and over-population. It is because of this that they will choose their new leadership carefully, yet I doubt if the final outcome will be one designed to appease both Washington and the other Arab states.

The most promising single development in Egypt since I wrote this book is the construction of a canal that extends all the way from Lake Nasser at Aswan nearly as far as Alexandria, which has facilitated an irrigation project nearly doubling the country's arable land by reclaiming desert. The land that has known marvels of engineering for 5,000 years — possibly much more — has seen little need to trumpet this achievement, yet it is considerable, and is, I believe, the beginning of what will one day culminate in the reclamation of the entire Sahara, which was, after all, fertile savanna ten millennia ago.

As always, modern Egypt and its multitudinous woes exist alongside remains of the greatest civilization ever seen on earth, and these are the reasons no one ought to miss an opportunity to visit the country. No matter how many times I go there, I never cease to find myself in tingling awe at the sight of the pyramids and vast temples that still stand as testament to the genius of men who died a thousand years before the birth of King Solomon, and lived in a civilization compared with which our own and every other throughout history seem but a paltry insubstantial thing.

The tide flowing against orthodox Egyptology, whose origins and first waves are recounted here, continues to gain converts willing to look differently and more deeply at the wonders of ancient Egypt and attempt to understand the minds responsible for them. A fine English translation of Schwaller de Lubicz' masterpiece on symbolist Egypt, *Le Temple du L'homme (The Temple of Man)*, which contains the only explication of ancient Egyptian philosophy ever attempted, was published a few years ago. And the man single-handedly responsible for challenging the legitimacy of orthodox Egyptology and establishing a rival discipline, John Anthony West, has successfully kept alive his argument for re-dating the construction of the Great Sphinx to circa 10,500 B.C. The whole argument for Egyptian civilization being a legacy from an earlier and now "lost" civilization is given in full here, and has also gained much ground since *River in the Desert* was published. While John Anthony West's work remains, in its scholarly integrity and elegance, by far the most important in the field, there have also been significant contributions by people like Robert Bauval, Graham Hancock and Rand Flem-Ath.

The cultural heritage of Iraq has all but gone now, trashed by the remnants of Saddam's army and by U.S. and U.K. troops. It is a crime of the first order, perhaps unparalleled in its wanton mindlessness, and stands as a grim harbinger of what could easily happen in Egypt. The country's monuments are already endangered enough by the toxicity of modern industrial air and the rising water table since the Aswan Dam's construction. The tombs on the west bank at Luxor are now frequently closed to protect them from the damage caused by humidity from tourists' perspiration. They may have to close permanently, but that is a hard decision for a country whose sole industry is tourism. The money spent on the Iraq War would have been more than sufficient to build special protective screens for the remains of Egypt's glory, and enough maybe even to wipe out AIDS in all of Africa too. One likes to think that a planet free of warring politicians might realize its responsibility to generations yet unborn for handing them a place in better shape than it was when we acquired it. But global big business has no use for culture. It has no use for us either, except as consumers; and it has no use for the planet, except as a warehouse of resources to plunder and sell. I still find terms like "liberal" and "idealist" complimentary — in America it seems now they are insults — and I find myself dreaming with increasing frequency of how things could be, of a world without borders and governments, ruled by philosophers not merchants. In such a world the treasures of ancient Egypt would be cherished above all other treasures, and every attempt would be made to preserve and restore them. Because we do not own them; we have merely borrowed them from our children and their children in turn.

The ancient Egyptians believed so profoundly in the virtue of their civilization that they built its monuments to last forever. To see the extraordinary extent of what still does remain is to become convinced that these ancient people have something to teach us still, something we have all but lost entirely in our pursuit of material gains, something we desperately need to rediscover if we are to avoid engineering our own extinction. As the second greatest predator in all of history, humans ought to remind ourselves of the fate that befell our reptilian predecessor, which was too greedy and too big for its own good. Tyrannosaurus Rex would have made a far more apt emblem for the American Empire than the eagle, which is still not quite extinct.

We all have the same hopes and dreams, whether in the alleys of Cairo or the malls of America, and they are generally modest ones involving the quality of life and the future of our children. Our common humanity shines out above the miasma of money and politics, and it is to this that we should cling. Visit Egypt while you can, for it may not always be there to visit. What it offers is far more than the spectacle of extraordinary ruins, old stuff in cases, dead people wrapped like parcels; for what you will see, and what will abide with you long afterwards, is a glimpse of the limitless potential in human beings for both aspiring to and creating a better world. The Old Kingdom Egyptians built one; we can build one. Knowing it was done means it can still be done. I have no idea why we are not on the job right now.

PWR, Toronto 2006

AUTHOR'S NOTE

Since ancient Egyptian chronologies are still hotly debated, varying in some cases by as much as fifteen hundred years, I have tried to avoid giving dates except when absolutely necessary. With the names of the pharaohs, I have used the most common forms generally encountered, avoiding alternative throne names to spare the reader confusion. Just as Prince Charles is known as the Prince of Wales, he is also the Duke of Cornwall and much else besides. Here he would always be the Prince of Wales. I have attempted to standardize the transliteration of Arabic words, but when quoting another writer have retained that writer's spelling. I apologize for any irritation this may cause.

CHAPTER ONE

CAIRO: TEA IN THE SAHARA WITH MICHAEL JACKSON

Take the understanding of the East and the knowledge of the West — and then seek.

— GURDJIEFF, *VIEWS FROM THE REAL WORLD*

Arriving in a "developing nation" is becoming increasingly hazardous. It's got something to do with the fact that "developing" is what the country would like to be doing, not what it is doing. Avoiding disintegration and utter ruin is an ambitious aspiration in over half of the countries on the planet these days. A "developing nation" is a far more ominous prospect than is a "Third World country." Will it, you wonder, sitting in your airplane entertaining apocalyptic jet lag, have "developed" an airport, for instance?

Landing in Cairo is thus a very pleasant surprise. For a start, the *new* terminal looks like a giant suite in the Trump Tower. And instead of the brutal interrogations and muggings you usually endure at the hands of North American Customs and Immigration storm troopers, I was greeted with astounding courtesy, then ushered through a couple of brief formalities, and — scarcely ten minutes after landing — found myself seated in a snazzy limo hurtling off down a highway so modern I wondered if I'd flown to the future by mistake. It was a cool, starry night. Where were the crowded, boiling, dusty souks?

By midnight I had checked into room 715 at the Ramses Hilton, then the newest and tallest of all the new tall buildings in Cairo. I drew back the curtains, stepped out onto my balcony, and gazed down at the broad, dark expanse of Nile curving away beneath me. A vast skein of stars hung far above the river, diamond studs stuck in the shimmering black silk of night.

Across on Gezira, the Nile's island, ten thousand other lights twinkled. Down below, the Corniche hummed and hooted, teeming with cars and with people out to stroll or loiter in the cool breezes that mercifully float off the river even during the hottest months.

Cairo is a vast city, the largest in Africa, with over fourteen million souls, each face evidence of a meeting place of worlds — Africa, Europe, Arabia, and·Asia. It's a sort of cross between Paris and Bombay, glittering and grandly elegant at night, throbbing, chaotic, and sprawling by day. At dawn and dusk, those periods of mystery and transition, it can seem one of the most vibrant and exciting cities in the world.

There is something curious about them, these famous pyramids,
the more one looks at them, the bigger they become.
—GUSTAVE FLAUBERT, LETTER FROM EGYPT, 1849

1:30 A.M. How can you sleep on the edge of wonder? No one else was. It was still Ramadan, the Muslim month of fasting, and the streets were thronged with people walking off the heavy meals that would have to see them through the next long day, until the sun once more set over the minarets and the muezzin announced that Allah would let them eat again.

The wide, dusty tree-lined boulevard that leads out of Cairo to the untidy suburb of Giza is quiet. Outside the Blow-Up Disco a few men in *gelabias* and turbans appear to be arguing but are only talking emphatically in Arabic — the Cairene form, a high-speed, guttural burst at maximum volume. There is a mist around the streetlamps as my taxi careers past stray camels and cars shrouded with cotton dustcovers. A sense of excitement builds.

"See, pyramids," the driver says, offering me a fifth Cleopatra Mild.

I don't see at first, squinting into yellow haze. Then I make out a massive familiar form in the distance, which melts back into the heavy gloom as we turn off the main drag and climb a smaller, winding road. The battered car, with its shaggy fake-fur dashboard and dangling worry beads, comes to an abrupt halt in a desolate spot alongside a colossal crumbling wall.

"Where are we?" I ask. The driver gestures with his hand at the dust and the rocks.

Warily I climb out, and, as I slam the creaking door behind me, realize the wall extends up into the night to an invisible point impossibly far above. *The Great Pyramid of Cheops.* The words themselves inspire awe. A manmade mountain of stone built four thousand years ago — perhaps more, perhaps *much* more — on a scale yet to be equalled. The sight of it sounds a chord in my heart, and I feel tears running down my cheeks. Nothing prepares you for the towering majesty of the last surviving Wonder of the ancient world. It looks designed to outlast every work of humans that ever was or will be. Instantly it is clear why so many for so long have felt it must mean something: *two and a half million stones, each with an average weight of two and a half tons* ... But that is somehow not the point.

> *For it is no easy task to realise, however imperfectly, the duration of six or seven thousand years; and the Great Pyramid, which is supposed to have been some four thousand two hundred and odd years old at the time of the birth of Christ, is now in its seventh millennary ... It was as if one had been snatched up for an instant to some vast height overlooking the plains of Time, and had seen the centuries mapped out beneath one's feet.*
>
> —AMELIA B. EDWARDS, 1877

If, as Goethe suggested, architecture is frozen music, then Egypt contains some of the greatest symphonies in the world: compositions of soaring genius that mirror the grandeur of the universe and its Creator. Like the great cathedrals of Europe or the religious complexes of the Maya or the Incas, these structures are gestures of the spirit, their continuing existence alone attesting to man's affinity with the Eternal — even in the soulless wastes of the close of the second millennium A.D.

From the dense shadows at the pyramid's base a bleary-eyed man in a tracksuit and a turban like a large bandage appears. "Country?" he asks. I tell him. "Canada Dry," he says. "No, it's wet," I reply. He shakes my hand warmly, adding, "Welcome, friend. You are welcome here." I thank him, wondering where all this is leading. "Pyramid," he explains, pointing up at it. I nod. "*Great* Pyramid," he then confides, patting a block of stone the size of my kitchen. "*Very* old." Again I thank him. "You, me, climb?" he inquires, looking up, up, a certain foxy challenge in his voice.

"I never realized how big it was" is all I can say, still wiping away tears.

"*Very* big," he assures me. "*Very* old."

At this point, as if on cue, two other, plumper men appear — his agents perhaps — and we negotiate. The fee for the proposed climb is initially steeper than the pyramid itself. "Special for *you*," the more roguish-looking of the two "agents" keeps telling me. "Special for *you*, not for *any* tourist peoples." A deal is finally struck — ten Egyptian pounds, about five dollars or so and a good day's wage in most of Egypt.

Seemingly content, the "agents" retreat back into the night, and I am left with my escort up the Great Pyramid of Cheops, Sayeed. With the agility of a mountain goat on Valium, he hauls himself up onto the first block in the southeast corner, beckoning me to follow.

We begin to climb. I soon feel like a mouse clambering up a gigantic ruined staircase, slithering through dust, seeking out convenient nooks and crannies, hoisting myself up toward the great dome of stars above this yellow-brick mountain.

The thing about a pyramid, when you're clinging to its side, is that its peak always looks about twenty feet away, even when it isn't — and it usually isn't. After fifty minutes or so, elation has given way to terminal exhaustion.

My leg muscles are trembling in spasm, my heart is bouncing off my ribs like a mad caged bird, I'm gasping for breath and sweating profusely in the cool desert air. "Come," Sayeed keeps saying. "Come."

Finally we're on the summit, five hundred feet above the Giza plateau. I roll across the irregular surface, propping myself against the last great block. Sayeed smiles, offering me a cigarette. It's the last thing I want, gazing up at constellations, which seem unnaturally close and as hopelessly enigmatic as the symphony in rock fanning out in flawless symmetry beneath us. The apex of the pyramid is missing; it was believed by some to have been solid gold capped with some kind of precious stone. I stand where the eye sits upon the pyramid those Freemason founders placed so cryptically on the American dollar bill.

I am not the first person to climb the pyramid. I notice what Flaubert noticed, and wrote about: "One is irritated by the number of imbeciles' names written everywhere; on top of the Great Pyramid there is a certain Buffard, 79 rue Saint Martin, wallpaper manufacturer; in black letters; an English fan of Jenny Lind's has written her name." Weeks later I was to notice Rimbaud's graffito carved into the Temple of Luxor.

"I five childrens, me," Sayeed suddenly volunteers. "All strong." He rubs his belly, and I know what is required.

"*Shukron,*" I tell him — "Thank you" — handing over a little baksheesh, that mysterious extra all transactions in Egypt seem to need. The top of the Great Pyramid is a good place to ask for it; after all, we have to go back down.

The return journey is not the journey up. My legs are shot, muscles quivering uncontrollably at every step. When I look below — far, far below — it suddenly dawns on me how very dangerous all this is. One wrong step and I'll bounce from stone to stone all the way to the bottom. And that's a long way.

The fear is tangible — perhaps a price one must pay for trampling over unknown millennia of mystery. Dust, sweat, a pounding heart, lungs valiantly pumping. A step six feet down into utter blackness. A loose stone, my fingernails cracking as I clutch wildly for support. It seems much farther going down, eerily so. Flaubert was right. So was Florence Nightingale, that intrepid soul, who observed on her trip, also in the 1840s, that the pyramids looked "as if they would wear out the air, boring holes in it all day long."

I flop from the last stone onto flat rock — ground, sweet ground. Ushered by Sayeed into a hut like a small garden shed, I find more people within than I would have thought it could contain, all huddled around a sulphurous oil heater. Among them I notice Sayeed's "agents."

"All good men," the fattest and clearly most senior man announces, gesturing at the hunched forms with their disastrous teeth and hopeful smiles. Beyond him, through an unpaned window, an edge of the pyramid climbs at its faultless angle. Here are its current keepers, cringing at the sight of my camera, offering tea and cigarettes instead of initiation into the mysteries. What we have been doing is obviously not legal. It is hard to say which has decayed most over the centuries, mankind or the Great Pyramid of Cheops.

> *It is truly a house of initiation in every sense, but that is not to say that the Great Pyramid was never used for anything else. Theodolite it may have been, astronomical observatory, in one sense or another, it almost certainly was. And there can scarcely be any doubt that pyramid-construction — even if not that of the Great Pyramid itself — lay at the very basis of the sudden rise of Egyptian civilisation in the third millennium B.C. Indeed, of all the various subsidiary theories proposed, only the long-familiar tombic, treasury and granary theories seem decidedly unlikely.*
>
> —PETER LEMESURIER, *THE GREAT PYRAMID DECODED*

Before the Battle of the Pyramids in 1798, Napoleon Bonaparte addressed his troops: "Soldiers, consider that from the summit of these pyramids, forty centuries look down upon you." Time itself, it was said, feared the pyramids. Originally encased in polished white limestone — which must have been a staggering sight, a vast gleaming crystal — the Great Pyramid has presided over Egypt for as long as we know, indifferent to every conqueror, indifferent to the long centuries themselves. It was already an ancient monument when the biblical Abraham visited Egypt, as the texts suggest he did; and it was still there when Napoleon defeated the Mamelukes in its shadow at the close of the eighteenth century.

Bringing with his army a team of scholars and scientists, Napoleon helped usher in the modern wave of interest in ancient Egypt that, much assisted by the discovery of Tutankhamen's tomb in the 1920s, has continued to the present day. Between the seventh century, when the Arabs who conquered Egypt in the name of Islam stripped the casing stones from the pyramids to build the mosques of Cairo, and the Renaissance, the monuments of Giza lay unnoticed beneath drifting sands at the desert's edge. It is hard to understand how. Perhaps their essential mystery and all that it still entails is an answer. What are they? What are they for? What do they mean?

The existence of the Giza pyramids is sheer effrontery, even to modern man. The reaction they elicit has often been hostility. Even Herodotus, writing five centuries before Christ about something as far away from his own time as we are from him, confidently proffers old and unsubstantiated gossip as truth.

Cheops' supposed ego has been a problem for many writers — as if the Great Pyramid were some ultimate macho threat. Such a bastard was this Cheops, according to Herodotus, that, short of cash for his ambitious building projects at one point, he made his daughter work as a prostitute to help him out. Upset but dutifully compliant, she asked of all her clients a further fee besides what she was expected to turn over to Dad — a block of stone with which to build her own pyramid. Hers still stands at the foot of her father's more substantial effort. Is the story true? Well, there are more than a hundred thousand blocks of stone in the pyramid associated with Cheops' daughter ...

Like everything written about the Great Pyramid, nothing in Herodotus can be proven, though much can be disproven. As Peter Lemesurier points out in one of the most recent books on the subject, the most common assumption, that the pyramids were tombs, is the most easily disproven. Even Herodotus, the earliest historian to write about the Great Pyramid, records he was told categorically by the Egyptian priesthood that Cheops, or Khufu, as he's also called, was never buried in the pyramid at all. He was apparently interred on a secret, subterranean island beneath the waters of the Nile. If he'd wanted his tomb to avoid attention, you can't help but ask, why would he have constructed the largest building on earth to house it? If the body was never there, that might explain why the Arabs who broke into the pyramid's upper passageways some twelve centuries after Herodotus found that it *still* wasn't there. The sarcophagus was empty. This could mean that the mummified body had been removed, either for safekeeping or by robbers looking for precious objects often wrapped in the mummy shrouds. But Egyptian sarcophagi were often buried empty. In 1954, for example, an alabaster coffer was discovered in the tomb chamber of Sekhemket's unfinished pyramid at Saqqara; it had been carefully sealed, although it was found to be empty when opened. The same is true of the sarcophagus of Cheops' mother, Queen Hetepheres, discovered at Giza.

Some pyramids *were* tombs, but the Great Pyramid is very different from any other pyramid in Egypt. Even that first night, as I contemplated the astounding structure for the first time, something made my bones tingle. Thinking about the story of a king who died, of a corpse placed in a tomb whose door was sealed with stone, of a god whose body subsequently disappeared from the tomb without a trace, I couldn't help but feel how uncannily similar it was to the tale told about a certain man from Galilee.

> The average Oriental regards the European traveller as a
> Croesus, therefore as fair game, and feels justified in pressing
> upon him with a perpetual demand for bakshish, which simply
> means "a gift." The number of beggars is enormous, but bakshish
> should never be given either to adults or children, except for
> services rendered or to the aged and crippled; and the government
> appeals to the tourist by public placards not to encourage the
> habit of begging ...
>
> — BAEDEKER'S *EGYPT*, 1929

I've seen more beggars during a ten-minute walk in downtown Toronto than I saw throughout my whole three months in Egypt. Since Prime Minister Gamal Abdel Nasser's revolution in the mid-1950s and the subsequent reforms and refinements of his successors, the government of Egypt and the principles of Islam have taken care of the poor, even if it has been, as I was often told, at the expense of everyone else.

～ɔ

The Eighth International Congress of Orientalists was held in Stockholm during the summer of 1889. The Egyptian delegation travelled to Sweden via Paris, where the members stopped over to visit the World Exhibition. The four Egyptians spent a week exploring the French capital, climbing Alexandre Eiffel's new tower, which, as they noted, was twice the height of the Great Pyramid. In the meticulously laid out parks and pavilions of the exhibition, they inspected all manner of merchandise and the latest machinery on display.

Only one sour note sounded in their report. Amid all this orderly grandeur, they discovered the Egyptian exhibit, a winding medieval street with overarching houses and even a mosque, built by the French. "It was intended," a member of the Egyptian delegation wrote, "to resemble the old aspect of Cairo and so carefully executed that even the paint on the buildings was made dirty." The painstaking reproduction of a Cairo bazaar was complete even down to the genuine chaos resulting from donkey rides. At one franc a pop, the attraction created such havoc among the throng of visitors that the director of the exhibition had to order them restricted to a certain number each hour.

All of this thoroughly disgusted the Egyptians, but their final embarrassment was entering the mosque to find it was only a facade. "Its external form as a mosque was all there was," the visitor noted. "As for the interior, it had been set up as a coffee house, where Egyptian girls performed dances with young males, and dervishes whirled." After this experience the visitors avoided the exhibit.

When they reached Stockholm for the congress, however, they found worse things in store. They themselves became the exhibit. Invited to participate in the proceedings as scholars, they spoke in their own language and were openly derided. A delegate attending from Oxford was even moved to write, "I have heard nothing so unworthy of a sensible man as ... the whistling howls emitted by an Arabic student of Al-Azhar of Cairo. Such exhibitions at Congresses are mischievous and degrading."

There are many other examples of the way Middle Eastern visitors found themselves treated by nineteenth-century Europeans. Rifa 'a Rafi al-Tahtawi, an Egyptian scholar who spent five years in Paris in the 1820s, observed, "One of the characteristics of the French is to stare and get excited at everything new." In another book he elaborated further: "One of the beliefs of the Europeans is that the gaze has no effect."

Our failure to understand the Orient, to impose upon it a false picture based upon our unwillingness to penetrate its reality, continues to this day and is best exemplified by the reactions of tourists. To many, Egypt is merely a colourful, charming, but distastefully chaotic and dirty display laid on by primitive people for their amusement. Of course, with five thousand years of continuous civilization behind them, the Egyptians have a very different perspective of the world. It is largely their patience we do not comprehend, and it is our Western impatience that threatens them.

A senior Egyptian cabinet minister remarked to me, "You in the developed countries are increasingly making those of us in the developing nations feel that there is no place for us on this planet." A poignant statement.

Many times, President Hosni Mubarak himself repeated this fear, adding that the removal of the Iron Curtain between East and West may result in the coming down of another Iron Curtain between north and south. Egypt, as Westernized as it is, compared with most of its neighbours, identifies itself with the south, with those African countries that contain the vital sources of the Nile, and with its Arab coreligionists. As aid is diverted from the south to help rebuild Eastern Europe, this identification will only intensify.

Egypt has immense economic problems — that is the first thing anyone there will tell you — and the Egyptians are attempting to deal with them as best they can. One cannot help feeling that if we in the West had their problems, we'd have already been crushed by them.

As I drove through the midday heat of Cairo, past skyscrapers and donkey carts carrying watermelons, from cloverleaf intersections through crowded medieval bazaars where vendors squatted beside sacks of spice,

I thought of all this. I thought of the patience that is such a noticeable trait in the Egyptian personality, and of the odd on-again-off-again unity that persists within the astonishing diversity of the Arab world. It's been said that Egypt is the only true Arab nation state, that the rest are just tribes with flags; but that was not and is not my experience. I went to Egypt searching for its past, but I found myself increasingly tangled up in its present, even its future. The age of the pharaohs seemed less and less distant from the turbulent present. The descendants of the pyramid builders seemed just as intent on making their presence admired and respected by their neighbours, using ideas and diplomacy instead of stone.

The last [pyramid] appears small compared with the other two,
but viewed at a short distance and to the exclusion of these it
excites in the imagination a singular oppression, and cannot be
contemplated without painfully affecting the sight.

—ABDEL LATIF, TWELFTH CENTURY

Had I read the writings of Latif, that observant physician, beforehand, I might not have been so keen to spend a night in the inner chamber of the Mycerinus Pyramid. Through the magic of baksheesh, however, I arranged just that, finding myself a little after midnight walking unsteadily down the narrow entrance shaft with a blanket and a flashlight, hearing the heavy door slammed and locked behind me. The Egyptian Antiquities Organisation doesn't like you doing this sort of thing; it was even harder to bribe my way into the Great Pyramid.

The passageway descends steeply for 130 feet, straight through bedrock at the base of the pyramid. Walking horizontally for a further 65 feet, you reach a chamber at the centre of the structure, then descend to a second one cut out of bedrock and lined with granite. This is presumed to have been the burial chamber; and here I settled down to spend a restless night.

Not much is known about Mycerinus, or Menkaurē, as he is sometimes called, though Herodotus recounts numerous legends, one of which tells that the pharaoh was informed by an oracle in his youth that he had only six years to live. To outwit the prophecy, he ordered that lamps be kept burning day and night, making night day and extending the six years to twelve. I could have used one of those lamps down there.

The "smallest" of the three pyramids in the Giza complex, Mycerinus' is still one of the largest buildings on earth, over 350 feet across at its base. Lying there, watching my flashlight fade against the twinkling red granite of what looked like a Romanesque barrel-vault ceiling, I could feel the oppressive weight of those millions of tons of stone above me.

Booming silence. Utter darkness: a terminal night unlike anything outside a sensory-deprivation tank. I coughed merely to assert my existence, hearing the odd, powerful resonance of sound within so much rock. Hard and warm, this rock that surrounded me smelled profoundly of old sweat, old bodies, old earth, and new urine. At one point I felt I was in the heart of some vast, foul, and ancient machine, at the focal point of raw and massive energies, complex alien designs.

Breathe slowly, I told myself, and do not panic: You are buried as surely and securely as any pharaoh. Yet it did not feel like a tomb — more like a place of fierce initiation, an opening into Mystery. The experience was both unnervingly thrilling and draining.

I must have slept, deep and dreamlessly, for above me, beyond a jaundiced electric beam, my "host" suddenly stood, all teeth and turban, anxiously urging me to leave before his superiors came on duty. It was not yet dawn outside — the Hour of the Wolf, when deaths most often happen — yet the countless lights burning in the steel-black sky all but blinded me.

> *My duty was now to take the shortest road to Egypt with the*
> *news, and the knowledge gained that evening in the palm wood*
> *grew and blossomed in my mind into a thousand branches,*
> *laden with fruit and shady leaves, beneath which I sat and*
> *half-listened and saw visions, while the twilight deepened,*
> *and the night …*
>
> —T. E. LAWRENCE, *SEVEN PILLARS OF WISDOM*

Emerging from the warmth of the pyramid into the cool air of the sleeping desert, I found my man, Mahmoud the camel driver, waiting, as arranged, with a camel called Michael Jackson and an Arab stallion with no name. Looking haughtily unenthusiastic about the whole business, Michael Jackson knelt on his bony front legs, allowing me to hoist myself onto his hump.

As the rosy tentacles of dawn clasped an increasingly blue dome of enormous sky, the three pyramids materialized far behind us, looking like a painted backdrop through the morning haze. Michael Jackson lurched and swayed beneath me.

"Like sheep, no?" said Mahmoud. Right: ships of the desert. "Come," he urged, trotting ahead. "We take some tea soon with Colonel Qaddafi. Yes?"

I hadn't thought of getting to Tripoli this way, but there was now indeed nothing but two thousand miles of sand between us and the good colonel in Libya. Soon the sand stretched to the horizon on all sides, so soaked in sunlight that it glowed yellow even when the sun was obscured by clouds. Rocks, sand, shells, proving the area was once a seabed: that's all there is in the Sahara al-Gharbiya Desert. Besides the mighty silence.

"It make me happy here," Mahmoud confided, patting his stallion. "This all for me. What is money? Money is sheet?" He smiled, revealing the decaying dental nightmare in his mouth. He was eighteen or so — he wasn't certain — with a wife, two children, one camel, and a horse to support.

Around noon we stopped, literally in the middle of nowhere, so Michael Jackson could eat the fodder he'd been carrying and Mahmoud could make some mint tea in a jagged and filthy tin, building a small fire with dried camel dung and sticks also plucked from one of the capacious camel bags.

"You like?" he asked, gesturing at the wilderness. I nodded. The mirage circling our horizons made it seem as if we were on an island set in a shimmering, lonely ocean.

With the immense solitude came an immense peace. The bobbing, hypnotic pace, the caressing warmth of the wind and sun: I nearly fell asleep, all but falling off. Mahmoud laughed; I laughed. It suddenly seemed we'd been ancient travellers crossing this desert together since the beginning of time. If we'd emerged into the twelfth century, I wouldn't have been surprised.

Night swooped out of the sky with terrifying suddenness. We made camp next to a useful dune. Dinner was bread and dates around another little fire, literally shit-hot with camel dung. Huddled in blankets by the dying embers as the desert air cooled drastically through 20 degrees, Mahmoud attempted to play disco hits on a battered set of small panpipes, but the plaintive tiny notes seemed as lonely as the blazing stars isolated in that great black mystery above us.

"You know some song?" he asked.

Michael Jackson burped in his sleep. I shook my head — a useless gesture in the dark — reciting instead the poem by T. E. Lawrence: "I loved you, so I drew these tides of men into my hands and wrote my will across the sky in stars / to earn you Freedom, the seven-pillared worthy house, that your eyes might be shining for me / When we came."

"Yes," said Mahmoud, doubtfully.

"Lawrence," I told him. "You know Lawrence of Arabia?"

"He make record?"

"No. That's probably where he went wrong."

"I like too much Michael Jackson," Mahmoud announced. "That's why I name camel after heem."

He proceeded to pipe out an atonal version of "Billie Jean." I lay back, feeling the planet was my pharaonic ship of millions of years, ensnared by a net of starlight.

The night was chillingly cold but beautiful beyond words. When I awoke, the wind whispering in my ear, Mahmoud was curled up behind me, one arm draped around my shoulders for warmth.

Late the next day, as the shabby outskirts of Giza and the world finally reappeared, I had half a mind to turn Michael Jackson around and hope the kettle was still boiling in Tripoli.

To amuse the crowd, Mohammed Ali's jester took a woman in a Cairo bazaar one day, set her on the counter of a shop, and coupled with her publicly while the shopkeeper calmly smoked his pipe ... On the road from Cairo to Shubra some time ago a

young fellow had himself publicly buggered by a large monkey
— as in the story above, to create a good opinion of himself and
make people laugh.

—GUSTAVE FLAUBERT, LETTER FROM EGYPT, 1849

Such scenes as Flaubert describes are unthinkable in modern Cairo. So is the sexual jamboree he appears to have enjoyed in brothels all over Egypt. Today, even belly dancers are considered highly risqué; the clubs that employ them are occasionally targeted for harassment or worse by fundamentalist Muslims. *Playboy* magazine is still banned.

With Ali, a young government employee who had been married just a month, I tried to discuss sex. We were visiting the Hadika Al-Khaldin fair in Cairo's Al-Darasa area one evening. The fair was a rippling lake of light and colourful tents packed with families out to enjoy the cool of a Ramadan evening.

As we threw hoops in an attempt to win a bottle of Palmolive dish detergent he said, "I never knew a woman before my wife." Hadn't he wanted to? "Oh yes, of course. But it is not possible. A woman here must remain pure or she is nothing. No man will marry her." He was always looking at attractive women, I noticed. Did he love his wife? "She is my wife," he said, fishing with a rod, line, and eyelet in a bucket of numbered tags with hooks. "She will give me many children. I will love my children." He won a plastic dish.

Farther on, a man on a tiny stage emblazoned with huge lurid images of a wizard-eyed character in a turban attempted to hypnotize a rabbit with his fingers. Ragged and hardly more than eighteen years old, the man widened his bloodshot black eyes and held the rabbit with one hand while stabbing the air near its head with two grimy fingers. Beside him, two girls decked out in garish synthetic veils tinkling with fake gold piastres kept giggling. Finally the rabbit went stiff and the man produced two long thin black snakes from a filthy sack, placing them around the creature's body. But the rabbit was having none of this. To the hysterical amusement of the girls, the rabbit kept emerging in terror from its trance, easily and instantly shaking off the snakes. The hypnotist shouted angrily at the girls, who hid their mouths behind hennaed hands. He went through his "ritual" again, this time stilling the rabbit long enough to wrap one snake around its neck and the other, longer one several times around its palpitating torso before it shook off the trance and wriggled free again. The crowd by now was losing interest.

The hypnotist suddenly lunged at the nearest giggling girl, slapping her face a resounding blow that turned laughter to tears. This amused the bystanders far more than the act had done, besides tearing open her blouse to reveal a brief glimpse of small, full brown breasts mottled with grime and sweat. The other girl just laughed harder. The hypnotist picked up the rabbit once more and rolled his eyes.

Ali stared at the crying girl, who was carefully concealing herself and touching her stinging face with exaggerated gestures of pain. Perhaps it was all part of the act? A girl like that would be easy to seduce, no? I inquired. "They are dirty … down here" — Ali pointed at his crotch. "No one want a girl like that … Also, they are with the *zaar*. They have bad powers. Very dangerous."

The *zaar* was a spirit cult I'd heard of from a friend. But I thought it existed only in the villages of northern Sudan. According to Ali, it was widespread in Cairo among working-class women, who used its rituals to gain power over men. Did he then believe that women should not have power over men? Looking profoundly serious, he quoted the Koran, Sura IV: 34: "Men have authority over women because Allah has made the one superior to the other, and because they spend their wealth to maintain them."

Did he believe this? "It is different now," he said. "But most men still believe this in their hearts." His wife worked, he told me — also for the government — but he did not like the idea of her being around other men. Economic necessity dictated that she work; he would prefer that she stay home. It turned out she was more qualified than he — he'd never gone to college — and her prospects were theoretically better. Ali was obsessed with continuing his education as soon as he could afford to do so. I wondered how much this was an issue of male pride.

We paid to enter a shabby hall of mirrors and went from one curving glass to the next, laughing like children at the distortions of our images. How had he met his wife?

"Her parents know mine. Also we work in the same office. That make things easier." But surely she wouldn't always work alongside him? I came to understand, however, she might easily do just that, jobs being scarce and promotion something you only dreamed about.

"I want to get out of this country," he confided, his tone loaded. "I like to come to Canada." I heard this many times, and, as I always did, I pointed out that Canada and the West were not what he imagined they would be. Canada may have been once, but now it wasn't. He looked despondent. "I worry," he said. "I worry for my future here." He indicated his stomach, and I realized that "here" meant the ulcer he suffered.

We walked down to Khan Khalili, the medieval bazaar adjacent to the ancient Al-Azhar mosque, which still housed the world's oldest university. There the light of learning had been kept burning throughout Europe's Dark Ages. As we ate kebabs and babaganoug — eggplant salad — Ali's stomach kept bothering him. "I have no chance," he kept saying. "Our economy is in ruins. Only the poor are better off now. Also, I like your women — they are so free." I urged him to reconsider the culture he would be leaving, the expenses he'd encounter in an alien land. "It's too old, this country," he replied. "Too old. And like all old things, it's tired now. Sometimes I think maybe too tired to live much longer."

We strolled into the narrow winding lanes of the bazaar, the same ones reproduced for the Paris exhibition a hundred years earlier, past noisy merchants extolling their wares — "Just looking. Not buying. Come, friend. Come. I show you something you never see before" — even I'd seen a brass plate before — past outdoor cafés all but blocking our path, through smells and sights that had not altered in five hundred years. At the Feshawi coffeehouse, immortalized, and once patronized, by Egypt's Nobel Prize–winning novelist, Naguib Mahfouz, we wove our way past crammed tables to a tiny dark back room, ordering mint tea and a pair of narghiles (water pipes). Dominated by an extraordinary wooden structure inlaid with mother-of-pearl and ivory and resembling a mini-mosque holding a large mirror, the cramped room was decorated with large ancient photographs, one of which showed the original owner wearing a tarboosh and sitting astride his horse. Puffing on tobacco cured in molasses that is kept alight by pieces of burning charcoal you're forced to keep shifting around in the pipe bowl with giant tweezers, we talked on about the state of modern Egypt.

"In Nasser's time," Ali sighed, "things were different. Then there was so much hope. Now there is no hope." He was too young to remember Nasser's time, but I didn't say so. Instead, I told him that his sense of despair was universal, that I felt it in Canada just as much as he did here. He didn't look as if he believed me. Since smoking a narghile is an involved business, our lapses into silence were frequent, broken only by the steady gurgling of the water cooling the smoke. His sadness was infectious.

Back in the swarming lanes, we passed a deformed beggar with two thumbs on each hand. The stream of exotic sweat-slick faces and the myriad odours of spices and perfumes pouring through each alley, with its overarching intricately carved *mashrabiyas*, its worn and ancient flagstones, thrilled me again as only the East can. Ali yet again turned his head to watch a beautiful face pass by.

"Come on," I pursued, "surely you must have opportunities?" I meant with women.

"Only the opportunity to dream," he answered. I asked about the possibility of having two wives or more. We'd stopped in a juice bar that specialized in a concoction of mashed strawberries in sugarcane juice.

"Koran recognizes that a man wants more than one wife," he replied. "But it makes it impossible for him to have. You are allowed four wives — *if* you treat them all equally. That is, of course, impossible. So no one has more than one wife now. In Egypt today even one wife is too much."

Next to the juice bar was a long, narrow store belonging to the most inept taxidermist I've ever come across. His animals were nearly unrecognizable, bent into impossibly unlifelike postures. One was a ratty-looking rabbit smoking a miniature narghile. Behind them, in distressingly tiny cages, were tiny live flamingos and baby owls. The price: a dollar or so.

Past giant cones of dried dates, stalls full of leather and brass goods, haunches of meat swinging as butchers carved off tomorrow's dinners, still working at 1:00 A.M., we came across another packed café, where, amid the smoke of smouldering charcoal and the steaming coffees and teas, a couple of tourist girls laughed brazenly with three sleazy Egyptian playboys who clearly fizzed with testosterone.

"How about foreign girls?" I asked Ali. "You've got a shot at some action there surely?" He just looked away. I'd either offended or embarrassed him.

Beyond us, in the open square, the green neon lights of a mosque showed the faithful within still discussing the beneficence of Allah, His many mercies, His omniscient greatness. I knew Ali, like everyone else, prayed at least five times a day; was his God's all-knowingness a problem when he entertained the thoughts I knew so often plagued his mind? But I had no right to ask.

We went our separate ways, and I was left in the hectic streets, surrounded by so much genuine and simple joy it saddened me that my friend could not see the riches he had compared with the poverty I would have to return to. Was this condescension on my part? Was I just one more foreigner, no different from those who had attended that Paris exhibition?

CHAPTER TWO

HEARTS WITH WINGS

The land of Egypt is in a state of turmoil these days. The face of Cairo is that of a stranger, one that I hadn't encountered on my previous travels here. I know the language of the city and its dialects, but the people seem to be speaking a different language. I see the city as a sick man on the point of tears, a terrified woman afraid of being raped at the end of the night. Even the clear blue of the sky is thin, with clouds laden with an alien fog that has come from distant lands ...

—THE FICTIONAL VENETIAN TRAVELLER VISCONTI GIANTI
DESCRIBING CAIRO IN 1516. FROM THE NOVEL
ZAYNI BARAKAT BY GAMAL AL-GHITANI

"There are *bassassin* everywhere," Mokhtar told me, as he wrapped a length of turban around my face and adjusted the old *gelabia* he'd brought over to the hotel. A *bassass* is a spy. Mokhtar had promised to take me to witness the gathering of a Sufi *tariqa* — the word means "way to attain union with God."

Sufism is a mystical sect of Islam that is all but outlawed in most strictly Muslim countries, although it has gained popularity in the West through the writings of Gurdjieff and others who adapted its rituals to suit their own needs. The word comes from *suf*, the crude woollen garments worn by itinerant holy men. One aspect of Sufism is a veneration for the Prophet that goes far beyond the tenets of orthodox Islam. Many Sufis came to regard Muhammad as the eternal manifestation of the force that created and sustains the universe, and the only channel by which God may be approached and known. Inevitably, supernatural qualities were thus conferred on Muhammad, something both the Prophet and mainstream belief had been careful to avoid. Like members of other mystical sects, the Sufi ascetics cultivated an ecstatic union with the divine through various disciplines and an overwhelming love of God. Their philosophy of the faith was developed from the eighth century on by defining mystical experiences. Some even believe Sufism is in fact the ancient Egyptian priestly wisdom adapted to Islam. Quite late in its development came the designation of saints — an aspect that still appeals greatly to ordinary Muslims. Besides major poets like the Persian Rumi, the order produced numerous Sufi masters who were, and are, believed to possess spiritual powers and the ability to perform miracles. The tombs of these saints — there are several in Egypt — have become places of pilgrimage. This reverence has led to some abuses in Sufism, so modern Muslims seeking to purge Islam of superstition have effected a decline in the sect among the educated classes throughout the Islamic world. However, it retains a powerful hold on the masses, as do the *zaar* and other cults. Because of the *bassassin*, fear of whom, whoever they are, seems to affect the private lives of many Cairenes, it was necessary for us to take great precautions before visiting this Sufi *tariqa*.

We were accosted rudely in the hotel lobby by a security officer, who apologized to the point of grovelling when I pulled aside the cloth covering my face. Both Mokhtar and I concluded that my disguise was convincing enough. He, too, had exchanged his business suit for the rough garb of the fellahin; he was something in "Research Planning," whatever that is.

We drove across Cairo through another hooting, squealing rush hour, heading up to the plateau of the original city fortress, or Citadel, where, low behind Muhammad Ali's gigantic, imposing mosque, a sunset of pale smouldering gold turned the smog into a sprawling wreath of gilded mist. Halfway up a steep hill leading past the City of the Dead into old Cairo, we parked on a patch of waste ground where a house seemed to have simply collapsed of its own accord. On what must once have been a section of wall, a young woman sat with a cabbage the size of a beach ball balanced on her black-veiled head and a miserable-looking chicken, its legs tied together, under one arm. Perhaps it had been her house?

"Ask her," I urged Mokhtar.

"You don't talk to *those* women," he told me. "Their husbands would cut your balls off and eat them. Anyway, houses are always falling down here. Mud brick is fine as long as it doesn't rain." Fortunately it doesn't often rain in Cairo — but it *does* rain.

The City of the Dead, Cairo's necropolis, covers many square miles and looks at first glance like a large walled village of vaguely prosperous houses. The buildings contain only tombs. On holidays, families can still go over to their deceased relatives' homes and include them in their festivities.

As we passed one of the necropolis gates, a stout woman in about an acre of black *abaya* staggered out carrying an army-style gasoline can (stamped WD — War Department — 1943) and two huge snot-nosed babies. Behind her, at least six more children were beating up a donkey.

"What do the dead want with gasoline?" I asked Mokhtar.

"Oh," he said, indicating the woman, "she probably lives there."

"What do you mean, *lives there*?"

"Housing shortage. People are renting out places there now. It's not cheap, either. You have to put about three thousand down just to get in, then it's around thirty pounds a month, which is steep for almost anyone."

Mokhtar, I learned, paid three pounds a month for his spacious three-bedroom apartment overlooking the Nile, although he was making at least a thousand a month. Rent control here means the rent stays at what it was when the place was built. Little wonder owners are not inclined to do much in the way of maintenance.

"So," I asked him, "you mean people *live* in mausoleums? What about the tombs?"

"I hear they make serviceable dining tables." He laughed. "Honestly."

We turned into a dark, twisting alley where the eaves of ancient houses nearly touched above us, blocking out what little light was left in the sky. No one was paying any attention to us, a real novelty for a foreigner in the Orient. Old men sat in their doorways smoking *sheesha* pipes and shooting the breeze. An occasional mule tottering beneath the weight of two big sacks of earth or vegetables or grain would make us flatten ourselves into the nearest recess while it passed. The smell of cooking wafted from windows and passageways. The place was such a labyrinth I'd need a thread to find my way out again.

> *A would-be seeker asked a Sufi:*
> *How long will it take me to arrive at the point*
> *of true understanding?*
> *The Sufi answered:*
> *As soon as you get to the stage where you do not*
> *ask how long it will take ...*

> —IDRIES SHAH, *A PERFUMED SCORPION*

"Keep your voice *down*." Mokhtar sounded serious. "What we are doing is illegal enough without you talking about brothels. There aren't any anywhere anymore. Well," he whispered, "there *used* to be a great African whorehouse near the American embassy — naturally — but they shut it down recently."

"African?"

"You wouldn't catch Muslim women doing that. They had all these slave girls from the Sudan in there ..."

"*Slave* girls?"

"Don't be so surprised. The slave trade still goes on in that business. Just like in your country."

I asked him what the place was like.

"Great — I mean *terrible*." He suppressed an odd giggle. "The girls used to lie on the billiards table with their legs open. Some of the marines were great billiards players. One girl could hold in three balls and fire them out so accurately they let her play that way ..."

"Bullshit."

"No. It's true. But it *was* a depraved place. They're terrible women, those Negro women. You'd think they'd be upset by what they were made to do, but I think they actually *enjoyed* it. You know, one of them could even push a banana up her thing and spit it out in slices. Another used to lie on the bar and drink beer with it. Another would *even* —"

"Okay, Mokhtar." I got the picture. No wonder the place was closed down. "Sounds as if *you* had a good time?"

"Me? Certainly *not*. I was merely an observer of human nature."

I finally got Mokhtar to confess that his observations of human nature had extended to getting laid. And I think he hated me for it. I might have squeezed the details out of him, but we arrived at our destination. Looking all around in a manner so furtive anyone watching would have known we were up to no good, Mokhtar suddenly bundled me up a short stone staircase and through an open arch that led into a long and very dark passage. At the end we came to an ancient door studded with large metal knobs and thick enough to hold off an army with battering rams.

I said, "*Now* I die?" I wasn't really joking. No one knew where I was, and I hardly knew Mokhtar from Mephistopheles, *or* the people who'd introduced me to him, for that matter. I didn't like the fact that he'd frequented whorehouses; no good Muslim would do such a thing. But then, no good Muslim would be involved with Sufis, either.

Silencing me with a gesture, my escort pulled a creaking metal ring until it appeared to come away in his hand and then recede back into the heavy wood. The sound of a distant bell ringing solved this enigma. Soon footsteps could be heard shuffling slowly toward us from within. A voice like the bark of an old dog with laryngitis uttered two syllables through the wood. Mokhtar replied with a simple "*Aiwa*." "Okay," or as close to an approximation of "yes" as Arabic seems to allow itself.

A recalcitrant bolt was drawn back, a key turned, and the mighty door was dragged open a couple of feet. Then the turbaned head of a man old enough to have known the Prophet personally appeared in the space.

The umber skin on his face looked like desiccated mud flats, and he wore a Solzhenitsyn-style beard the size, shape, and colour of a small cumulus cloud. Behind him I could make out an open courtyard and, on the far side, a house with heavy carved shutters. It was dark, apart from a dim yolky light framed by an open door. Squinting first at me, then at Mokhtar, the old man growled again, revealing three lonely teeth like thick spent matchsticks. The door didn't appear to open any farther, so, following my companion, I squeezed through the gap, and the two of us helped the old man, who wore what resembled a black academic gown over a white satiny *gelabia*, heave the monstrous door shut again. We slid back a bolt as thick as my arm, and he turned a key as large as a squash racquet in the kind of lock you see in bad parts of New York City.

"Wow," I remarked. "*This* must have been made when a door still *meant* something ..."

I followed Mokhtar and the old man across flagstones worn smooth by the feet of centuries and into the house. The place was huge, and palatial, if run-down. It certainly wasn't what I'd expected, given the area we'd been walking through. The ancient woodwork was exquisitely carved with Islamic patterns and, in places, inlaid with stained ivory and dusty mother-of-pearl. The curving masonry was similarly festooned with geometric and floral designs. I later discovered the place dated from the fourteenth century. That was probably also when it had last been cleaned. Down corridors we went, our pace as painfully slow as the old man's, and up an uneven staircase missing so many stones that some steps were virtually three feet high. Another corridor contained a huge mercury-backed mirror in a frame so ornately carved that it must have constituted someone's lifework. The mercury had worn so badly that when I looked, half my head was missing.

Finally, we were led into a tiny room containing two cheap metal folding chairs. The old man grunted, hawked, and shuffled noisily off.

"Not much room for a gathering here," I said.

Mokhtar just nodded toward what I'd taken to be a carved wooden panel at the end of the room. "Look," he told me, somewhat smugly. The panel was actually a kind of *mashrabiya* window, the kind used by women sequestered in purdah to look out while remaining unseen. Through the delicately fashioned peepholes I could see a large hall-like room lit by dozens of candles or oil lamps in turquoise glass shades hanging from the roof beams. Below, some thirty feet beneath where we sat, two dozen or so men in lavishly coloured silk caftans and blood-red turbans sat in a circle around an old white-bearded man. This figure was dressed entirely in black robes, with a black turban so large it looked like a bag of laundry on his head. "That's the sheikh," Mokhtar whispered.

"Are you sure we're supposed to *be* here?" I had grave doubts.

The sheikh appeared to be talking in a low, even tone to the men around him. The hall was constructed from floor to ceiling in pale white marble and even contained, at one end, a small fountain, also of marble. Its waters, though soundless from our vantage point, sparkled in the bluish light.

The sheikh's voice suddenly rose several octaves, and he broke into what sounded like a song. This atonal wailing yodel was clearly a big hit. His audience started swaying to and fro, clapping their hands, and eventually even singing along. Mokhtar and I drew up our chairs and looked down on this ridiculous spectacle in silence.

Now I'm not sure if my eyes deceived me or not in the poor light, but I could have sworn that the old sheikh didn't stand normally; rather, he seemed to float up to his usual height and then lower his legs to the ground beneath him. The other men certainly stood in the conventional manner — some with the obvious effort of old age — and, once they were all standing, proceeded to walk in their circle around the sheikh, slowly at first, but gradually gaining momentum until they were virtually running, old and young alike. This continued for some minutes, and then, as a loud chanting began, they started to weave in and out as they ran, still keeping their circle perfectly symmetrical. The effect, from above, was of an unbroken human braid. Their movements grew faster and more complex, as did the chanting, until I found it impossible to believe that anyone, let alone anyone as old as some of these characters had to be, could be capable of such faultlessly choreographed and sustained physical exertion. They couldn't have been better synchronized. As they spun and weaved, even their robes seemed to swirl and billow in unison.

Faster and faster the circle turned until it was one continuous blur of colour.

Then, with a loud clap of his hands, the sheikh stopped the men completely. No one teetered, no one appeared remotely winded, let alone tired or dizzy. The sheikh held up both hands, palms facing out. He next made a slight movement, as if pushing an invisible wall, and began to turn around very slowly, continuing the same movement with his upraised hands. The section of the circle he faced would rock noticeably, as if he were pushing the men themselves. This went on until the old man had turned several times and the whole circle swayed like flowers in a breeze.

He lowered his hands until they were parallel with the ground and started clenching and unclenching his fingers violently. I was wondering why when I saw what looked like liquid begin to shoot from his fingertips, as if he were flicking a basin of water. Turning again, he showered the circle of men with … what? Sweat was the best I could come up with. He must have incredibly sweaty old hands, I told myself. He then clapped his incredibly sweaty old hands twice, and the circle of men once more sat down. So did the sheikh, in the conventional manner.

Just then, following a spectacular demonstration of throat-clearing, the old creature who had let us in materialized near the doorway and barked something at Mokhtar.

Mokhtar looked visibly shaken. "We've been invited to go downstairs," he told me.

"What do you mean?" I said. "We've been asked to *leave*?"

"No. The sheikh has summoned us to join the *tariqa*."

"But how could he have … I mean, *he hasn't left the room …*"

Meekly I rose and followed Mokhtar and the old man. I hoped the athletic segment of the gathering was over. I hoped I didn't have to speak to the sheikh *(So, what's it like being a Sufi then? Nice, is it?)*. Was I expected to become the human sacrifice in stage two of their ritual?

Following the old man gave me much time for reflection and observation. I reflected on what I'd just seen. Pretty quickly I observed that we were heading back via a different route from the one we'd taken on our way in.

We passed a wall I'd never seen before, and it was certainly a wall I'd have remembered. On it was emblazoned a mural from floor to ceiling that, judging by the leprous condition of the paintwork alone, had to have been executed when Shakespeare was still a toddler. Pharaonic paint jobs are in better shape. As far as I could make out, the corrugated and peeling shapes depicted a fat heart with wings, hovering over a glade pullulating with wild animals who clearly wanted to take a bite out of it. There were certainly tigers, bears, jackals, crocodiles, and leopards. And there were bits of what could have been pterodactyls, carnivorous giraffes, and sabre-toothed hippopotamuses. An odd spirit of unity prevailed among them. In fact, they all seemed oblivious to one another. It was that big, juicy, winged heart they wanted. Yet the expressions on their faces conveyed a depressed resignation; they knew they'd never get near the heart. Even the tiger, who was nearer than his fellows, looked somewhat foolish, as if he knew he was wasting his time. Clearly, the mural was symbolic of something. But what?

"Hey, Mokhtar," I said. "What's a winged heart mean?"

"The soul in love with God" was the answer, delivered deadpan. At least it was better than those grotesque images of Jesus performing open-heart surgery on himself with his bare hands.

Descending a wooden staircase that creaked beneath our feet like choral music by dying cats, we passed a grandfather clock made, according to the faded lettering painted on its face, in Birmingham in 1823. Its hour hand and pendulum were missing.

Pulling aside a tapestry decorated with a large and complicated tree full of birds, the old man revealed a narrow archway leading into an area so dark it could well have been an entrance to the Underworld.

"If there's anything you feel I should know, Mokhtar," I said, "feel free to tell me. For example, why are we in this unlighted dungeon?"

"Do not be scared."

"Who's scared? I'm not scared — unless you think I *should* be scared?"

We walked like blind men, pausing when our guide did. A muffled fiddling with metal objects, punctuated by Olympic hawks that propelled pieces of the old man's lungs around the invisible space in worryingly numerous directions, resulted in the opening of a door about four feet from me. Light so dense it seemed almost liquid poured out in blinding waves.

We are above the skies and more than angels ...
Although we have descended here, let us speed back:
*   what place is this?*
— JALALUDDIN RUMI, THIRTEENTH CENTURY

We had been led into the marble hall where the sheikh still sat with his devotees, a point within a circle, like the ancient symbol used by occultists to designate the sun. Immediately facing the door we'd just emerged from stood porcelain bowls raised five feet high on lacquered stands and holding clods of blazing magnesium ribbon. As a fine thread, magnesium is the flash in old-fashioned camera flashbulbs. I was about to tell Mokhtar I'd just about had it with this farce when I realized the sheikh, beneath his preposterous black turban, was standing by my side.

"The mind is a monkey," he said in faultless English. It struck me as an odd statement. Had he meant to say "manqué" or something else? I glanced at Mokhtar. He'd bowed his head reverently.

"A monkey?" I repeated, smiling inanely at the sheikh. His eyes, set in a wizened, noble old Semitic face, seemed much younger than the rest of him. They were clear, bright, full of humour, yet I had the curious sense that no one was looking through them. Eye contact is a profound form of communication, yet, as my eyes met his, there was no communication between us at all. The only analogy I can offer is that of looking into the eyes of a mad person.

"The heart cannot fly with a monkey on its back," said the sheikh, his voice gentle, soft, and low.

The mural came to mind. But the human heart didn't have wings or a back upon which a monkey could sit; yet at that very instant I saw a ferociously clear mental picture of my mind as a restless and mischievous monkey engaged in countless unrelated, pointless activities, unable to stop itself, incapable of not responding to an unending stream of stimuli. A monkey, of course, has no set goals in life. It is not the least bit bothered by a lack of continuity, any absence of achievement. Morality and ethics are no problem, either.

This mind flash took maybe a second, but it thoroughly unnerved me. In the sheikh's eyes I next saw something that convinced me beyond all doubt my thoughts and his will were, at that moment, one and the same. I don't think I've ever felt such raw panic. *Tame the monkey*, I recall telling myself. But *was I the monkey*? Never again will I wonder what it's like to lose one's mind. No thought can be trusted — including *that* thought.

"The best way to tame monkey is to make him climb up and down a pole until he gets exhausted," the sheikh confided. His tone was that of a man who's learned everything the hard way.

This latest remark left me baffled and increasingly bad-tempered. What pole? It wasn't even *fair* to the monkey …

"Come," the sheikh told me, lightly tugging my elbow, "our ring of power is ready to receive you. There are voices in eternity that need to speak of many things to those who'll listen."

I felt about six years old as the sheikh took me by the hand and led me across the marble tiles to where the others still sat, their eyes half-closed, not registering me or Mokhtar or any other intrusion. I had a strong urge to say, *Can I sit next to Mokhtar, please, sir, we're friends.* I recalled experiencing the same feeling on my first day in school.

As it happened, the circle wriggled apart to make a space big enough for Mokhtar and me to sit together.

"You're so lucky, my friend," Mokhtar whispered.

"What's going on?" I hissed back. "This is weird stuff. *Too* weird."

Without warning, a man who could have been James Joyce's twin brother in Arab drag leapt up and started rocking back and forth on the balls of his feet, shouting, "Allah! Allah!" at the top of his lungs. He reminded me of a cheering sports fan. I half expected to hear rival supporters encourage their boys in the same fashion: "Siva! Siva!" After all, religion is a team sport.

The man shouting for, or at, God, far from being silenced for his disruptive behaviour, was joined by others, until everyone apart from Mokhtar, me, and the sheikh was rocking and roaring out his God's name. It reminded me of a passionate woman in the throes of a ferocious orgasm.

Looking at Mokhtar, I realized he realized what I realized: we could hardly continue to sit down. Within a moment both of us were bobbing along with the rest of the circle, hollering for Allah. I hoped Allah wouldn't mind my doing this. These, and other bizarre anxieties, flew like mosquitoes through my mind as I swayed and chanted, an imposter among the faithful.

After ten minutes or so I found the name of Allah I'd repeated a hundred-odd times began to sound as if it were repeating itself independently of me. My brain fizzled with inane streams of consciousness as my lips uttered God's name. *The mind is a monkey*, I remember telling myself. *But who am I? Who is I?* The vibration of the chant in my chest was beginning to kindle an extraordinary sensation of well-being, a warm glow like love, or finding a large cheque in the mailbox. I felt great, and I shouted out for Allah without even having to think about doing it. I dimly recalled a similar feeling of confusion and joy when taking acid. When I *could* think, my thoughts made no sense. Gradually this fuzzy warm feeling changed. My mind shifted to a state of abject panic. I tried at one point to stop the chant and found with bemused horror that I truly couldn't. *Was I chanting*, I wondered, *or being chanted?* I could hardly hear my own thoughts at times, and when I could, I found myself lost in long-forgotten memories from the distant past, which wove seamlessly into entirely unrelated thoughts, vivid sexual fantasies, angry feelings connected with incidents and people I hadn't thought about in years or even decades, all of them as immediate as if they were really happening. Yet the whole boiling stew that was my mind simultaneously recalling everything it had ever retained seemed remoter and remoter from the "me" who perceived it. The sun glowing in my heart overpowered my life now, my sole reality. That and the name of Allah speaking itself through my lips. My awareness of the room and everyone in it dimmed.

At some point I noticed people were beating their breasts in frenzy, and the noise of chanting pounded like the deafening roar of jet turbines. But then I noticed I, too, was pounding my chest with my fists, tearing at my clothes, jerking like a person with Saint Vitus' dance.

Only when I found myself staring directly into his eyes did I see the sheikh, immobile, a black outcrop of rock at the centre of a tempest-torn forest. This old man was more than I could comprehend. In some way he controlled everyone in that room. His power was tangible, emanating from him toward each of us like the spokes on a wheel. Or did it flow from us to him? You could almost see the energy. I could not decide whether the power was good or evil. It did not feel like either.

Whatever was happening kept shifting gear, too, changing its mood but always appearing to be heading somewhere. All the hysterical rigmarole we'd been participating in seemed to conjure up a force field of energy needed to get us to that obscure ultimate destination.

The controlled chaos now appeared to be getting out of control. Some of the men were beginning to salivate, frothing like epileptics. A man opposite me suddenly collapsed in a shuddering, untidy heap …

I must have done the same thing, for I next found myself sprawled on the bare marble with my nose buried in Mokhtar's hairy calf. The sheikh stood once more, walking slowly around the ring of tangled bodies. He looked bigger, younger, and altogether more potent than he had earlier. When he clapped his hands this time, the sound was almost deafening. Instantly everyone sat up and resumed his former calm, cross-legged posture. Some of our clothes were torn, and only the sheikh still wore his turban; the rest, mine included, lay scattered around us all like multicoloured rocks.

"Allah Akbar," the sheikh said, his voice rich with power. He continued in Arabic, an odd-sounding Arabic, for some minutes, then switched to English: "The bridge across worlds has been built. The light is with us. The light has dispelled all darkness. The light that was before all things shines once more …"

In fact, the room was now in almost total darkness. Only one dim oil lamp still burned, and were it not for the abundance of white marble, you'd have had trouble seeing your own feet.

"The light is the bridge," the sheikh continued. "The blessed who walk in light are now ready to cross over. Who among you will summon them?"

"What *now*?" I whispered at Mokhtar. "What's he going on about?"

"Ssssh! He's invoked the djinn. You must keep quiet now."

"The gin?" I presumed there were easier ways of ordering cocktails, even in Islamic nations.

"Djinn are powerful spirits who rule the other worlds. Now *sssh!*"

Humour, of course, is a nervous reaction. I'd always pictured djinn as turbaned phantoms that lived in magic lamps. Something like an electric shock suddenly sparked deep inside my brain.

A moth made love to the oil lamp's dim, flickering flame. By its vague strobe light I saw the sheikh had closed his eyes and was sitting quite rigid. A couple of men were swaying slightly again and muttering under their breath. Then, for a moment, I had the distinct impression a figure on a large horse had galloped silently across the far side of the room.

"How can you expect God to be pleased with you when you are not pleased with Him?" a voice like the sheikh's appeared to ask me explicitly.

Emerging from the sheikh's body seemed to be another, larger body. When I looked closely, it appeared to be merely a trick of the light.

Was I supposed to answer? I didn't; anyway, I didn't *have* an answer. I felt as if I'd been touched by some vast force, fierce yet gentle. It left me with an extraordinary sensation of calm. Dead calm.

The rest of the proceedings — a series of dialogues — was in Arabic and seemed not to concern me anyway. I sat in my cocoon, content with the peace that I didn't even try to understand.

～〜ʋ

"Well?" asked Mokhtar, when we stood once more in the darkened alley. I just shook my head. "That sheikh has great powers," he said, as if the thought had never occurred to him before. "He can bring the dead back to life."

He got no argument from me. We'd left the *tariqa* as furtively as we had entered it. I didn't have any more questions about Sufism. It was enough to know that the magic of ancient Egypt lived on.

Back in my hotel I was thinking about how Moses was reputed to possess all the magical knowledge of the Egyptians, having been raised as a prince among them, and I came across a story preserved in a document called the Westcar Papyrus, written in the early part of the Eighteenth Dynasty, around 1550 B.C., but containing stories that date from the period of the Great Pyramid. One of these, related by a Baiu-f-Ra to the pharaoh Khufu (Cheops), concerns an event during the reign of the pharaoh's father, Seneferu.

One day Seneferu was feeling down, and he sought out all the nobles of his household for something to cheer him up. As they could come up with nothing, he summoned Tchatcha-em-ankh, his head priest, a magician of great powers. The priest suggested his pharaoh try taking a cruise on a nearby lake in the royal barge.

"For," he urged, "the heart of thy majesty will rejoice and be glad when thou sailest about hither and thither, and dost see the beautiful thickets which are on the lake, and when thou seest the pretty banks thereof and the beautiful fields, then shall thy heart feel happiness." The priest begged that he be allowed to organize this cruise for his master, saying he would equip the vessel with twenty ebony paddles inlaid with gold and twenty of the best-looking virgins in the land to row them. Decked out in their finest jewels and dresses made merely of net, these babes would propel the pharaoh around the lake, singing to him — and probably doing a little more besides.

It was an offer the pharaoh could not possibly refuse. All went well on the lake, we're told, until one of the girls accidentally dropped her favourite turquoise ornament in the water. Distraught, she and the others ceased rowing. The pharaoh by now was enjoying himself immensely, his depression quite lifted. He promised the girl he'd get the ornament back to her and had Tchatcha-em-ankh summoned to the barge.

After hearing of the disaster, the priest

> spake certain words of power, and having thus caused one section of the water of the lake to go up upon the other, he found the ornament lying upon a pot-sherd, and he took it up and gave it to the maiden. Now the water was twelve cubits deep, but when Tchatcha-em-ankh had lifted up one section of the water on to the other, that portion became four and twenty cubits deep. The magician again uttered certain words of power. and the water of the lake became as it had been before he had caused one portion

of it to go up on to the other; and the pharaoh prepared a feast for all his royal household, and rewarded Tchatcha-em-ankh with gifts of every kind.

The story dates from around 2800 B.C. The Westcar Papyrus copy of it also dates from a period long before that of Moses, who parted the Red Sea like walls, one on the right hand and one on the left. The same papyrus also contains a story from the Old Kingdom about a magician called Teta, who demonstrated to Cheops' son his power to bring the dead back to life. This was certainly long before Jesus and the miracle of the raising of Lazarus. Long before.

That night I went to sleep feeling we live in many worlds at once, some an endless night, some still teeming with wonders, with the light of that innocence we knew as children, then lost, only to spend our lives striving to find it again.

CHAPTER THREE

POETRY AND THE DUST OF SORROW

[The Nile] flows through old hushed Egypt and its sands,
Like some grave mighty thought threading a dream.

—LEIGH HUNT

EgyptAir, the internal line, is not for the faint of heart. Nor is it for the nonsmoker. The plane to Aswan took off like a V-2 rocket, and as soon as the No Smoking sign was switched off, the Egyptian contingent on board, regardless of seating, lit up in unison, as if on command, smoking with furious dedication throughout the next hour. Judging by the anguished barking of lungs, many of them couldn't handle the pace. An aging American marine colonel reading *Stars and Stripes* sat next to me with his wife. They spent the entire flight loudly deploring this gross violation of their right to smoke-free air, glaring around menacingly at each flaring match. I ventured to point out good-humouredly that the marines were not exactly an environment-friendly outfit themselves.

"Thass pinko talk, boy," the colonel snapped, looking me over as one might a six-foot turd. "We do what we *have* to do. These goddam *Ee*gyptoes oughta be mighty grateful we saved their asses from the Israels. Worthless bastards — can't even obey a simple Non Smoking sign. No wonder the country's in such a godawful *mess.*"

I didn't dare light the cigarette I had been about to pluck from my shirt pocket. The colonel ordered over a flight attendant. I thought he was going to complain about the feverish square of cheese between two curling bone-dry slices of something resembling bread with which we'd just been presented. Instead, he demanded the smokers in the nonsmoking section be told to butt out or get out. She was an attractive woman — Egyptian women, when you can see them, often are — and she didn't hide the fact that she thought the colonel was a prime asshole. She looked at me, as if wondering whether I might be the asshole's son. I silently dissociated myself, rolling my eyes and pointing at the Marlboros in my pocket. She then leaned over and muttered to a couple of nearby smokers, who looked perplexed and carried on smoking.

"*Goddammit!*" the colonel growled, thrashing his *Stars and Stripes* until he'd succeeded in turning over a page, making a brutal knife-edge crease in it. "I'd like to put this whole damn country in my unit for a year," he told himself. "Then we'd see a different place all right ..."

"But it wouldn't be Egypt," I suggested, asking if he thought the whole world should be just like America.

He looked at me as if I were raving mad, beat the newspaper into submission, and settled heavily back in his chair. His wife smiled nervously, visibly shrinking in her seat, half of which was occupied by her husband's massive elbow. She knew this vacation was not going to be fun.

Named *Aton* (the sun), our plane, containing more cloud than the whole of North Africa, cruised through a dawn of blinding beauty over the snaking mercury thread of the Nile far below, following in under sixty minutes the entire vast course of Egyptian history all the way down to the edge of the great Nubian Desert.

Landing in Aswan was like landing on the moon: a pocked and haunted wasteland looming upward until it became all that was visible. Despite a low, fiercely brilliant sun, the morning air was unexpectedly pleasant for somewhere so near the equator in May.

The Cataract Hotel has every modern comfort. Large and small apartments for private families. Extensive hall and reception rooms. Library. Billiard rooms, etc. Fireplaces in hall, saloons and the principal rooms. Electric lights throughout the house running all night. Perfect sanitary arrangements approved by authorities. Can accommodate 60 visitors.

　　　　　　　　　　　　—THE EGYPTIAN GAZETTE, DECEMBER 11, 1899

Winston Churchill, Czar Nicholas of Russia, the Aga Khan, Prince Philip, King Hussein of Jordan, Henry Kissinger, Agatha Christie, and Colonel Muammar Qaddafi all stayed at Aswan's Cataract Hotel, some on a regular basis. By 1912 the place was being called "the finest winter resort in the world," albeit in the hotel's own ads. The lung-draining climate, the unparalleled beauty of the view over the Nile's first cataract, and the sheer elegance of the hotel attracted crowned heads, potentates, the rich and famous from all over the world. There's something irresistible about hotels with a history. Besides, there's almost nowhere else to stay in Aswan. Expecting the place to be a miserable letdown — renovated in Early Burger King Baroque or something — I was shocked to find that it had been upgraded to a more comfortable version of its original elegance.

It's a pity that the architect responsible didn't restore the guests along with the building. What is it that makes modern tourists wear clothes they'd never be seen dead in at home? Who'd dream of entering the Four Seasons in a tasselled sombrero and a tight Day-Glo-pink terry-cloth teddy? What happened to white linen suits and panamas? The terrace of the Cataract once teemed with them, especially at sunset, when the light is almost solid and the white sails of feluccas flutter against ultramarine waters curving past the yellow rocks of Elephantine Island beneath the high drama of a wounded sky.

The terrace was famous as a meeting place in those far-off days of elegance. "Meet you at the terrace" became a byword. One misses it all the more since the terrace has scarcely changed in eighty years, still featuring a string quartet struggling to keep its instruments in tune in the heat, while a staff better dressed than those they now serve bring round drinks on silver trays. Of course, the old guests were probably an appalling bunch of pompous snobs. The manager found an anecdote about a certain Lord Benbrook so inordinately amusing that he regaled me with it three times. Benbrook was a frequent visitor to the hotel, and he arrived on the terrace one evening in the 1920s to find his favourite table taken. He approached the intruder and said stiffly, "I'm sorry, but this table is reserved." The occupant, who had the misfortune of being American, replied, "Since when?" To which Benbrook responded, "Since twenty years!" Now, of course, he'd be told, "Tough shit, bub!"

In 1937 the Nazi general Erwin Rommel stayed at the Cataract for more than a month. One of his fellow guests at the time was the Aga Khan III, who was honeymooning with his new bride. For Rommel, however, this was a working vacation. Admired even by his nemesis, Field Marshal Bernard Montgomery, for sheer military genius, Rommel was working on his "Desert Fox" legend even back in '37. I spoke to an ancient local who claimed to have escorted Rommel on a safari to the western oasis of Al-Khārga during his stay at Aswan. What he did on this trip, according to my informant, was observe and make notes on the various camel-train routes. He realized the Arab traders knew the desert better than anyone else. It was information he would eventually make brilliant use of during the North African campaign. According to the old man, he was a nice guy, too, a real gentleman.

Howard Carter, discoverer of Tutankhamen's tomb, also stayed at the Cataract. He, though, in the opinion of one doddering retainer who claimed to remember him, was a real asshole.

No one appeared to remember Agatha Christie, who stayed there over many winter seasons while her second husband, an archaeologist, worked in Upper Egypt. I managed to get her old rooms, suite 338, which were lovingly restored with dainty four-poster bed and original furnishings, including ceramic washbasin and water jug, although it seemed wiser to wash in the gigantic new bathroom with marble tiles, royal-blue ceramic fixtures (including bidet), and gold-plated fittings.

The writing room was an eerie place to work. In a large glass-doored bookcase there was even the sort of book that had probably been in the room when Agatha had scribbled away at the very same desk: *Among the Wild Tribes of the Afghan Frontier* by Dr. Pennel; *Indian Village Crimes* by someone who called himself simply Benn. There were also more recent tomes on the lines of *Agatha Christie: Das Leben einer Schriftstellerin — spannend wie einer ihrer Romane*, plus, naturally, many volumes of Agatha's own books — in every language except English. I felt her rather prim spectre looking over my shoulder as I wrote up the day's notes. I apologized for never having read any of her books and picked up a German translation of *Death on the Nile* to start that night. Part of the novel is set in the hotel, and the film version, starring Peter Ustinov, was shot there. From the balcony, where Agatha must have taken breakfast each morning, I looked out over a vision of exquisite beauty: the braided blue river, the little boats, the sculpted rocks of the island with its ruins dating from pre-history to Greco-Roman times, and the Qubbet al-Hawa, or "Dome of the Wind," mountain dominating the horizon. This sand-covered eminence — deep, fine, yellow sand dotted with black volcanic stones — marks the edge of the vast Western Desert that stretches with hardly any interruption all the way to the Atlantic Ocean. The hourglass sands of eternity, perhaps.

Just as the desert begins at the Dome of the Wind, so ancient Egypt itself once began at Elephantine Island, the first inhabited area of the region and home of Hapi the Nile god. All goods transported from the interior of Africa into the land of the pharaohs headed for Elephantine, and all military expeditions dispatched to handle any problems in the south and east were mounted from the island. You look out on five thousand years of history from the Cataract Hotel. No wonder Aga Khan III, who died in Europe in 1957, asked in his will to be buried in the landscape he had loved to gaze upon every winter for much of his life. Unfortunately, his marble mausoleum, which took two years to build and resembles a large mosque, now vies with the mountain itself for dominance of the horizon.

His widow, the Begum, still visits the hotel each year, sitting for hours on the lower terrace path staring across at her husband's tomb in mournful silence. She is never to be disturbed.

Aswan, of course, is actually best known now for its dam — or rather its High Dam. The first dam, now called the Low Dam, was completed in 1902. The High Dam is called the High Dam because it is higher than the Low Dam. Much higher. The Low Dam caused some minor problems when it went into operation; many Nubian villages found themselves under fifty feet of water, for example. This, however, was nothing compared with what the High Dam did, indeed is still doing. That first day when I went to look at it, I concluded only that it was very big indeed and probably contained enough concrete to rebuild Warsaw. It supplies all the electricity in Egypt, with enough left over to power countries like the Sudan. Anyone attacking Egypt would certainly place it high on his list of things to blow up. This explains the heavy military presence in Aswan and the dozens of camou-flaged fighter-plane hangars dotted around the airport. The soldiers patrolling the road across the dam get very upset with anyone using a video camera. For some arcane and probably technical reason, still cameras are permitted. The dam seemed to me by far the most boring structure in all of Egypt, and I wondered why anyone would bother to visit it. Some days later, however, I began to grasp its symbolic significance to various interest groups. The military, I suggest, may well be there to protect the dam from their fellow Egyptians.

Fare thee well, my dear and holy Philae. I never loved a place so much ... thank God for all we have felt and thought there.
—FLORENCE NIGHTINGALE IN A LETTER FROM EGYPT

My first sunset in Nubia. Violent crimson rivers of fire burning across the pale topaz firmament above Aswan, above the inconceivable vastness of those desert wastes beyond. The flames slowly fade, now dark bloody veins in the quivering blue-black marble of heaven's dome, which is endless and yet nowhere. The bare little boat that will carry me to the great temple of Isis at Philae bobs in the basalt waters.

Out across the star-spattered lake into an eternal night. Nothing but the wind and all those unfamiliar constellations. The sky is upside down. Then, with the heart-wrenching beauty of a vision, the little island slides into view, bathed in blinding light.

It literally takes my breath away. I gasp, as at some dear familiar sight, lost for a lifetime, then found. Ulysses comes home. "What thou lovest well shall not be reft from thee …" Unbidden, another line from Ezra Pound also sears through my consciousness: "Out of all this beauty something must come …" The boat docks at the foot of steps leading up toward the entrance into arcana, the bridge across worlds. I have, it seems, passed the curve of Time.

In these serene courtyards, the goddess Isis was still being worshipped when Rome lay in ruins and goats grazed in the remains of the Colosseum. When the last priests departed their island temple on the southernmost border of Egypt, realizing that three thousand years of continuous civilization had finally come to a close and their world now belonged to the Christians, some say, they carefully effaced certain reliefs and hieroglyphs, taking their mysteries with them. On the stunning central pylons that remain, only the gigantic figures on the western side are chipped away, symbolically erasing the past, leaving intact only the eastern side, the unknown future where the sun rises.

As I stand in the central courtyard, its rows of subtly perfect columns leading toward the quiet magnificence of the main entrance — so eerily similar to some of the great Inca and Maya temples — the powerful lights dim off and the first thundering chord of the son-et-lumière show resounds from speakers cunningly concealed all over the shadowed island. The ancient stones glow palely beneath the fierce magnesium flares of heaven. Pulsing electric diamonds hammered into the void, the stars of Upper Egypt rage, one of them shooting south in a fiery arc.

At once I see white-robed priestesses emerge from the inner sanctum, their arms upstretched, invoking a power that wove the fabric of all things. But it is, once more, only a trick of the mind, of the night, for as a hundred lights glow slowly into life, the yawning gateway to that Great Secret is empty.

Even the hamminess of the sound track that booms from every corner cannot mar the profound and tangible sense of living magic that still permeates this place after twenty centuries of neglect. Isis has not left her island home.

Written in the kind of neo-Shakespearean favoured by terrible Victorian poets, the English son-et-lumière is worth avoiding. "She comes holding in her hands two large jugs," intones a shrill female voice. I thought of Dolly Parton. "O Nile, you used to come inside my walls," Isis says, apparently innocent of any ambiguity. Perhaps the writer consoled himself by such devices. God knows, he must have needed some consolation after churning out this, announced by another fourth-rate repertory actress: "Let them bring forth virgins wearing heavy wigs and we shall embroider our joy on their shoulders." *Embroider our joy on their shoulders?*

Yet at such a moment, under such a flawless sky, the world of legend seems all too close. It is possible to believe gods once dwelt among men. I never thought to ask in which language the commentary had been written originally. As dud dialogues between gods and goddesses pursued us through the sublime temple and its grounds, nothing could spoil the soaring exhilaration in my heart. Philae, as many visitors have noted, is a hard place to leave.

Later, as I walk the darkened bazaar with my thoughts, I notice the sand blowing up against street corners, doorways, sleeping animals, reminding the whole town that it stands on vast desert shores, alone and insignificant. I smell fresh bread baking, corn being cooked over charcoal, frankincense, coriander, saffron … I feel oddly at home, here on the edge of human history.

Silence fell on the three of them. They looked down to the shining black rocks in the Nile. There was something fantastic about them in the moonlight. They were like vast prehistoric monsters lying half out of the water. A little breeze came up suddenly and as suddenly died away. There was a feeling in the air of hush — of expectancy.

—AGATHA CHRISTIE, *DEATH ON THE NILE*

In Agatha's old chintz-covered four-poster bed that night I cracked open the German version of *Death on the Nile*. After a few pages I grew increasingly perplexed. It appeared to be a novel about Germans who all had English names and lived in England, where everyone else also spoke German. I wondered how P. G. Wodehouse would sound in Russian. Damon Runyon in Chinese? It got me wondering about the English translations of Arabic writers I'd read. It got me wondering about *any* translations. By the time Hercule Poirot had appeared, sounding like Herman Göring on bad drugs, I apologized to Agatha and tossed the book aside.

Then the phone rang. It was a repro version of the sort of appliance used when the hotel had originally opened, and the receiver felt like a barbell. Someone called Shoukry was waiting for me in the lobby. I didn't know anyone in Aswan, let alone anyone named Shoukry. The reception manager kept telling me this Shoukry had an appointment and had been waiting for over an hour already. Egyptians, as I've noted, are patient people.

Dressing hurriedly, I took the grand old elevator down to the lobby and found myself greeted warmly by a man resembling Eddie Murphy in thrift-store clothing. He claimed someone I'd also never heard of in Cairo had told him to make sure I had a good time in Aswan. He spoke almost flawless English (and, I noticed later, five other languages), exuding a gentleness and decency I found irresistible. I invited him for a drink on the terrace.

The Nile below was black and silent, rained on by the light of too many stars. At an adjacent table a German girl with breasts like zeppelins barely covered by a baggy tank top was engaging an American guy possessing enormous hair in a drunken conversation.

"I like one day to fuck inzide her pyrameed," she said quite loudly. "Zat be 'mazink, ya?" She leaned back in her chair, displaying her formidable chest to full advantage.

"The energy, man," her friend remarked. "The fuckin' energy must be a mindblower."

The girl was about to reply when her chair toppled over, throwing her backward, headfirst, on the hard stone floor. Everyone on the terrace — at least every man on the terrace — rushed over, partly, no doubt, because the girl's tank top had wrapped itself like a bag around her head, exposing her breasts and nipples like cigar butts. Blood was beginning to seep through the cloth around her head, and someone called for a doctor. The American guy stood, shaking his extravagant hair and saving, "Oh, wow, man. Oh, wow."

The waiters were clearly fascinated and embarrassed. Shoukry bent down and very gently pulled the girl's top from her face, attempting to cover her chest. The material wouldn't reach, however, so he then tried pushing her breasts under it.

"Hey, asshole," the American shouted. "Leave her fuckin' tits *alone*, man."

The girl sat up suddenly, dazed, rivulets of blood winding down over her face. "Fuck," she said. "I zink I hurt my 'ead, ya?"

"Oh, wow," her friend said once more. "Like, wow!"

Soon a doctor arrived, and the couple were escorted through revolving doors into the hotel lobby. They were clearly not guests.

"Who exactly are you?" I asked Shoukry.

"I've seen that girl in the town," he replied. "She makes much trouble for herself dressing that way. People here do not understand. Not even a prostitute would behave and look the way she does. Nubian people feel ashamed for her ... that she has no respect for herself."

I dropped my original question and asked him what he did for a living. After he'd explained for five minutes, I was still no wiser. At one point I thought he had something to do with rockets, but what he'd actually said related to "dockets." Arabic being a very imprecise language, Egyptians can often seem irritatingly vague, even in English, but it's not deliberate. Burdened with a bureaucracy that penetrates every aspect of life, many people have jobs that defy description. Words like "chit" and "docket" crop up frequently, as they do in India. But the British weren't the ones who brought bureaucracy to Egypt. Egyptians often say with some pride that they have the oldest bureaucracy in the world, which a glance at documents from pharaonic times, proclaiming stupefyingly petty rules, taxes, and regulations, easily confirms. Shoukry turned out to be a friend of Mokhtar, my entrée to Cairo's Sufidom; he referred to him as Hussein — which was, in our terms, Mokhtar's surname, but in Arabic terms, his formal name.

I never knew how to address people; and they never knew what to call me. I was Mr. Paul to some, Mr. William to others, and occasionally just Robert or Roberts. Everyone I met immediately proffered a business card, but the name on it rarely corresponded to the one their friends or associates used. Shoukry, for instance, was generally called Samir by everyone we encountered, though he never told me not to call him Shoukry. His business card, on the other hand, proclaimed him to be Muhammad Abd-al Shakka. It contained about fifteen telephone and telex numbers, but no title, company name, or even address. Since every other person in Egypt is called Muhammad, or variants of the name, like Mahmoud, conversations can be very confusing.

There was one point, however, upon which he was very clear: He was Nubian, *not* Egyptian. Nubians, as I was to find, are extremely proud of being Nubian and extremely disdainful of northern, or Lower, Egyptians. It is the classic north-south syndrome. The Egyptian equivalent of Polish jokes are stories hinging on the stupidity of Upper, or southern, Egyptians when they visit Cairo for the first time, say, or just try to make sense of the modern world in general.

There is, in addition, the question of colour. Nubians are so black that many seem dark blue; many Cairenes, on the other hand, could pass as Greek or southern Italian without much trouble. As in India, colour as an issue is tied up with caste and class, but far more so than we in the West can really understand through our own brands of racist thought. The term "black" has no real meaning in Egypt, its equivalent being "Negro" or "African." Nubians are not considered Negro or African, nor are Ethiopians, northern Sudanese, and most Muslim Blacks. This is, to some extent, racially correct, but geographically it makes no sense. Although Egypt *is* in Africa, to call an Egyptian "African" is as insulting as calling an Iranian an Arab. Egyptians use the terms "Negro" and "African" in the same mildly perjorative way that Jews call Blacks "*Shvartzes*" and Blacks call Jews "Hymies." Far from feeling inferior to the northern Egyptians, Shoukry was quick to impress upon me, the Nubians think of themselves as a superior culture. He even hinted about a move toward Nubian independence; although when I inquired if Nubia had *ever* been an independent nation, he couldn't answer, instead pointing out that several of the later pharaohs were Nubian, as if this proved the case for independence. In an age when national boundaries had little meaning, ancient Egyptian influence extended deep into the Sudan, to Ethiopia in the east and Libya in the west. Nubian independence, I suggested to Shoukry, would now create a country even worse off than the Sudan and Ethiopia — although it's hard to imagine such a place. He shrugged this off with a knowing smile.

It took a while to get to the heart of the matter. The Aswan High Dam, by blocking the Nile on such a prodigious scale, created a lake of gigantic proportions. An entire valley disappeared beneath Lake Nasser. Many Nubians were forcibly relocated from villages they'd inhabited for millennia and installed in hastily constructed concrete settlements, where they felt their traditional way of life was being deliberately destroyed. Such compulsory migrations had already occurred twice before, in 1912 and 1932, when the earlier Low Dam and subsequent modifications to it were under way. In 1962, however, the scale of upheaval was tremendous, and the sneaking suspicion that the rulers in Cairo didn't give a damn about anything but their dam crept into the Nubian consciousness.

Nubians are fine, gentle, noble people with graceful manners and generous hearts. Their current posture of suffering underdog, however, seems to suit them in a curious way. It ennobles them further in their own eyes, somehow justifying their long run of underachievement as a "nation." They have, after all, been resting on their laurels now for about two thousand years.

"Nasser built the dam with Russian help," Shoukry said, returning yet again to his favourite subject. "But it was more a political gesture of Egypt's independence. For the Russians it gave access to the Mediterranean, of course."

The High Dam transformed Egypt's economy from an agricultural to an industrial base in a single stroke. Although the idea for the project dated back to the thirties, it took Nasser to make it a reality. It complied with his program of establishing Egypt as the most potent force in the Arab world. Today it is hard to imagine Egypt without the High Dam. While Nasser's concerns were primarily international, he is now best remembered for his domestic achievements.

On the other hand, President Mubarak has continually declared his mandate to be one of internal social and economic reform, but he will probably be remembered for his "triumphs" in the field of foreign affairs. Shoukry seemed to like Mubarak, but unlike most northern Egyptians he despised Nasser. (Everyone loathed Anwar Sadat, to my surprise.) For Shoukry, the High Dam had come to symbolize everything he hated about Nasser and the uncaring north.

"He didn't care about the Nubian people," he said. "He didn't care even about Egyptian culture."

Like his two successors, Nasser was a military man, a pragmatist. The country, despite appearances, is still in truth a military dictatorship, albeit a benign one. Aware that the High Dam would submerge some of the finest examples of pharaonic architecture in his country, Nasser believed that the economic benefits far outweighed petty cultural concerns. It took a global cry of outrage and the assistance of UNESCO to salvage what now remains. The temple of Isis at Philae was transported stone by stone to a higher island. What I had seen, and been so intoxicated by, was really a reconstruction, a sort of fake, but employing authentic materials. It is a measure of the care and skill involved in this enormous undertaking that you would never guess you were not seeing the original temple on its original island. But only days later, visiting the staggering monolithic temple of Rameses at Abu Simbel, did I truly appreciate the miracle UNESCO had pulled off in Nasser's Egypt. Even so, while the director of the Egyptian Antiquities Organisation in Aswan will not admit it, dozens of major temples could *not* be saved, and are gradually dissolving beneath the waters of Lake Nasser. In return for their financial assistance to UNESCO during the salvage operation, various countries were also "given" any temple they could carry away. Shoukry told me he'd travelled to Spain a few years ago to visit the temple he'd once played in as a child. So poignant, so Nubian a gesture, that was the only occasion upon which he'd ever travelled outside Egypt.

"Nasser was all show," he said. "Without UNESCO there would be nothing left now. Nothing."

He also pointed out that it wasn't just the Nubians and the valley temples that the High Dam messed with. It was the entire ecology of Egypt.

Herodotus and countless others since have said that Egypt is a gift of the Nile. Actually it is a gift of what is now Ethiopia, whose mountains and topsoil, eroded by rain, were transported by the Nile and deposited in fertile alluvial layers along its course for countless millennia, especially in the broad fan of the Delta region, where the richness of the soil was once legendary. I use the past tense, as Shoukry did, because this process ceased with the completion of the High Dam. The business of harnessing the Nile began in the late nineteenth century when Muhammad Ali, founder of the "royal" dynasty that vanished with King Farouk after the 1952 revolution, constructed two barrages at Qanater, a little north of Cairo. With the completion of the Aswan High Dam in the early 1970s, the Nile thus became effectively one of the world's longest stretches of canal.

Most people agree that the country *had* to build the dam. A burgeoning population needed perennial irrigation, not the ancient seasonal irrigation the Nile had always provided. But along with the agrarian systems and continuous cultivation of crops made possible by the dam came a dramatic increase in the use of fertilizers and pesticides in the newly irrigated lands. Right now, only 25 percent of the water passing through Aswan reaches the sea, such is the demand on the country's main source of water. Flood irrigation practices, combined with insufficient drainage, have pushed up the water tables, bringing salts in contact with plant roots. What was intended to increase crop yields is reducing them, and what was supposed to produce more fertile land is in fact rendering once-fertile land barren.

As if demonstrating his Nubian generosity, Shoukry added that these problems were, at present, most severely felt at the other limit of his country, the "end of the line," the Delta. There, ironically, the pressure to reclaim surrounding desert along the boundaries of the fertile wedge has exacerbated this salinization problem. Excessive watering of these reclaimed lands, most of them at a slightly higher elevation, has washed down saline water, adding to local water-table problems. With the buildup of nitrates in groundwater and chemical residues in the soils, Egypt faces the same nightmare that intensive agricultural practices have created in many other countries.

And Shoukry hadn't finished his lecture. The need to conserve water is so great in Egypt, he said, that the Delta region is seeing an exponential increase in these problems. Of the many impossible choices now facing the powers that be, one involves the control of aquatic plants in the thousands of miles of irrigation canals. These plants reproduce at such a rate that they would choke the entire water-distribution system in one summer. There are only two ways to get rid of them: hack them down mechanically at enormous cost in time and labour, or zap them with poisonous chemicals that do the job overnight but are also banned in most countries.

As if all this weren't bad enough, Egypt's population increases by around one million every ten months, and therefore towns and villages also have to expand. But expand where? In the Delta the choice is limited solely to the agricultural lands. Compared with India's hungry billion, Egypt's 56 or so million seems trifling ... until you look at where they have to live. Imagine if the only habitable and arable land in America were Rhode Island.

"What to do?" Shoukry asked, his shoulders rising to ear level and his palms open as if testing for rain — something one rarely has cause to do in Aswan.

"Suicide? Emigration?" He thought I was serious.

"I once thought of going to Canada," Shoukry continued in a confidential tone, "but I realize I can never leave Nubia. We will solve our problems, with the grace of Allah."

I was glad he felt optimistic, because I didn't. I wished I hadn't answered the phone. It was Agatha's fault.

"Let's go into town?" he suddenly said, in an almost unseemly cheerful tone.

"It's 1:15 A.M.!"

He appeared not to understand what I'd said, knitting his brows. Then he announced that this was the last night of Ramadan. Tomorrow was a major holiday, a feast day, a party.

I wondered what Shoukry and anyone in the country had to party about. Fasting for a month certainly does make you keen to eat. Never underestimate Egyptians, though; they're party animals at heart. Always have been, as pharaonic art records so vividly.

CHAPTER FOUR

THE GRAND ILLUSION

La vie est vaine.
Un peu d'amour,
Un peu de haine,
Et puis bonjour.

La vie est breve.
Un peu d'espoir,
Un peu de rêve,
Et puis bonsoir.

—AGATHA CHRISTIE, *DEATH ON THE NILE*

Imagine Hercule Poirot saying *that* in German! Agatha, I realized after several days in her old rooms, was a profoundly unhappy and disillusioned woman. If the novel she set there is anything to go by, Aswan aggravated the cynicism and melancholy in her. Shoukry did the same for me. There is something melancholy about Nubia.

On the back of Shoukry's antique motorbike I saw Aswan's nightlife hopping, even at one-thirty in the morning. All along the corniche, where the tourist cruise ships were moored, elaborately decorated calèches, their quilted-leather seats packed with laughing people, clip-clopped through the warm air. The bazaars were packed with Aswanese doing last-minute shopping for the end-of-Ramadan feast; butchers carved off huge slabs of lamb from swinging carcasses; the tiny one-chair barbershops were busy, too; and the clothing stalls were doing a brisk business. Everywhere were laughing faces, children overexcited at being allowed to stay up late. Little boys rode through the narrow dusty lanes on mules; at one point a weathered desert shepherd drove his flock of fat-tailed bedraggled sheep into the packed market, creating a havoc that no one minded in the least. We strolled amid this joyful anarchy, buying charcoal-roasted corn and waving to the importuning merchants. Everyone seemed to know Shoukry, and innumerable holiday greetings were exchanged. Ali Baba Meets Christmas, I thought. In the distance a roar of voices rose above the eclectic hubbub, and we soon came across what looked like a demonstration of two hundred or so white-clad men shouting slogans and waving banners as they poured around the faded elegance of one of the city's main squares near the Military Sporting Club. It was and wasn't what it seemed; they were fundamentalists chanting *Allah Akbar*, God is Great, demonstrating their faith. The proximity of fundamentalists, the champions of Egypt's rural poor, to the rich world of the Nile cruise ships could spell trouble, Shoukry told me, steering his motorbike away from the marchers as we returned to the Cataract. There had already been an outbreak of violence in the Fayyoum Oasis between Christians and Muslims. A mentally retarded Christian had molested an eight-year-old Muslim girl, and the fundamentalists had blown the incident out of all proportion; in fact the same man had molested a Christian child not long before. It was put around that the girl had been killed, and fundamentalist youths had used the excuse to murder a few Christians and loot their stores. Most Egyptians are wary of the fundamentalists, particularly during Ramadan, when emotions run high. But that night in Aswan saw no trouble.

As we'd agreed, Shoukry picked me up very early the next morning, and we went to his mosque for feast-day prayers. I'd spent a restless night in my rooms, at one point convinced a little old lady was watching me from the shadows.

It was a relief to find the city streets thronged with people all dressed in new clothes and with freshly barbered hair. The normally scruffy country kids danced and sang in parks and along the riverbanks, showing off their clean, brand-new *gelabias*, exchanging candies and laughter. The mosque was packed and the atmosphere very different from that of our Western churches: the earnestness of the devotion was tangible and anything but solemn. When the service was over, many remained within the mosque's cool marble walls, debating finer points of Islamic doctrine. Outside, the local children were now engaged in horse races up and down the hectic streets.

Shoukry and I headed for the river, where we crossed the sparkling waters on a packed little vessel to a large island and Shoukry's home village. It was tradition, he said, to go visiting your friends and relatives on this day. The "bus" that took us across the island — an Edenic oasis lush with fields and fruit trees — was an old pickup truck packed with shy women and laughing children, one of whom gave me a special kind of flower, the customary gift on such a day.

The classic Nubian villages spared by the rising waters south of the High Dam are extraordinarily beautiful. Built of mud brick, with barrel-vault roofs and domes, the houses flow organically around broad shaded courtyards. The village lanes, covered in fine ochre sand, twist past walls painted in vivid shades of blue.

So harmonious, so intricately constructed, yet so simple to build, these houses were the inspiration for the designs of Hassan Fathy, Egypt's most internationally famous architect, whose book *Architecture for the Poor* outlined a plan to enable every peasant to build his own house in a traditional style for an affordable sum. Ironically Fathy's designs were taken up by the rich in places like Arizona and the south of France, where they were expanded into lavish villas. In Egypt they have been adapted for numerous tourist villages.

Those built for the peasants by the government ran into problems outside Nubia; no one wanted to move into them, complaining they looked like tombs. Unlike the concrete prefabs built to house Nubians who had lost their homes under the waters of Lake Nasser, the traditional designs are cool and spacious, capable of being added on to as a family expands. We first entered the house of Shoukry's sister, were greeted with a warmth and affection that was almost overwhelming, and were shown into a room containing only two beds and a TV. The floor was covered in the finest deep yellow sand, soft on the feet and easy to clean. Tea and a large narghile were brought by a shy, beautiful girl who covered her face when she laughed and kept staring at me with unfeigned fascination.

"I want you to hear our music," Shoukry announced, hauling a cheap ghetto-blaster from under a bed and shuffling through a boxful of cassettes. "The Bob Dylan of the Sudan," he announced. To the accompaniment of music sounding like a fusion between Middle Eastern and African, I heard this:

> *Hello, good friends, allow me to introduce myself. I am Abdul Karim al-Kabli from the heart of Africa. My country is big in area — almost one million square miles — with different climates, different regions, tribes, different dialects, and artistic temperaments, and it is natural that all beats are in variety and colourful. Our music is mainly based on the five tones, the pentatonic tones in the piano. Our folksinging mainly preaches about generosity, bravery, faithfulness, and love. The strong influence of the environment can always be felt. I hope the few examples I will be giving will mean something to you.*

The music — drums, discordant strings, but certainly no piano — changed pace, evoking a plangent bittersweetness. "This beatless poem with the title of 'The Poet,'" Sudan's Dylan explained, "goes like this":

> *Why did he awaken the sorrows to suffer, the loneliness of night and wild imagination? Why is he walking among the night caravans whispering to the ghosts and dark shadows? He's so simple and innocent that he's captivated by the smile of a child;*

while he's very strong and enduring to conquer generations to come. He's always bending his head and bowing for the beauties of the life. The dust of sorrow has been created and a touch of inflammable passion was added. Then fate cried loudly, Be a poet, and the dust of endurance and sorrow became a poem …

The song continued in the Nubian language, a poignant lament that captured perfectly that melancholia I felt so keenly.

Shoukry seemed pleased to see me visibly moved. A breeze blew the little net curtains; in the doorway a blinding rectangle of primrose light contrasted the cool dark interior with the fierce world outside. Sweetmeats were next served with kharkady, a kind of hibiscus-flower drink not unlike rose-hip tea in flavour.

In various other dwellings, similar yet all different in minute and charming ways, we experienced the same hospitality, puffing on cigarettes or water pipes, drinking countless cups of tea. TVs were always on, usually watched only by the older women.

Finally we reached Shoukry's own home, its main room dominated by a fridge of commercial proportions and a formidable teak wardrobe carved with mind-boggling intricacy. I asked him how such a massive structure had been hauled through the narrow doorway — clearly it had been built in the room — and he laughed, telling me a typical north-south joke: Some Nubians have been elected to a political position and are having their first meeting in Cairo, discussing a subject of grave seriousness. All they can think of, however, is how the enormous conference table they are sitting around could possibly have been carried into the room. That was the joke.

Changing into a *gelabia*, Shoukry suddenly looked like a proper Nubian now, in his Nubian home. We sat in an open archway where the cool passing breeze made it hard to believe the temperature beyond our shadowed space had reached 110 degrees Fahrenheit.

Most Nubians, I learned, have two jobs: one across the river in the city, usually in some government office; the other cultivating the figs, dates, lemons, mangoes, onions, tomatoes, okra, henna bushes, doum fruit, and other trees that grow in such abundance on their own small family lands.

Nature provides richly here, and there was not the sense of discontent with life that I heard from so many other Egyptians. The melancholy that is so much part of the Nubian soul resembles that embedded in the Celtic soul — an incentive to poetry, to bittersweet reflection on life's sorrows and the endurance required to live with them.

Shoukry dreamed of raising the money to build a Nubian-style tourist village on the island. Each unit could be constructed, he insisted, for less than five hundred dollars. He'd once interested a wealthy American in the idea but had never heard from the man again. I felt he was more comfortable with the thought that his dream would always remain just that — a dream — than he would have been with realizing it. Climatic changes had also resulted in recent heavy rains in Nubia, something almost unheard of previously, causing the mud-brick villages much damage. Indeed, the whole concept of mud brick was suddenly being questioned. Shoukry's Nubian Hotel would not be so cheap to build after all, particularly if stone had to be used on the outer walls as it was in much of his own village now. Nubia was dissolving.

That evening, back in Aswan, we sat in the Aswan Moon Café on the river's edge, while the real moon, a classic Islamic crescent, hung above the terrace, a neon brooch stuck in night's black silk, so bright you could see the dark globe it clung to. Frogs croaked; the steel rigging of boats twanged to the bobbing water's rhythm. Across from us loomed the grotesque design of the new Oberoi Hotel, part temple, part giant water tank in appearance. The water tank was supposed to hold a restaurant, Shoukry told me, but it doesn't. There were supposed to be rules about what you can build in Aswan, but there aren't. The charm of the city is being gradually eroded. "Take the new seven-storey police headquarters right in the heart of our city," he said with disgust. "It's an eyesore, but who's going to argue with the police?"

It was a problem that much of Egypt, outside Cairo, is beginning to face, particularly in the construction related to tourism, which is the first major sector to encourage privatization. To Shoukry it was yet another of these melancholic Nubian issues, insoluble and evidence of a government that didn't really care. Shoukry's concerns were on the same level as my irritation at having to hear Zamfir endlessly piping out "Don't cry for me, Argentina" from the Muzak outlets of almost every hotel I stayed in. Nubian pride, like any other pride, is intractable. Shoukry's only upbeat topic was the Nubian Museum currently being built by UNESCO at a cost of $25 million to house Nubian artifacts collected from all over Egypt. The fact that UNESCO and not the government was building the museum was fodder for yet another mournful Nubian irony.

Nothing in Egyptian sculpture is perhaps quite so wonderful as the way in which these Abou Simbel artists dealt with the thousands of tons of material to which they here gave human form. Consummate masters of effect, they knew precisely what to do, and what to leave undone. These were portrait statues; therefore they finished the heads up to the highest point consistent with their size. But the trunk and the lower limbs they regarded from a decorative rather than a statuesque point of view.

—AMELIA B. EDWARDS, 1874

Handsome heads, ugly feet ...

—GUSTAVE FLAUBERT, LETTER FROM EGYPT, 1849

Why would anyone name a condom after Rameses? The man had around two hundred children. Rameses, when mentioned, is usually Rameses II, the Great, whose monuments extend from Memphis near Cairo all the way down to Abu Simbel, one hundred-odd miles from the present border with the Sudan. The flight from Aswan is short — you go up, throw down a juice, land — yet it gave me the opportunity on one hand to see how wild and bleak the desert south of the Nile's first cataract really is, and on the other to glimpse the magnitude of Lake Nasser. Almost the size of Delaware, it's one of the largest man-made lakes in the world. I found it easier to imagine just how much must now lie beneath its waters after that.

TO TEMPELS [*sic*] proclaims a sign just outside the miniature airport. It was obvious from the start that all this place was about was the temple complex. You pile off the plane into a bus that heads straight to the site; no one's going anywhere else, and although there are rather rudimentary "tourist willages," no one but the purist intent on seeing dawn's first rays strike the colossi stays here. Rameses II reigned around the early twelfth century B.C. and the Abu Simbel complex was completed during the thirty-fourth year of his ascension. Why he ordered it built here, so far from his capital, is not clear. Anyone travelling into Egypt from the south, however, would certainly have appreciated that its ruler was a man not to be trifled with, and perhaps that was part of the point. Leaving the bus, you plod across burning sand and rock around a small mountain before you even see the temples. Clever, this, because the effect is all the more dramatic. Sailing up the Nile, as Amelia Edwards did, must have provided an infinitely more dramatic view. No photograph can convey the megalithic proportions and awesome beauty of these structures. Even the 1929 Baedeker, normally somewhat restrained in its enthusiasm, gushes over them. But what we now see represents really two marvels of engineering: the original construction 3,200 years ago, and the feat accomplished in the 1960s, when the temples were literally sawed up into more than one thousand giant blocks and moved nearly sixty yards higher, to be reassembled about two hundred yards back as the waters of the Nile began to rise behind the High Dam. So skilfully was this achieved that the first ray of dawn still penetrates sixty yards inside the temple on the equinoxes to illuminate miraculously the statues of Rameses and his consort. The assembled hordes who come to witness the spectacle basically support the continued existence of the town for the other 363 days, when almost no one stays overnight.

The two temples are similar in appearance, the smaller one dedicated to Hathor, consort of the sun god Ra and identified with Nefertari, Rameses' wife. Religion was the family business. The intricacy of the recessed chambers and passageways and the subtlety of the painted murals, their colours unretouched and unnervingly vivid after more than three millennia, are done little justice by the stifling heat and the oppressive presence of whining tourists herded like sheep by guides spouting anecdotal nonsense. I wanted to escape to a spot beneath a tree and overlooking the lake, where I could contemplate the staggering facades in peace.

Noticing a little door beside the main temple into which a few people kept disappearing, however, I decided I'd missed something. Next to the door was a self-congratulatory plaque placed by Nasser to celebrate the salvaging of the temples on behalf of humankind. Had mankind, in the form of UNESCO, not intervened, in fact, there would now be merely a signpost on the spot pointing into the lake and saying THIS WAS WHERE THE ABU SIMBEL TEMPLES USED TO BE.

Through the small door I found myself in a long, low concrete passageway. At the end of it was an unbelievable sight: an enormous concrete dome, reinforced by steel struts, circled by metal catwalks. I wondered for a moment whether I had stepped into the operations centre of some top-secret nuke shelter. The whole mountain was man-made! Everything you think you're seeing outside is a shell, a facade, a movie set. The fact that people are allowed to see behind the facade shows contemporary Egypt's dual sense of pride — in its unequalled past and in its increasingly technological present. It's a good idea to visit this bewildering behind-the-scenes world *after* visiting the illusion created by it. Despite my initial shock, I found the experience uplifting, and I left the site with a double sense of awe, and optimism. Like finding the Wizard of Oz really was the wizard he was.

I sat in the hot breeze beneath the shade of some acacia trees waiting for my fellow tourists to return to our bus. Behind me, leading down to the waters of Lake Nasser, the steep hillside was strewn with tourists' trash — candy wrappers, countless dented plastic mineral-water bottles, all carefully swept out of sight but not away. A sly-looking man approached me with an armful of coloured beads for sale and a hangdog attitude suggesting I should buy some out of recognition of his poverty. In some way — I didn't like him — I saw the trash as his fault. I asked him why the locals didn't help keep the place tidy; he shrugged as if the matter were irrelevant. I waved his beads away.

"American?" he asked. I shook my head, and he went through several other nationalities. He seemed to be trying to establish that I came from the wealthy West and he was merely a poor Oriental. The problem with the Americanization of the world is that those in the developing countries who watch American films and TV end up feeling not that they should work hard and be enterprising and gain what the West has the way the West obtained it, but that they will never have it and that Westerners owe them a living.

The facade of Abu Simbel is a useful metaphor, stretching beyond the transplanted shell of the temples. The whole town exists for tourists to visit the temples; the one main street is broad and clean, festooned with signs that recall the celebrations held when the removed and restored complex was finally unveiled. Yet off the streets, carefully concealed, is the garbage that reveals a country that doesn't really care enough about itself. Pride and optimism about the past and the glorious future are tempered by a lazy hopelessness regarding the present. That's what colonialism does. The man with the beads grew angry with my refusal to buy his shabby little goods and stomped off to bother other tourists. Perhaps I *should* have bought something?

Back in Aswan, at the Cataract Hotel, I went for a drink in the dark, opulent bar. The barman, a handsome Nubian who resembled Harry Belafonte, was clearly having problems with two very drunk German couples. As he served me, one of the German men shouted loudly for four beers — "Vier Bier!" — no "please," no courtesy. The barman, who spoke excellent German — and French, Italian, English, Arabic, and Nubian — rolled his eyes at me. He was soon embroiled in a dispute over the bill with the four Germans, who laughed among themselves as if dealing with an idiot. When they had finally staggered off, rudely throwing some money on the floor, he returned to me.

"American?" he asked. I told him Canadian; he looked relieved. "I am Nubian," he said. "*They* were German — ugh! No manners. They drink here all afternoon and think I am trying to trick them into paying for two more drinks than they had. You know what — I buy those beers out of my own pocket rather than listen to *that!*"

Saturday, 9 March 1850. *Assuan. Reached Assuan threading our course between the rocks in midstream; they are dark chocolate-colour, with long white streaks of bird-droppings that widen toward the bottom. To the right, bare sand-hills, their summits sharp against the blue sky. The light comes down perpendicular into transparent depths. A negro landscape.*

—GUSTAVE FLAUBERT, TRAVEL NOTES, 1850

There's something about Aswan that makes you want to stay a very long time; you always have the sense you've not seen all it has to offer. Sheila McKay, an American woman in her early fifties, obviously felt this way. She came fifteen years ago and fell in love with the place and with the Nubian people, and she obtained a job teaching English at a local school. She lives in a tiny apartment just back from the corniche, up several flights of dilapidated concrete stairs. Not married, she doesn't suffer the suspicious curiosity she would in Cairo.

Shoukry admired and respected her for the work she was doing. Her temperament seemed ideally suited to that of the people she worked among. Casual to the point of old hippie sloppiness, she had a finely structured face prematurely lined from years in the fierce sun and long brown hair streaked with grey, pulled tightly against her head by one of those worked-leather clasps once sold on every San Francisco street. What special kind of loneliness had driven her to spend her life here? I never asked, and she never volunteered the answer.

The three of us went to visit one of the most fascinating of all ancient Egyptian remains, the "Unfinished Obelisk." During pharaonic times Aswan was the site of the major quarries of special red granite that was shipped down the Nile to be used in constructing particularly important sculptures or architectural features in the great temples and pyramids. Of all such works, obelisks are perhaps the most impressive. Made from solid blocks often more than thirty yards long, they were capped with gold and covered in hieroglyphic encomiums to whichever pharaoh commissioned them.

At the edge of the northern quarries in Aswan, carved out of the bedrock on three sides but still lying in place, is what would have been the largest obelisk ever erected. Just before it was finally removed, a crack was discovered in it, and the megalith was simply abandoned. Had it been completed, this obelisk would have been one single gigantic piece of granite nearly fifty yards long and fifteen feet wide at its base. It would have weighed well over one thousand tons. The project, with all the labour involved and the problems of transportation, seems almost unimaginably difficult.

Those who subscribe to theories of assistance from extraterrestrials are hard put to explain away the abundant evidence of ancient Egyptian stone-cutting techniques found at this site. Rock was quarried by drilling a series of holes around the monolith involved — they're clearly visible around this obelisk — then inserting wooden stakes in the holes and soaking them with water, which made the wood expand, cracking the stone block away from its bedrock. The rough stone was then pounded smooth with balls of dolerite, a rock harder than granite. Many of these balls have been found, but it's still not clear how, or with what, they were themselves originally shaped into tools. Most archaeologists concur that some basic yet sophisticated technique of working with exceedingly hard abrasives was employed: carborundum or even ground gemstones. The Egyptians had not developed steel, but they *had* devised a method of tempering copper to the hardness of steel, a method no one since has been able to reproduce. It has also been suggested, though upon little evidence, that they set teeth made from gems into their copper saws and drills. Knowing all this merely makes the massive undertaking you see in the Aswan quarry all the more majestic. Although the monolith must have cracked because of some hidden fault line, I had the impression someone must have been in deep shit when the crack was found.

Who commissioned it three thousand-odd years ago? How would it have been moved, let alone transported hundreds of miles up the Nile?

"Some say it was intended for Hatshepsut, the only woman pharaoh," Sheila said. She had a great interest in Hatshepsut, whose mummy might have been discovered in the Valley of the Tombs of the Kings on the very day we spoke. If obelisks had some phallic significance, as seems a little too obvious and twentieth-century an explanation, then Hatshepsut would have needed the biggest one available to bolster her somewhat shaky position in dynastic history.

That evening, as the sun was sinking over the Dome of the Wind, the three of us took a felucca ride on the blood-red waters of the Nile around Elephantine Island. The enormous ghostly white triangle of the sail flapping overhead in a cooling breeze, the dark shapes of the ancient ruins and rocks rising up around us, the twinkling lights of the Cataract terrace, all combined to evoke a sense of awe that is uniquely engendered by so much in Egypt.

"This is why I came to Aswan," Sheila confided. Then, looking affectionately at Shoukry, she added, "This and so much more." She seemed happy, but happy in that bittersweet way all the inhabitants of Nubia seemed happy.

Later we visited the temple of Isis at Philae again, the final bastion of the ancient Egyptian faith. Shoukry showed me what is now thought to be the last known inscription in the sacred hieroglyphs. With these spare pictograms, still to the very end so close to the original image they represented, the written language of ancient Egypt, virtually unchanged in three thousand years, simply vanished from the face of the earth. After the Roman Empire was officially Christianized under Constantine the Great in the first half of the fourth century A.D., the process of conversion began, first by edict and then by the sword. Egypt had been raped economically by the Romans, but her religion had remained unscathed. Now the priests moved south, setting up camp on their island fortress at Philae, protected by the loyal Nubians for two hundred years. In A.D. 550 an edict of the Byzantine emperor Justinian converted the temple of Isis to a Christian church, and crude Coptic crosses were carved everywhere, even on the altar, putting an end to the most enduring and sophisticated civilization the world has ever known. It's hard to understand the evangelizing fury of the followers of Jesus Christ as they smashed the stone symphonies of ancient Egypt, as if their very beauty were a threat as potent as Satan.

The son-et-lumière was in Arabic that night, so I was spared banality, free to meditate upon the serene splendour of this magic island amid the shadows of the moon-pale stones. It's almost as if, by being moved to a new island, the temple has shrugged off its desecration and returned to its former power and beauty.

Sheila told me it was rumoured that certain Freemasons had been behind the move to finance the temple's relocation and that they still held their rituals of Isis worship here on certain occasions. There were nights, she claimed, when no one was permitted to visit the island. Shoukry confirmed this, happy that the past was only hidden and not dead. Nubian independence is tied up with Nubian dependence, of course. The past, with its Nubian pharaohs, conjures up for these southernmost inhabitants of Upper Egypt a daydream of a time when their pride did not have to grapple with obstacles like independence or dependence. Perhaps, they fantasize, such a time will come again. So close are they to the animism of the vast dark continent below them, their allegiance to any of the major religions has always been tenuous at best, I suspected. Whatever replaces Islam — if or when it happens — they will still march to the beat of a different drummer, just as the rhythms of tribal Africa throb at the heart of Abdul Karim al-Kabli's Middle Eastern music, making the dust of sorrow a poet.

～～つ

I'd heard there were newly restored Nubian temples three hours south of Abu Simbel that would soon be open to the public, and I had been trying to arrange a meeting with the Aswan director of the Egyptian Antiquities Organisation since I'd been in town, hoping to get permission to visit them. The man proved elusive, but I assumed the holiday period probably accounted for this. I was wrong.

With Shoukry's help, I tracked him down one morning in a café near his office. A disreputable-looking greybeard with something of the old colonial Egyptian about him, he literally refused to look at me as Shoukry explained what I wanted and showed him my Cairo government press credentials. The streets were full of weary-looking people, the general atmosphere one of lethargy. According to Shoukry, it takes the metabolism a while to readjust to eating during the day after a month of fasting. The director muttered a few dismissive phrases and returned, with a rudeness quite un-Egyptian, to chat with his cronies. Shoukry told me he had instructed me to make an appointment with his assistant.

That evening, the assistant showed up an hour late in my hotel lobby. A standoffish character with a limp handshake, spectacles so thick they were almost opaque, and the intellectual presence of a junior clerk, he was so evasive his attitude soon struck me as downright ludicrous. Eventually he admitted there were two temples that had recently been restored by a British team of archaeologists and that they would be open to the public as soon as a road had been built through the desert. I indicated my willingness to hire a Land Rover and a guide if I could go there now.

"Not possible," he kept repeating. "What's the big secret?" I asked. He smiled lamely, saying, "No secret. You bring letter from Cairo." I asked about digs currently under way on sites around Aswan, only to meet the same response. Eventually he conceded that German, French, British, and American units were working in the area. On what? He smiled again, looking away and playing nervously with his fingers. What about the temples still under Lake Nasser? Could one scuba dive to see them?

"There are no temples there," he muttered, irritated. "We rescued them all." I told him that everyone knew there were many temples still down there. He denied this again, looking at his watch.

"You're sure you *are* the assistant director?" I asked jokingly. He was sure. How long had he had the position? Fifteen years. How had he got it? He'd studied ancient Egyptian history at college. "Then how come you don't appear to know anything about the subject?" I asked bluntly. He ignored the question and rose to leave.

"What was *that* all about?" I said to Shoukry when the man had gone.

"These government departments are all at odds with each other. They've had so much trouble with journalists in the past that they are unwilling to talk about anything unless Sayeed Tawfiq, the national director, gives permission, and he rarely does. I understand their position," Shoukry confessed, his Nubian generosity coming through once more. "They don't wish to risk their jobs."

"So my press credentials mean nothing?"

"Wrong government department. The Antiquities people come under more international criticism than most departments, mainly because of lack of funds. The government hates international criticism; so does Sayeed Tawfiq. He can do what he likes."

I came to understand the situation more thoroughly later, but even at this stage certain things were clear. Unwilling to turn over everything to foreigners with the money to excavate and restore, the EAO had to put up with constant flak about its lack of adequate concern for existing sites and for properly excavating new ones, let alone the touchy issue of those sites lost forever beneath Lake Nasser. The world tends to view the antiquities of ancient Egypt as the property of all mankind. The EAO views these matchless ruins as exclusively Egyptian property. It's a classic Egyptian double bind, another hopelessly insoluble problem. The Egyptians need foreign money and expertise to support the EAO, yet they also resent needing it and like to make it clear to foreigners that they are only invited guests: their permits can be revoked at any time or not renewed for any reason. So often after this encounter I wished I could see Egypt the way I'd first seen it, as a simple tourist, content with the facade. Who really wants illusions shattered? As the Arab chieftain, Hassan-i-Sabbah, the Old Man of the Mountain, leader of the Hashishi, the assassins, said, "Nothing is true. Everything is permitted."

CHAPTER FIVE

THE PRISON OF HISTORY

All know the monstrous worships that defile
the Egyptians. They adore the crocodile,
the ibis gorged with snakes. In awe they gape
before the golden image of an ape,
where broken Memnon twangs to dawning skies …
They spare the woolly race and won't permit
the throat of any goatbitch to be slit,
but unrebuked at meals of human flesh they sit.

—JUVENAL, *FIFTEENTH SATIRE*

I'd booked myself on a cruise ship run by a major hotel chain. I intended
to take the obligatory Nile trip from Aswan to Luxor — not the best way of
seeing the remains of ancient Egypt, since the civilization essentially developed in the opposite direction from north gradually to south over the long
centuries. This route would be showing me history in reverse.

The morning I was due to transfer to the ship from the Cataract Hotel,

Shoukry came with a friend's car to help me with my bags. I hadn't asked him to do this, and I got the feeling there was more to his gesture than merely a professed sadness at seeing me leave; Egyptians have a rather endearing tendency to become your best friends within minutes. It became obvious, as we reached the ship, a floating hotel, rectangular, high in the water like a Mississippi riverboat, that he wanted an excuse to come on board. Although these radiantly opulent vessels were moored by the dozen all along Aswan's hectic corniche for much of the year, dropping one load of tourists to pick up another, it was nearly impossible for a local to board them and get a close-up glimpse of what his country offered rich Westerners. From the pavement, someone like Shoukry could watch bikini-clad women sit with men in Ray-Bans and Rolexes sipping drinks around the thimble-sized swimming pools on upper decks; or, at night, the same tourists dressed in tropical elegance, in luxurious restaurants with wine and heaped plates of strange foods. But they could get no nearer than the gang-way before being ordered off by one of the ever-vigilant crew members.

I felt this was unnecessary, considering the inordinately low crime rate in Egypt. The hassle rate, however, is inordinately high; and this was the excuse for the verbal brutality the curious Nubians were frequently sub-jected to by their fellow Egyptians — yet another cause of the Nubians' melancholy grievance against the wicked north, where most of the Nile sailors originated. Even accompanying me, Shoukry was subjected to a rather humiliating interrogation; indeed, only my insistence that he be allowed on board as my friend prevented his being dismissed, like any other cabdriver, at the entrance. The lavishness of the ship embarrassed me on Shoukry's behalf. Once we had deposited my bags in a cabin that con-tained everything one might find, apart from space, in a five-star hotel room, including a TV, I invited him for coffee in the lounge. The air-con-ditioning made him shiver, and he was clearly uncomfortable being served by his countrymen with the same obsequious grandeur as any Westerner. He tried to make up for it by chatting with the waiters.

All men are equal in Islam (as they allegedly are in Judaism and Christianity), and while there are obviously class divisions, the barriers between men aren't the same as those I'd been conditioned to after twenty-seven years of growing up in England. The mosque is the great equalizer, and, praying up to five times a day, most Egyptians spend far more time being equal than we in the Christian West do. Shoukry's patent uneasiness saddened me. He soon finished his coffee and made an excuse to leave. We promised to write to each other, knowing we wouldn't.

"This is a good boat," he said, as if he'd seen many. "You will have good experiences on this boat."

I unpacked, then went out onto the upper deck. It was some hours before departure time, and my fellow passengers were just beginning to arrive. Most would come straight from the Cairo plane. I dozed beneath an awning, cooled by a pleasant dry wind.

"Do you think anyone *reads* the Dr. Dolittle stories anymore?" said the most archly upper-class English voice I think I've ever heard, awakening me from some reverie.

"Didn't they make a *film* about them with Rex *Harrison*?" another similar but oddly familiar voice inquired.

"*Yerse*, I think you're absolutely *right*. They *did*."

I opened one eye to find three old women of the male sex leaning over the starboard railing. They were accompanied by a younger man, who was, in every detail, ostentatiously homosexual in a way that only the English can be. I hadn't seen anyone quite like him since the late 1960s. The older man, whom I'll call Clarence, the owner of the familiar voice, was an ancient but sprightly don I'd served time under at Oxford. I'd always known he was gay, as so many of his colleagues seemed to be in those days, but he had never flaunted the fact and certainly never let it intrude upon his academic duties. The author of several major historical biographies, he was one of the most respected and eminent of my tutors. I could hardly avoid saying hello, although I hadn't seen him in nearly twenty years. Apart from a rather ludicrous tropical getup, he'd scarcely altered and greeted me as if he'd last seen me a week before, indeed *expected* to find me on the banks of the Nile in Nubia. His companion, whom I'll call Trevor, the man with the caricature accent, turned out to be a Cambridge professor of Italian literature, an expert on Dante. The third older man, whom I'll call John, a thick-set, wall-eyed, rather sinister fellow, was, I learned, one of Britain's foremost experts on Middle East politics, an economist and consultant to multinational corporations, as well as a familiar face on TV news and talk shows whenever the cauldron boiled over — which was often. His companion, Pierre — a French musician, as it turned out — was the blatantly effeminate one. I realized then and there, with a mounting sense of horror, something quintessential about cruises: you're trapped with your fellow passengers. Floating palaces can be floating prisons.

My other shipmates, gathering now in the bar for a welcome drink of kharkady, did not look promising either: rich East Indians working in Saudi Arabia, laden with video equipment and obnoxious children with incongruous accents from their American-run schools; aged Californian couples with expensive luggage and skin, whose reactions to everything were polarized between awe and disapproval; a clan of edgy Italians who kept strictly to themselves and constantly complained about the food; and an Egyptian Copt who'd lived in Canada for twenty years and was bringing his Canadian wife and children to his homeland for the first time. He was a calm, handsome, and dignified man, obviously proud of his heritage, quietly delighted that his family were overawed by the majesty of the civilization his ancestors had helped build.

At this get-to-know-each-other gathering, we were introduced to our guide. Syed was a self-important man in his late twenties who imagined himself to be thoroughly Westernized, a notch above his fellow countrymen, disdaining their company, revelling in that of his Western "friends." As a guide, he was useless. He resented being asked questions — mainly because he couldn't answer them — and most of all he resented people who could see through his Western facade and the facade of his professional abilities. He had set speeches he delivered at certain points in each site we visited, information we could have gleaned for ourselves after ten minutes with a guidebook, spurious anecdotes he expected us to listen to with rapt attention, and lame jokes he'd obviously employed a thousand times before. He grew petulant when his flock strayed or talked among themselves during his "lectures." He was especially miffed at John, the Arabist, and was painfully aware that what I came to think of as "our group" knew far more than he did and had no time for his ill-informed performances. Syed knew I was writing a book and was revoltingly eager to please me, insisting several times that I mention him in it — to help his "career."

He didn't really want this career, it seemed to me. He had a wife and child in Cairo whom he rarely saw. And, being on the Nile with Westerners most of the time, he wanted me to know, allowed him too many "opportunities" with the women he guided. "Different woman every cruise," he bragged; then, growing implausibly grave and sad, he added, "But this is not good when a man has a wife and child." On this cruise he was unduly attentive to the thirteen-year-old daughter of one of the East Indians, who thought she could still wear skimpy tops and tight shorts with impunity.

I wondered where Syed's cabin was. Although he dined in the restaurant, he slept somewhere below decks with the rest of the crew. The job obviously didn't pay well; he relied on the substantial tips handed out by passengers at the end of each cruise, as he was quick to point out to us that first day. The ship was barely half-full, and he instinctively knew our little group's reliance on his services was such that we'd be unlikely to tip him much, if anything.

When we finally shipped anchor and set off, the broad curve of the Nile flowed like molten turquoise past the vessel, past the ochre walls and endless sands of Nubia, spattered here and there with the billowing sails of zigzagging feluccas slowly bouncing from shore to shore: a combination of colours so rich and elegant it must have driven countless landscape painters mad and eluded ten million rolls of Kodak. The sands of the desert seem to hold the sun, shining even when there is no sun.

Our first stop was the stately Ptolemaic temple of Kom Ombo. Unlike the other major temples along the Nile, Kom Ombo is not surrounded by a town. Situated at a bend in the river, it appears suddenly, seeming all the more impressive after the miles of burning empty countryside preceding it, and looking all the more serene with nothing but irrigated fields on all sides, the Nile lapping at its feet. The early evening light made the

Greco-Roman-like columns glow, intensifying the many patches where original paintwork still looks as brilliant as it did well over two thousand years ago, reminding us that all these stone marvels were once covered in a riot of singing colours in marked contrast to the monotones of the vast desert sands in whose midst they were built. The ancient Egyptians loved colour and made sure, by grinding their paints from actual minerals — turquoise, malachite, lapis, and others — that their temple murals would not fade beneath the harsh sun.

Kom Ombo is dedicated to two separate divine triads: the crocodile-god Sobek at the head of one, the falcon Haroeris, a version of Horus the Elder, at the head of the other. Herodotus tells us that the Egyptians seemed to have an ambiguous attitude toward crocodiles. In some parts they were feared and detested, killed whenever the opportunity arose; but in others, especially the Kom Ombo area and the Fayyoum Oasis, they were held to be divine, offered sacrifices, and even tamed, pampered with necklaces and jewelled earrings. As John Anthony West notes, "Egypt's view of evil was complex, sophisticated and cyclical." While representing death, the crocodile also implies the resurrection that cannot take place without death.

For Syed, Kom Ombo was more about crocodiles than anything else. Marshalling us before a small chapel dedicated to Hathor and now used to display several gnarled, loglike mummified crocodiles found in the surrounding necropolis, he made some remark about not worrying because they'd just been fed, as well as numerous irrelevant comments he considered amusing.

John and the others walked off in exaggerated disgust. I trailed along, learning far more. On the outer wall of the ruined sanctuary chambers, there stands a relief that is both famous and perplexing. It depicts the Roman emperor Trajan kneeling before a deified version of the high priest Imhotep, who was the legendary "first physician" and the architect of King Zoser's step-pyramid at Saqqara, and two goddesses. Near it are representations of what have been traditionally described as medical instruments, largely due to Imhotep's connection with medicine. But, as John pointed out, the drills, massive shears, saws, knives, and other, similar tools might have enabled someone to perform an autopsy on an elephant but not a tricky operation on a living person, let alone the detailed ophthalmic work implied by the presence of Horus, the divine oculist, whose "eye" is among the best known of ancient Egyptian symbols.

Back from these reliefs, the five of us tried to scale a battered staircase at the rear of the temple and were suddenly subjected to the angry imprecations of a turbaned official. Apparently a tourist had recently died plunging from the ledge above these same steps. Anxious to promote an image of tourist Egypt as a haven of safety, which it in fact is, the authorities were unnaturally touchy about discussing or even admitting such incidents.

Notions of hospitality across the Middle East include the host's responsibility for anything that may befall his guests. Wherever I went, I found also that the most trifling failures were reacted to with exaggeratedly defensive, and often irritatingly inappropriate, measures. The same curious emotion lies behind the complicated yet utterly wrong directions someone will invariably give you in Egypt when you ask how to reach a place he has never heard of. To admit ignorance is a humiliation beyond countenance. Only the appearance of dignity is being preserved here, not the substance.

Rejoining Syed and the rest of our shipmates by a well where the sacred crocodiles were once kept in reptilian luxury, we got a taste of our guide's barely concealed truculence. Just to spite us, it seemed, he spent an unnecessarily long time explaining the function of the Nilometre, an ancient device that basically kept tabs on the height of the river, warning of potential floods or droughts. No mystery there.

The vendors waiting outside the Kom Ombo complex are among the most terrifyingly persistent in all of Egypt, mainly because they have so little time to accost tourists between cruise ship and temple entrance. Warned about the costume party to be held that night, I succumbed to purchasing a *gelabia* and several accessories, being obliged to negotiate for nearly twenty minutes before obtaining a price that was remotely reasonable.

Back on board, we headed into a sinister night that seemed to rise out of the very waters around us. Soon the ship began to lurch and shudder, navigating a stretch of the river where, owing to the drought in Ethiopia that year, the Nile was treacherously low. As people prepared for the costume party, most of them donning embarrassingly tacky belly-dancer or pharaoh getups supplied by the crew, the ship proceeded in a slow and tortuous fashion. In the oppressive gathering gloom, rolling erratically, we passed a vessel like ours that had stuck on a sandbank and was now listing at forty-five degrees, her passengers evacuated to the shore by dinghy. The sight spooked my fellow travellers, who all sat drinking nervously in the bar in their garish outfits.

Besides me, only Pierre in our group had donned a costume, parading about now like a caricature of a fellah with thin pencilled moustache and a scarf wrapped clumsily around his head. The others on board clearly hated his overt homosexuality, his loud camp comments, his very walk. And they just as patently hated all the rest of us for being associated with him *and* for sounding far too English as well.

Even I began to sound far too English for my own liking. To remedy this, I sat with Nagy, the Canadian Copt, who'd invited me for a drink. His wife, Rita, was of German descent; watching her children's reactions to everything they saw clearly gave her immense pleasure. They were obviously prospering in Canada. Nagy said he'd arrived there from Egypt with less than twenty dollars in his pocket — all the government would let him take out — and no possessions. Now he owned a large house in one of the expensive suburbs of Toronto and a small manufacturing plant. He made a practice, he wanted me to know, of hiring Coptic immigrants who were in the position he had once been in.

The persecution of Christians in Egypt was, he insisted, appalling: one of the least-publicized scandals in the world. I reminded him that one of the most powerful men in the current cabinet, Boutros Boutros-Ghali, was a Christian, but Nagy dismissed the example as mere tokenism. The man was minister of state for foreign affairs, he said, and not empowered to do anything about the domestic situation of his fellow Christians, who were suffering in countless insidious ways. Their only strength was in the field of banking and finance, Nagy claimed, because Muslims did not trust other Muslims with their money. "Banking and finance" sounded better than many fates I could think of. Outside these areas they were severely restricted, I learned; Coptic employers, for example, are obliged to hire a higher percentage of Muslims than Christians; Coptic gynecologists are forbidden to examine Muslim women. Was his obvious bitterness about all this the reason he had waited so long to bring his wife and family back to the land of his birth? He'd never had the time, he answered. It was clearly a half-truth. I felt sure he'd not wanted to embarrass himself by showing his homeland in its current state of poverty, often backward, shabby, and pathetic.

"You know," he said, more for his family's benefit than for mine, "this is a poor country, but it tries hard with the little it has." It was a refrain I'd heard already countless times. I guessed that his experiences of looking up distant relatives in Cairo had been difficult. One third cousin, who was hoping for help emigrating to Canada, had brought him a gift of twenty pounds of pistachio nuts. He sighed. "I gave them away." He still loved his homeland, and I think this trip had somewhat saddened him. He realized he could never return again because, magnificent as Egypt's monuments were to them, his wife and children made it clear they felt themselves in an utterly alien land.

Surviving the shallows around the town of Silwa, our ship returned to a more even course, and the costume party commenced after dinner. It was a ludicrous and lacklustre affair, passengers hitting the disco floor like extras in a cheap Bombay movie. Syed — and the rest of the crew, for that matter — couldn't keep their eyes off the young East Indian girl, a cheap tinsel Cleopatra. Her young breasts all but fell out of their sequined bra as she boogied, and the diaphanous shreds of chiffon left little mystery about what was below her waist. The pedophiliac lust of the Egyptians was in stark contrast to her charming innocence of the effect she had on them. Even her parents seemed blissfully oblivious to these ravenous stares and the slavishly attentive service their table was receiving from every waiter on the floor.

We arrived at the town of Edfu a little after eleven that night, mooring alongside a small and hectic fairground: a tiny Ferris wheel, a miniature merry-go-round, brilliantly lit stalls, and the shrill warbling quarter-tones of Arabic pop blaring from a dozen crude speakers.

"How de*light*ful," Trevor said, this assessment thoroughly endorsed by his three friends.

"We simply *must* go for a *troll*," said Pierre, with theatrical enthusiasm. "There'll be *boys!*"

"Yerse," Trevor replied. "Gives cruising the Nile an *entirely* new meaning, doesn't it."

Pierre and I were still in our party clothes, but we all headed for the exit, where the gangway was just being swung onto the corniche. The noise from the fairground was formidable.

"Not possible to go ashore," the purser announced, rather sternly. He was greeted with incredulity. The tourist police, he informed us, had forbidden anyone to leave the cruise ships; something wasn't safe. What that "something" was he either couldn't or wouldn't say.

"It's like being in a bloody *concentration* camp," Pierre muttered, sweeping grandly back upstairs with the other three.

I asked the purser what was really going on. He glanced behind me and, in a confidential whisper, said there'd been trouble with a previous cruise ship. Some "gays" — he used the term — had propositioned a calèche boy for sex, it seems, and there had been a dispute over money. This incident had ended with the townspeople marching angrily to the ship and beating the crap out of the men in question. Thus, no tourists, especially not gay tourists, were now being permitted ashore at night.

Back on the upper deck, somewhat misguidedly, I related this to the four brooding and now tolerably drunk friends. I regretted it instantly.

"So we're *prisoners!*" Pierre huffed, pouring three fingers of scotch into his already full glass from a bottle he clutched between his legs. For a moment I thought someone was about to suggest hiring a lawyer. Only John the Arabist was philosophical about the situation. He'd lived in Cairo for sixteen years during Nasser's time and had clearly experienced far worse things.

"Egyptians are fairly *peaceable* people," he told me. "Except when they *aren't.* Then *any*thing can happen. And anything *tends* to happen, *oddly* enough, around Ramadan. One finds that, having *lost* this extraordinary desire to *avoid* unpleasantness, they can really turn *quite* nasty." He went on to describe a gruesome murder he'd once witnessed that had stemmed from an argument over the price of bread in a Cairo bazaar. "The man became *totally* deranged," he recalled. "It was *all so* out of *proportion*. Exactly like this business *here*."

Resigned, I sat on the deck overlooking the blaring incandescent fairground and the shadowy town surrounding it, talking with John, or rather listening to him, while the others grumpily amused themselves calling out drunkenly to passersby on the corniche.

Horus was worshipped under many forms and is an extremely complex deity, but his fundamental and overriding role is easily expressed and grasped: Horus is the realized divine principle: the matured seed carried by Isis and fecundated posthumously by Osiris, the mortal god. The innumerable forms and aspects of Horus may be understood as stages in the process of spiritualization.

—JOHN ANTHONY WEST,
THE TRAVELER'S KEY TO ANCIENT EGYPT

Setting off along the Edfu corniche behind Syed and the others, we noticed a sign that read: THE TOWN OF KIND MEETING WISHES YOU AN ENJOYABLE TIME.

"*Well*," Pierre shrieked, "they're certainly going about giving us one the wrong way, *aren't* they!" All of us laughed, but I don't believe anyone found it funny.

Dedicated to Horus, the temple of Edfu is the best preserved in Egypt; indeed, it is the most intact temple of the ancient world anywhere. Apart from effacements, smoke damage, vanished paintwork and gold leaf, it stands much as it did over two thousand years ago, an awesome and overpowering structure redolent of the might and mysteries possessed by those who constructed it. The site itself seems to have been sacred ground as far back as the Old Kingdom, but most of what now stands dates from the Ptolemaic period. Unlike any other remaining temple, Edfu still possesses large sections of its original outer wall, indicating how secluded from the general populace these realms of the pharaoh and his priests actually were.

I could imagine fear and wonder in the eyes of the common people who approached these sacred confines in ancient times. Here more than anywhere else in Egypt you feel that you are trespassing on forbidden ground.

Shaded from the fierce sun, the inner courtyards are cool and increasingly dark as you proceed in toward the sanctuary, where narrow holes make dramatic use of the blinding light outside to cast incandescent beams on reliefs and shrines. The enormous polished-granite falcons that guard the outer pylons and stand at the far end of the great court just outside the vestibule still emit an aura of fierce power. As with my experiences in the pyramids, I felt here not the sanctity of initiation but rather the sheer muscle of the cosmic forces connected with it. You feel very frail and human standing next to those falcons. As John Anthony West states so succinctly:

> *The falcon is the chief symbol of Horus, who represents the manifold aspects of resurrection. This is the triumph of the divine over the temporal. Horus, born of Osiris, and yet older than his father, avenges his father's murder by Set, who is associated with the cycles of time and the imprisonment of spirit in matter. So the falcon symbolizes this role — the falcon that strikes in silence, without warning and with incredible swiftness, and then carries away its prey into the eye of the sun itself.*

West and others who believe that, like Christ, the Egyptian priesthood spoke directly and symbolically to the initiated and in stories or parables to the multitudes, are vindicated at Edfu by the unique series of reliefs that appear on the walls of the outer western corridor. This is one part of the temple interior that members of the populace were probably permitted to enter on certain special occasions.

Here, the myth of Horus is depicted in what appears to be a dramatic story form, his battle with Set portrayed as combat with a giant hippopotamus. Leviathan and so many other mythical monsters came to mind. Scholars are divided over the issue of whether there actually *was* drama as we know it in ancient Egypt, but these vibrant, action-filled reliefs certainly lend credence to the theory that there was. Indeed, many of the larger Egyptian temples have even been used as stage sets in recent years. It is hard to imagine they weren't originally employed to present sacred performances of some sort.

The only performance I saw at Edfu, however, was Pierre's — he seemed determined to confirm the very worst his fellow passengers suspected of him. In the streets of the bustling little town he continually approached any good-looking man or boy unfortunate enough to cross his path, rubbing his palms together in an obscene gesture and shouting, "You want *zigzag, habibi*?" Rough translation: "You wanna fuck, lover-boy?" I could see our ship being stormed by another angry mob if this continued. I took Syed's advice, trailing behind the four musketeers and starting up a conversation with the East Indian couple, whose daughter, in drum-taut shorts, was causing a commotion among the locals herself.

Indra, her mother, kept talking about how similar these Egyptian temples were to the ones she'd grown up with in southern India. "Except *there*," she said, incredulous, "they are still one hundred percent functioning. Here, they seem not to be in use."

I let it drop. Her comment wasn't even strictly true; I'd seen Californians (one assumes) meditating cross-legged at a number of temple sites. And Shirley MacLaine is still "using" the Great Pyramid.

Over lunch Pierre began to complain loudly about the service, the food, his cabin, the ship, anything that crossed his mind. Even his three friends, particularly John, began to suggest he cool it.

Hiding in my cabin, its window a giant TV tuned in to Egypt, I was relieved when we finally began to slip out of Edfu, heading north down the Nile toward Esna. Brown-skinned children swam near the banks while their elders toiled languidly in narrow patches of irrigated land, plowing or drawing up water with levered devices as old as the land itself. The kids waved at our ship, as I remember once waving at trains, no doubt wondering, as I used to wonder, where these mobile strangers were from and where they were going. But I never sensed the yearning in these children that I had once felt myself, the yearning to travel off forever with strangers, regardless of their origins or destination.

Esna. Wednesday, 6 March 1850 ... *We go ashore. The town is like*
all the others, built of dried mud, smaller than Kena; the bazaars
less rich ... School above a mosque, where we go to buy some
ink. First visit to the temple, where we stay but a moment ...
———GUSTAVE FLAUBERT, TRAVEL NOTES, 1850

Flaubert stayed "but a moment" at the Esna temple because, as he neg-
lects to mention, there wasn't much of it to see in 1850. David Roberts'
famous watercolours and sketches of Egyptian monuments, executed
around the same time, show it almost totally buried in silt, and people
occupying the hutlike spaces left. More than at any other site in Egypt
today, here you can get some idea of the effect of hundreds of years of successive flooding and the resulting silt deposits. When Napoleon passed
through, only the roof and uppermost parts of columns were visible; subsequent excavations dug out the Hypostyle Hall, but the rest of the temple
still lies buried beneath the modern town that grew up on and around it.
The temple is now situated at the bottom of what resembles the beginnings
of a construction site for a skyscraper, and although what remains is
impressive enough, I found it contained little of interest. Begun in 150 B.C.
under the Ptolemies, it was constructed mostly under Roman rule, and the
last inscriptions date from around A.D. 200 — almost a few months ago by
Egyptian standards.

As Clarence pointed out to me, apologizing for Pierre's behaviour in the
process, by far the most interesting reliefs are on the ceiling above the
extreme left- and right-hand aisles. One appeared to depict a slug with two
human heads and some sort of tree sprouting from its back; another
showed what looked like a centipede, or snake with many legs, wearing a
crown. The late Egyptians were overly fond of complex word games, and
cut into two little doorways at the far north and south ends of the vestibule
are examples of reliefs in cryptographic script, employing visual puns with
words that use a hieroglyphic image of either a crocodile or a ram in their
formation. No one has yet managed to solve these riddles, but the leading
contemporary expert on Esna, Serge Sauneron, calls these particular texts

"gruesome examples of the excesses achieved in graphic cryptography." Indeed, excess is everywhere at Esna, the figures of gods and humans alike attaining a meaty voluptuousness encountered almost nowhere else in Egypt and clearly implying that, at this late stage in history, religion had descended from the spiritual to the carnal, as it had right across the whole Roman Empire. As we examined the martial friezes on the exterior walls typical of most Egyptian temples, Clarence indicated a traditional manacled band of prisoners whose heads were being clubbed by the king. In this case they would presumably be Egyptians for a change, since the king involved was the emperor Domitian.

The town I found far more charming than Flaubert described it, although, by his own account, he was far too busy catching syphilis from a number of sources to notice much. The streets were steep and the bazaars more authentically Oriental (again, admitting that old Paris-exhibition mentality of the Westerner). It was while we were walking back through the dust and bullying merchants that, to my horror, Pierre actually picked up a teenage boy and disappeared into an alley with him.

Over lunch, he looked quite deranged, flushed with his "conquest" and going on about similar sexual exploits in Egypt before. "*John,*" he trilled, "remember the first time I was *raped*? When we were staying at the Winter Palace in Luxor that *year,* and I came back with my *gelabia simply* all covered in *blood*? It was *so* delightful, darling." It certainly didn't sound much like a "rape" either.

Everyone seemed to be getting a trifle weary of Pierre by now.

"You told *me* the first time you were raped was by your *uncle,*" John snapped grumpily, shunting food around his plate. He'd had trouble sleeping and was definitely not in a good mood. I wondered about the nature of his relationship with Pierre.

"Oh, yes, *that,*" Pierre replied, somewhat chastened.

On the outskirts of Esna is the only lock on the Nile between Aswan and Luxor. We found ourselves queued up behind several other cruise ships, a considerable period of waiting ahead since the low water level lengthened the period each ship would have to spend passing the lock. The surrounding countryside was unusually lush and fertile: green fields, waving palms, a small, riverlike inlet heading toward the town and flanked by prosperous-looking mansions with gardens full of flowers and fruit trees. On the banks below, small boys called up at us, soliciting pens and anything else we might like to throw down.

Nagy and Rita suggested I accompany them and their children on a walk around this part of Esna. "It'll give you some idea of what these small towns are really like," Nagy said. The East Indian couple and their nubile daughter decided to string along. At first we were importuned by countless scruffy kids all wanting to be our guide, but a brutal character with many missing teeth and hideous scars who had something to do with the lock chased them away. One rather sweet-natured boy reappeared along the mud path leading into town, and we agreed to let him guide us.

The streets here, where the town gradually dissolved into the country-side, were broad, dusty, and chaotic with horse-drawn calèches, animals, cars, and people. It was obviously a market area, lined with little fruit and vegetable stalls, barrows that sold luridly coloured soft drinks of various kinds, and, farther along, a large open space thronged with yelling people amid hundreds of cagelike wooden crates containing the reddest tomatoes I've ever seen. It was an auction, Nagy explained. The price for one crate: around a dollar.

Again, the East Indian girl's shorts began to attract much fevered interest, but it seemed benevolent enough. Nagy warned her father that she should probably consider returning to the ship and changing, but the man didn't appear to understand him, continuing to wave his video camera in all directions. Nagy, ever concerned to avoid any form of potential unpleasantness, then told the man to be careful whom he pointed his camera at.

"Generally no one minds," he explained, "but if you tried to film the wife of an important man — the mayor, a mullah, for example — you could find yourself in a lot of trouble. These people are not like those in Aswan or Luxor or Cairo; they're far more backward here, and many are fundamentalists. So be careful, eh?"

The Indian again, whether through incomprehension or wilful stupidity, ignored this warning, too. Apart from shy stares and enthusiastic cries of "Hello, how are you?" and "What country, pliss?" from passing schoolchildren, however, we encountered nothing but courtesy and geniality. Led by our little guide through a maze of winding medieval streets, we passed numerous open rooms where carpenters were at work carving elaborate items of furniture with tools that belonged in museums. Almost every door we passed, each hundreds of years old, intricately chiselled and studded with ancient pyramid-tipped nails, would have fetched a fair price in the West. At a bakery, where a dozen people ghostly with flour kneaded dough, loading the flattened slabs into blazing wood-fired ovens with implements like large flat shovels, we were offered fresh hot bread and greeted with happy smiles.

An official-looking man approached us at one point, and Nagy spoke with him in Arabic. Apparently he only wanted to be sure we weren't being bothered by our little guide. The boy looked anxiously up at Nagy, who explained to the man that we'd hired the little urchin, and he was doing an excellent job.

Reaching the far end of the corniche, we came across someone reshoeing his donkey, which was harnessed to a cartload of fat, shiny eggplants, while several old-timers sat outside a tiny café watching, puffing away on gurgling narghiles. The workday was winding down, and other, similar little establishments all along the riverside were packed with tea drinkers, smokers, and soldiers in uniform playing *sheshbesh*, backgammon. Returned to the ship, we heard the cries of a dozen muezzins summoning the faithful to evening prayers, reminding them, as always, that God was indeed great.

The interlude had been a pleasant change from the ordered life on board and the tourist Egypt of Syed, its clichés and platitudes. It left me with another image of Esna, one of timeless simplicity, a life free of modern aggravations and rich with the traditional values, the peace and order implicit in orthodox Islam, which the big cities have eschewed in the name of progress. Part of me yearned to stay there, fend off the future until another life.

Before long, we had passed through the lock and were heading off into the night for Luxor. Thebes, the capital of ancient Egypt for much of its history and the site of its most magnificent remains. *Thebes:* the name kept ringing in my head, sent chills down my spine. It was a name that seemed to echo across history with the force of *Athens, Rome, Byzantium* ... My mood of anticipation was marred only because I had to have dinner with Syed, who made a last and desperate bid for a celebration of his talents in print, revealing that he was also a poet, scribbling one of his masterpieces on the back of a bill, dating and signing it for me. It read:

> *Later today*
> *Comes tomorrow*
> *By the evening*
> *In the silence of midnight*
> *To whisper*
> *Late yesterday*

Roll over, Ezra Pound.

CHAPTER SIX

SYMPHONIES IN STONE

We arrived at Luxor on Monday, 30 April, at 8:30 p.m. The
moon was rising. We go ashore. The Nile is low, and there is
quite a broad stretch of sand between the water and the village
of Luxor; we have to climb the bank to see anything. On the
bank, a short man accosts us and asks to be our guide. We ask
him if he speaks Italian. "Si, signor, molto bene."

The mass of the pylons and the colonnades looms in the
darkness; the moon, just risen behind the double colonnades,
seems to be resting on the horizon, low and round and motionless,
just for us, and the better to illumine the horizon's great flat
stretch.

—GUSTAVE FLAUBERT, TRAVEL NOTES, 1850

In fact, Flaubert arrived on April 29, according to his diary. I quibble because 140 years later I arrived on the same date. If the name "Thebes" conjured up visions of an incomparable past, that of Luxor reminded me of a cheap synthetic fabric. Essentially it is the Arab town that grew up around the ruins of Thebes, sprawling mainly along the east bank of the purling Nile. My first sight, through that giant TV-screen window in my cabin, was a rosy-fingered dawn casting pale fuchsia light on the low mountain range of the west bank. Few buildings were visible there.

The ancient Egyptians called the west, the region of the setting sun, Amenti. It was the domain of Osiris, god of the dead, also known as Khentamenti, Chief of the West. Apart from that of Akhenaten, the heretical "monotheistic" pharaoh, all burials in dynastic Egypt took place on the west bank. Within the mountain range I watched through dawn's mist lie the great pharaonic tombs: the Valley of the Kings, the Valley of the Queens, the Tombs of the Nobles, the Temple of Queen Hatshepsut, the Colossi of Memnon, the Ramesseum, and more. In fact, if you include the mighty Luxor and Karnak temple complexes on the east bank, Thebes and Luxor contain more than 85 percent of the remains of ancient Egypt. Looking out across these Western Lands, I could comprehend the ancient Egyptian preoccupation with death as the goal and apotheosis of life. They were still forbidding yet powerfully attractive, hostile yet enticing.

I decided to go out alone in the early morning light, one of the best times to view and photograph the great Egyptian monuments. The ship was quiet, and so was Luxor. Thanks to construction engineers from China, there is now a new corniche along the water's edge rather than the broad stretch of sand Flaubert encountered. As I climbed the steps to street level, the breathtaking pylons and columns of the colossal Luxor temple rose up, bathed in soft golden light filtering through a delicate mist, the shadows on its western side defining the exquisitely carved colonnades, massive hieroglyphic reliefs, rows of sphinxes, towering statues, and the serene harmony of the whole vast complex.

The low, rickety gates were locked, but in a booth nearby a hostile old man in a white turban, who looked as if he'd used tar as toothpaste for many years, growled at me, beckoning with a long, gnarled finger. "Ticket ticket," he said. With great effort, many groans and sighs, he walked the three yards to the temple entrance and unlocked a book-sized padlock to admit me.

The inner compound looked deserted — something to be devoutly wished of Egyptian sacred sites — and even the surrounding town displayed few signs or sounds of life. Like most midnight ramblers, Egyptians are not early risers. As someone had advised, I avoided looking to my right at the temple entrance, walking to the left down the avenue of sphinxes that once stretched nearly a mile to the Karnak Temple of Amon, creating a sacred complex whose dimensions are not equalled on earth.

Now the avenue extends only a few hundred yards, and sphinxes in various states of ruin can be seen in fields, backyards, and dumps all the way to Karnak if you walk the ancient route. All the sphinxes, with their human heads on lions' bodies, appeared identical in size. One guidebook suggested they were so perfectly matched by the stonemasons that they looked as if they had been poured from a mould. This seemed true, too, until I noticed that their human faces were subtly different, one even distinctly fat and jowly. Like the gargoyles on Gothic structures in Europe, had the sphinxes been endowed with the characteristics of local personages? I wondered. Actually most of the faces are essentially that of one man, Amenhotep III, with the bodhisattva smile reminiscent of the great Indian sacred sculptures, or the tantalizing transcendent mystery implicit in the smiles of da Vinci's *Mona Lisa* and his *Saint John the Baptist.* That smile, reflecting a sublime inner secret, never changes on the sphinxes, but the face around it does — perhaps making Amenhotep III into Everyman?

Finally turning around, I faced the shattering magnificence of the temple's numinous entrance. Slowly I retraced my steps, picturing myself part of an ancient procession, the regularly spaced sphinxes on either side passing like the steady beat of enormous drums. Before the towering pylons, to the left, stands a single obelisk, once part of a pair. Flaubert explains what happened to its partner in his travel notes: "The obelisk that is now in Paris was against the right-hand pylon. Perched on its pedestal, how bored it must be in the Place de la Concorde! How it must miss its Nile! What does it think as it watches all the cabs drive by, instead of the chariots it saw at its feet in the old days?" Flaubert was eleven years old when the obelisk was dismantled by French naval officers and engineers in 1832 to be transported to France. Its arrival caused enormous interest. In fact, since the ship carrying it sailed up the Seine from Le Havre to Paris, docking in Rouen for a few days, he might even have visited it on board, as many of his fellow citizens did. To me, the remaining obelisk seemed lonely, too, a widow at the end of a long and happy marriage. The colossus to the right of the pylons is of the ubiquitous Rameses II, and now, unobscured by the plundered obelisk, it looks all the more imposing. The wrecks of other colossi line the outer wall and are due for total restoration ... someday.

Across the length and breadth of this pylon wall is, as usual, a martial frieze in relief. This one, however, is exceptionally grand. One can only imagine how dramatic it would have looked when freshly carved and covered in vibrant colours. It depicts the Battle of Kadesh, an event, like so much of ancient Egyptian history, over which there is much dispute.

Rameses II, forewarned that a coalition centring on the Hittites and the nomadic Bedouin was forming itself in Anatolia (now Turkey) to invade his kingdom, gathered his army and marched through Palestine, intending to nip this nuisance in the bud. Outmanoeuvred by the enemy, betrayed and abandoned by his own army, we're told, Rameses prayed to Amon for assistance. Since no one had done more for Amon than Rameses, particularly in the field of temple-building, the god readily agreed to help him, descending into Rameses' body and giving him the strength to vanquish his foes single-handed, killing thousands and pitching chariots into the Orontes River. Yet, we learn, even after this total rout the battle somehow goes on for another fifteen years. Finally a peace treaty is signed and Rameses — evidently still working on his two hundred-odd children — takes a daughter of the Hittite king as wife, meting out other terms favourable to both sides. The problem all this raises is whether these events are to be taken literally or symbolically.

As in the legend of Cheops' burial in the Great Pyramid, there are again striking parallels here with the myth of Jesus. It's worthwhile quoting a section from Sir Alan Gardiner's translation of the invocation to Amon spoken by Rameses before the battle and carved beneath this scene on the pylons of the Luxor temple:

*I invoke thee, O my father, Amon! I find myself in the midst of
great multitudes of strangers; all the nations joined against me.
My cohorts have forsaken me, not one of my charioteers has
looked back to me, and when I summon, none harken to my
voice. Yet I believe that Amon is worth more to me than millions
of soldiers, and the hundreds of thousands of chariots, more
than countless brethren and youths united with one heart! The
work of many men is nothing! Amon is greater than all!*

> *My voice reaches unto Hermonthis; Amon responds to my call,
he stretches forth his hand to me and I rejoice; he calls out from
behind. "I hasten to thee, to thee, Ramesses Meriamon ["beloved
of God"]. I am with thee! It is I, thy father, my hand is with thee,
and I am of more avail than a hundred thousand men. I am the
lord of strength, lover of valour. I have found a courageous heart
and I am content. All that I desire will come to pass."*

That Amon has much in common with the Judeo-Christian concept of the
one God is made clear by an incantation surviving in a Late Kingdom document called the Leyden Papyrus; stanza 600 says of Amon that "he gives
birth to everything that is and causes all that exists to live."

It's important to have this other perspective on the nature of ancient
Egyptian beliefs, particularly if you find yourself as moved as I often was
by the deep spirituality I found in the tombs and temples of Egypt, and
particularly at Philae, Luxor, Karnak, and the Giza pyramids. Otherwise it
is easy to become oppressed by these monuments and obsessed with the
suffering one imagines was inflicted on the peasants and slaves who built
them. The grandeur of Egypt quickly becomes a pile of stones, as one
German tourist on the beach at Hurghada told me: "You zee vun, you zee
dem all." In fact, there is no specific evidence to suggest the Hebrews were
ever enslaved in Egypt or that the Exodus occurred. There is no evidence
of slavery in pharaonic times until comparatively late in Egyptian history.
Only Cecil B. DeMille ever thought the Hebrews were forced to build the
pyramids.

Thus, I entered the Luxor temple looking not for pharaonic one-upmanship, but for evidence of spiritual concerns, arcane knowledge. That first morning I wanted just a first impression. The magnificent striding colossus of Rameses II with its unusually vivid sense of motion dominates the court he constructed. Now, incongruously, the same court also houses the little mosque of Abu al-Haggag, from which a muezzin starts his call as I pass; then the soaring colonnade, its twin line of pillars raising my spirits with their fluted stone all the way to heaven; Amenhotep III's Peristyle Court, broad, majestic, echoing with the invocations of a thousand years' devotion to union with God; beyond it the forestlike Hypostyle Hall, leading into a series of small chambers and the Inner Sanctuary itself, where the stones feel full of intense superhuman power; then, at the far end, another pillared hall leading to what is known as the Triple Sanctuary, the place where, according to some symbolist interpretations, Amon, the "hidden," makes flesh out of spirit, the place where the Three-in-One of the New Testament are one and yet three. So impressed was the poet Rimbaud that here, up on the far right, he carved his name in bold capitals into the hard grey stone of a lintel.

I felt dazed at this point, my head spinning. I'd never realized the temples of Egypt were built on such a scale. It had taken me over an hour to walk through the complex. In comparison, anything in Greece seemed puny and lacking in resonance, in the mystic.

Wondering how to photograph myself for the family album in front of the entrance pylons in this magic light, I noticed a man halfway along the avenue of sphinxes surrounded by serious cameras. As I approached, I could see him scowl; he wanted to be alone here, too. I asked him whether he'd mind taking a snap. He grunted, looking at my idiot-proof fully automatic Nikon as if I'd handed him a turd. I posed, then asked him where he was from, what he was up to.

A Swiss magazine had sent him to photograph a massive colour spread, he told me between gritted teeth. Did he like Egypt? At this he exploded, cursing everyone and everything he'd encountered — the dirt, the chaos, the hustlers, the incompetence, the bureaucracy. "And *now*," he shrieked, "that idiot at the gate won't let me to bring in my large-format because he says I have no permit for professional equipment!" I offered to find out whether my government credentials pulled any weight. "I been every-where," the photographer hissed, "but I never encounter anything like *this*!" He must have meant "everywhere" in Europe.

At the gate the turbaned official turned my documents sideways, upside down, back to front, then waved approval. The photographer hefted his mighty large-format from the hut where he'd been forced to leave it and sighed gratitude. I wanted to infuse him with what I felt, but looking at the professional baggage he was forced to lug around wherever he went, I decided he'd probably be incapable of appreciating any trip.

I sat for a while in the little garden behind the temple. Date palms, mimosas, broad-leaved banana trees, oleanders, and lemon trees shaded me in deep green coolness from the ascending sun. Arabian jasmine diffused its perfume everywhere, and doves cooed under its leaves. Two old men sat puffing on a narghile as the city behind them came to rowdy life. Stalls full of fake antiquities and spurious papyri opened up; horse-drawn calèches packed with schoolchildren clip-clopped down to the corniche, horns honking, brasses jingling; roadside food stands cooked up *foul* beans and onions to be served in oven-fresh pita halves. The sounds and the smells and the sights were intoxicating.

Back on board ship, I breakfasted with The Four. Pierre had calmed down somewhat and was enthusing over old times spent in Luxor with John. His delight in the city infected the rest of us. We set off on our last day together in high spirits that even Syed's disgruntled obsequiousness could not dampen. This, after all, was the day he'd be collecting his tip.

ع

The Valley of the Kings on the west bank of the Nile certainly looks like a good spot to be buried in, if you want to discourage fiends and relatives from visiting your grave. Abandoning the pyramid tomb as too conspicu-ous apparently, the ancient Egyptians turned to hollowing mausoleums out of solid rock, which they'd often done before, but not building anything over them. The new idea worked well visually. The Valley looks so wasted and desolate at first glance that some of my fellow tourists doubted that our driver had brought us to the right place.

Most of the major tombs have modest entrances: tunnels descending through solid rock cut as smooth as butter. As you edge cautiously down, you can't help but marvel at the technology involved, unless, of course, you suffer from claustrophobia, in which case you're frothing at the mouth after three minutes. Without iron or steel, using probably flint or possibly tempered copper, these tomb builders seemed to have thought nothing of burrowing straight into the rock face, keeping measurements almost flawlessly accurate for six hundred feet or more. Only when you've plodded down some tunnel for fifteen minutes do you realize it is merely a foyer. Beyond this "entrance" there are huge chambers teeming with paintings illustrating the *Book of the Dead*, the map instructing the soul on what to expect on its journey through the next world. Often these continue all the way to the pharaoh's final resting place, a titanic sarcophagus usually carved out of one solid piece of granite the size of a Chevy van.

Rather than deal with the pungent aura of mystery around these tombs, one tends to think of more practical matters. What happened to the thousands of tons of chips they must have hacked out? More important: remote and wild as the valley looks, it is only a half day's stroll from downtown Luxor, so how could such mind-boggling efforts of excavation have been expected to go unnoticed? Even killing everyone directly involved in the digging wouldn't have solved the problem. Clearly the whole of Thebes knew what was going on. Every single tomb was plundered, either partially or totally. A glance at the treasures found within Tutankhamen's modest little grave, itself twice robbed thirty centuries ago, explains why there was no shortage of people willing to risk life and limb in order to steal what no living man was ever supposed to see again.

Directly above Tutankhamen's bachelor apartment of a tomb stands the entrance to the epic resting place of Rameses VI. In fact, it was debris from the excavation of this prodigious tomb that concealed Tutankhamen's for three millennia more.

Rameses VI's tomb was clearly a major attraction to the tourists of antiquity. Clarence, translating from the Greek, pointed out numerous graffiti. "Hermogines of Amasa has seen and admired the tombs," read one, "but this tomb of Memnon, after he had examined it, he more than admired it." The usually silent Trevor added that the writer must have confused Memnon, the Greek name for Amenhotep, with Rameses VI. Farther on another ancient traveller had inscribed, "I, the torchbearer of the very holy mysteries of Eleusis, son of Minucianus, the Athenian, having visited the tombs long after the divine Plato, the Athenian, have admired and given thanks to the gods and to the most pious emperor Constantine who has granted me this." There was a long-winded charm about these mementos from men who two thousand years earlier had experienced precisely what we were experiencing. Some, admittedly, assumed a more pompous tone: "Ephiphanius saw nothing to admire but the stone," read one, and right across a painted serpent was written, "I, Dioscorammon, saw this folly and it puzzled me."

What puzzled and irritated Syed was our mirth at and fascination with these aspects of the tomb, which weren't included in *his* tour. As he regaled his flock with some anecdote connected with a pair of immense winged, crowned serpents, I noticed he'd slipped his arm around the Indian girl, and none too innocently — although *she* did not seem bothered.

It's not necessary to know exactly what you're looking at in these tomb paintings to appreciate their extravagant beauty and vibrancy, but it helps.

The Book of the Dead is a collection of ancient texts of charms, spells, and formulas from the sixteenth century B.C. It shows the various stages through which a soul passes after death, the various trials and tribulations that culminate in a "last judgement." Here the heart of the deceased is weighed in a balance against a white feather, the symbol of truth. If the scales remain stable, the soul merges into Osiris and takes its place in a paradise. If not, …

Just outside the Valley of the Kings, built against the same extraterrestrial cliff face, stands the mortuary temple of Queen Hatshepsut. Resembling a postmodern architectural experiment in New Mexico or Arizona, with its sheer ramps and subtle deference to landscape, this transcendently beautiful monument commemorates the only female pharaoh, Hatshepsut of the Eighteenth Dynasty. As daughter of Tuthmosis I, she married her father's son and heir, Tuthmosis II, who died before she could bear him children. Instead of stepping down at his death, she reigned as the king's widow for a number of years before taking the unprecedented step of declaring herself pharaoh. Twice before in Egyptian history queens had reigned for brief periods, but they'd never called themselves pharaohs. This posed a semantic problem for a start, since, like "king," "pharaoh" was an exclusively male noun. Hatshepsut solved this by having herself frequently depicted as a man, with the royal false beard, and making it clear in other ways that she was boss.

Where the martial frieze would normally be we find instead in her temple an exquisite painted relief of the puzzling "Expedition to the Holy Land of Punt." Still bearing traces of the original paintwork these magnificent reliefs show Hatshepsut travelling to a foreign land with its inexplicable mélange of alien races and its exotic or barbarous merchandise and animals. She also sets up statues in Punt, "thereby," according to John Anthony West, "extending the civilizing influence of Egypt, and so accomplishing by peaceful symbolic feminine means what the pharaohs accomplished by symbolic conquest."

Like Rameses II's Battle of Kadesh, the expedition to Punt may be entirely allegorical. No one is sure where Punt was. Emmanuel Velikovsky, the bane of archaeologists, has suggested that Hatshepsut was in fact the biblical queen of Sheba, and the land of Punt, Palestine. He also thinks Hatshepsut's temple is a version of Solomon's temple, which would explain its grandeur and beauty. It is indeed beautiful.

Today in the precincts, beyond the great ramps, a hot-air balloon was being inflated with roaring blasts of flame. Emblazoned with the Pepsi logo and King Tut's head, it was a crude and jarring presence amid such splendour.

John pointed up the cliff face of Deir al-Bahari, north of the temple, saying there was something there we had to see. Much to Syed's annoyance, our little band set off up the steep path followed by Nagy and his family, and arrived hot and out of breath at a little cavern that was invisible from the ground. Here, John explained, the workers who built the temple may have enjoyed their lunch and a rest, shaded from the midday sun. They also doodled on the walls.

"*Outrageous!*" Pierre exclaimed. "How utterly *charming*." He was look-ing at a graffito that clearly depicted a man sodomizing a figure bent over in front of him. No matter what Pierre liked to think went on in the cav-ern, I later learned that the second figure has been unarguably determined to be that of a woman. Moreover, the carving is thought to be a proletar-ian comment on the notion of a female declaring herself pharaoh. Since very little remains of secular Egypt, this cavern reminds us that human nature changes very little.

Completing his lacklustre performance in an unexceptional tomb in the Valley of the Queens, Syed, glaring at Pierre, observed that some men were also buried in this valley. "So we know that they had *those* type of men even in ancient Egypt," the guide said, his comment greeted by a few guffaws and sniggers. When it was time to take our leave of Syed forever, Pierre handed the man one very crumpled Egyptian pound note. The rest of us were very slightly more generous.

Sitting on the back terrace of the Winter Palace Hotel later that after-noon, overlooking its lush verdant garden and secluded pool, John decided we should take a felucca back across the river to visit the Tombs of the Nobles, where one could find some of the most enchanting works of art in the world, he said. "If they were in *Greece*, they would be world famous."

The old Winter Palace, now on the brink of total restoration by the same company responsible for the Cataract in Aswan, was always a hotel, not a palace, but is nonetheless palatial, its cavernous lobby redolent of faded splendour, its ragged corridors leading to billiards rooms, smoking rooms, ladies' rooms — all the amenities that made it popular with the Brits of Empire, King Farouk, and other past luminaries. John lapsed into a mournful silence, staring out over the palms, as much a part of that lost past, it struck me, as he was of a present he clearly despised.

CHAPTER SEVEN

THE KNAVES AND THE GRAVES

Necropolis ghosts were hideous — all those unappeased officials and unrewarded warriors, priests unjustly punished and noblemen betrayed by near relatives, or, even more common, the ghosts of robbers killed in the act of violating a tomb.

—NORMAN MAILER, *ANCIENT EVENINGS*

Like the gondolas of Venice, Nile feluccas are often extravagantly decorated, painted, and varnished, strewn with handwoven rugs and colourful cushions. As the raucous sounds of Luxor and its swarming streets receded behind us, the Nile flowed broad and slow on all sides, its waters a muddy green. High above, the vessel's towering white triangle of sail sought out the torrid breeze, propelling us in a snaking course toward the tranquil west bank. The carcass of a buffalo floated slowly past, two white vultures pecking at its bloated neck with their sharp, bloody yellow beaks. Men sat fishing with long makeshift rods in the shade of palms.

"*Goodness,*" said Clarence, "who'd eat anything that swam in *this*?" Pierre protested that the waters were sacred, that we should all be sure to pour a handful over our heads: "That way, darlings, you can *guarantee* you'll come back to Egypt." John smiled, adding, "I think *I'll* not bother this time."

On the muddy shores of the west bank we got into a lengthy argument with two taxi drivers who each claimed our felucca boy was his brother and therefore he deserved our business. Hearing what we intended to pay, the older man dropped out, leaving us with a grubby character in his late teens who became the beneficiary of Pierre's limitless fund of sexual innuendos.

The land on this side is lushly irrigated and fertile for at least a mile, right up to the edge of the desert mountains. Bumping along an uneven road, we passed a collection of newly built houses of mud brick in the Nubian style. Ordering the driver to stop, John explained these were designed by Hassan Fathy and intended to house the villagers from Sheikh Abd al-Qurna, up on the slopes of the Theban necropolis. The trouble was the Qurnawis refused to leave their traditional homes. Like other Egyptians who refused to inhabit Fathy's neo-Nubian mud-brick housing-for-the-poor, the inhabitants of Qurna had their reasons; but in this case it wasn't because they felt the dwellings resembled tombs. For over three thousand years the Qurnawis have made their living not by toiling in the fields of the floodplain, but by engaging in a far more lucrative business high up on the burning slopes among the desolate crags of the ancient burial grounds.

At the close of the mummification ceremonies, when the body of a deceased pharaoh or noble was finally placed in his tomb, the priest recited these words: "You live again, you revive always, you have become young again, you are young again, and forever." These high hopes of immortality assumed an undisturbed tomb and an intact mummy as essential. Nearly always such hopes were dashed.

Leaving the prosperous fields behind, we drove toward the edge of the Great Western Desert, where the macadam road stops at the foot of high, dust-covered slopes. Proceeding on foot, with the sun burning out of the ground through the soles of our shoes, we slowly made our thirsty way up. You don't see the village of Qurna first; you hear it. Barking dogs, the bleat of baby goats, excited screams of children playing, wailing music crackling from speakers with the audio-fidelity of Chatty Cathy dolls, billowed in a tangled dust cloud of sound over the toasted boulders above us. You're almost in the village before you see it, and even then, its sand-coloured walls of sun-dried brick blend into the hillside. The place hasn't changed since Giovanni Belzoni, explorer and exploiter of Egyptian antiquities, wrote this description of it in 1820:

> *The people ... live in the entrance of such caves as have already been opened, and, by making partitions with earthen walls, they form habitations for themselves, as well as for their cows, camels, buffaloes, sheep, goats, dogs, etc ... Their dwelling is generally in the passage between the first and second entrance into a tomb. The walls and the roof as black as any chimney. The inner door is closed up with mud, except a small aperture sufficient for a man to crawl through. Within this place the sheep are kept at night, and occasionally accompany their masters in their vocal concert.*
>
> —GIOVANNI BELZONI, *NARRATIVE OF THE OPERATIONS AND RECENT DISCOVERIES WITHIN THE PYRAMIDS, TEMPLES, TOMBS AND EXCAVATIONS IN EGYPT AND NUBIA*, 1820

The landscape here is almost two-dimensional, its details erased by blinding sunlight. Yet all around and beneath Qurna's mud foundations lie the Tombs of the Nobles, the rock-cut burial chambers of ancient Egypt's viziers and administrators. Farther west, not half an hour by foot, are the Valley of the Kings and the Valley of the Queens. In these places Qurnawis have made their living for hundreds of centuries, plundering tombs, removing amulets and scarabs, papyri, and precious jewellery, ritual objects of every description. They sold their booty to the antiquities dealers back across the river in Luxor. Cunning and cautious, they rarely encountered trouble from the authorities, handing out baksheesh to the police and hawking only a few objects at a time to avoid arousing suspicion. No matter how much they removed from the tombs, the locations of which were their closely guarded secret, there always seemed to be more. The mine was inexhaustible.

And the Qurnawis have been in business for as long as the source of their supply has existed. Threats of imprisonment and torture have had little effect on the thieves of Thebes, whether they came from the ancient priesthood assigned to guard the tombs three millennia ago or from the modern Egyptian Antiquities Organisation. On the tomb of Amenhotep, son of Hapu, an inscription written nearly four thousand years ago reads in part: "[Trespassers in my tomb] shall not receive the honours which are given virtuous men; they shall have no son to succeed them; their wives shall be raped before their eyes ..." Whoever plundered Amenhotep's tomb either couldn't read or couldn't care less. Business was business.

From the 1860s on, when European tourists began to visit Luxor in increasingly large numbers, the demand for the commodities of Qurna boomed. One villager in particular, Ahmed Abd al-Rassoul, acquired both enormous wealth and a dubious kind of fame. In 1871 Ahmed was tending his herd of goats on the slopes of the necropolis and went looking for a kid that had wandered away from its mother. These slopes are not exactly the best place for animals to wander; they are full of deep shafts dug as ancient tomb entrances. It was down one such shaft, forty feet deep, that Ahmed spotted his baby goat. Clambering down, he noticed weather-worn fragments of ritual objects and, scraping away the sand, discovered an opening sealed with stone and plaster. He chipped out a small hole and looked through to find a chamber stacked with mummies and a staggering cache of treasures as far back as the narrow beam of light enabled him to see.

With his brother, Muhammad, he began removing the objects and sailing to Luxor with a few pieces at a time concealed in baskets of vegetables. For the next ten years the two brothers continued to visit the cache, getting richer each time and eventually dealing exclusively with one man, a Turk named Mustapha Agha Ayat.

A resident of Luxor, Ayat was a resourceful fellow. He had somehow contrived to have himself appointed consular agent for Great Britain, Belgium, and Russia, representing the interests of nationals from these countries when they travelled in Upper Egypt. The main benefit of these positions, however, was that they gave Ayat diplomatic immunity. This he exploited to the fullest, buying and shipping antiquities through Egyptian Customs to an international clientele.

Unfortunately, neither Ayat nor the brothers Abd al-Rassoul knew much about pharaonic antiquities. They were certainly unaware that the royal funerary papyri, shawabti figures, scarabs, and canopic jars bearing names of Twentieth Dynasty kings were objects rarely seen in the marketplace. The existence of such pieces had been long suspected, but very few had been found before.

News of their sale on the black market eventually reached Gaston Maspero, then director of the Egyptian Antiquities Service, as it was originally named, and he realized a discovery of immense importance had been made and was being systematically looted. Using an undercover agent as well as the Luxor police, he swiftly narrowed down his list of suspects to Mustapha Ayat and the Abd al-Rassoul brothers. Ayat, of course, was diplomatically immune from prosecution. The brothers were not.

On April 4, 1881, they were arrested. After the police searched their homes unsuccessfully two days later, they sent the pair in chains forty miles south to the town of Qena to be interrogated by the resident police administrator.

By all accounts, this brutal examination was pure black comedy. Ordered by Maspero to preside over the event, Daud Pasha, mayor of Qena, was obliged by a savage skin disease he suffered to sit through the proceedings submerged up to his neck in an enormous jar of water. The brothers could hardly have fared worse at the hands of ancient Egyptian authorities. Torture was still used to extract confessions even by the late nineteenth-century colonial government. Tied, beaten, burned on the head by red-hot iron pots, Ahmed still had scars to show a decade later.

But despite everything, the trial was a failure. Supported by a large contingent of their fellow villagers who had travelled to Qena, the brothers were finally released into the custody of their family. Numerous character witnesses had established the men as highly respectable and incapable of defiling ancient tombs. It was only later, when Ahmed tried to claim that his sufferings at the hands of the authorities entitled him to a half share of the proceeds from the plundering — rather than the one-fifth share Muhammad and the rest of the family had originally agreed on — that a violent and vocal squabble broke out. Soon the fraternal dispute became common knowledge. Muhammad, probably realizing it was only a matter of time before news of it reached the Antiquities Service, decided his best course was to confess and try to save his own skin. Visiting Daud Pasha secretly in Qena, he was promised immunity from prosecution, so he spilled the beans and fingered his brother as the ringleader.

On July 6, 1881, Muhammad led Emil Brugsch, a German Egyptologist employed by the Antiquities Service, to the site of the cache. Aware that Ahmed was well liked in Qurna and that Muhammad's confession could easily spark a bloody vendetta, Brugsch was edgy as he descended by rope into the deep shaft. Stooping to pick his way through the low chamber, he saw by the dim, flickering light of his candle the bodies and the treasures of more pharaohs than any modern man had ever laid eyes on.

Scattered everywhere were bronze bowls and other vessels, wooden shrines, intricately carved statues, canopic jars with elaborately sculpted lids depicting deities with animal heads. Before he'd gone more than two steps, a brilliantly painted coffin bearing the name "Neskhonsu," the wife of the Twentieth Dynasty high priest, materialized in the candlelight. Moments later he was gazing on the coffins of Queen Henttowy and the pharaoh Seti I. Abandoned in a corner was a funerary tent in which mortuary services had once been conducted. It bore the name of Queen Esemkhebe.

Although only ten feet wide, the chamber proved to be nearly 700 feet long. By the time Brugsch had reached its far wall, he had passed the coffins of some of Egypt's most illustrious rulers: Amenhotep I, Tuthmosis II, Ahmose, and even Rameses II, the Great. As he later said, it all seemed a dream, impossible to believe. Gaston Maspero concurred: "Like him, I ask myself if I am not dreaming when I see and touch the bodies of so many rulers of whom we thought we always would know only the name."

The discovery was of such magnitude that the Antiquities Service decided to ship the entire contents of the chamber up to Cairo as soon as possible, to prevent further pilfering. When the first boatload sailed off down the Nile, it caused an extraordinary reaction among fellahin in the tiny villages through which the vessel passed. They lined the riverbanks,

women wailing and tearing at their hair, men firing shotguns into the air
— almost a traditional funeral, a last tribute to the pharaohs who were
leaving Thebes forever after three thousand years.

Ironically Muhammad Abd al-Rassoul was rewarded with an appointment as chief of the Antiquities Service guards and a gift of five hundred
English pounds in cash. His brother Ahmed supposedly returned to a quiet
life as a shepherd.

Supposedly. Over a century later the international antiquities market is
still being supplied by the men of Qurna, albeit in a far more covert manner, and the villagers refuse to be resettled in the agricultural life urged on
them by the government. The new free homes still await them in the verdant floodplain beneath those parched, forbidding cliffs. No one would be
surprised if another secret cache should be discovered one day.

What Ahmed Abd al-Rassoul stumbled across, however, is probably
unique. It's generally believed that the ancient priests, attempting to stem
the tide of tomb robberies and to protect the mummies of their divine
pharaohs, removed the contents of countless tombs to one single secret
location they could more easily guard.

Tomb-robbing seems to be among the oldest professions. Three and a
half millennia ago the Abd al-Rassouls of the time were doing a thriving
business. Around 1500 B.C., the royal architect Ineny, construction supervisor on the tombs of pharaohs Amenhotep I and Tuthmosis I, wrote, "I
supervised the carving of the tomb of His Majesty in a solitary place, none
seeing, none hearing." Optimistic as Ineny's words sound, he could hardly
have failed to be aware that even as his inscriptions were being carved,
thieves knew exactly where the tombs were located and were merely biding
their time until it was relatively safe to plunder them.

There's also evidence to suggest that many of these ancient break-and-
enter stunts were inside jobs, involving the very police and priests who
were supposed to be guarding the necropolis. Hence robberies were
rarely reported, and little official action was ever taken against the plun-
derers. In addition, considering the awesome nature and value of the
treasures sealed up in the tombs, a pharaoh's family members must have
been sorely tempted to retrieve some of this wealth for the living to enjoy.

Either way, late in the New Kingdom, between 1200 and 1085 B.C., tomb-robbing had become so flagrant and widespread that something clearly had to be done about it.

Interestingly enough, the details of what was done have come down to us nearly complete, recorded in one of the most engaging series of papyri ever to have survived from ancient Egypt. Discovered at Thebes in the 1850s, the Papyrus Amherst records the confessions elicited from several men accused of tomb-robbing. The tale of corruption in high places that led to the investigation is just as interesting as the actual confessions. In August 1126 B.C., tired of hearing constant rumours about large-scale thievery in the Great Necropolis, the mayor of Eastern Thebes, a certain Pa-ser, decided to investigate the extent of these sacrilegious violations. It was not really a decision he had a right to make. Being on the west bank, the necropolis lay within the jurisdiction of Pa-wero, the mayor of Western Thebes. It seems Pa-ser had grounds to believe that his western counterpart was involved in the robberies himself. The two mayors also seem to have been bitter rivals.

Here is one of the confessions extracted during Pa-ser's initial interrogations. The name of the accused man is unfortunately lost:

> *Now in the year 13 of the Pharaoh my Lord, four years ago, I agreed with the carpenter Seteknakht [to rob the tombs of the Necropolis. We searched] and we found the tomb of [the King] and of the Royal Wife, Neb-khaas. It was protected and sealed with plaster, but we forced it open. We opened their coffins and the cloth in which they were wrapped and found the noble mummy of the King, equipped like a warrior. There were many sacred eye amulets and ornaments of gold at his neck, and a mask of gold upon him. The noble mummy of the King was covered completely with gold and silver, inside and out, and with inlays of all sorts of precious stones. We took the gold which we found on this noble mummy of this god, and his eye amulets, and the ornaments which were at his neck and on the wrappings in which he lay. We found the Royal Wife similarly adorned and*

we took all that we found on her, too. We set fire to the wrappings.
We stole their equipment, which we found on them, objects of
gold, silver and bronze, and divided them among ourselves.
We divided the gold we found on these two gods and on their
mummies into eight parts ... Then we crossed over to Thebes.
A few days later the district superintendents heard of our stealing
in the West and they seized me and imprisoned me in the office
of the Mayor of Thebes.

—HIEROGLYPHIC TEXTS IN T. ERIC PEET, *THE GREAT TOMB*
ROBBERIES OF THE TWENTIETH EGYPTIAN DYNASTY, 1930

The extremely deferential terms this robber used are probably due to the situation in which he found himself, but they do raise interesting questions. He referred to the pharaoh and his wife as "gods," as if this were society's accepted view of them. Then wouldn't the act of violating their tomb be tantamount to an assault on religion itself? If the might of the priests of Amon did not deter such robbers, this may be convincing evidence of that religion's arcane and elitist nature. Perhaps the thieves of Qurna felt so far removed from the religion of court and temple, so excluded from its mysteries and rituals, that it meant little to them. Or were their actions symptomatic of a society on the brink of decay? The torture and painful execution that followed guilty verdicts after such investigations and trials also did little to stem the tide of necropolis robberies. Knowing that many of the tombs contained treasures that would have made Tutankhamen's stash look like Woolworth's jewellery counter, and that most of the plunder was merely melted down for its gold, one realizes not only the prodigious wealth of the pharaohs but also the extent of what has been lost forever.

After extracting such confessions, Pa-ser, the mayor of Eastern Thebes, should have had himself a pretty watertight case. Far from it. He learned instead that Pa-wero, over on the west bank, had some pretty heavy friends: the vizier, Kha-em-wese, for example. And the vizier took a dim view of Pa-ser's allegations, especially since they implied he, too, was party to

Pa-wero's misdeeds. Pa-ser was nothing if not persistent, continuing to produce fresh evidence and new culprits. It took him, however, four years — and the appointment of a new vizier — finally to prove his suspicions. Parts of the transcripts from these trials survive. It is ironic that the papyri recording them surfaced in various museums after having been sold on the Luxor antiquities market by thieves who had stolen them from Theban tombs.

For four thousand years this trade has survived in Thebes, and pharaohs who were expecting to outlast eternity hidden from mortal eyes have found themselves instead in most unquiet graves. A song engraved on the walls of several Middle Kingdom tombs contains, perhaps, more truth than any ancient Egyptians could have ever allowed themselves to contemplate:

> *What has been done with them? …*
> *What are their places [now]?*
> *Their walls have crumbled and their places are not —*
> *As if they had never been.*
> *No one has [ever] come back from [the dead],*
> *That he might describe their condition,*
> *And relate their needs;*
> *That he might calm our hearts*
> *Until we [too] pass into that place where they have gone …*
> *[Let us] make holiday and never tire of it!*
> *[For] behold, no man can take his property with him,*
> *No man who has gone can return again.*
> —"THE SONG OF THE HARPERS," TRANSLATED BY MIRIAM
> LICHTHEIM, *JOURNAL OF NEAR EASTERN STUDIES* XXIV (1945)

But even this song has other levels of meaning; for example, the harpers are blind.

One last anecdote concerning the tenacity of the thieves of Thebes: twenty years before his discovery of Tutankhamen's tomb, Howard Carter recorded in his journal a tomb robbery that took place on the night of November 24, 1901, in the Valley of the Kings. Guards placed outside the tomb of Amenhotep were surprised by a group of armed men who threatened to kill them if they moved or raised the alarm. The men broke into the tomb, cut open the royal mummy, smashed another, and escaped with their plunder. Unfortunately for the robbers, they had been recognized by three of the guards. They were Ahmed and Muhammad, the Abd al-Rassoul brothers. This identification was in itself not sufficient evidence on which to charge and try the men. It took the manic diligence of Howard Carter, using a mixture of archaeological techniques and detective work, to build up a viable case. Twenty years after they'd been caught at Deir al-Bahari, the brothers Abd al-Rassoul were finally convicted of pursuing the family business.

⟡

When we stopped to purchase tepid soft drinks from a black-veiled woman with tattoos covering her wizened face who called us over to the tiny square window of her house, John inquired if any members of the Abd al-Rassoul family still existed in Qurna. She scowled, spat a ball of phlegm the colour of gravy into the roasting dust, and delivered a machine-gun volley of Arabic that seemed to consist of one word about six thousand syllables long.

"She says yes — *basically*," John informed us.

"There *did* seem to be rather an *excessive* number of caveats attached to it, did there not?" Trevor complained.

"*Yerse*," John confessed. "She *claimed* an Abd al-Rassoul owes her money and that she would far prefer to pluck out this particular chap's eyes than allow his name to *soil* her lips. *However*, she did tell me where to find a chappie who — or so he *claims* — actually worked for Howard Carter on *Tut's* bloody tomb."

Pierre pouted. "Oh no, *not* another one of *those*, Johnny, please! I simply couldn't bear to hear that tiresome old story *again*!"

Clarence and Trevor were keen to visit the man, and John told Pierre he'd become jaded and should think of others who were here for the first time.

The old man was called Khadry, and he was indeed old. In fact, John established that he'd known the Abd al-Rassoul brothers personally; he kept referring to them, however, as "jackals." Khadry invited the five of us to take tea in his tiny house, where we sat on a monstrous sofa, stuffed with what felt like rocks, beneath a large blurred photograph of the Ka'aba in Mecca. The shade was welcome, as was the mint tea. He'd obviously recounted his Howard Carter stories ten thousand times, and as John translated, I heard nothing that I hadn't already read somewhere or other.

I urged John to get him onto Carter's personality: was the man really celibate, for example. Khadry grinned toothlessly, slapping his knee, then answering in a roundabout fashion that implied both boys and the occasional "dancing girl" enhanced Carter's domestic life from time to time.

How did he and Lord Carnarvon get along? Not well, it seemed, not at all well. Carter, Khadry suggested, wished to marry Carnarvon's daughter, Lady Evelyn, but the lord put an end to their relationship because Carter was from a lower-class background.

How much stuff from the tomb had both men managed to keep for themselves and smuggle out? Quite a bit.

Khadry chuckled, embarking on an epic fit of coughing. Then he disappeared into a back room, from which he emerged with a small cardboard box. Inside were three objects wrapped in heavy cloth. Two were painted ivory figurines; the third was an extraordinarily ornate spoon, also in painted ivory, with thin bands of gilding. We all examined them. The workmanship was of exceptional quality, particularly on the faces of the figurines, and they did seem extremely old.

John pronounced them genuine antiquities or among the best fakes he'd ever come across. But were they from Tut's tomb? The old man merely giggled at the question, wrapping the objects carefully and replacing them in his box. Pierre, huffing throughout this, declared there was only one way to find out the truth: he offered the man three hundred dollars for the contents of the box. Khadry simply laughed, taking his treasures back to wherever they'd come from. When he returned, Pierre persisted, asking him to name a price, but the old man wasn't playing.

"You know," John said as we emerged into dazzling light, "I'm *inclined* to think we've just handled the real McCoy. Never known a Qurnawi to *not* try selling fakes. *Never.*" The peddling of fakes was now almost as lucrative a business to the villagers as the trade in genuine artifacts had once been. There was a tacit understanding between buyer and seller that they *were* fakes — the price alone established that — accompanied by a sort of willing suspension of disbelief on the part of both. Most tourists, of course, would perpetuate the lie when they returned home, showing their friends "a genuine Eighteenth Dynasty bronze" they'd managed to smuggle through Customs. The best place to see just how authentic-looking a fake can be is the shop inside the Egyptian Museum in Cairo.

At the foot of the dusty slope leading back up to Qurna, we traipsed to the entrance of the first of the Tombs of the Nobles that John had wished to show us. "About *bloody* time," Trevor said. "I was wondering what had happened to *them.*"

The reason the Tombs of the Nobles are hardly ever included on standard tours of the necropolis is that few of them are open, and guides rightly assume their flocks will be suffering from terminal exhaustion and cultural overkill by the time they've "done" the Valley of the Kings, the Valley of the Queens, Hatshepsut's temple, and the other must-sees. This is a shame, a consequence of poor tour scheduling and the lack of concern of tour operators for their clients, most of whom will visit Egypt only once in their lives. Luxor and Thebes deserve at least a week of anyone's time, presuming an interest in ancient Egyptian culture is what impels people to travel there in the first place.

In contrast to the overpowering temples and the supernatural splendour of the pharaonic mausoleums, the Tombs of the Nobles offer a glimpse of the more human side of life in dynastic Egypt. All these tombs have "guardians" living nearby who, for a little baksheesh, will readily agree to open those that the Egyptian Antiquities Organisation has ordered closed — usually because they are in a poor state of repair, somewhat unsafe, or not yet equipped to allow tourists easy access and the benefit of electric light. Many of these turbaned guardians with their shifty grins and swirling blue *gelabias* easily produced large sheets of polished metal or mirrors with which they skilfully reflected sunlight into the recesses, illuminating the most interesting murals and reliefs, without the aid of electricity and in the same manner probably used by the artists as they created them 3,500 years ago.

The tomb of Ramose is the best known and seems generally to be open. Ramose (1550–1310 B.C.) was vizier to both Amenhotep III, of the Eighteenth Dynasty, and his son Amenhotep IV (who became Akhenaten, the heretic). As the position of vizier was the highest rank within the administrative system of the time, his tomb is relatively lavish, with broad pillared halls and an impressive range of superb reliefs. During the latter part of Ramose's life, the so-called Amarna period, Amenhotep IV became Akhenaten and banished the priests of Amon and their pantheon, moving his capital upriver to Akhetaten (Tell al-Amarna). There, he declared the official worship of his kingdom to be of one god alone, the Aten or "solar disk." Ramose's tomb reflects the artistic styles of both periods, through either conviction or expediency. The Amarna style is unmistakable; the pharaoh, who is believed to have been badly deformed by a rare ailment, is depicted with a grotesquely enlarged head, a potbelly, and a body that is effeminate in a revolting way. It's possible that, like Goya's royal portraits, these images of the pharaoh reflect the artists' personal disgust. The solar disk, which Akhenaten is frequently shown worshipping, is represented as a circle emitting spokelike rays that end in little hands. The image is somehow repugnant and spidery, certainly not an uplifting emblem of the One God. Despite this, many historians like to believe that Akhenaten was a forerunner of Moses, a pioneer of organized monotheism.

The Amarna style conveys a more Western sense of naturalism in its depictions of people, animals, and the objects of daily life. At the same time it lacks the ritual grandeur of the conventional style, which manages to elevate even the most quotidian scene to a level of spiritual significance. The tomb of Ramose offers a rare opportunity to see the two styles side by side and to observe what is perhaps the earliest example of the movement from the sacred to the secular in art. Admittedly this came about largely because Akhenaten dismissed the gods who would normally have adorned such tombs, which forced artists to portray everyday life, real people. For whatever reason, and for the first time, artists became concerned with conveying three dimensions on two-dimensional surfaces.

Hands become more than mere glyphs, the right now distinguishable from the left; heads are more than mere outlined profiles; children are no longer just small people with their thumbs always in their mouths.

And Akhenaten's chief queen, Nefertiti, is accorded status equal to her husband's. She is known to have wielded much power — possibly over her husband as well as the court — and the portraits of her, especially those made during the late Amarna period, have guaranteed her fame for all time as one of the toughest and most beautiful women who ever lived. Indeed, the painted limestone bust of her ranks alongside anything by Bernini or Michelangelo.

But what John was so eager to show us were the more traditional reliefs flanking the left and right walls of the entrance hall. Unpainted except for the eyes, these highlight the genius of their unknown creator and the purity of the stone he worked on. Many reliefs or murals one sees in Egypt are skilled, workmanlike jobs; occasionally, however, you encounter the work of a master, an artist of the highest calibre. Such are the Ramose reliefs. John was right: if they were anywhere else in the world, especially in Greece or Italy, they would be counted among mankind's greatest artistic achievements. Scenes from the vizier's life, traditional enough in themselves, are depicted with such infinite subtlety that the artist somehow manages to grasp the very joy of life itself. Hair flows like water in the stone; human love is portrayed in all its deep tenderness merely by the gentle placement of a woman's hand around her husband's shoulder; the abundance of gifts from the natural world is expressed by a still life of dead geese, their fragile necks drooping from a table laden with flowers, fruits, and other foods. Nothing is lost on this artist. The delicate fold of a cormorant's wing, the fecundity of a good harvest, the sweet hum of the lyre. The sculptor has captured them in stone for all time.

"One *cannot* help but feel," observed Clarence, himself in raptures, "that Ramose was a man upon whom *nothing* was wasted."

"Yes, *absolutely*," Pierre agreed, as excited as a child. "And, *Clarence*, don't you think also he knew enough about art to hire *this* chap to carve these for him? They are simply *exquisite*. Exquisite."

And they were. Everyone thanked John profusely. It was the high point of our day in Thebes. John looked unusually solemn, muttering about how he feared the reliefs would be lost to pollution if the government didn't do something very soon. "*Jesus*," he said, "the whole bloody necropolis is going to vanish within our lifetimes, the way things are going."

This is true. It is yet another problem the Egyptian Antiquities Organisation faces. Every day, it has been estimated, tourists in Tutankhamen's tomb leave behind twelve gallons of sweat. The murals there are beginning to crumble. In other tombs the story is the same. More damage has been done to the monuments of ancient Egypt in less than a century than during the entire three or four thousand years of their existence. The great tombs may even be permanently closed in the not-too-distant future, and the pyramids and temples will have to be encased in Plexiglas domes if they are to survive at all. There is serious discussion about creating facsimile tombs for the tourist hordes.

With this sobering thought we returned to our ship, intending to be anything but sober before we finally disembarked. The four were staying overnight at the Winter Palace and catching a train to Cairo the following day. Knowing this, I booked myself into the Hilton, a mile upriver, near the Karnak Temple — a precaution against Pierre, the Midnight Rambler.

Later that night, after a second useful session in the bar of the Winter Palace, we hired two calèches and were driven north along the darkened corniche to attend the son-et-lumière at Karnak.

Karnak. The very name is like an earthshaking gong. Dedicated to the supreme god, Amon, Lord of Creation, Karnak ranks with the Great Pyramid as the most powerful of all Egypt's symphonies in stone. Outside, stretching back from the short, broad avenue of massive sphinxes leading to the towering silhouettes of the huge entrance pylons, is a wide square where taxis, cars, buses, and calèches wait for their passengers. Here, some of the world's most persistent hustlers attempt to lure you into "their" shops, which form a blindingly bright strip along the far side, or strive to convince you they have some genuine Eighteenth Dynasty antiquities — but not *on* them, you understand, because of the authorities. These ancient artifacts can be seen in their homes, just a short walk away. It won't take you long. Their ancestors were pulling the same con when Amelia Edwards and Flaubert were in town. Yet it still works.

As we stepped down from the calèches, with their Christmas-tree lights, springy quilted-leather seats, their framed Koranic slogans and photographs of Arabic movie stars and musicians, tourists of every nationality were being given the old rap, or led by the elbow toward Rasheed's Egyptian Bazaar or Abdul's Papyrus Museum. A group of teenage Swedish girls who all looked like young Brigitte Bardots had two vendors' touts and a local playboy each, and they were shaking their heads so often in so many different directions that they formed a blond hairstorm in the wilderness of dark faces.

John had a knack of saying no as if he meant it. The lone hawker who misguidedly approached us with a bale of plastic papyri got halfway through his pitch and gave up dejectedly, seeking out easier marks.

Soon we were huddled in the crowd by that first pair of mighty sphinxes, the temple now merely a colossal shadow. My resistance weakened by many gins, I felt a creeping sense of awe, as if we were about to witness some rare momentous event — the descent of the gods, perhaps. Without warning, shattering chords of imperial music poured into the night from powerful speakers concealed in the shadows.

VOICE: *May the evening soothe and welcome you, O travellers from Upper Egypt.*

An electric torrent poured up my spine.

VOICE: *You will travel no farther because you are come. Here, you are at the beginning of time.*

A dark-peach light illumined the sphinxes and the vast pylons. I felt transported back three thousand years, a participant in some real festival at the house of Amon, not a tourist being entertained.

VOICE: *Here was conceived, and lived, the Great Week of the Creation of the World; and the Separation of the Earth from the Waters. You are at the House of the Father.*

And I could feel it. Unlike the one at Philae, this son-et-lumière had intelligence and power. Maybe a little too much power.

VOICE: *In this House of the Father each pharaoh thought of himself as a son, and wished to leave his mark upon it. Each added, superimposed, over-*

did, outdid, through a span of twenty centuries. The result is this fabulous labyrinth of facades and passages, esplanades and corridors, perspectives and detours; to which only priests and pharaoh had access. But the Egyptian is at ease in the circumvolutions of the divine. He is at home with the Science of the Beyond. He has a taste for side exits, secret passages, concealed staircases, the phosphorescent gloom of tombs. The vade mecums, *the guidebooks for the journey which accompanied the mummy, are called* Book of the Dead, Book of the Gateways, Book of the Caverns, Book of the Night. *They are the only books ever to attempt to produce maps of the other world.*

Then, a shuffling throng of bodies, we were ushered down, past the decapitated sphinxes, through the central portal and into the Great Court, with its triple shrine to the Theban Trinity of Amon–Mut–Khonsu. Here, the vastness of Karnak first begins to sink in. The hairs on my neck stood up in the warm, scented air.

VOICE: *The solemn threshold you have just crossed was forbidden to mortals. The City of God was a fortress where a whole garrison of mystic votaries watched over the great divine scheme of things — sunrises, eclipses of the moon, dynastic chains, the barque of night, the bounds of immortality.*

The sound track had a supernatural quality, an ability to address my innermost thoughts. As lights played up and down, revealing and concealing temples, colossi, obelisks, colonnades, I had the mounting impression that I was indeed on holy ground.

VOICE: *And if one of you this evening were to voice the question that you are whispering in your hearts, "Who art Thou, Amon?," the answer would seep from these walls, these lintels, these pedestals, these secret chambers, these piled ruins — for the answer is written everywhere in a thousand different hieroglyphics.*

Then came many voices, near and distant. The voices of the omnipresent Amon.

AMON: *"I am the father of fathers, the mother of mothers, and the bull of the seven celestial kine. I opened my mouth to speak in the midst of silence. I caused to be that men should have a path on which to tread. I opened the eyes of all, that they might see. My right eye is the day. My left eye is the night. And the waters of the Nile flow from my feet."*

A dozen voices told their stories, a mosaic of human and divine history within this great mosaic of arcane stone. Entering the Hypostyle Hall, I began to weep silently at the incomprehensible magnitude of the grandeur surrounding me. Above, as if seen through a forest of giant redwoods, a saffron moon glowed within its pale halo, a perfect ring of light circling it. I understood what that robust Victorian pioneer Egyptologist, Amelia Edwards, had meant.

> *How often has it been written, and how often must it be repeated, that the Great Hall at Karnak is the noblest architectural work ever designed and executed by human hands? One writer tells us that it covers four times the area occupied by the Cathedral of Notre Dame in Paris. Another measures it against St. Peter's. All admit their inability to describe it; yet all attempt the description. To convey a concrete image of the place to one who has not seen it, is, however, as I have already said, impossible. If it could be likened to this place or that, the task would not be so difficult; but there is, in truth, no building in the wide world to compare with it. The pyramids are more stupendous. The Colosseum covers more ground. The Parthenon is more beautiful. Yet in nobility of conception, in vastness of detail, in majesty of the highest order, the Hall of Pillars exceeds them every one ... You are stupefied by the thought of the mighty men who made them. You say to yourself — "There were indeed giants in those days."*

All I can do is agree with Amelia.

The Hypostyle Hall was executed largely by the pharaoh Seti and completed by his son, Rameses the Great. Beyond it, the temple precincts extend as far as one can see. In silence we wove through the labyrinth of courtyards, past the broad dark expanse of the sacred lake and, finally, up to a pavilion from which we could see the entire expanse of the holy city bathed in a rose-hued light like that of the dawn itself. The voices from ancient evenings continued on all sides, recounting the unimaginable sweep of history these stones had witnessed, describing the processions and festivals that marked the passage of the sacred year and the Nile's seasonal ebb and flow, reciting poetry written by lovers of God and man.

VOICE: *Your love is in my heart like the reed in the arms of the wind …*

The beauty was excruciating. The age of the pharaohs scorched the mind, stretched out all around as far as my eyes could see, a matchless culture of impossible glory, as alive now beneath the star-webbed night sky as it had always been.

VOICE: *May these hieroglyphics come to life once more to bid farewell to you, new pilgrims to Upper Egypt, like a sudden flight of a myriad sacred birds, their spread wings sprinkling the droplets of the river like a benediction.*

I felt blessed indeed. And certainly more like a pilgrim than a tourist.

"Where does one *go* to sign up with Amon?" Clarence said, as we stumbled in a daze back through the darkened towers to where the other world awaited.

"Yes," Pierre murmured. "*I'd* certainly join. *John*, why don't we *revive* the worship of Amon when we get *home*?"

"The archbishop of Canterbury wouldn't approve," replied John.

"Well, *fuck* him. We won't let *him* convert when it all takes off."

"I rather think," Trevor added thoughtfully, "that no one could *afford* to worship Amon in the manner to which he's been accustomed *these* days. I *mean, look* at this place! *Who* could finance building *this* in England now?"

"Oh, pooh!" Pierre trilled. "We'll just adapt Westminster Abbey. It'll have to do."

"Compared to *this* place," Trevor told him, "Westminster Abbey seems like a rather modest log cabin, does it not?"

This banter covered what we knew we'd all felt that night. If Amon was not present within those walls, then someone equally influential certainly was. We parted for good in a very restrained and English way, and the four rode back into Luxor. Refusing sixty offers from calèche drivers, I walked the mile or so down darkened, silent streets toward the Hilton. My spirits were still so high I could feel them spilling all over the heavens; in my heart was a glow that felt a lot like love.

CHAPTER EIGHT

SACRED SCIENCE AND HIGH WISDOM

The Egyptians of old thought like men a hundred feet tall.
We in Europe are but Lilliputians.

—JEAN-FRANÇOIS CHAMPOLLION, 1828

Qui non intelligit, aut taceat aut discat.

—JOHN DEE, 1564

John Dee was astrologer to Queen Elizabeth I of England. He was also one of the most learned men in all of Europe during the late sixteenth century. The above motto, from his most arcane and mystical work, *Monas hiero-glyphica,* translates roughly as "Let him who does not understand this either be silent about it or learn." In the eyes of some contemporary schol-ars it is an exhortation that should be heeded by most Egyptologists currently working on the many aspects of ancient Egyptian civilization. Traditional Egyptology has increasingly come under siege by an army of

"Neo-Renaissance thinkers." Their ranks include, of course, a fair number of cranks and charlatans; but they also include many serious men and women whose diligence and insight into the metaphysical basis of dynastic Egyptian culture have resulted in an outpouring of books and articles that call into question almost every premise of modern academic scholarship concerning the pharaonic world. Their arguments are cogent and powerful.

At the forefront of this potential revolution is John Anthony West, who, as I write, is convinced that he now has irrefutable evidence to prove the case he has been building for the last twenty years. A novelist and playwright, he also terms himself an "independent Egyptologist" and has written two books on the subject: *Serpent in the Sky: The High Wisdom of Ancient Egypt* (Harper and Row, 1979) and *The Traveler's Key to Ancient Egypt* (Alfred A. Knopf, 1985). It is from these works that I have drawn much of the material for this chapter. Of the hundred or so books I have read since first becoming infatuated with the world of the pharaohs and Egypt in general, West's were among the handful I ultimately found most useful and enlightening. They were also the only ones in which I found elegantly articulated the powerful emotional truths I had experienced on my travels, at first not comprehending their meaning.

> *Egypt was a land of tradition where the same things went on recurring indefinitely ... they very rightly maintained that there had been no change since "the time of the god."*
> —PIERRE MONTET, *ETERNAL EGYPT*, 1964

The science of Egyptology is a relatively recent phenomenon in the academic world. The reason for this is simple enough: from the disappearance of the Egyptian priesthood until the nineteenth century no one was able to translate the hieroglyphs. After Herodotus visited Egypt in the fifth century B.C. many Greco-Roman writers followed in his footsteps, returning with their impressions of what they had seen and experienced. Many of these writings survived in some form and comprised a good part of the classical education received by Renaissance scholars. Apart from the poet Juvenal's misanthropic satires, these ancient fragmentary accounts unanimously concur that ancient Egypt was the cradle of the civilized world, the original well of all wisdom. (One reason for Juvenal's disaffection with Egypt may have been his exile from Rome; he presumably viewed Egypt as his prison.) In Plato's *Timaeus*, the Greek philosopher and lawmaker Solon is rebuked by an Egyptian priest for thinking of the Greeks as anything more than children when it came to matters of learning and history. Even so, the average well-educated person today is still taught at school to believe ancient Greece was the birthplace of Western civilization. We can comprehend the *Greeks* — that's why — and we can comprehend them because we can translate their language, which means we can *think* like them.

In the ancient accounts that survive, it is clear that knowledge of the hieroglyphs was either lost by the beginning of the Christian era or protected by a code of secrecy imposed on the few who still had access to it. The early church father and mathematician Clement of Alexandria wrote treatises that reveal some familiarity with Egyptian mathematics; and in the fourth century the Greek writer Horapollon produced a work on hieroglyphs that showed he understood the manner in which they contained the complex symbolism of Egyptian thought in an encoded form.

As Christianity began to dominate the shores of the Mediterranean, knowledge of the ancient traditions went underground, although it seems likely that esoteric groups, such as cabalistic, hermetic, alchemical, Masonic, and, later, Sufi orders kept some of the wisdom alive far from the ever-watchful eyes of the church. As late as the twelfth century, the Byzantine mathematician Rhabdas was employing a system to derive square roots that had been used previously only in Egypt. As John Crowley in his brilliant novel *Aegypt* so aptly suggests, there is perhaps more than one history of the world. Far from the sight of ordinary men, beyond the reach of scholarly research, arcane knowledge could well have been handed down from master to disciple in an unbroken chain for more than two thousand years. The rituals of Freemasonry and Theosophy are to some extent embellished versions of those used by the priests of Isis thirty centuries ago.

After Christianity's influence in Egypt was replaced by the sword of Islam, very little of value was written about the ancient civilization. Indeed, its monuments were ignored so scrupulously, gradually allowed to vanish beneath sands and silt, that it is almost as if they became invisible to the followers of the Prophet.

Nonetheless, the odd intrepid European did manage to make the dangerous and harrowing trip to the land of the pharaohs, returning with all manner of fanciful tales, gossip, rumour, and versions of old legends. One claimed the pyramids were in fact the granaries of Joseph described in the Old Testament. It is hard to imagine the architect able to convince his client that a structure consisting of 99 percent solid stone and 1 percent storage space would be ideal for a granary. Another, more intriguing tale brought back during this period was that the Great Pyramid had been built in antediluvian times by a pharaoh who'd been warned in a dream of the imminent deluge and had enshrined in its structure all the knowledge of his time to preserve it for posterity.

There was, however, little that could be termed scientific about such visits to Egypt. The sole exception is that by John Greaves, an English mathematician and astronomer who journeyed there in 1638–39 to confirm contentions in many classical documents that the Great Pyramid was in effect a model of the earth, containing standards of measure based upon actual knowledge of the circumference of the planet. Unfortunately Greaves' attempts to gain accurate measurements were thwarted by the accumulated debris and drifting sands that obscured the pyramid's base by that point.

As travel to Egypt became slightly less hazardous, more adventurers risked the journey, and the first serious attempts were made to decipher the hieroglyphs and understand the civilization responsible for such superhuman feats of architecture. The first "modern" man to devote most of his life to this study was probably Athanasius Kircher (1601–1680), a German Jesuit and one of the last scholars whose erudition could truly be called Renaissance in scope. While his fellow Jesuits were busy persecuting anyone suspected of dabbling in esoteric ideas like hermeticism, Rosicrucianism, and so on, Kircher was able to do nothing but study such subjects, publishing dozens of books about his work with apparent impunity.

His obsession with the hieroglyphs and his attempts to link them to the symbolism of the hermetic schools led him to acquire a number of rare Coptic manuscripts. Studying this all-but-forgotten language, he eventually concluded — quite rightly as it turned out — that it was derived from the ancient Egyptian and that it followed that the hieroglyphs would have a phonetic as well as a symbolic meaning. He believed he had found the key and produced various translations of hieroglyphic texts that, since no one was in a position to verify or refute them, were regarded only as tantalizing novelties. While subsequent scholarship has proved Kircher's linguistic theories wrong, his overall grasp of the nature of Egyptian thought did not deserve the derision it has since consistently received.

Napoleon Bonaparte seems an unlikely figure to be credited with having founded Egyptology as the serious study we consider it today, yet he did. His reasons for conquering Egypt in the name of the French Empire, or despite the British Empire, were partly connected to one of his lesser-known interests. He was a Freemason, as were many eminent figures of that era, and he shared the conviction of most Masons that the source of the secret brotherhood's wisdom lay in the mysteries of Egypt. Although his military campaign ultimately ended in disaster and a humiliating naval defeat at the hands of Admiral Horatio Nelson, it also generated a wealth of material produced by the legion of scholars and artists he had brought to Egypt along with his army. The emperor also managed to spend a night in the King's Chamber of the Great Pyramid, experiencing something that disturbed him profoundly, according to some accounts.

While Napoleon continued on the bloody course that led to his eventual downfall, French scholars and draftsmen were at work on a series of volumes called *Description de l'Egypte*, the last of which was published in 1830. For the first time Europeans could see what before they had only read about. On page after page, lavish and architecturally precise engravings portrayed the magnificence of the ancient Egyptian ruins. Suddenly Egypt was all the rage, launching trends in everything from fashion to furniture design and architecture.

It also opened up the market for antiquities. Under English mandate Egypt became safe for travellers, and another kind of foreign invasion began, one that is still in progress. Digging up the tombs and sacred sites in these early days was pretty well open to anyone with a shovel and the inclination to do so. The spoils from such indiscriminate treasure hunts now form most of the great Egyptological collections in America and Europe — a fact that irks contemporary Egyptian scholars whenever they brood over it. Although the gloomy Cairo Museum is crammed to the rafters with all manner of pharaonic treasures, artifacts, and monolithic sculptures, many of the most important examples ever discovered are still liberally scattered around the world. It must be said, however, that most Islamic Egyptians, even up to the present day, have shown remarkably little interest in the remains of their spectacular pre-Islamic past. At times I felt that nothing existing before Islam was remotely relevant to many of the people I met. Under the British-installed native pashas, numerous temples depicted in the *Description de l'Egypte* were dismantled to supply stones for factories, housing, and offices that frequently were never even built; and in the countryside no one seems to have minded the fellahin pursuing an age-old practice of burning limestone blocks to extract their lime.

But despite Egypt's accessibility during the early nineteenth century, the progress of scholarship was still impeded by those impenetrable hieroglyphs. The race to be the first to crack the code lured some of the most eminent scholars of the day and produced many disappointments and dead ends. Attention was frenziedly focused on the Rosetta Stone, a black granite commemorative tablet discovered during Napoleon's expedition in 1799. Dating from the late second century B.C., during the reign of Ptolemy V Epiphanes, it was inscribed in three languages: Egyptian hieroglyphs, demotic or Egyptian vernacular, and ancient Greek. Although the Rosetta Stone was badly damaged, with no single line complete, enough of the Greek survived to show all three languages reproduced the same text.

It was still not until 1822 that a young French linguist named Jean-François Champollion declared he had finally found the key that had eluded scholars far older and more experienced than himself for so many years. But Champollion was a rather extraordinary character. From the age of eleven he had been obsessed with Egypt, announcing confidently that *he* would be the one to decipher the hieroglyphs. Utterly single-minded, he spent twenty years mastering all the languages he thought might assist him on his mission. Arabic, Chaldean, Syriac, Amharic, Sanskrit, Pahlavi, Parsee, Persian, and, since there were those who claimed the ancient Egyptians were originally from China, even Old Chinese. He was, we're told, fluent in them all. He was also familiar with Kircher's work, and like the Jesuit father he had immersed himself in Egyptian culture to such a degree that he was able to think like an Egyptian, so much so that many people he encountered had the distinct feeling he was the reincarnation of someone from dynastic times, a belief he confessed to sharing himself.

With the announcement of his breakthrough, he experienced not instant acclaim and recognition but that resistance to new ideas that has plagued science for three centuries now. A scholar who has based his life's work on a theoretical foundation that is suddenly proved completely wrong is incapable of accepting the evidence that undermines his own years of labour. Modern physicists may now have adapted to working in a realm where no law or theory is absolute; such mental flexibility has yet to spread to other scientific disciplines. Champollion was an early victim of what people like John Anthony West are still facing. It took thirty-five years, long after his untimely death at the age of forty-two, for the young Frenchman's work to be generally accepted by the majority of scholars.

By 1880 Egyptology was fully recognized as a legitimate academic study, chairs for it instituted in all the major universities, organized expeditions replacing the random and destructive excavations of treasure-seeking adventurers. The major papyri were translated and published; Egyptian history was gradually pieced together, although the question of a correct chronology is still hotly debated. And some scholars began to probe the baffling intricacies of pharaonic religion, striving to assess also the nature and extent of Egyptian scientific and philosophic knowledge. Here, opinion began to diverge most sharply.

The quote from Champollion that opens this chapter, written after his stay at Thebes, reflects what he felt about the calibre of ancient Egyptian thought. Heinrich Brugsch, the German Egyptologist, concurred with

Champollion and the hermetic tradition, convinced that all the gods, monsters, animal-headed deities, and other weird and wonderful images seen in tombs and temples were actually symbolic renderings of a rich and profound spiritual science, a wisdom that transcended the limitations of modern religion and included a genuine understanding of the mysteries inherent in creation, life, and death.

On the other side of the academic fence were people like Gaston Maspero, French director of the Antiquities Service, who believed the ancient Egyptians were scarcely a step away from cannibalism and savagery. The translator T. Eric Peet declared with absolute conviction that they were "essentially a nation of shopkeepers" — although it's hard to imagine anyone who had stood in the Great Hall at Karnak thinking *that*.

But these views were well in line with the conventions of the day. Darwinism had just taken root, and "evolution" was the buzzword. Modern civilization, its foundations in the rational science and speculative philosophy of ancient Greece, was held with absolute conviction to be the most advanced yet seen on the face of the earth. This new "history" was a downward path leading back to caves and apes. The Egyptians were a long way back down that path, so it followed they must have been a good deal nearer the caves and the apes.

In archaeology preconceived ideas are almost always dangerous, for the excavator can never be sure of finding what he has set out to find, or of proving what he wants to prove. Dig with hope, but dig with an open mind.
— T. G. H. JAMES, KEEPER OF EGYPTIAN ANTIQUITIES,
BRITISH MUSEUM

After the discovery of Tutankhamen's tomb in 1924, and subsequent smaller but significant finds, the rapid advance of modern science began to play an increasingly important role in Egyptological research. The patronizing vision of Maspero, Peet, and others was called into question more and more as scientists from other disciplines began to apply their skills to the vast amount of information on ancient Egypt that had steadily been piling up in universities around the world.

German scholars deciphering the first medical papyri unearthed had been revolted and amused by what they saw as absurd and barbaric practices, such as applying dung and other vile things to wounds, inflammations, and infections. With the discovery of penicillin and antibiotics, however, another generation of doctors was much impressed by such treatments. And it was intrigued. The Egyptians were extremely specific about what kind of dung or fungus to use on what kind of ailment. Before long, advances in modern neurology established that the Egyptians had also possessed detailed knowledge of the workings of the human nervous system and the bodily functions controlled by specific areas of the brain. In the fields of astronomy, high-energy physics, and molecular biology, similar reappreciations of the extent and profundity of ancient Egyptian science are appearing with increasing regularity, and will doubtless continue to do so.

As science became more and more specialized, dissecting a universe that had once been viewed as a unity, it became impossible for orthodox scholars to engage in cross-over scholarship without being branded dilettantes and ultimately hounded from the establishment. Egyptologists generally know little of particle physics or advanced genetics. Thus, those scholars from outside the academic establishment are more willing to risk the disapproval of orthodoxy and familiarize themselves with the aspects of many disciplines that have a bearing on the study of ancient Egyptian civilization. As holistic thinking returns, particularly in physics and the arts, the late twentieth-century mind is beginning to grasp the kind of cosmic view necessary to comprehend the ancient Egyptian mind, with its deeply symbolic modes of expression, its numerical mysticism, and its elaborate, highly developed mythologies employed to express thoughts too deep for words.

That our view of the ancient world is undergoing drastic upheaval is evinced by the works of John Anthony West, as well as other recent studies. As West has stated, what Egyptology lacked was a Unified Field Theory, something that would pull together all the many areas of

Egyptian knowledge, from astronomy to zoology, and place them in a cohesive master plan. What he discovered, however, was that this master plan already existed, in the work of an obscure Alsatian mathematician and philosopher named R. A. Schwaller de Lubicz, who formulated what amounted to a total reinterpretation of ancient Egypt during a protracted on-site study of the Temple of Luxor between 1937 and 1952.

Each of us [orthodox Egyptologists], within the little sphere of his speciality, must have the courage to verify the elements with which he is most familiar; he must check, on the site if necessary, the assertions made by M. de Lubicz and must call unselfconsciously for help from colleagues and technicians able to throw light on the domains which formerly have been closed to him; above all, he must not reject a priori as inconceivable that which exceeds his understanding … The symbolism of M. Schwaller de Lubicz … is not a simple personal and fantastic interpretation of facts, but conclusions drawn from precise and objective evidence which up to now has escaped the acumen of Egyptologists.

> —ARPAG MEKHITARIAN, *CAHIERS DU SUD*, NO. 358, DECEMBER 1960

Hieroglyphic writing first appears in the beginning of the First Dynasty … Almost from its inception it gives the appearance of being fully developed … All the elements appeared together at the same time.

> —DICTIONARY OF EGYPTIAN CIVILIZATION, 1962

Egyptian civilization was not a "development," it was a legacy.

> —JOHN ANTHONY WEST, *SERPENT IN THE SKY*

Few orthodox Egyptologists have taken such an enlightened stance as Arpag Mekhitarian; Schwaller de Lubicz' work was written off by those I spoke with as "nonsense" or "madness." It has never been refuted, merely ignored. What is it then that so annoys the establishment, and what so intrigues John Anthony West, Schwaller's principal champion?

Generally I shall divide West's interpretations of Schwaller into two broad categories. First, there is the contention that Egyptian civilization appears fully formed because it was an inheritance or legacy from a previous and now lost culture, Plato's "Atlantis." I use quotation marks, as West tends to, because it is the civilization of "Atlantis" that is meant by the term, not the geographical location. West and Schwaller both predate the beginnings of Egyptian civilization to around 30,000 B.C., which conforms to what Herodotus was told by the Egyptian priesthood, who said that in their history "the sun had twice risen where it now set, and twice set where it now rises." This remark is interpreted as a description of the passage of one and one-half precessional cycles, the 24,000-year period during which, because of the earth's axis-tilt, the apparent position of the universe around it slowly changes, east in effect becoming west. The two scholars also maintain that the Great Sphinx and the temple complex adjacent to it — and possibly the Great Pyramid — date from before the Flood and are remains of this earlier civilization. They believe that Egyptian symbolism was closely aligned to astrological periods, the lion's body of the Great Sphinx constructed during the age of Leo, the bull's bodies relating to Montu, the Old Kingdom god, from the age of Taurus, and the later rams of Amon from the age of Aries.

Second, West and Schwaller insist that:

> *Egyptian science, medicine, mathematics and astronomy were all of an exponentially higher order of refinement and sophistication than modern scholars will acknowledge. The whole of Egyptian civilization was based upon a complete and precise understanding of universal laws. And this profound understanding manifested itself in a consistent, coherent and inter-related system that fused*

science, art and religion into a single organic Unity. In other words,
it was exactly the opposite of what we find in the world today.
—WEST, *SERPENT IN THE SKY*

This latter aspect of West's extension of Schwaller's work is largely based on the studies of the Temple of Luxor published in the 1950s by Schwaller in three volumes entitled *Le Temple de l'Homme* (*The Temple of Man*), and presented in a far more comprehensible form by West in *Serpent in the Sky: The High Wisdom of Ancient Egypt*. West's book includes his own subsequent discoveries and theories as well as a wealth of mathematical and architectural drawings, photographs, and other documentation.

What Schwaller discovered at Luxor ostensibly complies with Protagoras' dictum that "Man is the measure of all things." Through exhaustive measurements and studies of the hieroglyphs, he proved that the temple represents an architectural configuration of man, including such arcane knowledge as the location of the ductless glands, of the energy centres called chakras by the Hindus, and of the acupuncture points upon which Chinese medicine is based. He also discovered the astronomical orientations of the temple; and he showed that the geometry of its construction was based on the proportions of the human body, with figurations and inscriptions physiologically located.

It was in effect an image of Adamic man, or humanity before the fall from unity with the divine; and in its proportions and harmonies the temple told the story of the creation of humanity and its relation to the universe. The incarnation of the universe in humans, Schwaller claimed, was the fundamental theme of all revealed religion, the human body being a living synthesis of all the vital functions of the universe. In West's words, "It is a library containing the totality of knowledge pertaining to universal creative powers, embodied in the building itself." The temple also reflects the primordial struggle that takes place in all religions between the quintessential antagonists: light and dark, yin and yang, gravity and levity, Ormazda and Ahriman, Christ and Satan, Quetzalcoatl and Tezcatlipoca, Vishnu and Siva, Horus and Seth. The temple is about the resolution of polarities, the return of the many to the One.

Indeed, Schwaller discovered that the ancient Egyptians understood the functions of pi and the Golden Section a thousand years before the Greeks, which led him to contend that Platonic and Pythagorean knowledge of numbers and wisdom was derived from the science of ancient Egypt. The essential mystery of the Creation, how the One produced the many, West explains, can only be represented through numbers. As early as 1917, Schwaller had produced a treatise on numbers in which he explained that they were merely names applied to the functions and principles upon which the universe was created and maintained, that from the interplay of numbers result the phenomena of the physical world. He stated that to understand properly the successive steps of creation, one must first know the development of abstract numbers.

This is essentially what lay behind the cult of Pythagoras, who was far from being the mere math teacher presented to schoolchildren today. The ancient Egyptians disliked imprecision and abstraction, and although their language was capable of more subtlety than ours they were fully aware that only through numbers could the greater mysteries be portrayed accurately. We can now talk or write about things entirely beyond our comprehension: "infinity," for example, which is an abstraction; or "zero," which is a negation; or even "the square root of minus one," which is both abstraction *and* negation. The Egyptians would have shuddered at such folly. However, through the understanding of numbers, West shows that they were able to demonstrate the actual process of creation itself and the subsequent vast and complex interplay of relationships between natural and cosmic rhythms, stars, planets, metals, colours, sounds, types of vegetables and animals, and parts of the human body.

One plus one does not equal two in the Pythagorean/Egyptian system. The process by which one becomes two — the mystery of creation itself — actually implies three. Yes, one plus one equals three. The "becoming" of one *becoming* two is a third force, establishing relationship, and the ubiquitous concept of the Trinity. There can be no two without three, the relationship. Just as male plus female is not a relationship; they require love or desire for that. An artist and a canvas are not a painting; will or inspiration, the third force, creates the painting and forges the trinity. Similarly sodium and chlorine together are not a chemical reaction; affinity creates the salt. So, while the ancient Egyptians admitted that the creation of the universe was the only ineluctable mystery, the Primordial Scission, they believed all else was in principle comprehensible through the understanding of "relationship." West writes:

From the standpoint of everyday experience, we are aware of the universe as an incredibly diverse system made up of a multiplicity of apparent unities. A duck is a unity, made of a multiplicity of cells, each of which is a unity made up of a multiplicity of molecules, each of which is a unity made up of a multiplicity of atoms, each of which is a unity made up of a multiplicity of "particles" for whose description ordinary language will no longer suffice. Seen one way they are particles, or unities; seen another way, they are modes of behaviour of energy; and it is energy that is now regarded as the ultimate unity underlying the material universe.

He next extends the same line of thought into the macrocosmic universe: duck, earth, solar system, galaxies, and thus to universe, the ultimate unity.

Understanding this, West and Schwaller assert, the ancient Egyptians were aware that the third force, the one that reconciles the polarities, is consciousness, which is what, paradoxically, also creates duality in the first place. From the three comes four, the triangle becomes the pyramid, the symbol for the material world, used extensively in Egyptian number mysticism and mythology — from the four orientations to the four "elements," the principles that account for matter and describe its inherent nature, not, as is commonly believed, the notion that earth, water, fire, and air were actual elements.

The figure of a square inscribed inside a circle represents passive, potential matter contained within unity. The cross upon which Christ is nailed, West elaborates, is the "cross of matter, upon which all of us are pinned. Upon the cross, the Christ, the cosmic man, is crucified. By reconciling its polarities through his own consciousness, he attains unity."

When people speak of esoteric knowledge being enshrined in architectural structures, this is what they mean. Schwaller's studies at Luxor convinced him that, evident everywhere in measure, proportion, and harmony were the numerical relationships that conveyed such complex and hermetic ideas. And in the hieroglyphs he found similar messages, often so arcane they could be unravelled only by what he termed "transparency," the matching up of glyphs and reliefs on one side of a wall with those appearing on its opposite side.

Needless to say, such theories would not be greeted with open arms by the academic establishment, containing as they do an understanding of the "high wisdom" outside the tenets of orthodoxy, besides an eclectic multi-disciplinary approach quite beyond the abilities of most Egyptologists, with their rigid groundings in conventional anthropology, linguistics, historical chronologies, and the increasingly narrow specializations of archaeology.

Applying his system beyond the Temple of Luxor, West shows how Schwaller's research confirms all manner of things that have long been debated by orthodox Egyptologists. One of the most convincing is that temples were not destroyed or reliefs vandalized by succeeding pharaohs to blot out the achievements of their predecessors but were systematically dis-assembled or carefully effaced according to astrological dictates, once their function in the great scheme of things had passed. Since no two temples are alike, and most show evidence of many hands, many historical periods of addition and subtraction, overlaying and refinement, this theory is immensely complicated, partly because the documentation to prove it is, though copious, still incomplete.

At the Philae temple the process of effacement seemed to me indis-putable, the gigantic figures on the western pylon carefully chipped away with a mason's skill, while the figures on the eastern pylon were left intact. In other places only ritual headdresses were effaced, as if their symbolic meaning had become either redundant or should be hidden from the uninitiated who would soon invade the sacred precincts.

Acts of vandalism by Christians and Muslims are very different in nature — the work of thugs with sledgehammers — and generally affect hieroglyphs portraying ithyphallic figures and other images offensive to the newer religions. Equally obvious is the difference between a temple that has been carefully dismantled, stone placed on stone in an orderly fashion, as at Kom Ombo, and one that has been destroyed by earthquake or natural disaster — like the outer pylon of the Ramesseum at Thebes. Because of subsequent excavations at some of these sites, West has provided in the books early photographs that show the stones as they originally were after being dismantled.

Schwaller's work even managed to explain the extraordinary impression of movement I noticed in the striding colossus of Rameses II carved from a single block of granite in the great courtyard of the Luxor Temple. This feeling of the statue advancing is heightened by the somewhat ruined colossi flanking it, which appear rigidly static. Schwaller's study revealed the colossus was based upon a rigorous symmetry from "every angle except when viewed from above. The illusion of 'advance' is created solely by the twist of the supporting dorsal stela and the positioning of the feet — an instance of the astonishing command of technique common in Egypt."

If Schwaller de Lubicz's work is so powerfully reasoned and backed up by exhaustive documentation then, why is it so scorned by the Egyptological establishment? John Anthony West recounts an amusing anecdote that may sum up the answer to this question.

Early in his research, but before he'd studied *Le Temple de l'Homme* in any depth and begun collaborating with Schwaller's stepdaughter, Lucie Lamy, West obtained an interview with the late T. G. H. James, keeper of Egyptian Antiquities at the British Museum (where the cream of dynastic remains, imperial booty, are still stored). The official assured West that "in his opinion, and in the opinion of all other Egyptologists, Schwaller de Lubicz was mad. His work was repudiated in entirety." West said he realized this, but that it seemed to him everything was backed up by a mass of documentation, documentation that had been checked and supervised on the site by an orthodox Egyptologist, Alexandre Varille, and by an architect, Clement Robinson, chief of excavations for the French Egyptological mission in Egypt. Had this documentation, West inquired, ever been disproved?

James admitted that it had not, but that if any Egyptologists could be bothered to disprove it, the task would easily be accomplished. They were, however, all too busy to waste their time on patent madness. Recognizing this was an impossible argument to pursue, West asked James to give him an instance where, even without formal disproof, he could substantiate an error. The man then confessed he had not actually read *Le Temple de l'Homme*, and, furthermore, did not know of any Egyptologist who had. West then pointed out that at least one respected and orthodox Egyptologist, Arpag Mekhitarian, secretary of the Egyptological Institute in Brussels, had gone on record after the book had been published, saying Schwaller's work demanded serious study and deserved the courtesy of a formal refutation if such a thing was possible. "Ah, yes," James replied, "Mekhitarian is something of a mystic. He might well say that."

The establishment, it seems, is almost afraid of Schwaller de Lubicz and John Anthony West. Only the orthodox Egyptologists themselves know just how flimsy the foundations of their work really are; the whole structure could collapse like a pack of cards at any moment. And it possibly has done just that. By their resistance they also reveal another and perhaps more deep-seated fear: the possibility of there *being* ancient wisdom at all, and the implications for their lives if what West and Schwaller have posited proves to be correct.

Currently West is striving to provide the kind of proof that the establishment academics will not be able to ignore: artifacts from the antediluvian or "Atlantean" period. This, of course, relates to the other section of his work, which contends that Egyptian civilization was a legacy.

Egyptologists generally agree that the ancient civilization *does* appear fully formed, the hieroglyphs showing no development and the architectural feats of the Great Sphinx and Giza pyramids refined, perhaps, yet never matched again in size and complexity. But they choose to view the progress of the dynasties as a development, most seeing the Middle Kingdom, the age of Rameses and Tutankhamen, as the "golden age" of Egypt.

West, on the other hand, looks on this period as a marked step down from the earlier age, when an increasing emphasis on the material gradually corrupted the purity of the spiritual aspects of the culture. He suggests that the Middle Kingdom represents a kind of decadence similar to that manifested by the late Roman Empire in contrast with the scientific and philosophic achievements of the ancient Greek civilization from which it had grown. All languages that we are able to study show distinct stages of development, growing increasingly rich and complex and often then deteriorating. The hieroglyphs do not follow this pattern. In fact, the earliest examples are among the finest in detail, subtlety, and symbolic elegance.

The time will come when diligent research over long periods will bring to light things which now lie hidden ... Many discoveries are reserved for ages still to come, when memories of us will have been effaced. Our universe is a sorry little affair unless it has something for every age to investigate. Nature does not reveal her mysteries once and for all.

—SENECA, *NATURAL QUESTIONS*,
BOOK 7, FIRST CENTURY A.D.

They couldn't hit an elephant at this dist —

—LAST WORDS OF GENERAL JOHN SEDGWICK
AT THE BATTLE OF SPOTSYLVANIA, 1861

Schwaller had contended that proof of the earlier civilization, the real source of Egyptian knowledge and culture, could be found by examining the Great Sphinx and the temple complex south of it. Both are unlike anything else, in terms of structure and design, found in any other location throughout the whole of Egypt, with one exception. The evidence placing their original construction in a period long preceding that of Old Kingdom Egypt was, Schwaller claimed, to be found in the erosion visible on their stones, which was caused by water and not, as was commonly accepted, by wind or blown sand. Even the water erosion from capillary action — an alternate orthodox theory — would not have resulted in such extreme effects. Armed with this, John Anthony West set out to vindicate Schwaller's thesis and, in the process, to attack conventional Egyptology by striking its Achilles heel: chronology.

Reviled and slandered by the academics, whose proprietary attitude toward ancient Egypt resembled Howard Carter's sense of territorial imperative with Tutankhamen's tomb, West realized that it was not a sympathetic archaeologist he needed to find after all. Schwaller's theory was work for another scientific discipline altogether — geology.

But geologists initially proved no more receptive to a dilettante without letters behind his name and with a dubious theory to propound, until West approached Dr. Robert M. Schoch of Boston University. Schoch heard West out — extraordinary enough in itself — and then, while still highly skeptical, agreed to accompany him to the Giza plateau for a look at the Sphinx. What he found, much to his surprise, was sufficient evidence to suggest that Schwaller and West at least had a case.

Intrigued now, Schoch prepared the formal applications for permission to conduct elaborate seismic studies with sophisticated equipment never before employed in Egypt. Along with Dr. Thomas Dobecki, a Houston geophysicist, Schoch and West made three trips to Cairo, performing a complex series of seismographic tests on and around the Great Sphinx. After analyzing these and other data, Schoch reached the conclusion that the core body of this massive statue could not have been carved later than 7000 to 5000 B.C., and quite possibly dated to an even earlier period. At the very least, this placed its original construction some two and a half millennia before the date generally accepted by orthodox Egyptologists. It also placed it a few thousand years outside the traditional beginnings of ancient Egyptian civilization entirely, implying the existence of a highly advanced culture in the area about which nothing whatsoever was known.

Schoch and Dobecki stood firmly behind their conclusions, presenting them at the annual meeting of the Geological Society of America on October 23, 1991. Schoch was careful to dissociate himself from West's more speculative statements and the "Atlantis" theory (which he referred to as "the A-word"), and his account of his Sphinx studies was well received by other professional geologists, many of whom offered support and encouragement. While forewarned by West, however, Schoch was not prepared for the outraged reactions his hypothesis immediately elicited from archaeologists and Egyptologists, some of which amounted to little more than gratuitous insults and accusations of charlatanry and sensation-seeking.

One very prominent scholar — who would deny it if named — told West, "I don't care what data you have, I won't believe it." But those who went on record were at best distressingly unscientific. "That's ridiculous," Peter Lacovara of the Boston Museum of Fine Arts' Egyptian Department told the *Boston Globe*. "Thousands of scholars working for hundreds of years" had studied the topic (an exaggeration, to say the least); "the chronology is pretty well worked out. There are no big surprises in store for us." Carol Redmount of the University of California at Berkeley informed the *Los Angeles Times*, "There's just no way this could be true," adding that Schoch's conclusions flew in the face of "everything we know about ancient Egypt."

There was even an article in Cairo's *Al-Ahram* that allegedly stated that the chairman of Boston University's Archaeology Department, Dr. James Wiseman, had said Schoch was not a member of the Boston University community. He is, of course, not a member of the Archaeology faculty, but he is a tenured associate professor in Boston University's College of Basic Studies, Division of Science and Mathematics, and the author of numerous papers and several books, some of them standard texts in the fields of paleontology and stratigraphy. He was not a man used to being treated the way John Anthony West was used to being treated. And he did not like it; nor did he back down.

West, on the other hand, gleefully jousted with the orthodoxy, hoisting his old persecutors on their own petards. "An Egyptologist's opinion of Dr. Dobecki's data," he told one newspaper, "is about as relevant as a proctologist's." He was right, and fully aware he'd started the scientific equivalent of a civil war. Unlike a Velikovsky, who craved the approval of academia for his radical theories, West had come to despise an establishment that "monopolized truth at the expense of truth." The last thing he wanted was its approval. "It's like wanting to be Hitler's friend," he once told me. "If they weren't such idiots, I'd have to call them criminals. Rationalism is irrational, and the Enlightenment is the most ironic term for any period in history; it began the real Dark Ages ..."

After Schoch's initial presentation and the subsequent media interest it generated, the Egyptological establishment clearly decided it had to respond formally — before someone noticed that the whole premise of the discipline had been challenged as forcefully as Einstein's special Theory of Relativity had challenged Newtonian physics, and no defence had so far been offered.

The Great Sphinx is generally accepted as a project of the Fourth Dynasty pharaoh, Khafre, or Chephren, dating to around 2500 B.C. The evidence for this is, however, surprisingly circumstantial. Like the chronologies and much else, convenience seems more often a motivating force in archaeology than does a genuine search for the facts. As in many other areas of our lives, facts are often an inconvenience.

It was determined that the task of trashing Schoch's hypothesis and salvaging an entire science should fall to Dr. Mark Lehner of the University of Chicago. Being probably the world's leading expert on the Great Sphinx, he had more to lose than most. Few of his colleagues presumably realized just how much more he had to lose. But John Anthony West certainly did.

Dismissed as a "New Ager," someone who would believe anything that the establishment dismissed, West is in fact more impatient and scornful of most so-called New Age thinking than are his detractors in the orthodoxy. Formidably erudite, he has nonetheless a somewhat austere intellect, focused and irreducibly concise when he is discussing his work. Content to let Schoch bask in the limelight of media interest, he was not about to sit back and watch the geologist suffer abuse from those who had abused *him* for nearly twenty years. The showdown between geology and Egyptology was set for February 7, 1992, at the annual meeting of the American Association for the Advancement of Science, to be held in Chicago. Although he would not be allowed to sit with Schoch on the podium, West made sure that the professor was armed to the teeth and prepared to fight dirty if it came to that.

The AAAS meeting is the largest scientific jamboree in the world, with hundreds of scientists presenting state-of-the-art research in forums on everything from astrophysics to zoology. Frequently there were several symposia in progress simultaneously in the warren of conference rooms deep below the massive Hyatt Regency Hotel. None, however, attracted more interest than the one listed as "How Old Is the Sphinx?" in the program. The participants were Schoch, Dobecki, Lehner, and a geo-archaeologist called Gauri from the University of Louisville. Lehner had wisely refused to pit discipline against discipline, unearthing someone he imagined embodied both disciplines to back him up. He may well have wrecked a career in the process.

It is customary at such august gatherings for papers being presented to be made available beforehand for those attending the presentations. Dr. Schoch produced an extensive document, not only detailing the work carried out at Giza but also reviewing objections to their hypothesis and systematically refuting them. Dobecki provided a document of robotic starkness, ostensibly a list of data from the seismographic studies in language that appeared to view adjectives as a shameless luxury in any written communication. If Lehner supplied a paper, no one seems to have noticed it. Gauri's contribution, apparently untitled, began:

Nearly 70 L of a medium with the following composition was prepared: KH_2PO_4, 0.5g; NH_4Cl, 1.0g; $MgCl_2$, 0.06g; $FeCl_2$, 4.0g; sodium lactate, 3.5g; yeast extract, 1.0g; sodium ascorbate, 0.1g; sodium thioglycolate. 0.1g; L-cysteine, 0.1g, resazurin, 1.5g per liter of water. To this medium, nearly 45 min before inoculation with the microbe, we added oxyrase EC-100, which is a preparation of frozen, partially purified bacterial membranes that removes dissolved oxygen from aqueous environments. A concentrated culture of Desulfovibrio desulfuricans was then added to this medium. This broth was then poured into the bag so that the monument was completely immersed in it.

Christ! I thought, these geo-archaeologists don't fool around. If this was the refutation of Schoch's hypothesis, I hoped Schoch would understand it, because I certainly didn't. It sounded as if Gauri had soaked the Sphinx in some sort of wizard's brew. Since the statue is around 60 feet high and 250 feet long, I hardly dared imagine how he'd achieved this, let alone why no one had noticed such an astounding event. "The bag was then removed," I read on, "and the monument surface washed off with a garden hose. After this treatment, the monument lost the black color without loosing [*sic*] any surface details of sculpture. Some yellowishness is still present at isolated sites, perhaps representing gypsum, but we considered it unnecessary to repeat the experiment."

Only then did I notice a subheading reading "Studies on the Great Sphinx of Giza, Egypt," followed by two pages questioning not only Schoch's hypothesis, but apparently the current state of knowledge about the weathering of rocks in general. Some other monument had been immersed in whatever-it-was and then hosed down, emerging cleaner. Gauri had photocopied his paper from a scholarly desktop job, not bothering to eliminate the material surrounding it. After a final thirty-word paragraph assuring the reader that Schoch was full of shit, even if no one could prove it, another subheading proclaimed "Stone Treatment Using Epoxies." It seemed more promising than Gauri's ruminations on the weather in Egypt eight thousand years ago, but ended in the middle of its third sentence, which left me wondering whether historic buildings in the United States would be saved from the ravages of pollution by epoxy treatments or not.

There were also illegible notes scribbled in the margins. One could only assume that Gauri was a sloppy operator or that he resented having to defend the party line against an interloper like Schoch.

The morning got off to an amiable enough start. Lehner presented the orthodox position, which, with nothing to oppose it yet, seemed reasonable enough. He, however, did seem defensive about something. Then the proceedings continued with Schoch showing slides and discussing things like "surficial calcareous duricrust." The only thing comprehensible to a layman was that his studies had utterly convinced him that the Sphinx was carved thousands of years before the date Egyptologists claimed for it. He conceded the structure was most probably restored by Chephren around 2500 B.C., as were other buildings that also dated from several millennia earlier. And he was adamant that his seismic data did not lie.

Dobecki confirmed all this, or appeared to, his talk consisting of terms like "seismic refraction investigation," "wave propagation method," "refraction tomography," and other technical arcana that everyone present either understood or did not dare question. At least he was brief.

As Lehner had been. That morning he had refused to discuss the whole business with me before the forum began, sounding just this side of rude and distinctly that side of edgy. On the podium he looked calm and confident the way only those who are virtually paranoid with anxiety can manage. It was not Schoch's geophysics that seemed to bother him, either.

Publicly stating his respect for John Anthony West's scholarship and acknowledging that there would have been no Sphinx Project without him, Schoch deplored New Age gullibility and indiscrimination, dissociating himself and West from healing crystals, gnomes, space aliens, and the rest of La-La-Land. He studied rocks, he stated. And that was all he did and all he had ever done.

Dr. Lehner, he mentioned, studied the Sphinx, but that was not all *he* had ever done. Lehner's interest in Egypt had originated with his connection to an organization known as the Association for Research and Enlightenment (ARE), the foundation set up to perpetuate the teachings and work of the psychic and mystic Edgar Cayce. Reportedly ARE and its members had even helped subsidize part of Lehner's college education, the intention being that he would further the association's Egyptological work. He even wrote a book, now hard to obtain, called *The Egyptian Heritage*, which purportedly recounted Cayce's psychic readings concerning Egypt.

Somewhere along the way, it seems, Lehner lost his faith, embracing the orthodox dogma of Egyptology, rejecting ARE and all it stood for. Apostates always have axes to grind. Now, for Lehner, the appearance of Schoch's data must have been a nightmare worse than Scrooge's Christmas Eve.

Edgar Cayce claimed that ancient Egypt was the civilization formed by survivors from Atlantis, that the pyramids and the Sphinx were constructed around 10,000 B.C., and that, furthermore, beneath the Sphinx was buried a Hall of Records containing all the Atlantean documentation. Schoch visibly shudders when the "A-word" is mentioned; yet among his seismic studies is the indication that a previously unknown chamber or chambers exists some thirty feet beneath the paws of the Sphinx.

Little wonder Lehner spent more time emphasizing that he had come to realize Cayce was wrong through his own studies of accepted facts than he did proving Schoch was wrong with these same accepted facts. His main argument consisted of asking where the evidence of this earlier civilization could be found. Where were the pottery shards? The peoples living in Egypt around 6000 B.C., he maintained, were hunters and gatherers. They did not build cities. He characterized Schoch's work as "pseudoscience."

Even a mile from the AAAS conference, in Chicago's Field Museum, are examples of pots from the predynastic cultures called Naqada I and II, about which nothing is known, although they are confidently dated to around 3500 B.C. The pots are carved from solid rock — basalt in some cases — and are flawlessly symmetrical, often ovoid in shape. While they are among the most beautiful objects ever made by human hands, one wonders how a society of "hunters and gatherers" without metal tools made them, let alone *why* they made them. Any museum curator will admit that no one knows how a narrow-necked vase was hollowed out of solid basalt, particularly since no one knows how to do it now, even with diamond-bit drills and lasers. Such pots have survived without so much as a chip or scratch for five and a half millennia; how can anyone be certain that they had not survived another five and a half millennia before ending up in the Naqada tombs where they were discovered by the pioneer Egyptologist Flinders Petrie?

By the time Gauri delivered his refutation of Schoch's hypothesis, even those in the audience who knew nothing of the background to this squabble sensed something was wrong. Gauri had apparently abandoned the argument in his printed paper for another one involving "yardangs," a term meaning natural rock formations. Not an accomplished speaker, Gauri defended his discipline in a way that clearly amazed the normally deadpan Schoch, who started shaking his head and wincing as if in pain. Schoch later explained that Gauri had really committed professional suicide onstage, claiming, among other things, that the Sphinx had originally been a natural rock formation that was eventually embellished by carving, thus explaining Schoch's weathering data. In fact, far from refuting Schoch's studies, this endorsed them: even Lehner would deny the Sphinx had been a "yardang." There was not a single Egyptologist who disputed that the statue had been carved from bedrock. The head alone had conceivably once protruded above ground level.

Only the participants in this extraordinary conflict understood its implications at first. The result seemed to most a dead heat. Yet what occurred was not argument but contradiction. Schoch's hypothesis was met only with Lehner's dogmatic assertions. In other words, Egyptology failed to defend itself, merely restating its traditional position.

At 2:30 P.M. on February 7, 1992, for all intents and purposes, an entire scientific discipline collapsed. It may take years for this to sink in, but the media were intuitively aware that science had been replaced by emotion. The *New York Times* observed that after the symposium there was a "hallway confrontation in which voices were raised and words skated on the icy edge of scientific politeness." Dr. Mark Lehner was telling John Anthony West not to meddle with things only those with Ph.D.s are qualified to meddle with.

Watching an aspect of science rarely presented on public television, I was struck by two things: one, Lehner clearly wished that West would vanish from the face of the earth; two, West knew more about ancient Egypt than Lehner ever would. Far from being a difference of opinion between two intellectuals, it more closely resembled the futile attempt of two different species to communicate with one another. West walked off laughing; Lehner seemed less than amused and has yet to discuss the subject further with me or anyone else.

Possibly he senses West will take no prisoners in this war. While he now feels he has vindicated Schwaller's hypothesis and can let Egyptology pick up the pieces, West still has scores to settle. Not long ago Lehner was featured in *National Geographic* with his computer reconstruction that "proved" the Sphinx's head was a definite likeness of Chephren. Not necessarily disputing that Chephren restored the Sphinx, having its face recarved in his own image, West and Schoch find Lehner's computer methodology spurious. Using an identical procedure, they planned to show that the head of the Sphinx is really a likeness of Elvis Presley, and they waited for the conclusions of the New York forensic specialist they had sent to Giza. The police expert specialized in the reconstruction of faces from decomposed cadavers, and he predicted that the original face of the Sphinx would not resemble any known portrait bust of Chephren. Or of Elvis, for that matter.

At the end of February 1992, results of the forensic reconstruction were released. The Sphinx's face is neither that of Chephren nor Elvis. It is a stylized face, in the tradition of many other sculpted portraits of Egyptian pharaohs. Which simply goes to prove what computer buffs are fond of saying: garbage in, garbage out.

West hopes the work he has done with Schoch will encourage someone to apply for a permit to excavate the Sphinx site. Only when objects unlike any previously found are unearthed will the "lost civilization" theory gain universal acceptance. In the meantime, rather than fight with those he views at best as a confederation of dunces, West is working with an associate of Steven Spielberg on a documentary film and, otherwise, prefers to conduct tours of Egypt for anyone interested in finding out whether life in contemporary New York City is an improvement on life in ancient Thebes. John Cleese recently took forty of his friends on one. Generally, West finds, people return from such tours wondering how Darwin ever managed to get a single soul to take his theory of evolution seriously.

The Egyptians themselves claimed to date back to an age of gods, which was followed by a steady degeneration. This explains why their culture was so archly conservative, determined to resist change, because the golden age lay *behind*, not ahead. It is the exact reverse of modern thinking.

Any understanding of ancient Egypt is incomplete without at least a glimpse of what *might* have lain behind it, and what it *may* still have to say to us forty centuries later. If there is an explanation for the indescribable power of a structure like the Great Hypostyle Hall at Karnak, then it surely lies in the symbolist interpretations of Schwaller de Lubicz and John Anthony West. The power most certainly there, as so many have attested, defies any rational explanation. For those, like me, who have seen in the pharaonic world something more than a race of brutal megalomaniacs, the symbolist schism provides an alternative explanation, grander in scope and implication than the dry, unimaginative, and depressing world academics so often picture.

Giving me an analogy for what he felt contemporary Egyptology is up against, John Anthony West compared modern scholars to Martians studying baseball: "They'd be able to work out the principles and rules of the game, the cult of the black socks and the white socks, but they'd never be able to work out what the process was really about and why it was being played if they had no conception of games on their planet."

CHAPTER NINE

THE PROFESSOR AND THE HERETIC

*The King of the Gods [Amon] is a [true] god, one who takes
cognizance of one who is cognizant of him, who favours him
that serves him, and protects him who follows him. He is Re, his
body is the sun-disc ...*

—OLD KINGDOM TEXT

*One of my fervent desires in my teaching or writing of ancient
history is that the novice or reader will be confronted time and
again by the factual evidence, as much or as little as it is. Read
the scholar's or the novelist's romanticized version of the story
and enjoy it fleetingly — then discard it, and turn and ferret
out the truth.*

—PROFESSOR DONALD B. REDFORD,
AKHENATEN: THE HERETIC KING, 1989

Waking early in the luxury of the Hilton, I took a walk along the manicured banks of the Nile in the cool morning breeze. Feluccas were already busy out on the slow, broad green river, ferrying produce from outlying villages to the markets of Luxor. Stained mauve and rose, the low mountains that guard the Valley of the Kings far on the western horizon struck me as even more mysterious than usual after my evening in the Karnak Temple. One of my purposes in staying on at Thebes/Luxor was to get some idea of what a conventional academic Egyptologist's life is really like. I'd chosen as my main subject Professor Donald B. Redford of the University of Toronto, director of the Akhenaten Temple Project, which has been in progress since 1966.

In the hotel's extravagant lobby, with its fountain and marble, I was approached after breakfast by a man representing the American Express travel office, which kept a branch — a desk, really — in the Hilton. His name was Hussein, and he seemed to have taken it upon himself to explain certain things to me. "You will meet many people here in Upper Egypt," he said, "who wish to talk to you. All they are wanting is to practise their English, not to bother you. For you see we are poor people without the benefits of education, and the only way in which we can improve our skills in language is to talk to our foreign guests. I hope you will not take offence at this and remember that it will be of great help to our people."

He seemed genuine, but in that depressed, melancholy way I'd encountered in Nubia. Then he offered to find me a good guide. I declined, thanking him and pointing out I would be spending most of my time with various archaeologists in the area. He announced that his grandfather had worked with Howard Carter, was the last man alive to know him, and would be happy to meet me. Almost anyone old enough to remember the 1920s now claims to have worked with Carter.

My car soon arrived, and I told the driver to take me to Beit Kanada, the Canadian Institute in Egypt's headquarters in Luxor, giving him the directions I'd received in Cairo. We drove toward the Karnak Temple, which looked more mundane in the brightness of day, its massive stones a bland mud colour without the benefit of dramatic lighting, but its dimensions no less awesome. The son-et-lumière restores the colour and grandeur of the original structure and probably shows the temple more authentically than daylight ever can now. Skirting the massive exterior walls on the eastern side, we veered off the hardtop onto a bumpy dust road that wove past an untidy collection of mud-brick houses, heading through long, spiky grass across an uneven patch of wasteland. Dogs barked and grimy children chased our vehicle, getting even grimier in its dusty wake.

Struggling in first gear up an incline, we arrived at a dilapidated Nubian-style mud-brick structure enclosed by a wall and flanked by garagelike out-buildings in the shadows of the towering Karnak Temple's deserted eastern wall. Compared to the palatial French, German, and American missions I'd seen, this was a humble abode indeed. An ancient but dignified Egyptian in turban and *gelabia* was cutting up vegetables in the shade of a crumbling veranda. With great courtesy he ushered me through a tiny doorway, across a cluttered courtyard, showing me into a darkened room containing a huge table around which sat half a dozen young men and women eating *foul* beans and eggs. Professor Redford sat at the head of the table. Wearing only stained cotton pants and labourer's workboots, he was exceptionally friendly and looked every bit the eccentric genius with his long white hair and beard framing a sun-savaged face. He introduced me to the others — students from Europe and North America assisting with the dig. This was, in fact, their first full day on the site. Others were still due to arrive. Redford invited me to join them in breakfast; they'd been up working since 5:30 A.M., so this was a fairly substantial meal. Work would continue to 12:30 when, after a break for lunch, there would be a siesta until 4:30 in deference to the heat. The day had a rigid, almost military schedule. From 4:30 to 7:00 P.M. everyone was expected to write up his notes for the day, then have dinner and turn in early.

Redford had been working on the present site since 1975, proving in 1976 that it was indeed where Amenophis IV had erected his great temple to the sun disk, the "Aten," before changing his name to Akhen*aten*, abolishing the pantheon of the priests of Amon and moving his capital downriver to Tell al-Amarna or Akhetaten. Redford's discovery received international attention, it being previously assumed all traces of the temple had been destroyed after Akhenaten's mysterious death and the reinstatement of the worship of Amon. Interest in Akhenaten had always been great, many seeing the pharaoh as the original monotheist, a precursor of Moses and even a Christlike visionary.

Redford's subsequent scholarship presented a very different picture of the man, one that even angered those with romantic notions. Redford's Akhenaten is an indolent, deformed paranoiac with a severe Oedipal complex and a morbid fear of the powerful priesthood of Amon that had dominated his father, Amenophis III. Besides his physical ailments, he was the second son and not expected to succeed to the throne. While the eldest son was raised in the court, Akhenaten was probably brought up far from his father's court, in Heliopolis, the old capital and centre of the earlier worship of Re, whose body was the sun. But his older brother died young.

Redford interprets Akhenaten's advocacy of the exclusive worship of the sun disk as primarily a desire to supersede his father, who had used the sobriquet "Dazzling Sun Disk" in the same way Louis XIV termed himself the "Sun King." The sun disk is ubiquitously termed "my father" by Akhenaten, associated with him on countless reliefs and hieroglyphs.

Redford also believes he has detected a sinister totalitarian aspect to Akhenaten's rule that more closely resembles state atheism than monotheism. For example, the fanaticism of the new worship entailed holding all audiences, meetings, and ceremonies in the open, unprotected from the burning rays of the sun that turn Thebes and Akhetaten into infernos for much of the year. This led the Assyrian sovereign Ashuruballit I, who had sent a delegation to commence relations with Egypt, to write an amusing remonstration to the pharaoh: "Why are my messengers kept standing in the open sun? They will die in the open sun. If it does the king good to stand in the open sun, then let the king stand there and die in the open sun. Then will there be profit for the king! But really, why should they die in the open sun? ... They will be killed in the open sun!" Clearly the Assyrian delegation reported back that the ruler of Egypt was out of his tree.

In spite of Akhenaten's love of poetry and his own poetic talents and his fostering of the arts, Redford sums him up as someone who "in spirit remains to the end totalitarian. The right of the individual freely to choose was wholly foreign to him. He was the champion of a universal, celestial power who demanded universal submission, claimed universal truth, and from whom no further revelation could be expected. I cannot conceive a more tiresome regime under which to be fated to live."

Redford's work at the site has enabled him to arrive at his radical interpretation of Akhenaten. He has concentrated on piecing together the *talatat* — the term, of uncertain origin, is used for small stone blocks, many inscribed with reliefs, that faced the temple walls — found at Karnak and previously discovered as fill in later pylons. Along with the study of existing material, the work continues.

But that first morning the work was not continuing. Redford's briefcase containing the season's permits to dig and other official documents required by the labyrinthine bureaucracy of the Egyptian Antiquities Organisation had been stolen in Cairo airport. Sounding as optimistic as possible under the circumstances, he said he'd been assured he could commence work the next day. Seasons are brief, and the painstaking nature of on-site work makes it imperative that the archaeologists achieve as much as possible in that short time.

An air of benign chaos seemed to reign in the house. When the students had left to organize their modest living quarters, Redford confided that his helpers could be as much of a problem as the work itself. Their personal dilemmas and adjustments to the food and climate often slowed things down. But these were just a few of the myriad hazards in an Egyptologist's life. I asked Redford about the house. He admitted it was modest by international standards; Japanese Egyptologists researching designs for their own mission had once come to view it as an example of what to avoid. Canadian government money had built it, but it would revert to the Egyptians at the end of the operation. "That won't happen," he added, "unless I let the site go fallow for more than five years."

I arranged to meet him early the following day for a tour of the excavations. "We're working a huge site," he explained, "concentrating on the domestic part of the temple. There are a lot of small houses — the dwellings of priests — and a few shrines. Also, at a certain level, there is the Akhenaten temple itself."

I asked about the *talatat,* and he said they were still finding fragments. Could he reconstruct anything yet? "We could reconstruct one corner now," he replied. "About a sixty-metre [two-hundred-foot] stretch on either side of the southwest corner. We could in fact put it right back together."

Sayeed Tawfiq of the EAO apparently wanted this done as soon as possible. "But," Redford sighed, "there's a problem, and I don't know how to solve it. The water table is quite high, you see, and unless we have some kind of impervious ceiling level, the salts are inevitably going to come up and destroy the reliefs. It's a major problem. I've had all sorts of chemical engineers come along, but no one can give me reassurances about how to avoid it." He looked so frazzled and careworn that I did not pursue the issue.

Back at the hotel, I found a government representative waiting for me. I never caught his name since his poor command of English, combined with a useful stutter, made 50 percent of what he said unintelligible. With spectacles like the bottoms of Coke bottles, buck teeth, and many pens in his shirt pocket, he struck me as an Egyptian nerd. Under the mistaken belief that I was writing a tourist guidebook, he insisted on taking me on an inspection of the local hotels. Nothing I said could dissuade him from his task, so I trailed along with him. (I suspect he had some sort of vested interest in the hotels we visited.)

The manager of the Isis, a sprawling and execrably designed structure in an ugly part of Luxor, gushed with enthusiasm over his hotel. I couldn't understand why. First, the elevators wouldn't work, so we had to climb innumerable staircases and plod down many corridors smelling of old air-conditioning, fitted with broadloom joined together with strips of unmatching carpet. Second, we couldn't visit any of the rooms because the manager was unable to locate anyone with keys. "Houseman!" he kept shouting up and down the empty labyrinth, finally changing his cry to "Housewoman!" with no better results. The pair insisted on showing me restaurants and discos, which looked much like restaurants and discos. Finally it was my turn to insist — on leaving. I asked the nerd to do something useful, like arranging appointments for me to meet the local governor and the local head of the Antiquities Organisation.

In the bar, where Zamfir was once more piping out "Don't Cry for Me, Argentina," a burly, snub-nosed American introduced himself to me, Captain Bill Spreadbury. It was a while before I realized he was the pilot of the hot-air balloon I'd seen being inflated in the precincts of the Hatshepsut temple. "It's an eight-passenger pilot and fuel aircraft," he said, somewhat defensively. The fact that it *was*, technically speaking, an aircraft had contributed to the incredible complexities of starting up this operation in Egypt. "By far the best way to see Thebes," was Captain Bill's motto.

The Englishman who had conceived the entire project now operated a similar one in Dubai and was in the process of starting up in Jaipur, India. He had valiantly waded through a morass of bureaucracy to get things going in Luxor.

"The most perfect weather conditions in the world for ballooning," Captain Bill maintained. Though he confessed that even with these conditions, flights were frequently cancelled. "Weather reporting here is so bloody unreliable," he said. "You know, there are times when the temperature has reached sixty-eight degrees Celsius [154 degrees Fahrenheit]! But there's a law in Egypt that says all work must stop if the temperature exceeds fifty-two [125 degrees Fahrenheit]. So, of course, 'officially' it's never reported as above fifty-one point five." He laughed hard and raucously.

It must be a strange existence, I suggested, stuck in Luxor all alone. He'd been a "shooter" for Time-Life magazines once, he claimed, although I got the distinct impression he'd been a mercenary at some point as well. He was, he said, "a man without a country," adding, "but it's bad for your health to have no roots." Occasionally he went over to run the operation in Dubai, and he'd done some stunt work in movies as well as various kinds of promotional work.

"I sailed around the States with a globe of Mars for a Schwarzenegger movie," he said. "And next I'm gonna be in Venezuela three months for a whiskey company, flying around with a hundred-foot bottle of scotch above my head." Once he'd been hired by King Fouad of Saudi Arabia for six weeks to provide a novel entertainment for His Majesty's guests. "But the king only decided to fly twice in the six weeks — what the hell! It still cost him eight hundred dollars a day to have me there."

After a few more drinks he was recounting other exploits, such as smuggling arms into Afghanistan in small planes, landing on roads at night.

He wouldn't say who was paying him to do this, but it seemed more likely that it was one of the Arab countries than the CIA. He spoke a lot about his time in the Gulf states, where princes would leave Ferraris abandoned by the roadside if they ran out of gas. Expertise with racing-car engines seemed to be another of Captain Bill's many talents.

Perhaps Vietnam, or some similarly awful experience, had set him on this lonely road. Like so many Westerners one encounters in remote parts of the world, he had a special sadness that was counterbalanced by the knowledge that he'd never be able to return to a "normal" life back home. Behind his ebullient tough-guy facade, there was a badly scarred sensitivity and sensibility. Yet you'd probably never really get to know him. As I got up to leave, he invited me to take a balloon ride. We agreed I'd go whenever the weather was next suitable. "It's the only way to see Thebes!" he shouted after me.

⌁

Even in May, the desert cools down as much as 20 degrees at night. I walked through a cool mist pouring off the Nile across Karnak's fields and twisting streets. In a predawn light everything seemed illumined by a steel blue that reminded me of day-for-night sequences in films. It wasn't as easy to find Beit Kanada on foot as I'd imagined. I plodded along dusty footpaths dissecting the fields around the tiny temple dedicated to Mut, goddess of night. Wherever I looked, there were the fractured remains of lintels, sphinxes, columns, monolithic sculpture of various kinds. How much of this area had ever been properly excavated? I wondered. There's probably enough in Egypt to keep archaeologists busy forever.

Redford's site lay about five hundred yards from his house, on the other side of a little canal, no more than a ditch really. When I finally arrived, Akhenaten's ancient father, the carotene sun, was already burning threads of cirrus cloud low in the east over Luxor; and the pharaoh's newest foe, the man whose rebarbative portrait of him must be disturbing his rest in that dateless night, was standing over a deep square hole from which twenty or so local children, supervised by a fierce turbaned man with a stick, were removing earth in wicker baskets. Students with theodolites and clipboards were dotted around the shadowy landscape.

"God," Redford sighed when he noticed me. "You can't keep anything clean here. As soon as I leave each season, the villagers fill up my holes with garbage. They even pull out my marker pegs for fun. They've just no interest in this stuff. It's *amazing*. I always have to spend the first few weeks just putting the site back in order." I asked him why this was. "It doesn't exist for them," Redford said. "They're just not interested in anything before Muhammad."

I inquired about the local labour, wondering who paid them. It came out of Redford's budget: "I give the little boys three-fifty a day — that's nearly two bucks — the men with hoes get four-fifty; skilled diggers, fourteen … and the big boss over there gets fifty." The big boss, or *reiss*, had worked with Redford for many years. "I couldn't do it without him. He's the best." He said I should talk with the man if I got the chance. The *reiss* had recently discovered a large and important cache of Middle Kingdom statues while supervising the clearing of a well in the Karnak Temple, and he was garrulously proud of the fact.

The professor walked me around the gigantic site, past many steep-sided pits that, lacking fences, struck me as dangerous. "Yes," he admitted when I pointed it out. "I fell in one last year. Almost broke my neck." Safety was one of the many luxuries he couldn't afford. He began to explain what his project entailed: "We'll go through maybe seven building phases here, representing the site from, say, the seventeenth or eighteenth century B.C. all the way down to Alexander the Great, when this whole area was abandoned."

I asked how one went about getting permission to dig. "Oh, you can request sites here. It's not like with the Greeks, who tell you to go wherever they feel like allowing you to dig. You present a formal proposal, and the Egyptians don't particularly care where you get the money from. The only problem is if someone else wants the site, too, they never like to say no, so they *may* divide what you want up, giving half to each."

Could they divide it after you've been working on it? "No," Redford said, then corrected himself. "Well, I shouldn't say that, because it *did* happen to me."

Several years ago, Redford had been informed that part of his site was being given to an organization called AWARE — the American Women's Archaeological Research Expedition. "They were all filthy rich," he said, clearly amused. "Widows from Aspen, you see. There were about five of them; none had taken any courses whatsoever; they had no university backing; and most of them didn't even have university degrees. But they did have the money. Their leader was a woman called Diane Smith, who claimed she'd been a ballerina. In fact, she was a chorus girl who'd caught the eye of Walter Susskind, the conductor. He married her and promptly died. Then she married the inventor of the Titan rocket, and he died, leaving her all his money. She was then apparently about to marry Robert McNamara of the World Bank, but that didn't work out so she ended up marrying the then–director general of Antiquities here — which of course got the whole group an immediate in, and they chopped off part of my territory and gave it to them." He laughed, but he clearly hadn't found it so funny at the time.

"Because they were all feminists, you see, they wouldn't allow any men to help with digging on the site." He indicated his own substantial labour force. "*Ridiculous*, see. They came down here with the most expensive equipment and lived in a luxury cruise ship they'd hired on the Nile. Anyway, after the second day their theodolite broke, so they flew it back to New York to be repaired and sailed off up to Aswan for a party.

"It went from bad to absurd — you can do some serious damage to these sites if you don't know what you're doing. *Eventually* the Egyptians woke up to the scandal. When they returned for a second season, the authorities pussyfooted about renewing their permits. Now, every year in a forlorn sort of way, one of these girls will come back and ask if they can renew digging. Diane Smith died of cancer a few years later, so she may have known then that she was in for it, pursuing a last dream, that kind of thing. They all came up to Toronto to meet me once, because I suppose they realized they were treading on my toes. Tried to smooth the way by inviting me to a big party at the Hilton. The *Hilton*!" I realized he was laughing at the idea of himself in a place like the Hilton. He was a humble, unassuming man in many ways, modest about his accomplishments.

I worked my way around to the subject of John Anthony West and Schwaller de Lubicz. Redford groaned, arranging a loose white *kaffiyeh* on his head to protect it from the fierce, climbing sun. It gave him the appearance of a davening rabbi. "Oh God," he said. "Those idiots. And de Lubicz, there's another fool. You know, these fringe groups are the bane of our existence: the Velikovskyites, the Von Danikens of this world ..." I tried to discuss Schwaller's extensive documentation, but he waved the subject away like a fly.

Most of the contact he'd had with such groups, he told me, was with Rosicrucians. "They're a little more intelligent," he conceded. "They don't reveal themselves too often when they request to meet me and tour the site. But the dead giveaway is their inordinate interest in Akhenaten and the Amarna period — that's where they claim to derive their philosophy and rites."

I asked about the effacements I'd noticed at Philae. "But you can find that here," Redford said. "It was just the Christians — you know, destroying the demon of the pagan religion. There was an Egyptian who did a useful thesis on effacement, using measurements of the pick sizes as a datable criterion. There's a part of the temple here that was used as a domicile in the Middle Ages, and all the owls on the hieroglyphs there have two slashes through them. Doesn't the owl mean death or something? Even today the villagers here don't like owls in their houses."

A student approached with a surveyor's rod and said, "What I want to do is shoot back to that old line and double-check. Okay?"

The professor nodded, adding some kindly encouragement. He was probably a popular figure at his university.

I attempted to return to the subject of the origins of Egyptian civilization and the "symbolist" view. Redford mopped his brow with the soiled *kaffiyeh*, as the heat was building ferociously, and started talking with animated enthusiasm about work currently under way in the Nile Delta region. "That's the coming thing," he said. "I'm off there for a week when I finish here. It's incredibly exciting what's going on there. *That's* the place to be. They're trying to show contact with Asia in prehistoric times, and they've already got an excavation that shows contact with North Syria at a very early date. It's going to rewrite the history books." Though not, I thought, the way John Anthony West would like them to be rewritten.

"The rise of the pharaonic state was one of the most dramatic episodes in Egyptian history," Redford explained patiently. "And it looks as if the catalyst was Mesopotamia. That's where they got the ideas for the creation of the hieroglyphs. The evidence from the Delta is earthshaking — I can't wait to get there! At one site they've uncovered North Syrian pottery, flint industries that show a northern influence, and also architectural pieces — great clay nails with painted ends. These have been absolutely unknown in Egypt before now, but they're known in Mesopotamia. They'd build walls of soft mud and hammer these nails in to make mosaics." It seemed a far cry from West's "Atlantean" artifacts. "Also this season they found a huge *mastaba* [early form of tomb] under a village dating from the First Dynasty."

Redford looked thoughtful for a moment, stroking his beard and watching the chain of small boys pass up baskets of debris from one of the larger pits. "Of course," he eventually added, "they were only able to do this kind of work because Volkswagen gave them a lot of money and enabled them to put in well points to reduce the water table. Thank *God* for Volkswagen. I wish someone on our side would do something."

Money was a continual worry to Redford. His work could be shut down at any moment if even the meagre funding he currently received was cut off. I asked about the interest and publicity generated by his original discovery.

"Publicity backfires," he said. "When we made our original discovery that this was the temple of Akhenaten, it made the front page in the *New York Times*, and I was interviewed on TV and so on. Next year my money was cut off. Academia has a distinct aversion to high-profile activities. We've drawn so many blanks in trying to get corporate sponsorship and what not." While he did not say so, I imagined that presenting his work to boards of directors was not something he particularly enjoyed.

Some years ago, he told me, subordinates at the Canadian embassy in Cairo had been caught changing money on the black market three weeks after their arrival. The ambassador and his staff were sent home in disgrace, and Marc Perron, an old buddy of Pierre Trudeau, had been dispatched in his place to mend the fence. "Marc was a prince," Redford said. "A gifted man who loathed businessmen and idolized scholarship — which wasn't exactly what Ottawa wanted. The ambassador's residence in Cairo is a beautiful mansion, and Marc set up a kind of salon there, with concerts and exhibitions of art. When he knew I was having money troubles with the project, he put me in touch with Paul Desmarais, the head of Power Corporation in Quebec. He flew in by private jet on his way from China back to Canada. He was keen, excited by what I showed him. He kept up with me even in the heat of June — though his private physician and secretary didn't — and in the end he said that if there was any way he could help monetarily, all I had to do was send him my CV and a proposal. So I did it — two years ago — and I've not heard a word since. So what do you do with the rich? All of us here thought it was something to do with Desmarais' private secretary. He didn't like us much and was clearly bored silly when he came out. Everything is filtered through him, you see." He laughed again, unable to take the financial end *that* seriously.

Peering into the pits that dotted the site so dangerously, I knew I had no idea what archaeologists were up to in these excavations of theirs. "We take a section," Redford explained. "We dig a vertical face so you can draw all the levels, all the stages the area passed through. It's really the most important document to come out of a dig. You see" — he pointed out what looked to me like stray rocks and striated mud — "this was a priest's house — actually more of a large villa — and there, right there, is the shrine." The whole area, he said, gesturing toward the distant Nile, ceased to be a part of the city about the time of Alexander the Great. "Between the fourth to the fifth centuries B.C. there was a period of abandonment. We don't really know quite why. The domestic quarters went right down to the river, and before that they were even bigger."

Then he outlined the nature of what he believed to be the correct form of archaeology, fulminating against those who deviated from it. "It's painstaking work," he admitted. "Tedious and slow. Each square should have a qualified supervisor. That's what these students are doing. This is what distinguishes Kenyon archaeology, the school in which I trained. It's scandalous to see the way the French work here — it's just a bloody treasure hunt. They have *one* supervisor who *might* write a sentence a day. It drives me crazy thinking about all the evidence that is just *going*, lost forever."

Egyptologists, it seems, are not especially kind to each other. Reputation and fame obviously count for more than they should. Redford told me a story about a man named Alfred Lucas who was an important technician at the Cairo Museum during the early 1920s, a brilliant chemist who happened to be from a cockney working-class background. "Every day," Redford said, "Lucas would walk all the way from his lodgings to the Valley of the Kings. And every day Howard Carter would pass him in his big new car — never once stopping to offer him a lift. Not *once.*"

I pointed out that Carter himself was from a humble background, insecure of his social and academic standing, which might account for his apparent parvenu snobbery. Redford didn't seem to be aware of Carter's background and the fact that he was formally trained only as an artist. He then launched into a comparison with John Romer, the BBC popularizer of archaeology, saying, "He had no academic training either. Suddenly he's an expert, he's an Egyptologist." Apparently Romer had been shooting one of his idiosyncratic programs on a site being worked by one of Redford's friends, who happened to be in the middle of a divorce from a woman who was also a member of his team. "Romer shot all this footage of them arguing," Redford recalled, "and without them noticing. When the footage was screened, my friend had a fit, demanding Romer cut it out. Romer refused, saying it gave people an insight into what goes on at a dig. They had the most godawful fight, which ended with Romer taking my friend's Land Rovers across the river and refusing to give them back.

"Things can really get so childish out here. Tempers get strained after too long in Egypt. Kenyon used to say that no one should spend more than six months out here at a stretch."

A shout made us both look up. The *reiss* was chasing one of the boy workers with his stick, but the boy, dodging the blows, ran laughing up the steep incline where debris from the pits was being taken. "He's very strict," Redford commented. "You *have* to be with these kids, or they'd get away with murder. They're sweet people, though. Always happy, never tired. I've grown very fond of them over the years. Some of the ones I employed a decade ago come back to see me occasionally. They're all working in factories now, of course." Weren't any of them ever interested in looking for work with the Antiquities Organisation? "No," Redford replied, resigned to certain truths. "They have no interest, and the money's no good, even for those who manage to go to college. All they want are motorbikes, cars, stereos, and only the factories can pay for such things."

He decided we should all break for lunch. Back at Beit Kanada, Redford's wife, Susan, an attractive woman in her thirties, was coping with their new baby, who sat contentedly in a stroller shrouded with cotton fly-screening. A government driver who'd arrived to pick me up was trying to get her to give him one of her baby bottles — apparently an item hard to find in Egypt — insisting she could get others. Seeing us, he retreated.

"They can be so bloody grasping," Redford said, sinking wearily into his chair at the huge, pitted table. "They really think we're made of money. If they only knew how little we actually have in our terms …"

This was no Indiana Jones school of archaeology. There was precious little glamour here, and very little in the way of rewards, beyond the accumulation of knowledge. Perhaps dedication is its own reward. Everyone involved, how-ever, clearly *wants* to uncover another King Tut's tomb or dig up a major cache of artifacts or papyri. Redford had had his fifteen minutes of fame — not that he seemed to have been much impressed by it. The last fourteen years had been toil under the burning sun, much like one of Akhenaten's minions, and the painfully slow process of gradually building up a picture of the many lives once lived out on that now-barren strip of land.

Redford's young son, wearing a Tang orange-juice moustache, declared he was hungry. Students filed in, sighing with relief to be out of their first full day in the Theban inferno, and a servant appeared with piled dishes of simple, delicious food. Susan Redford, also a trained Egyptologist, was not going to be getting much work done this year, she confessed, what with the new baby and their son to care for. The heat didn't seem to bother them, but hygienic food and water were a constant worry, along with the flies. Among her many duties were the drawing of site plans and the supervision of the day-to-day running of the operation, dealing with the endless demands of bureaucracy, paying taxes for the workers, and so on.

A year or so before, she told me, she'd gone to the tax office. The man there, after a pathetic search peering through stacked mountains of files, had apparently lost the relevant documents, finally remembering he'd noted their location on the wall in pencil. "When I went back the following year," Susan recalled, "we went through the same process until I reminded the guy he'd written the information on the wall. When we looked, of course, we realized the whole place had been totally repainted since." The table burst out laughing, but as I remembered my years in India, the story seemed familiar enough. At the time, such incidents can drive you to weeping hysteria.

Redford launched into another anecdote. One summer, during the period through which most Egyptologists leave Luxor to break new records for "hottest temperature ever recorded" on its own, some valuable antiquities were stolen from the German mission's storeroom. The Egyptians, saving face again, blamed the foreigners for their lax security, demanding that each expedition build an impenetrable bunker to government specifications.

"*We* had to pay for it, of course," Redford said, shaking his head, "but it would be the property of the government, sealed and locked by them, the only key in their possession. I was the first one back that year and found this new order waiting for me. So I built the bloody bunker — it's that garagelike monstrosity outside — with three-foot-thick walls and so on. Hardly anyone else bothered to do it, naturally, but there I was, saddled with it. Next thing I know, the local inspector arrives and demands his own office in the house for the *one day out of three hundred and sixty-five* when he'll come to open the bunker and have that year's finds locked away in it. He wanted a desk, the lot! *Amazing!* Then, of course, when they come to seal up everything from my storeroom, I realize, after they've locked their bunker and gone, that they've forgotten to put the *talatat* in. I mean, they're only the most valuable finds to come out of this dig. And they're *still* where they were! *This* is the kind of thing that can drive you crazy working here, if you let it."

It was the same facade of doing something while doing nothing that I'd encountered all over Egypt. When people don't know or care why they're doing what they're doing, they generally don't do it well. Truck drivers who would blast their horns to warn other drivers and pedestrians of their presence all day and night long would never dream of turning on their lights at night for the same purpose, becoming hundred-ton silhouettes hurtling almost invisibly through the blackness, under the misguided impression they were saving their batteries or lightbulbs. The Redfords had had more sinister experiences, too.

"Remember that antiquities inspector who tried to blackmail us?" Susan asked her husband. The man was used to receiving baksheesh from foreign expeditions in return for simplifying their lives. When Susan and Redford had refused to be coerced into this arrangement, he made their lives much harder, even accusing them of illegally removing antiquities and then trying to put them under house arrest. Fortunately Redford's good relationship with the general director, Sayeed Tawfiq, put a stop to this, and the inspector was eventually fired.

With staff, too, they'd had endless trouble. "Many of them are furtive alcoholics," Donald told me. "One man came to us as a driver, highly recommended. But I kept noticing my beer was disappearing. One day the fellow returned with our car looking as if someone had peeled both sides open like a sardine can. The friends he'd been with were clearly terrified, lucky to be alive. Yet the man insisted the vehicle had been parked, and he had no idea how the accident had happened. *Parked!* There's no end to their lying. I didn't want to fire him, but I had no choice. If word gets round that you're an easy touch, you're finished here. You end up treating most of them like children, which saddens me, but there you have it." He was the sort of man well suited to having a large family, and what with his students and his Egyptian helpers, he certainly had a prodigious brood to contend with here.

Outside, lurking, the nerd, I noticed, had joined my driver, and much as Egyptians usually seem to enjoy waiting, this pair were signalling obliquely that they'd now waited long enough. The Redfords invited me to join them for dinner that night. Susan Redford made me think of the old woman who lived in a shoe — except Susan was younger, knew what to do with so many children. One more mouth to feed would make little difference. Privacy was either not something the Redfords needed or, most probably, expected during their time in Egypt.

The nerd, his stutter vibrating his head like a tuning fork, managed to convey that he wanted me to have tea with the manager of the Winter Palace Hotel. I wanted to hit him, but it occurred to me that the manager of the Winter Palace might be a little more interesting than the manager of the Isis, so I agreed.

"What about my meetings with the governor and the Antiquities director?" I inquired as we bounced off through the dust, the searing air, the bleached brittle landscape.

"I have made telephone calls," I think he replied. "Yes, yes. There will be appointments. Without que-que-que-question."

"Hoo-hoo-hooray!" I said unkindly. He brought out the worst in me. He wasn't doing his government much good, either.

As it turned out, the manager of the Winter Palace was well worth meeting. A portly but compact and very elegantly dressed Egyptian, he reminded me of Adnan Khashogi. Chain-smoking cigarettes, he described his plans for the hotel, which seemed wholly admirable, and recounted his travels around Africa, the state of most of which made Egypt look like Switzerland, he assured me. I'd recently travelled through the Sudan and Ethiopia and had to agree with him.

"These countries will never catch up with the rest of the world," he stated flatly. "There's no hope for them, you see. But we in Egypt, poor as we are, feel we must help them. We cannot let them slide into oblivion like this. But the West doesn't seem to care, and America is just concerned with looking after its own interests. If those countries had oil, it would be different, very different, wouldn't it?" I had to agree.

He was waiting, he told me, for a man named Jean-Pierre to show up, a man he said I should meet. "He's a Frenchman," the manager elaborated, which I'd somehow suspected. Jean-Pierre, the manager told me, operated a novel and expensive tour of Africa that he'd devised himself. For $38,000 per head, he flew a maximum of sixteen people down the Nile in a seaplane, landing on the river so his passengers could spend the night at places like the Winter Palace. The trip started in Cairo and took in some of the Nile towns, flying on through the Sudan and terminating in Kenya. How did he manage to organize landing on such a crowded river? I wanted to know.

"It is not easy," the manager admitted. "We have to clear all traffic for him. Consequently he experiences many delays."

Obviously Jean-Pierre was currently experiencing one of his delays, because he failed to arrive that day — and there was no sign of him three days later, either.

~⌐

When I returned to the Redfords' at sunset, students sat cross-legged in a line upon a tarpaulin in the driveway, sorting and numbering the day's trove of potsherds. It seemed a restful enough way to end the day, but the sight of baskets full of muddy clay fragments was enough to dispel any notions I might still have harboured about the thrills of archaeology.

The professor grabbed a couple of beers from his fridge, and I followed him up the exterior staircase onto the flat roof, where a line of washing hung drying and various items of furniture were scattered with children's toys. The vast blurred disk of a Congo rubine sun was balancing on the shadowed walls of the Karnak Temple behind us and a smoke-scented breeze already carried a cooling hint of night.

"This is my favourite time of day," Redford confided, puffing contentedly on his pipe, gazing across the golden fields where outlines had once more returned. I told him about Jean-Pierre and his plane. "Rather him than me," he said, chuckling, telling me a story he'd heard recently about a Sudan Airways jet. The pilot had mistaken the White Nile for a runway and had made a perfect landing in it. The passengers, unhurt, had managed to clamber out onto the roof, where they remained all night. A passing motorist saw them the following morning, and boats were eventually sent across the broad, crocodile-infested waters to rescue them. Later that day, an Alitalia pilot flying through the Sudan noticed the aircraft in the river and radioed Khartoum, asking if they'd lost a jet. Certainly not, the authorities replied, and they'd know it if they had. Besides, since they only employed the finest pilots, they *hadn't*. Well, the Italian said, it's down there. The same afternoon the same pilot was flying back up the same route and, looking down, he saw the plane still floating in the river.

"But," Redford bellowed, "there were people on the wings painting over the Sudanese airline logo so no one else would notice their shame!" It was, he said, *so* typical.

What were his hopes for this season's dig? "By June," he replied, "We should have reached the Amarna period. It would be nice to find a new head, or even some more *talatat*. With this work you always hope to come across something major, but you can't let it dominate your days. For the students it's more of a problem. They really want to go home having actually *found* something no one's seen in three thousand years. A mountain of potsherds isn't much compensation for months out there in the heat and dust."

I wondered how he felt about what was currently going on in Israel, considering he was so close to the Arab world. His dream, he admitted, was to excavate in the Gaza. "Almost nothing's been done there on any serious scale," he told me, "and it's been in such a strategic position for so many millennia that I *know* I'd find something of major importance. But, I tell you this, I wouldn't tolerate those Israeli thug soldiers standing over the top of *my* trenches with their Uzis."

He'd worked in Israel years before with Kenyon's widow, I learned. As usual, they were employing local peasant boys to haul earth out of the trenches. One day an Israeli official arrived on their site with a roll of blueprints, and "without doing anyone the courtesy of telling them what he was doing there, he wandered around looking at his plans and our site. At one point he dropped one of his rolls in a trench and ordered one of the boys working in it to bring it up to him.

"Now, these were Palestinian kids, for a start, so they lost no love over Israeli officials. But the boy quite rightly said he was working for me and that the man would have to ask my permission for him to leave his work. The official got very angry, shouting at the boy and stomping off. Boys being boys, they laughed at him. Next thing I know, he's back with a couple of armed soldiers, and they're dragging this kid away.

"I stopped them and asked what the hell they thought they were doing. 'Arresting him,' they said. 'For what?' I asked. 'For laughing at the official' was their answer. I told them they'd better get the hell out. If I hadn't have been there, God knows what they'd have done to that boy — for *laughing*.

I think what's going on there is deplorable, in short. I love the Palestinians — they're simple, but they're decent people, and they deserve so much better than they're getting."

As a star-snared night poured over our heads from the east, the distant sounds of the Karnak son-et-lumière echoed beyond that vast black wall of stone in whose shadow Donald Redford has spent much of the last twenty years. As we walked back down to dinner, I asked him if he ever went to see the show anymore. "Oh, occasionally," he replied. "With guests usually. Although the last part takes place just over that wall there, and I think everyone who's ever stayed here has memorized it forever. I can't imagine going to sleep here without hearing it — " And he repeated word for word the parting voices that whispered their poetry across the sacred lake, bidding all pilgrims to the house of Amon good night, Godspeed.

Dinner was a pleasure, the Redfords' obvious erudition happily taking a backseat to the more anecdotal aspects of Egyptology. The entire science seemed strewn with bizarre eccentrics. A man who'd once headed up the French Institute in Luxor, I heard, looked like Mephistopheles — and dressed the part — and hung an enormous full-frontal nude portrait of his boyfriend in the dining room of his extravagant house. Donald Redford had once been invited by this man to dinner and, mistaking the nature of the invitation, arrived with ten other people. Rather than explaining he'd invited Redford on his own, the flamboyant Frenchman kept everyone eating hors d'oeuvres for two hours while his chefs prepared more food. "Of course," Redford added, "you had to eat with this homoerotic apparition looming over your head." Mephistopheles had, it seemed, succumbed to AIDS not long before.

Indeed, AIDS had become a major topic in Egypt of late, I learned, after an American professor at the University in Cairo had been caught with some very young boys to whom he'd thoughtfully transmitted the virus. "Last year," Redford said, "I came back to all kinds of rumours about AIDS clinics being set up right across the country, although Egypt has yet to admit any official statistics regarding the disease. Foreigners get the blame, naturally. We also heard that no one would be allowed a visa longer than one month without submitting to an AIDS test. Everyone was looking round to see who was cutting short their stays." It seems Egyptology has more than its professional share of homosexuals — another blow to the Indiana Jones image.

My image of hefty government and university funding for archaeological work had taken a beating, too. At times it looked to me as if Redford was all but subsidizing his own project.

But couldn't the Canadian government be of any assistance? I asked, probably naively. Redford did not have much time for the current ambassador in Cairo. "I hate the civil side of External Affairs," he fumed. "They're *swine.* It's all business, business, business. As far as the resident idiot is concerned, *we* don't count. All he's interested in is entertaining moneymen, people who generate the kind of profit measured in dollars."

I was to glimpse the Cairo diplomatic world firsthand myself later, but now I wondered if a government could really be so unsupportive of work that would benefit the country that had elected it for far longer than the proceeds of any financial deal. The conservatism of Prime Minister Brian Mulroney's Conservative party must be very far from the kind of conservatism that sustained ancient Egyptian civilization for four thousand years. As versed in that civilization as he was, Professor Redford must have found the new barbarism he faced all the more ironic.

In the acknowledgements section of his book on Akhenaten, he thanks a couple of government bodies for funding stages of his work, but it is two private individuals, one in the United States and one in Eire, who are thanked for "generous financial support … throughout our work."

I reread some of Redford's book that night in my hotel room, coming across a section in the preface that I'd either overlooked or forgotten:

> *Laity often suffer under the delusion that "scholars" constitute a special interest group that stands united whenever any of its members is attacked, and refuses to allow anyone without the Ph.D. "union card" to participate in its activities. Nothing could be further from the truth. The quest for knowledge (a pompous but apt phrase) through the application of reasoned scholarly*

method employs far more simple common sense than most people realize, and is therefore open to all. If professionals generally do it better, that is simply because they have had more practice; but it sometimes transpires that in a particularly thorny problem it is the unbiased amateur that makes a breakthrough.

He goes on to outline how the Akhenaten Temple Project got off the ground in 1965 due to the efforts of one Ray Winfield Smith, a retired U.S. Foreign Service officer. Smith had become interested in the thousands of *talatat* blocks that had already been found in the ruined temples of Akhenaten, and learning no scholar was then engaged in any serious study of the material, he resolved to make the effort himself. Convinced no human hand or eye could possibly reconstruct the jumbled blocks into the original relief scenes they depicted, he enlisted the aid of the computer, receiving assistance from IBM and funding and sponsorship from various sources. Physical reconstruction was not then viable, but Smith's indefatigable efforts of photographing each block to scale and coding the details of its reliefs to feed the computer eventually enabled him to match the blocks on paper into collages. A gigantic jigsaw puzzle began to take shape, rebuilding images of a period thought to have been lost forever 3,500 years ago.

This willingness to accept the work of "amateurs" — work that made his own possible — made me find his rejection of Schwaller de Lubicz all the more difficult to comprehend. But, what with Egyptian rules and regulations *and* funding problems, the world of Egyptology seemed far less fun than it must have been when Howard Carter discovered Tutankhamen's tomb. What had begun as an adventure had certainly ended up a science — in the narrowest sense of the term.

CHAPTER TEN

HOWARD AND PORCHEY: THE REAL CURSE OF TUTANKHAMEN'S TOMB

I inserted the candle and peered in, Lord Carnarvon, Lady Evelyn and Callender standing anxiously behind me to hear the verdict. At first I could see nothing, the hot air escaping from the chamber causing the candle flame to flicker, but presently, as my eyes grew accustomed to the light, details of the room within emerged slowly from the mist, strange animals, statues and gold — everywhere the glint of gold. For the moment — an eternity it must have been to the others standing by — I was struck dumb with amazement, and when Lord Carnarvon, unable to stand the suspense any longer, inquired anxiously, "Can you see anything?" it was all I could do to get out the words, "Yes, wonderful things." Then, widening the hole a little further so that both could see, we inserted an electric torch.

—HOWARD CARTER, *THE TOMB OF TUTANKHAMEN*,

NOVEMBER 26, 1922

I have seen yesterday; I know tomorrow.

—INSCRIPTION ON TUTANKHAMEN'S SHRINE

The discovery of Tutankhamen's tomb was for Egyptology what the first moon landing was for NASA. Every day for literally years the London *Times* carried prominent reports on the progress of the excavation. The whole world wanted to come to Luxor, to see the tomb, to meet its discoverer, and much of it did. The story has become legend, but there's more than one history of the world. Standing in the tomb the morning after having dinner with the Redfords, I considered the truth versus the myth. No stay in Luxor is complete without a visit to Tut's little tomb, not to mention an encounter with someone who "worked with Carter," so it's worthwhile briefly to examine the story behind the most famous archaeological discovery in history.

Howard Carter went out to Egypt when he was seventeen, hired for his technical proficiency in drawing for an expedition sponsored by the British Museum. Trained by his father, who made a living painting portraits of pet animals owned by the rich, the young Carter would sketch hieroglyphs, paintings, and reliefs on the walls of Hatshepsut's temple at Deir al-Bahari. From 1890 to 1898, he worked principally under the guidance of Sir William Matthew Flinders Petrie, one of the great pioneer Egyptologists, the man justly credited with bringing system, sense, and order to the field. Petrie frequently worked sites wearing only pink underpants and an undershirt to discourage curious tourists from interrupting his excavations.

A short, stocky man of great physical strength, Carter was himself a loner, humourless and dour, but with a driving energy and utter dedication to his work that made him invaluable. Some of the watercolours he produced hang in the Egyptian Department of New York's Metropolitan Museum. Punctilious, scrupulously faithful, they are absolutely devoid of life. By 1899, under Petrie's tutelage, Carter had made up for his lack of formal education and had become proficient enough in archaeology, Egyptology, and the basics of the hieroglyphs to be appointed by the Antiquities Service director, Sir Gaston Maspero, to the post of inspector of monuments in Upper Egypt and Nubia. All went well until 1903, when Carter's career in the Egyptian Antiquities Service abruptly ended.

Flinders Petrie surrounded himself with women, believing the female temperament was best suited to the nature of his work. With his wife and three young women apprentices, he had been recording hieroglyphs at Saqqara when their camp was entered by several drunken Frenchmen one night. These men eventually tried to force their way into the women's quarters. Petrie summoned Carter, who arrived as soon as he could with some Antiquities Service guards. A fight broke out during which one of the Frenchmen was knocked down by a guard. Next day the men filed an official complaint with Gaston Maspero against Carter and the guard. The French consul general demanded a formal apology. Since the French effectively controlled the power structure of Egyptian archaeology in those days, Maspero urged Carter to make a routine apology. But Carter, with that blindness to human and public relations and the exigencies of petty politics that blighted much of his life, refused point-blank. With deep regret, Maspero fired him.

The next four years saw the future discoverer of King Tut's tomb hawking watercolours, leading guided tours, and dealing in antiquities whenever he could find them and had the money.

George Edward Stanhope Molyneux Herbert, former Viscount Porchester, fifth earl of Carnarvon — "Porchey" to his friends — was seven years older than Howard Carter. He also had more money. Far from being forced to scrape a living from menial jobs in 1907, the year in which he first met Carter, Porchey would never have to "work" in his life. At the age of forty he had done precisely nothing except travel the world in luxury, hunt on his massive estate, and socialize with his peers. A serious motoring accident shook him out of this aimless existence; he needed to get a life. Sent to Luxor for the winter climate, he soon developed an avid interest in Egyptology and resolutely determined to devote himself to exploring and excavating. This posed a problem since he knew almost nothing about archaeological practices. He approached Gaston Maspero for advice on hiring an expert. The director of Antiquities, eager to redress a wrong, did not hesitate to recommend the services of Howard Carter to him. Howard, needless to say, took the job. They made an odd couple: the handsome, charming, sophisticated, gregarious aristocrat and the gruff, dour, unsociable workaholic from decidedly humble origins.

As I've pointed out, archaeology in Egypt in the late nineteenth century, thanks to people like Petrie, was just in the process of becoming the modern science we know today. In many ways, though, Carter was a throwback to an earlier era best typified by someone like Giovanni Belzoni (1778–1823), his hero, whom he described as "the most remarkable man in the whole history of Egyptology." Indeed, in the first volume he wrote about the tomb of Tutankhamen, Carter devoted more pages to singing Belzoni's praises than he did to any other archaeologist, including his mentor, Petrie.

Belzoni was born in Padua, and his family intended him for the priesthood, but a roving disposition led him to seek his fortune abroad. In England he worked as a circus strongman, apparently studying engineering by night. In 1815 he had invented what is described as a hydraulic waterwheel, convincing himself that this labour-saving device would be a big hit in a place like Egypt. He lugged the enormous prototype from England to Cairo to demonstrate its superiority over traditional devices to Egypt's broad-minded ruler, the Turk, Muhammad Ali. However, the main trouble with the invention was that it wouldn't work. Belzoni found himself stranded in Egypt with no money and no obvious means of making any.

His next career move was into "archaeology," where he was soon developing a thriving business shipping antiquities of all kinds back to England for British consular officials. He uprooted obelisks (dropping at least one into the Nile while transporting it downriver), columns, monolithic sculptures. He scoured the Valley of the Kings, terrifying the normally fearless and vicious thieves of Qurna since he thought nothing of cranking off a barrage of rifle fire at anyone who stood in his plundering way. Besides expending liberal quantities of gunpowder, Belzoni preferred to deal with the sealed doors of tombs by slamming through them with battering rams. In a revealingly nostalgic observation on this period, Howard Carter once wrote, "Those were the great days of collecting. Anything to which a fancy was taken, from a scarab to an obelisk, was just appropriated, and if there was a difference of opinion with a brother excavator, one laid for him with a gun."

Much as he would have denied it later, Carter never ceased to subscribe to Belzonian principles at heart. Another source of his admiration for the Italian — and a method he was able to employ himself without fear of censure — was the man's highly systematic manner of working and the lavish scale of his undertakings, with their hundreds of fellahin labourers working virtually around the clock seven days a week.

Carter was not without a deeper, almost mystical, side to him, though, when it came to appreciating ancient Egyptian art. Speaking of the paintings in the tomb of Seti I, he once remarked, "These are not, of course, as some fools have actually *suggested* to me, the creations of crazed brains, but symbols with a dignified and recondite meaning, for which only the ancient colleges of priests could furnish the true key." Schwaller and West would agree.

Belzoni, like almost every archaeologist who had laboured in the Valley of Kings before or since him, had adamantly maintained there were no more undiscovered tombs left to find there. Carter, who would also later claim he'd exhausted the Valley after finding Tut's tomb, was convinced he was wrong about this, certain himself, from his studies in the chronologies, that at least one tomb had never been found, that of the boy pharaoh Tutankhamen. With Porchey Carnarvon's money, he began a maniacally systematic search of the Valley, mapping it out in a grid, determined to excavate every spot not yet touched. Ironically he wanted to start just below the mausoleum of Rameses VI first, having noticed evidence of workers' huts beneath the debris dumped from this enormous tomb, but was reluctant to close it off for the duration of his excavation. It was, as already mentioned, one of the major tourist attractions in the Valley. Instead, Carter spent the next sixteen years — with a brief hiatus during the First World War — digging up the rest of the Valley, obsessively faithful to the squares on his grid. His toil yielded scant compensation in finds, and it yielded a very poor return to Lord Carnarvon on his considerable monetary investment. Beset by the novelty of financial difficulties, largely owing to the war and a capricious stock market, Porchey told Howard he couldn't afford another season. It was over.

But Carter was not about to give in so easily, asking Carnarvon to let him take up the concession and vowing to finance the work himself. Moved by Carter's dedication and conviction, Porchey agreed to bankroll one more year. In 1922, returning to the debris beneath Rameses VI's tomb where he'd almost begun, eight days into his "last" season, Howard Carter entered the history books forever.

That is the conventional account of the discovery. How far does it correspond to the truth? After establishing he had indeed found what appeared to be a tomb with the original mortuary seals still intact, Carter recounted that he filled in the entrance passage, posted guards, and waited nearly three weeks for his benefactor to arrive from England before uncovering the door once more. The suspense must have been unimaginable during those three long weeks. At last he made an opening to establish whether he'd found yet another empty tomb, or merely a storehouse for odds and ends of no great value and perhaps left out of Rameses VI's main tomb above. After the team had established otherwise, we're expected to believe that Porchey and Howard resealed the exploratory hole and waited for the arrival of officials from the Antiquities Service, as they were legally bound to do, before finally entering the tomb. Does that sound like human nature?

Here's another version: According to Thomas Hoving and others, they broke right through that night, proceeding into the first chamber, then knocking through that wall into the main shrine, satisfying themselves they did indeed have the only intact shrine room and sarcophagus of a pharaoh found in modern times. Before leaving, they removed several objects, resealed the inner chamber, and only then closed up the main door.

The evidence for this? At least one major item from the tomb was seen in Carter's house long before it had been "discovered" during the lengthy process of exploring the inner tomb. And if photos of the original first chamber are studied, one can clearly make out the resealed section through which the shrine chamber was entered that first night.

And there's more. The first thing Carter recognized on discovering the tomb was that it had been robbed twice around three thousand years ago and resealed by the necropolis priests. After that the debris from Rameses VI's tomb had successfully protected it. The original robbers, however, had entered only the first chamber before perhaps being surprised by guards.

This accounted for the extraordinary mess of its contents, the thieves clearly looking only for small precious objects they could easily remove, ransacking everything else in their haste. They had, like moles, burrowed surreptitiously through a tiny tunnel in the gravel fill blocking the entrance passage, with very little light and even less time.

As news of Carter's momentous discovery spread, all manner of problems arrived in almost as great a number as the curious and the thrill seekers. Various dubious deals were swiftly made by Carter and Carnarvon, according to Thomas Hoving, among them the sale of exclusive rights to the London *Times* to cover the excavation, angering the Egyptian press and every other foreign journalist, and a covert arrangement with the Metropolitan Museum in New York to supply technical expertise in exchange for a substantial share of the treasures.

Now, government regulations at the time specified that 50 percent of the objects found in a tomb *that was not intact* would go to the archaeologist involved, the other half becoming the property of the Egyptian Antiquities Service and remaining in the country. Instead, Carter embarked on a belligerent course, increasingly thinking of the tomb as his personal property, denying access to visitors with letters of recommendation from Egyptian authorities, and so on.

Pierre Lacau, the new director general of Antiquities, and others began to rethink this division of spoils, claiming Tutankhamen's tomb was by definition intact and must therefore remain in its entirety the property of the Egyptian government. Carter would receive nothing for his years of toil, and Carnarvon nothing for his massive investment. Lacau became Carter's nemesis, their mutual dislike blossoming into full-fledged hatred over the ensuing years. Thus, Howard Carter can be held almost single-handedly responsible for the difficult relationship that persists to this day between foreign Egyptologists and the Antiquities branch of government. But this was also a time of great political turmoil in Egypt, with five governments coming and going between 1925 and 1930 alone, a time that witnessed the growth of the nationalist movement that would eventually lead to Nasser's revolution in the early 1950s and the end of over two thousand years of foreign domination. The issue of allowing Egyptian antiquities to leave the country came to symbolize colonialism itself. A more prudent man than Howard Carter would have trod more carefully.

Porchey died less than a year after the discovery of the tomb, a victim not so much of the Pharaoh's Curse but of his own generally poor health coupled with pneumonia. As for all the others connected with the excavation who are widely believed also to have succumbed to this mythical curse, most of them happened to be in their late seventies or eighties when they died.

As Carter's rampaging offensiveness grew increasingly psychotic, people responded in kind. He worked himself to death in the stifling tomb, dressed generally only in his underwear, in homage to Petrie perhaps, and allowed himself to be irritated into blazing fury by constant and trifling interruptions.

Finally Carter went too far. He announced he was closing "his" tomb, erecting a massive iron door, locking it with the world's largest padlock, pocketing the key, and leaving for England. Lacau and his boys had been waiting for such an opportunity. Somehow they removed Carter's lock and replaced it with their own. Now Carter was locked out, his life's work apparently down the drain. Yet worse was in store. Herbert Winlock, director of the Metropolitan Museum, sent the following cable to Carter:

TRANSMIT STEVENS 08716

COMPANY COMMISSION 17642 BEHIND 68509 06262 FORTNUM MASON 75826 75821 04804 089 STOP. 19464 EGYPTIAN COMMITTEE MEMBERS STOP. 40762 MARQUAND IMMEDIATELY AND 39864 CAIRO STOP. 30816 SEVERANCE AND TROUT 39864 THEM YOU 04788 LORD 44856 FROM AKHENATEN. 21422 03627 THAT ACTUALLY. 19842 ORIGIN 21847. 19974.

The code had been worked out some years before for members of the Metropolitan excavation team to use in "emergencies." The telegram actually read:

TRANSMIT CARTER. TO BE KEPT CONFIDENTIAL. GOVERNMENT COMMISSION HAVE FOUND BEHIND [TOMB] FOUR IN CASE OF WINE FORTNUM MASON "SCULPTURE HEAD, CAPITAL PIECE" UNLABELED. MADE A BAD IMPRESSION ON EGYPTIAN COMMITTEE MEMBERS. IT WAS ANNOUNCED BY TELEGRAM TO ZAGHLOOL [THEN PRIME MINISTER SAAD ZAGHLUL] IMMEDIATELY AND SENT BY EXPRESS TO CAIRO. TO PROTECT YOU LACAU AND ENGELBACH HAVE SUGGESTED THEM YOU HAVE BOUGHT FOR ACCOUNT OF LORD CARNARVON, 1923, LAST YEAR FROM AKHENATEN. DO NOT KNOW WHETHER THEY BELIEVE THAT ACTUALLY. SEND ALL THE INFORMATION YOU CAN RELATING TO ORIGIN IF POSSIBLE. ADVISE US BY LETTER IF ANY INQUIRY IS MADE WE SHALL BE PREPARED.

Both cables are on file in the Egyptian Department of the Metropolitan Museum of Art. What had happened after his sudden departure was that Lacau and the Egyptian authorities started making a thorough check of all Carter's work to date, inspecting an adjacent empty tomb he was using as a restoration workshop and storage area for the items he'd removed so far from Tutankhamen's tomb. Initially, they were impressed with Carter's work: everything had been numbered, labelled, and crated meticulously.

Then, at the back of the storage room, next to numerous empty Fortnum and Mason crates — Carnarvon and Carter dined well in the Valley — they noticed a sealed box labelled simply RED WINE. The investigators almost left it alone until Lacau insisted it be opened. Inside, the box was stuffed with surgical gauze and cotton batting; within this Lacau found an almost life-size wooden head, covered with a thin coat of plaster and painted with such delicacy and skill that it almost seemed alive. It was a major work of ancient Egyptian art, perhaps one of the finest examples ever found. Yet why did neither the crate nor the object bear any identifying numbers or labels? The implications were obvious.

Everyone present was deeply shocked. Lacau suggested Carter must have purchased the item from a dealer in Luxor on behalf of Lord Carnarvon before he died. But was his offered suggestion merely a trap? Obviously Carter thought so, because he came up with various vaguely plausible explanations of his own. The suspicion lingered; but it was far from the rumours that had once been spread about secret planes landing daily in the Valley and flying out treasure by the ton.

Carter was finally allowed to complete his work on the tomb and, by all accounts, behaved in an exemplary fashion throughout the eight long years it took him to finish dismantling the sarcophagi and probing the rather disappointing mummy. When the task that had absorbed nearly thirty years of his life was finally concluded, Carter returned to England in 1932, and a year later fell sick. Although he did return to Egypt several times, declaring his next project to be the search for the tomb of Alexander the Great, he never again excavated. In 1939, in his mid-sixties, he died. Only a handful of people attended his modest funeral, one of them Lady Evelyn, the daughter of Lord Carnarvon.

The old man I'd met in Qurna believed Howard and Porchey had "stolen" numerous items from Tutankhamen's tomb. So do many other people. In the Metropolitan Museum's Egyptian collection there are ten works of art described in the catalogue cards as "probably from the tomb of Tutankhamen, but not positively identified in Carter's list." They are among the finest exhibits of their kind in the world. Everything removed from the tomb was supposed to be in Carter's list; there *was* no other list, and no one but Carter removed the contents.

In the museum's files is a private letter from Carnarvon in England to Carter in the Valley of the Kings, dated December 24, 1922, not a month after both men had first "peeked" into the tomb. Porchey writes about the various dignitaries who had congratulated him on the discovery. Then he writes that he had "put the ariel [a species of gazelle] and horse — *bought in Cairo* — into the wall case. They look very well. I have, after mature examination, decided that they are *early* 18th Dynasty and *must* come from the Saqqareh."

This is an Egyptological joke. To say that the two pieces of sculpture were thought, after "mature examination," to be *early* Eighteenth Dynasty from Saqqara, an area not used by any pharaoh since the Fifth Dynasty, easily a thousand years before Tutankhamen's era, was like saying "mature examination" of a Picasso had convinced him the painting dated from just before the Norman Conquest of England.

Two days before this letter, Carnarvon had written Carter another asking him whether he thought he would find "much more unmarked stuff" in the tomb. This clearly means items not bearing the pharaoh's cartouche or emblem, like the horses referred to in the subsequent letter. Obviously they couldn't remove anything bearing Tutankhamen's cartouche without hopelessly incriminating themselves.

Carnarvon's entire collection, according to the conditions of his will, was to be offered for sale to the British Museum. The museum, however, by an inexplicable manoeuvre of the solicitor involved, was given a mere seven hours to decide on a purchase the magnitude of which would normally take months of deliberation. The collection ended up in New York at the Metropolitan.

Some years after the purchase, Herbert Winlock, the Metropolitan's director, met the British Museum's curator of Egyptian art on routine business, and, according to Thomas Hoving, the subject of the Carnarvon collection came up. "Ah, yes, the Carnarvon collection," Winlock supposedly said, smiling somewhat sheepishly. After a pause he suddenly patted his side pocket, adding, "You know — it was really only a *pocket* collection." This anecdote was related by I. E. S. Edwards, curator emeritus of Egyptian Art at the British Museum.

One could not fail to be affected by the unmistakable proofs of human affection, human conviction and human fidelity to an ideal in these men of thirty-two hundred years before ... [Such works] preach a lesson of piety and deep conviction to an age of cynical materialism and unbelief.

—HOWARD CARTER

I've never been able to dislike Howard Carter. You had to know him to do *that*. And I felt his presence strongly many times as I wandered around the blazing moonscape of the Valley. He was certainly "a man more sinned against than sinning," but when you look at the treasures from Tutankhamen's tomb in the Cairo Museum, or at the coffin of the pharaoh still containing his mummy where it had lain in peace for more than thirty centuries, as Lord Carnarvon had wished, you cannot help but feel that he experienced a moment worth most men's lives. To have been the first human being to enter a place that was exactly as it had been the day the young pharaoh was buried: the flower garlands placed in the sarcophagus looking, as Carter noted, as fresh as if they'd been placed there the day before; to have seen the glinting gold of treasures the like of which no one had looked upon since the time of Moses; to have breathed air that was itself three millennia old … to have done all this was surely worth the price it cost him. Subsequent archaeologists might, however, have reservations about the price it has been costing *them* ever since.

I still can't help wishing Carter had married Lady Evelyn and lived happily ever after to a ripe and contented old age. The only companion he's *known* to have shared his house with, I'm sorry to report, was a singing canary that was eaten by a cobra just days before he discovered the tomb. Carter's fellahin workers made much of this "omen."

Schwaller de Lubicz, it's worth mentioning, also died after a cobra bite. It must have been the one time in his life he wished he knew less about symbolism.

CHAPTER ELEVEN

SHELLEY'S POEM AND CAPTAIN BILL'S HOT AIR

I met a traveller from an antique land,
Who said: Two vast and trunkless legs of stone
Stand in the desert … Near them, on the sand,
Half sunk, a shattered visage lies, whose frown,
And wrinkled lip, and sneer of cold command,
Tell that its sculptor well those passions read
Which yet survive, stamped on these lifeless things,
The hand that mocked them, and the heart that fed:
And on the pedestal these words appear:
"My name is Ozymandias, king of kings;
Look on my works, ye Mighty, and despair!"
Nothing beside remains. Round the decay
Of that colossal wreck, boundless and bare
The lone and level sands stretch far away.

—PERCY BYSSHE SHELLEY, "OZYMANDIAS," 1818

The nerd showed up an hour late, blaming the driver. This was the day I had my appointments with the local governor and the director of Antiquities, but something in the nerd's face told me I was in for a disappointment. Furiously rotating his worry beads until they almost began to smoke in his hand, he managed to inform me it was M-M-M-May Day, the workers' celebration.

"Workers?" I inquired. "What workers?"

Egypt did consider itself a socialist state, I remembered, but its proletariat was not exactly a united force for the continued improvement of social conditions. The rural peasants spent every waking hour toiling on their little strips of irrigated land just to stay alive. Almost everyone else in the underclass did next to nothing that could be loosely termed regular work.

"So g-g-g-governor is not available. Also d-director ..."

"So why did they give me appointments if they knew today was a holiday?"

He could not answer this. Possibly he hadn't even made any appointments. He grinned uncontrollably, the opaque spectacles and his Bugs Bunny teeth making him resemble a cartoon stereotype Japanese. Worry beads a smouldering blur, he suggested we go shopping in the bazaars. He would ensure I got the best prices, he repeated a dozen times. He knew I was not a happy unit. Just to keep things interesting, however, I agreed to his plan.

We drove into Luxor, walked down winding dusty streets through a gauntlet of hollering merchants, and arrived finally at a nondescript store festooned with handwoven tapestries. The owner, Ahmed, a sinewy man with bad nerves and dishonest eyes, ushered us into the gloomy interior. A dozen strip lights were flipped on, revealing a few thousand more tapestries and rugs, on every wall and piled all over the floor. There was a powerful smell of old wet rope. "Ah, esteemed sir, Your Excellency!" Ahmed said, indicating a chair in which I should sit, rubbing his hands like Uriah Heep. "Your Excellency will take coffee?" His Excellency nodded, then Ahmed screamed out something unintelligible in an entirely different voice. From behind a curtain appeared an unusual sight: an Egyptian girl of eighteen or so wearing tight faded Levis and a loose sleeveless T-shirt. Her hair hung down to her chest, and she had a cigarette between heavily made-up lips and Cleopatra mascara. Not something you see every day in Upper Egypt. Ahmed screamed something else at her, and with a faint curl of the lip she turned back through the curtain.

"My wife," Ahmed explained with an odd pride.

"Your wife?"

"Newest wife." Ahmed cackled. "She seventeen years. I" — he clenched his fist slowly and shook it — "sixty-seven year but *strong*." He made an obscene roll of his hips. "She like Hollywood girl, no?"

"A movie star," I agreed, thinking *Biker Babes in Heat*.

Ahmed seemed pleased that I, too, thought highly of his new wife. He next turned to the nerd and clasped him by the shoulders, declaring he was his greatest friend. The nerd looked uncomfortable, but then he always did. Soon Ahmed's wife reappeared with a tray of Turkish coffee, another cigarette between her lips. She bent to place the tray beside me, her top hanging so far open I could see her navel, let alone her conical, braless breasts.

Ahmed reclined on a mound of rugs, ordering his wife to show me tapestries. This was hard and dirty work; the windowless room soon filled with more dust than air. I looked at hundreds of numbingly mediocre woven rugs, with their lifeless birds, cartoon palm trees, and deformed ciphers of people, repeatedly asking to see only the best work. More coffee and three hundred cigarettes later, Ahmed's wife was caked in dust and sweat, and I'd found three pieces I didn't utterly detest. The nerd seemed edgy.

I asked the price of a hunting scene. Ahmed looked pained for a moment. Then, claiming *just* because the nerd was his closest and dearest friend, he'd let the piece go for a mere $1,800 U.S. I got up to leave. Ahmed shot over to my side.

"How much you like to pay?" he asked, gripping my arm too tightly. I told him I wouldn't insult him with an offer; I didn't have that kind of money. "How much you have?" he asked.

I told him to forget it, turning to go. The nerd hid behind a pile of discarded rugs.

Ahmed blocked my exit, saying, "How much you have, hmmm?" I told him I had a hundred dollars. He smiled the kind of smile that is not a smile at all. "Best price," he continued, "is — only for you — twelve hundred dollars. Take it, friend. You have VISA, American Express?" I told him I didn't believe in credit cards. Money is the poor man's credit card. Again I tried to leave. This time Ahmed pushed me back to my chair. I told him he'd better get his hands off me, and quick.

It struck me that this could turn quite nasty. As his wife poured me a fifteenth coffee, she caught me staring down her top and gave me a look somewhere between disgust and lust. Back and forth I went with Ahmed, telling him I wasn't bargaining; all I had was one hundred dollars, and the sum was not open to debate. Throwing murderous looks at the nerd, I finally decided to walk, whatever the consequences. I pushed Ahmed politely aside and headed out the door. Within a second he was on my arm. "Take it then!" he spat, looking physically ill. "Take it! One hundred dollars! I not care, I not need *money*." He was sick with anger, his pride or something deeply wounded. I tried to refuse, saying I had no wish to rob him, but he was already rolling the tapestry up in brown paper. As I handed over a hundred-dollar bill, the wife, who'd been in the recesses of the store, ran over screaming at Ahmed, trying to tear the money from his fist. Ahmed grabbed her by the throat with one hand, and with the other that held my money punched her so hard in the face that she reeled back, falling onto a mound of rugs, clutching her bleeding nose.

"That wasn't very Islamic of you, Ahmed," I said, but noticing the black void behind his bulging eyes, thought better of saying more.

Out in the fiery street I turned on the nerd, listing everything I couldn't stand about him. "From eighteen hundred to one hundred is quite a discount," I pointed out. "Would you have stopped me if I'd agreed to buy it for the original price?"

"M-m-m-must b-bargain," he told me, quaking, worry beads worn to amber cinders. He probably went through several strings a week.

I left him standing there. It occurred to me that what I'd paid was probably a fair price. The merchants of Egypt have lost all touch with reality when it comes to pricing. Because some rich foreigners, applying the standards of their own countries, scribble out traveller's cheques and hand over plastic without a second thought, vendors tend to quote any price that comes into their heads. If you've sold a $100 rug for $1,800, it's hard to let it go for $100 again. In a Cairo store I asked the price of a carved table — admittedly a nice one — to be told it was $250,000. It was worth $300 or $400 at the most, but how do you negotiate $250,000 down to $400?

⌁

If the Egyptian Museum in Cairo resembles a gloomy, massive, and cluttered warehouse, impossible to view adequately in a week for the sheer quantity of exhibits and the startling ineptitude of its cataloguing, then the Luxor Museum is almost its exact opposite. The building is small, ingeniously designed, and displays relatively few objects, each of them usefully identified and tastefully mounted under lighting that emphasizes their various delicacies and perfections without being obtrusive. An hour is more than enough to see everything, although one exhibit so captivated me I don't think I could ever tire of looking at it.

The statue of Pharaoh Thutmose III on the main floor is one of the finest ever carved in ancient Egypt. To me, it is one of the five greatest sculptures in the world. Its beauty defies description. Dating from the early fourteenth century B.C., it represents the pharaoh as a being eternally youthful, exuding a divine majesty and power and an aura of sublime spirituality. Again I found myself transfixed by that blissfully serene bodhisattva smile, reflecting an inner wisdom and a peace that passes understanding. The eyes are full of life, strength, splendour, yet they are profoundly compassionate, eyes that have seen God and thus love His creation. You gaze upon an image of perfected man, in whom all dualities are resolved, ruled by neither life nor death, the very goal of creation in human form. Standing there in the darkened museum before Thutmose III's radiant form, I found it ludicrous for anyone to suggest a society capable of creating such a powerful sense of mystical truth in stone was barbaric or backward.

The Luxor Museum also contains a reconstructed wall of *talatat* from

Professor Redford's Akhenaten temple, known, in the orthodox phonetic rendering of hieroglyphics, as *Gm.p3–itn*, and pronounced something like "Geena-paten." It too is profoundly impressive.

Inspired, I decided to return to the west bank on my own and visit the "Ramesseum," the giant mortuary temple of Rameses II that stands at the very edge of the floodplain. Literally one step takes you from green cultivated land onto the dust leading up to the Deir al-Bahari cliff face and the vast desert beyond.

Which brings me back to Percy Bysshe Shelley and his poem "Ozymandias." For the record, Shelley never visited Egypt — though any number of books state with utter conviction that he did. The focus of the Ramesseum and the poem is the famous fallen colossus of Rameses II. Besides the Great Sphinx, which was carved *in situ* out of living rock, this colossus was the largest statue in Egypt, shaped from a single solid block of granite weighing one thousand tons. When intact, the seated figure stood over sixty feet high. This monolithic chunk of rock was quarried in Aswan, transported several miles to the river, shipped by some kind of formidable boat downriver to Thebes, offloaded, carried another few miles to the temple, and then erected. I'd like to have witnessed this particular feat of Nineteenth Dynasty engineering.

"I met a traveller from an antique land," Shelley writes. Since the traveller was Diodourus of Sicily, a man John Anthony West describes as a "garrulous, second-rate Latin historian from the 1st century B.C.," the poet must have been brandishing his licence when he wrote. Diodourus, in his choppy account of Egypt, described the fallen colossus, attributing it to Ozymandias, a Greek corruption of Usermaatre, one of Rameses II's many throne names. As for the inscription, "Look on my works, ye Mighty, and despair," Diodourus either made it up or recorded an erroneous translation. No pharaoh ever wrote such things on his temple, although the claim "the like of this has not been seen from the beginning" is quite common.

As for the "frown" and "sneer of cold command" on the "shattered visage," none of the many statues of Rameses II, broken or intact, reveals an expression remotely like this. His features are sensuous, certainly regal, imbued not only with power but with the subtle inner strength of wisdom.

Shelley may have seen an engraving or sketch to complement Diodourus' account, but none of his sources was particularly reliable. Even in the first century B.C. there were no "lone and level sands" stretching far away; and as for "nothing beside remains," one could hardly call 4,600 square miles of imposing temple ruins "nothing," not to mention Rameses II's many other monuments which are strewn from the Delta all the way down to Nubia.

Clambering around this shattered marvel in the white heat of early afternoon, I found its size increasingly impressive. An index finger is three and a half feet long; the ear four feet; the circumference of the arm at elbow point is nearly seventeen and a half feet. It is big — very, very big. Not only that, the work is of exceptionally high quality. How it was erected baffled me; how it collapsed is easier to understand. The great earthquake of 27 B.C. also reduced the outer pylon of the temple's First Court to rubble.

Shelley's poem has contributed to the notion of Egyptian pharaohs as arrogant and boastful megalomaniacs. Rameses II, reigning for sixty-seven years, building temples and monuments on unequalled scale all over Egypt, is the easiest target for such attacks. If, however, one accepts the Schwaller de Lubicz/West thesis, it is necessary to understand properly the nature and function of kingship in ancient Egypt.

Despite all the monuments with their hieroglyphic encomiums, we know little about the individual personalities of most pharaohs, including Rameses. If we see the pharaoh as something like a combination of pope, tribal king, and CEO, his role becomes easier to understand. Even in primitive societies today where poverty is the norm, the king is kept in luxury, wanting nothing, because he symbolizes the prosperity of the whole tribe. In the history of the Catholic Church, most popes have been respected and even revered by the faithful. Similarly the CEO, not the assembly-line workers, runs the company — unless his mistakes come to be considered incompetence. A pharaoh referring to Amon as his "father" does so in the same impersonal way that Christ claimed, "My Father and I are One."

Rameses in particular is accused of having erased monuments constructed by other pharaohs, substituting his own cartouche for theirs, co-opting their achievements. But in the light of Schwaller's contention that buildings were assembled and disassembled according to astronomical cycles, Rameses' actions become less egotistical. It is true that he did "usurp" temples, often replacing the builders' cartouches with his own; but he also added to them, often giving full credit to their original builders. In other temples he replaced some cartouches and left the rest intact. If his intention had been to obliterate the memory of every king before him, he could have done so, considering the length of his reign, throughout Egypt.

More important, if what he did had been considered criminal, he would have been punished for it posthumously. The actions of Akhenaten and Hatshepsut were clearly viewed this way, and in the case of the former, attempts were made after his death to destroy all his works and completely erase his name from history. Hatshepsut's "crime" is less clear. Although her temples were left standing and continued to be maintained, selected reliefs and inscriptions were effaced. No attempt was ever made to usurp the works of Rameses after his death. It follows that those who persist in viewing this most prolific of pharaohs as the heartless tyrant of Shelley's poem are simply wrong.

Leaning in the hot dry air against Rameses' ear, I tried to reconstruct his mortuary temple in my mind's eye — the columns tall and clean, the pylons hung with bright, fluttering banners, the reliefs covered in vibrant blues, reds, yellows, and everywhere the glint of gold leaf. The magnificence must have overwhelmed all who saw it. Since ancient Egypt had few foreign visitors, Rameses was not building to impress the world. He was building for the glory of God and the uplifting of his subjects' hearts. Shelley's fellow Romantic poet Keats got closer to the reality of this ancient world when he wrote, "'Beauty is truth, truth beauty,' — that is all/Ye know on earth, and all ye need to know."

◦⌣◦

"Are ya ready to get high tomorrow?" a voice yelled at me across the Hilton lobby. It was Captain Bill. For a moment I thought he'd cracked up. I pretended he wasn't addressing me and dodged behind a large plant.

"High, high, high over Thebes," I heard him sing out.

Ah, yes. The balloon. I waved back and hit the bar with my captain.

"Weather sounds good," he confided. "Of course, that means nothing at all … but a desperate man believes anything." I asked where he intended to fly. "Hell," he replied. "Don't ask me that. I never know till I get there, do my tests. The atmosphere is like a layer cake, you see. And you don't wanna hit a layer movin' fast the wrong way — you're liable to end up two hundred miles out in the Sahara. That's a long, thirsty walk, bub."

Did I really want to ride a hot-air balloon over the Egyptian desert with Captain Bill? Despite the jokes, something about him inspired confidence. His was the gallows humour of the front-line soldier. He was one of those men who found danger romantic and assumed others did, too.

~~~

That night I took myself off for another fix of Amon at the Karnak son-et-lumière. The experience was every bit as powerful as it had been the first time, but I noticed something else that also touched me deeply. Sitting in the darkened pavilion above the shimmering vespertine sacred lake, the holy city spread out to the north in all its majesty, I watched a young woman in front of me seated next to an old man — presumably her father or grandfather. He was clearly suffering from severe back pain, and throughout the entire half hour or so the girl gently rubbed his bent old spine, stroking his soft, leathery neck and the thinning white hairs on his sun-painted head. Her tenderness moved me almost to tears, reminding me somehow of the poignant reliefs in Ramose the vizier's tomb. How pointless the soaring chords and inspired hymns of praise in stone would be without those little unremembered acts of kindness and of love that make us worthy to stand before the presence of God …

A soft breeze smoothed the ripples on the sacred lake to a mirror reflecting the burning geometries of the starry night sky. It seemed an image of the mind itself.

Back on the hotel lawns I sat watching a highway of honeyed light undulating across the broad dark Nile and back up to the tarnished moon, a fat luminous spider squatting in the centre of a jewelled web. Fireflies roved above the reeds like lighted cigarettes held by unseen hands. Magic, truth, mystery, an entrance into arcanum — why does Egypt always bring such things so close?

I could hear the eternal cry of every person who ever lived: *Who am I? Where do I come from? Why am I here? Where am I going?* Karnak, Luxor, Philae, Kom Ombo, Esna, Edfu. All of Egypt's ancient sacred sites provoke those questions. Perhaps they answer them, too.

～つ

Captain Bill had told me to be in the lobby at 4:30 A.M. sharp. I was. But except for the haggard night manager, no other humans were in sight. I sat reading brochures, counting the typographical errors on average per paragraph. When I awoke, it was 5:28, and Captain Bill towered over me looking intolerably well rested, hale, and hearty.

"Nope, bub. I said five-thirty," he replied when I told him he was an hour late. Maybe he *had* said 5:30.

A young English man and woman joined us. They were on their honeymoon, but they looked more like people whose main bedroom activity for years had been reading serious books while wearing sturdy pyjamas on separate sides of the bed. Both had that freckly anemic English skin that never tans but turns a painful boiling red after five minutes in the sun. Both wore small hiking knapsacks that looked empty.

Captain Bill boisterously herded us out into the night. The sky contained not even a hint of dawn. Luxor was sleeping soundly. Even the outsize Estate wagon that pulled up out of the shadows seemed drowsy and noiseless. The Englishwoman looked at me with horror, or so I thought, and seemed to be on the verge of screaming. Instead, she threw up a colourful stream of undigested vegetables over her husband's feet.

"She's feeling sick," her husband usefully explained.

Knowing how the Englishwoman felt, and feeling certain that Captain Bill's balloon would not feature a toilet, I wondered how she could contemplate this trip. And since all these so-called revenges of ancient potentates involve an urgency that overrides dignity, I worried about the consequences the rest of us might face trapped in a wicker basket six feet square with her for the next three hours.

The English couple looked like folks who worried about their health, what they ate, what they drank. Such people invariably get sick in the Orient. In fact, Egypt, because of its extreme dryness, is one of the healthiest environments in the world.

After two minutes the pungent tang of vomit scented the Estate wagon as we hurtled down to the corniche for the west-bank ferry. Two more passengers were waiting in the pitch-black shadows below the sidewalk on a little quay, near which floated the dilapidated hulk of something more like a huge covered dock with an engine than a boat. One was a man with many cameras around his neck and a Hindenburg moustache so large it looked in the gloom like a hairy bird flying out of his nostrils; the other was either a tall, effeminate boy with cropped, peroxided hair ... or a girl who'd been assigned the wrong body. The Englishwoman began to retch, emitting strangled, inhuman noises but nothing else. The peroxide blonde was introduced as Debbie. She turned out to be Captain Bill's colleague, observing his operation in Luxor before heading off to run the one in Dubai. Although she'd probably spent her childhood climbing trees, hunting squirrels with slingshots, and swapping baseball cards, she had a delicate, impish face, and a gentle, sunny disposition that offset her total lack of other female characteristics. The walking moustache eventually revealed himself as a German mortician on vacation; he wasn't much of a conversationalist — but that was probably an occupational hazard.

We boarded the ferry along with several Qurnawis in turbans and *gelabias* who looked as if they'd spent a night doing something that was taking its toll on their bodies. They sat hunched in a little circle, coughing continuously in rhythmic pattern, sounding like performers rehearsing some kind of avant-garde choral opus.

An engine louder than three pneumatic drills hammered into life, and the ferry lurched out across black, mist-wreathed waters. Captain Bill and I leaned over the unstable starboard railing smoking cigarettes. I asked him whether he thought the Englishwoman was in any shape to fly.

"Well," he said, rubbing his massive stubbly jaw, "I wouldn't want her doing the old technicolour yawn over Qurna. I can't imagine anything worse than having a torrent of spew land on your head first thing in the morning. Ruin your whole day. And knowing those villagers, we'd probably get blown out of the sky by bazookas. On the other hand, I don't fancy flying in a basket knee-deep with the second coming of yesterday's menu for three hours. We'll give her breakfast, and if it makes a reappearance, she'll have to follow us in the Jeep. Or maybe *on* the Jeep."

The ferry had nearly reached the misty middle of the Nile by now, and both of us began to stare in fascination at the large, vague silhouette of a cruise ship moving at a fair speed on a course that looked as if it would intersect ours in less than a minute.

"Bill," I said, "do you think our pilot has seen that?"

Captain Bill looked thoughtful for a moment. "I'd give it a fifty–fifty on the possibility scale. I don't think he's got around to installing the radar unit yet though. He'd have to install something to install it in first, of course."

"Fifty–fifty seems optimistic to me, Bill."

We watched as the ferry moved directly into the cruise ship's path, about thirty feet between us and the churning V of foam streaming from its towering bows.

"You're right," Captain Bill conceded. "I'll give you a million-to-one odds, bub. In fact …" He paused, then shouted at the top of his voice, *"Everyone, HIT THE GODDAMN DECK NOW!"*

Everyone did, seconds before a sickening crunchy thump shook the ferry like a toy, knocking it forty-five degrees off course into the huge bubbling wake of the cruise ship. Sirens and foghorns sounded, spotlights seared into life on the deck above. Voices called out through the night. I could hear our pilot and his crew repeating "*Inch' Allah, Inch' Allah*" over and over. The will of God, the will of God — as opposed to the incompetence of man. But neither the ferry nor the cruise ship stopped to check damage. Although heading now up the river rather than across it, our craft seemed miraculously to be in one piece. I kept thinking we'd find ourselves plunging into the fetid depths at any moment, but we spun back and resumed our crossing, the crew now giggling nervously, the Englishwoman groaning in a death agony, the mortician displaying a copious fund of rasping Teutonic curses, and everyone else looking at each other in disbelief.

"Happens all the time," Captain Bill announced. "The only vessels Egyptians should be licensed to sail are ships of the desert. Know why they're called that — camels?" he asked.

I didn't.

"Because they're full of Arab semen. *Get* it? Sea-men ..."

Looking at the mangled sides of the ferry when we'd finally docked on the west bank, I agreed. This wasn't our craft's first collision with something large and heavy. Parts of the hull resembled blackened aluminum foil that had been reused a few hundred times.

"Where's the goddamn Jeep!" Captain Bill roared, peering down the narrow dusty road to Qurna. "Those assholes shoulda been here half an hour ago!" We all sat down on picnic hampers. The odd taxi driver approached, offering his services. Everyone was yawning, except the Englishwoman, who wept silently, clutching her stomach. The mortician blasted his many camera lenses with canned air.

"I wonder what excuse they'll have for me this time," Captain Bill said.

After some minutes a long-wheel-base Jeep rattled into view. "I love these guys," Captain Bill told the guys who clambered from the vehicle, one of them incongruously dressed in white shirt, black bow tie, and cummerbund.

Passengers and packages loaded up, Captain Bill turned to the driver and said, "Howard Carter's villa, I think."

The enormous sky had turned iridescent steel blue by the time we reached a large open patch of flat gravelly ground adjacent to the house Howard Carter had lived in while excavating Tutankhamen's tomb. It was a charming Nubian-style villa surrounded by a wall enclosing lush spinneys of palm trees.

"Carter had this area cleared to use as a football pitch," Captain Bill explained. "Thoughtful of him, no? Makes a perfect launch pad."

From a box the captain extracted several small balloons, inflated them with a helium cylinder, letting them float up into the dawn while he watched their progress carefully. "It's a layer cake," he said. "Different winds at different heights." At length he shook his head. "Nope, it's gonna be the Valley today, friends."

We all piled back into the Jeep and headed around the curve past Carter's house into the narrow, forbidding opening beyond which lay the Valley of the Kings. Pulling up in the large parking lot opposite Tut's invisible tomb, the crew unpacked the balloon from its massive crate, unrolling a giant tarpaulin that covered half the lot to protect the fabric from scratches. Without anyone's noticing, two folding tables were set near the van, and the man with the bow tie laid out fresh croissants, smoked salmon, cheese, cold cuts, and fruit, alongside an urn of coffee. There were silver knives and forks, bone-china plates, cups, and saucers.

"Breakfast!" yelled Captain Bill, clapping his huge hands like a schoolteacher on a class outing.

Over the steep cliffs the sun was already burning although still out of sight, casting stark shadows that made me shiver. As we ate, Captain Bill's crew began to inflate the gigantic blue sack with roaring blasts of flaming gas. Slowly it billowed from limp, crumpled folds into a heaving egg that strove to escape the many ropes and hands. It was a magnificent sight, the brilliant blue against the pale, dry, yellow rock. The Englishwoman suddenly volunteered to stay on earth, as if the reality of what she would be facing had finally hit home.

The rest of us clambered into the basket. It was a sturdy affair, framed in stainless steel, cushioned, fitted with handholds, yet still a wicker basket. Captain Bill, now wearing aviator goggles and leather gloves, gave safety instructions and turned up the howling burners until the heat singed our heads.

Unlike airplanes, balloons take off so smoothly you don't even realize you've left the ground. The Valley receded beneath us, and the sun appeared low in the east softened by a morning mist. The barren place seemed still more enigmatic for all the treasures once contained all over that bleak craggy cleft. The silence was eerie, as if the earth were sinking and we were motionless.

"We're displacing 176,500 cubic feet of air," Captain Bill announced. "And these four burners use in one hour the same energy as two hundred three-bedroom homes consume in a year. Ladies and gentlemen, I have the Aswan Dam over your heads." He began to try rousing Luxor Airport ground control on a two-way radio. "Wake up, Luxor," he said, eventually getting a reply and the okay for his route. It all seemed rather vague, but knowing how few flights Luxor handled, it also seemed unlikely we'd encounter other craft.

Out of the valley we floated, rising and descending in and out of the layered winds. "It's a pilot's dream flying here," Captain Bill said.

Below us now was Deir al-Bahari, the cliff face housing Hatshepsut's mortuary temple, with its spare, modernistic terraces and the clean lines of its ramps. From this height, the relationship of buildings to one another in the Theban necropolis was far clearer, and the full extent of their original dimensions visible in the lines of long-vanished courtyards and walls invisible from the ground. Our captain was right. This *is* the only way to see Thebes.

We swooped down low over waking villages where children cheered and waved, over fields where fellahin were making the most of the early morning cool to tend their crops. The broad green strip of irrigated land on either side of the Nile seemed especially miraculous measured against the vast desert expanses stretching away on all sides.

Captain Bill took great delight in bringing us down to less than thirty yards above rooftops and little courtyards where villagers were washing or preparing breakfast. "I never tire of the pleasure it gives those kids," he said. "I love these people."

Heading toward the Ramesseum, we came in low above the fallen colossus. "There he is," said Captain Bill. "What a party animal that Rameses guy is — always facedown in the dirt every morning I come here." Tourists below waved and clicked off film. "Most photographed balloon in the world," the captain informed us proudly.

On toward the Nile we drifted, up and down, fast and slow, the burners alternately roaring and silent. At the Colossi of Memnon we paused, descending over the compound that contains the monolithic statues of Amenhotep III for an unusual view of these imposing though ruined works by a legendary pharaoh. His memory had vanished altogether by Roman times, the Romans incorporating what they found into their own myths. For them these statues represented Memnon, the son of Eos, the

Dawn, and Tithonus, who killed Antilochus, the son of Nestor, and was himself slain by Achilles.

The thinking behind this attribution is far from clear. Ever since the great earthquake of 27 B.C. the colossus was said to emit a strange musical noise at dawn, Memnon's greeting to his mother, Eos — possibly the result of temperature changes in the expanding stones. When the emperor Trajan visited the site and spent several days there with his wife, he was greeted, according to graffiti, by the "oracle" with a gonglike sound in the second hour after dawn. At the close of the second century A.D. Septimus Severus attempted repairs; he sawed the fallen colossus into blocks and clumsily re-erected them. After this, the dawn sounds ceased. Over sixty feet high, the Colossi still present a commanding if weather-beaten appearance, standing alone facing the open fields, invariably surrounded by tourists freed from their coaches for an obligatory five minutes.

Captain Bill turned up the burners, taking us high over the canals and clustered settlements that flank the Nile, then across the green, slow-moving waters of the river to descend toward Luxor Temple and float low across the city rooftops along the processional path to Karnak, swooping in to land with the gentlest thump not far from Professor Redford's huge Geena-paten temple site. From the air the vastness of Karnak, a city as much as a temple — in all its crumbling splendour brutally contrasted with the sprawling mess of modern Luxor — was more apparent than it can ever be from ground level.

The Estate wagon, with the pale Englishwoman inside, was waiting to take us down to the corniche, where we enjoyed another breakfast by the Nile, everyone strangely silent.

Within the hour I was waiting for the Cairo plane, wondering when I'd next be back in Thebes, the heart of the pharaohs' mysterious kingdom, if ever.

CHAPTER TWELVE

THE NEIGHBOURHOOD BULLY

Islam is a humanitarian religion which upholds many immortal principles such as freedom, social justice, human rights, forgiveness and great love for science and work. Islam is also known for its moderation and being far from extremism. Meanwhile, the deviant trends are known for their extremism, narrow-mindedness and their call for violence and hatred.

How could such groups be so strong to the degree that they almost disrupt the image of a religion with such purity?

What is more astonishing is that the real religion symbolised by Al-Azhar, thousands of teachers and professors of Islamic religion and all the media have not been able to disseminate the real principles of Islam, while the militants, who only depend on secret activities, have been able to gain more ground. Shouldn't this situation make us reconsider the way we present Islam? What is the role which the school should play and what should the mosques do? What is the role of TV and radio? We shouldn't care for the quantity as much as we care for the quality and

> *those who present it. The question which all of us should think*
> *about is: how should religious teaching be and how could we*
> *preach religion in the age of science, information and barrier-*
> *free communication?*
>
> —NAGUIB MAHFOUZ IN *AL-AHRAM*, APRIL 1990

Such deceptively reasonable broadsides by Naguib Mahfouz, Egypt's Nobel Prize–winning novelist, now appear regularly in the Cairo press. I'd first met him in 1988, before he'd received the prize, finding then a less cautious man than the one who was besieged in the spring of 1990 by the international media. Now his every utterance is scrutinized by the fundamentalist Muslim Brotherhood, a militant faction of which issued a death threat against him when the Nobel was announced. During the 1970s, when, along with his mentor, the great Egyptian man of letters Tawfiq al-Hakim, Mahfouz was urging President Anwar Sadat to make peace with Israel, the Muslim Brotherhood had also issued a death threat. The Brotherhood liked issuing death threats more than carrying them out.

Mahfouz has been constantly criticized by orthodox Islamic bodies over nearly six decades, during which time he has produced more than forty books. In 1959 the Al-Azhar authorities banned his novel *The Children of Gebelawi*, a satire on the hypocrisy of Judaism, Christianity, and Islam. (The *fatwa* was reissued along with the one banning Salman Rushdie's *The Satanic Verses*.)

In the eyes of fundamentalists, Mahfouz's novels are un-Islamic. They claimed the Nobel Prize resulted from an Israeli conspiracy to ensure that the Arabic writer most pro-Israel in temperament received the accolade. Actually contemporary Arab literature has been long overdue for such recognition. Certainly, however, the top experts on Mahfouz's work *are* all Israelis.

And this is not the only criticism levelled at him within Egypt. He is also accused of having remained silent during Nasser's oppressive rule, managing, unlike many of his contemporaries, to stay out of jail. On the other hand, his defenders in Israel and elsewhere maintain he consistently used allegory to criticize President Gamal Abdel Nasser's abuses of power and war-mongering. Arabic lends itself to allegory. So do repressive dictatorships.

In Cairo, Mahfouz is now treated as something of a national treasure. Everyone seems to know the rigid schedule he has followed for most of his career, and as I walked on the streets with him strangers frequently called out greetings. Anyone seriously interested in killing him, I thought, would not have a hard job. At 6:30 A.M. he leaves his modest apartment in the middle-class quarter of Agouza, walks the two miles or so to the Ali Baba café in Tahrir (or "Liberation") Square, across the Nile on the east bank in the city's hectic heart. There he takes coffee and reads newspapers until eleven, when he heads for his office in the *Al-Ahram* newspaper building. The office is more of a token gesture now as he writes little for the paper; today it is more a place where he can hold interviews and dispose of business. At four he returns home and writes until seven. He has not broken this routine, which stems from the years when he worked full time in the civil service before getting down to writing his novels. Only since 1971 has he enjoyed the luxury of making a living solely with his pen.

Back in 1988 I met him at the *Al-Ahram* office, being told to arrive at 11:05 A.M. *sharp*. In a room that somehow managed to be both Spartan and opulent, he sat in one corner of a titanic plastic sofa, a frail, dapper little man in dark glasses. Because of his severe deafness, I was eventually obliged to speak an inch from his ear, hearing my voice echo unnervingly in his hearing aid as he sipped Turkish coffee and puffed on Cleopatra Milds.

His major influences, he claimed, were the British social realists of the beginning of the century. John Galsworthy, H. G. Wells, and Arnold Bennett. His descriptions of the Cairo poor, however, had most often been compared to Dickens, but when I broached this, he maintained he'd never been able to finish anything by Dickens, saying, "His plots are distressingly artificial."

He emphasized that a writer must reflect the conditions of the society in which he lives. "Egypt is where Europe was in the late nineteenth century," he told me. "My books must be written for my audience. If I wrote like James Joyce, I'd have perhaps five readers." Perhaps. He lamented the pervasiveness of television and the general decline of the reading public.

Egypt seems to have leapt straight into postliteracy without ever achieving literacy along the way.

Arabic is a highly imprecise, ornate language, and any writer has to choose, ostensibly, between poetry and clarity. Mahfouz's work is famous for its clear, precise style and is consequently very easy to translate. Even his later experimental novels play more with structure than with style, changing points of view and time sequences as a means of reaching multiple levels of perception and consciousness. That and allegory are his hallmarks.

He staunchly maintained that Arabic literature, and his work in general, had little to say to the West, comparing the best of it to third-rate European writing. I pressed him for examples, and he shrugged, saying he never read third-rate literature. Arabs are relentlessly polite.

When I questioned him then about his conflicts with Islamic orthodoxy, he was more openly critical. He claimed his work had been wilfully misunderstood. This time, however, he was guarded, even evasive.

We met one evening in the Kasr al-Nil, a more upmarket café than the somewhat seedy Ali Baba, overlooking the Nile on the wealthy enclave of Zamalek Island. He held court here every Thursday night with a group of young writers and intellectuals, who were openly jealous of my presence, jealous of the Master's attention. In the interim since our last meeting the Salman Rushdie affair had ripped into Cairo's intellectual world. Mahfouz had been quick to denounce Ayatollah Khomeini's death sentence as an act of terrorism, defending Rushdie's right of expression as a writer.

The backlash was instantaneous. A writer for a London-based Muslim paper said that if Mahfouz had been killed in the first place, there would have been no Rushdie to deal with. This was echoed by a high-ranking Egyptian cleric, known to have terrorist links, who told a Kuwaiti paper that Mahfouz should have been executed under Islamic law when *Children of Gebelawi* first appeared in 1959. The Egyptian press softened these reports, allowing that Mahfouz could be forgiven, providing he repented. Accordingly Mahfouz was quick to repent, holding a press conference where he claimed that his comments had been taken out of context and rejecting any comparison between *The Satanic Verses* and *Gebelawi*. He referred to *Gebelawi* as "my illegitimate son," relegating it to a phase of his life that, he said, had ended thirty years before. He also pointed out that he'd not read Rushdie's book when he'd made his original remarks, saying, now that he had, as a Muslim he found it disgusting. In a later interview with a Cairo magazine he added that he could not tolerate Rushdie's "insults and calumny against Islam and the Prophet." Rushdie has now recanted in a similarly unconvincing fashion.

That evening at the Kasr al-Nil, he was unwilling to discuss the matter any further. He was similarly reticent about discussing his faith. I'd never had from his novels much sense of him as particularly religious, yet now he claimed to consider himself a good Muslim. Since the details of his day were so well known, I asked him where prayers fitted into this tight schedule, but he merely smiled.

"I'm just the man of the Prize now," he told me more than once. He said he'd been unable to work on fiction since I'd last met him. I think he was enjoying all the attention. Although he sent his daughters to Stockholm to collect the Nobel, pleading ill health, he had been extremely active back in Cairo, using his loftier new position to write about the conditions of contemporary Egyptian society more directly. Awarded the Order of the Nile by President Muhammad Hosni Mubarak, in recognition of the Nobel, he'd delivered a tricky little speech on the occasion, which caused a minor scandal. Expressing his gratitude for the honour and lauding Mubarak for promoting Egyptian culture, he said he hoped he would one day be able to reciprocate by congratulating the president on a victory over the problems that faced Egypt. In 1988 he'd been more approving of the president, likening contemporary Egypt to a group of drowning men struggling to reach the surface. "When Mubarak came to power in 1981," he told me then, "the men were thirty metres under water. He helped push them up twenty metres, but they've still got ten metres to go. But if the Egyptian people do not understand what Mubarak has done and is doing, they will fall into unsafe hands."

In 1990 Mahfouz seemed less enamoured of his country's leader, complaining of the man's passivity and his lack of success with economic reforms. "The people have no emotional attachment to Mubarak," he said, pausing to light yet another cigarette. "But in a curious way his lack of charisma is encouraging more popular involvement in government. We Egyptians want democracy, you see, but we are also afraid of it. Two thousand years of oppression do not do much for the national spirit. I think this country may not be ready for full democracy for a century or more. Mubarak has given us many freedoms — the journalists and artists in particular — but unfortunately the only people who really believe in him are those who need him. There is so much to be done, so many *new* things to be done, that he is not doing. They are the actions of a passive man, and that is not enough, I'm afraid."

I asked him why he wasn't writing another novel. He sighed, looking suddenly older and tired. "I find it very difficult to write a novel about our current situation. I wrote about Egypt when it was young and I was able to be somewhat provocative. I was young, too. Now it seems corruption is a part of everyday life, not just limited to the few. The newspapers are more interesting than most novels. Why read fiction when you have the real thing every day in the papers?" Mahfouz was a well-known newspaper addict himself.

He sounded like one of his own characters. The men in his novels are invariably defeated idealists, often vain and obsessed with their social standing, occasionally even criminals justifying their crimes as revenges on the rich, the exploiters. His women, on the other hand, are solid, reliable, strong, hardworking, and long-suffering. It was, after all, Mahfouz's daughters who picked up the Nobel Prize for him.

> *You shall not enter heaven until you believe,*
> *and you shall not believe until you love one another.*
>
> —THE PROPHET MUHAMMAD, QUOTED IN
> ABD ASSAMII AL-MISRY, *ISLAM: THE ONLY WAY OUT OF ANXIETY*

Islam gets a bad press in the West. I have spoken with a number of people who have actually said they feel Islam's not even a legitimate religion, rather a perverse cult. I sought out some Egyptian members of the Islamic establishment to ask them why they thought their faith was so misunder-stood outside the Muslim world. The first was Dr. Gamal Al-din Muhammad, secretary-general of the Supreme Council for Islamic Affairs.

The headquarters of the Supreme Council was a crumbling palace of a place in one of the quiet, gardenlike, shabbily genteel areas that central Cairo is surprisingly full of. In dire need of a coat of paint, the building was now a memory of its former grandeur, the marble dull, the alabaster cracked and faded. A tiny, shuddering elevator carried me up a couple of floors, and I was shown by a secretary into a ballroom-sized office sparsely furnished with dusty antique furniture and the kind of overstuffed arm-chairs Chinese politicians favour.

Behind a mahogany desk on which you could have played football sat Dr. Muhammad. He was an elegant man in his sixties, dressed like a mod-erate Arab leader in a very conservative suit and tie. He greeted me with typical Egyptian courtesy, extending a soft, dry hand, and in a voice that was a low but powerful purr indicated a seat beside the desk and offered me coffee.

Nothing happens in Egypt before coffee is served, so there's often an awkward waiting period unless you're a genius at small talk. Dr. Muhammad didn't seem to be the kind of man who had much use for it.

He introduced me to an immensely plump, moist man with unnaturally white skin, wearing a leisure suit he'd long outgrown, and owlish specta-cles. Would I mind if he used a translator? Dr. Muhammad asked. The plump man joined us and, short of quibbling over one word with his boss, did no translating at all throughout the interview.

Coffee soon arrived, and Dr. Muhammad volunteered an explanation of the Supreme Council's activities. He was an expert in Islamic jurispru-dence, he informed me, and the council had two goals: "One, we promote Islam in Egypt and around the world. Two, we establish and develop rela-tions with Islamic nations, through publishing books, pamphlets, and suchlike." His voice was almost inaudible, one of those rhetorical tech-niques that makes you listen more carefully. "I believe Islam is one," he con-tinued. "But its principles are not above discussion."

I asked my questions. Dr. Muhammad was not about to accept any blame for Islam's poor international image. That was the fault of Israeli propaganda and the Shiite fundamentalists. He was quite explicit about the relationship between the Shia Muslims and the orthodox Sunni: "The Shia sect is not a religious sect," he said firmly, his voice gaining volume. "Political circumstances caused this sect to come into existence. There is no difference in our forms of worship, but Shia is a political sect." So what was the difference? "It lies in the problem of ruling in an Islamic society," Dr. Muhammad answered. This sounded like a speech he'd given many times before.

"The Shia believe the ruler might be anointed, chosen by heaven. But we believe, as the Koran clearly states, that we must choose our rulers in a democratic way. That is the main difference. Shia is shaped by political influences." He dismissed the reasons for Shia's split from orthodoxy — a belief that leadership should remain in the Prophet's bloodline — as "folklore ... very far from Islam."

"I think, and it is a personal view" — he used this phrase frequently; he was a cautious man — "that the Shia sect or its followers want to present themselves as absolute authorities, and they don't accept free discussion. They want everyone to believe in their principles unquestioningly, especially that of the anointment of the ruler. They have political goals that are disguised as religion. Always throughout history the Shia sect has been divided, but we cannot make them our enemies; they are still Muslims. They testify there is no God but God, and that Muhammad is the Messenger of God. They pray, they fast, they do *zakat* [alms], they do pilgrimage." The five pillars of the faith.

I asked about his feelings toward Ayatollah Khomeini and the Iranian revolution. "We think," Dr. Muhammad replied, the plural presumably indicating his authoritative position in Islamic matters, "that Imam Khomeini or anyone who rules is *just* a ruler; he is obliged to obey Islamic principles. When the Iranian revolution happened, the Islamic world was happy because they thought it would provide a good example."

Clearly he didn't feel this was the case, but seemed reluctant to say anything further. When I pressed him, he changed direction.

"Egyptian people believe in moderation," he explained, "which is a

Koranic principle. More than any other country in the Islamic world, we have a mixed civilization, and we accept whatever can be in accord with our principles of Islam. We have no problems with the Western nations. We believe, in fact, that the beginnings of Western civilization came out of the Arabs from Andalusia." I was impressed by this gross generalization.

Leaping several centuries of history, Dr. Muhammad changed direction again: "We struggled for our freedom against colonialism … and I think we succeeded. We have independence; we are responsible for ourselves."

He looked grave. "The main problem, and it is a personal view, between the Arab world and the West is the problem of Israel. We believe that Palestine was an Arab country. I think, and it is a personal view, that this is a sword hanging over the necks of Arabs since forty years. We seek for justice, and we seek to make this problem vanish — for our present and for our future." This sounded rather ominous, I thought, wondering if the "translator" considered "vanish" the best choice of words.

Dr. Muhammad elaborated. "We want to take our time to develop our country, improve our economy and social conditions — why does Israel resent us?" He wasn't asking a question; he was stating the general Arab line on events in the Middle East. "Israel has made three or four wars against us," he went on, "and continually tried to extend its frontiers. The Israelis have never indicated at any time that they wanted to cooperate with us, so we are obliged to misunderstand them, as they are obliged to misunderstand us. We can live with them in harmony, as we have done with all kinds of creeds. The history of the Arabs has never shown any fanatic goals."

I asked about his views on the Palestinian question, but to him it was all part of the same issue: "If Israel's intentions are good, we can solve all problems. We know Israel is stronger than any Islamic nation," he said somewhat mournfully, "but what about the Palestinians? As Palestine contained Jews, so Israel can now contain Palestinians. None of the Arabic nations have any desire to fight now; they are too busy building their own countries. If Israel also has no desire to fight or to extend its territories, we can reach a solution based on the decrees of the United Nations, to establish another nation in Palestine on the West Bank. With guarantees from the United States. *They are our cousins.*" He could not have known that even as we spoke, Saddam Hussein and the Iraqi military were planning to invade Kuwait.

It wasn't clear to me who he thought of as cousins, the Palestinians, the Israelis, or the Americans. I asked if he felt the United States was the key to this "solution." "I feel very deeply," he replied, "that the U.S. can fulfill its commission."

We seemed to have strayed very far away from the topic of Islam's world image, yet I had the feeling that, in Dr. Muhammad's eyes, we were at the core of it. He was not to be swayed from this line of thought, so I asked about the relative military strengths of Israel and the Arab countries.

"Israel is too strong," he answered forcefully. "We are not permitted to reach their level. Israel has aggressed Iraq and Tunisia in the last three years. It has killed a Palestinian leader, and it possesses the atomic bomb. But if any Arab country wanted to reach this level of military strength, Israel will say she feels anxious about her security.

"It is just a personal view, but all Islamic nations are united against Israel. Israel possesses all the weapons of mass destruction, but we don't possess *any*. We, too, can be a very sincere friend to the Western world. We don't believe our differences are as great as some make out."

I asked whether he felt the famous Arab patience would soon run out. "Yes, we are patient," he agreed. "But not out of choice — we are obliged to be patient. From our experience of dealing with Israel, we have bad feelings about their intentions, and we think Israel has no desire for real peace. It wants to extend its territories; it wants to gather all the Jews of the world into Great Israel. This is a stated intention of [Yitzhak] Shamir. Since [Yassir] Arafat's announcement recognizing Israel and renouncing terrorism, we still have to live. The Palestinians have no territory. Arafat has nothing left to offer. I think it was Golda Meir who said, 'There is no such thing as the Palestinian people.' So what can we negotiate with? They don't want peace."

There was nothing more to say. What had started as a discussion about religion had ended in a political diatribe. It seemed that there was no separation of religion and politics in Egypt — or anywhere in the Islamic world for that matter.

*I have found an answer to every question ... I have found that
what they call defects in Islam are, in fact, merits and what they
thought conflicting doctrines are pearls of wisdom detailed for
thinkers. What they regarded as blemishes in Islam was a remedy for humanity that had long been shrouded in darkness until
Islam brought it out to light. My mental powers were possessed
by Islam. Its commandments, its illuminating teachings and its
truthful messages compelled me to have Faith in it and belief in
the tradition of the Prophet. I adhered to Islam willingly, without any compulsion, pressure or temptation. But I believed in it
as a result of reasoning, contemplating, deep thinking, studying,
scrutinising and checking. In this way, Islam got the upper hand;
in other words, the side of Islam religion tipped the balance.*

—AHMAD SHALABY, *ISLAM: BELIEF – LEGISLATION – MORALS*

Professor Dr. Ahmad Shalaby, head of the Department of Islamic History
and Civilization at Cairo University, is one of the foremost scholars in
Egypt. With a Ph.D. from Cambridge, he is the author of a ten-volume
encyclopedia on Islamic history, comprising the history of all Muslim
countries up to the present; another ten-volume encyclopedia on Islamic
civilization, which describes Islam's attitudes toward politics, economy, culture, social life, and international relations; a four-volume series on comparative religions; two volumes on Arabic language and grammar; and
numerous other single volumes on various, more contained subjects.

Dr. Shalaby lived in Ma'adi, a garden suburb up the eastern bank of the
Nile where minor diplomats and foreign academics tended to rent. Far from
the nerve-grating noise of the city centre, Ma'adi is quiet. Broad streets are
flanked by modest, relatively modern villas and low-rise apartment buildings, their courtyards shaded by flowering trees, their well-tended gardens
crowded with colourful plants. An air of bourgeois complacency seems to
prevail.

Dr. Shalaby's apartment, however, was in a tenebrous and depressing
structure that looked over a large pit probably intended for the foundation

of a postponed low-rise, and now a dump site for a bewildering array of garbage: dead refrigerators, mangled bicycles, rusty tin cans, oil drums, newspapers, even what could once have been a car.

Since the flats weren't numbered, and the crooked line of battered wooden mailboxes did not have one labelled "Shalaby," I was obliged to knock on the first door, then, receiving no reply, the second, which proved to be the right one.

A tall, imposing figure even in his eighth decade, Dr. Shalaby ushered me into a bizarrely furnished room. The whole of one wall was papered with a billboardlike photo of a waterfall; there was a television the size of an industrial stove; monstrous pieces of dusty French Empire–style furniture, legs and corners festooned with gilded curlicues, surfaces littered with various artifacts; bloated politburo sofas and armchairs in lurid pastels; cabinets crammed with glassware of a design that could be termed Venetian-Caribbean; and, on what wall space there was left, diplomas and a large framed photograph of the young Shalaby in academic robes.

Consumed by a fat armchair, I sat absorbing the room while my host disappeared to arrange refreshments. It's common in countries like Egypt to keep the heavy wooden window shutters closed during the heat of the day, but, lit by Sicilian-style chandeliers, this room took on an alien, disconcerting appearance. The gigantic waterfall, cascading behind one pink sofa and pullulating with chartreuse foliage, made me feel I was in the jungle dwelling of some tribal chieftain who'd once laid his hands on a guidebook to Versailles.

Returned with a tray bearing soft drinks and a plate of sugar slabs disguised as cakes, Dr. Shalaby proved a somewhat pompous, pedantic, and rambling interviewee. I began with my usual inquiry about Islam's image in the West.

"It is the position of Egypt," he began — not that this was remotely related to what I'd asked — "to be the centre of the Middle East, as well as the centre of Islamic countries in general. The Islamic countries are far closer to each other than the Christian countries, you see. I travel almost every month to some place in the Islamic world. We don't live in Cairo at all; we live in the very heart of the Islamic and Arabic world." I wondered if this meant he didn't actually travel at all, since there was no need. Instead, I asked him where he felt Israel fit in, being also close to the heart of this world.

Dr. Shalaby sighed deeply and grandly. "The position Israel is taking now," he intoned, looking pleased with what he was about to say, "was taken by the Crusaders — and they stayed here for two centuries." I thought I was about to get about five volumes' worth of history, but we skipped from the early Middle Ages straight to the present day. "Israel lives here," Dr. Shalaby continued, presumably meaning the Middle East. "It is a foreign country, foreign people. They may get victory once or twice — but one day they will be absorbed by the millions around them. Or driven away — *when*, we don't know, of course. But there's no doubt about this — there's a foreign body in the area. It is not good for them. They will kill us, we will kill them. But eventually they will be absorbed or driven away. Historically, psychologically, for me and for many scholars, *that's* definite.

"Israel lives just because of the support of the United States. Without that, it would come to an end very soon. We are quite ready to sacrifice five, six, seven millions of people — only we can't win against the United States. One day this will change. We believe the Americans are under Jewish pressure, but we hope that one day a good and just president of the U.S. will stop supporting Israel."

I told Dr. Shalaby that, from conversations I'd had with his fellow countrymen, I doubted 15 or so percent he was so ready to sacrifice in a war would want anything to do with such a war. But he continued:

"I'm a professor at Cairo University, and part of my work is to teach students that you prepare to sacrifice anything to get real freedom, and freedom now means not only internal freedom but freedom from this enemy. We made a treaty with Israel, but this treaty meant nothing to them. Any day they may do something against us. That's our position in this part of the world."

He began to sound quite crazed. "We are preparing some millions to be pushed under the earth — *young people* are ready to do that. They're just waiting for the order, as they did at the time of Sadat. This is the only way. Israel has not provided a way for us to cooperate with them. We're fed up.

I don't believe Israel wants peace for one minute."

He was certainly less cautious than Dr. Muhammad, judging by the embers glowing in his eyes. I tried to point out that there was a considerable peace movement within Israel, and that surely he couldn't generalize about a whole nation.

"I'm sure you've made a good study of the lives of Jewish people," he went on, inexplicably. "They can't think for peace; they may be forced to do peace. But they said recently, two or three days ago, 'We will do another war.'" I asked him where and who exactly had said this in Israel.

"For me," he continued, oblivious to the question, "the Arab world is getting to be one world. We don't want to attack, but we'll defend very strongly. We are quite ready — as are Iraq, Syria, and Jordan. We hope to avoid war, and we hope Israel has the same feelings. One day it will come to an end. We must be patient."

I disliked this old man. With his life nearly over, what did he care about the consequences of war?

Unbidden, Dr. Shalaby changed tactics. "One day," he said, the words reminding me of the beginning of a diabolical fairy tale, "I received some Jewish guests here. We were discussing the atomic bomb, and I told them that if they thought we could not have it as well one day soon, they were mistaken. But even if they use their bomb, the danger will come to them as well. Israel thinks it can do anything it likes against anybody. The truth is they can't be a sincere friend to anyone. That is their nature. Some of my professors at Cambridge were Jews," he announced, as if the news would astound me, "but they were very polite and decent."

Again I tried to interject. Wasn't he doing to the Jews what he claimed the West was now doing to Arabs? He didn't even flinch. He'd probably spent a lifetime being unquestioned, so the notion of being wrong never entered his head.

"We believe," he lectured on, "that Judaism, Christianity, and Islam all came from God, but something happened by the people. They did not keep with it. Much happened to the Christians; *more* happened with the Jews." I gathered what he was trying to say was that Islam, much like the ancient Egyptian religion it succeeded, was adamantly against change.

"You see," he went on, "we Muslims have the Koran, which is completely good and unchanged from the original. With the Koran we can correct any mistakes that may arise. We are getting much better now in writing our history and preparing our religion. With the help of Koran we are getting back to real Islam. Christians can't do that because the Bible's not there. The real Bible is missing."

I inquired if he was now talking about authoritative texts. He was, and perhaps in deference to my Christian feelings he added, "The nature of Christian people is good; we can cooperate with them." He paused, as if remembering something important, then proceeded diffidently, "Well, *something* happened during the Crusades — but *mostly* we can cooperate with them." He made the Crusades sound like a regrettable incident a couple of years ago. "There are millions of Christians here in Egypt — we're in contact with them.

"But the Jewish we cannot communicate with at all. From following history for four thousand years we cannot find cooperation between Jewish people and other people, Christians or Muslims."

I sat speechless, staring at one of the most respected Islamic scholars in the world, wondering what I'd hear next.

"All the religions have one God," Dr. Shalaby said, virtual glee in his voice now, "but the concept was changed by the Christians. They say three — hah!" He laughed. "Up to them. I was in the Vatican" — he pronounced it "Fattycan" — "two years ago, and I raised this question about Jesus. The idea was that Jesus went up after death, after *crucification*. He left the grave and went up. So I asked them, in Vatican, *what* went up, the body or the spirit? In other words, *what* came down? He is the son, son of God, spirit came down and entered inside Maria, was born. What went up — the person who lived in Israel and ate, et cetera? They said at Vatican they could not reply to me" — This I found hard to believe, unless he'd asked some Japanese tourists — "but after some time they wrote and said that what went up is the spirit. Body profits nothing, was killed, buried, would not come out. This is great change. It may put an end to the question of three Gods. I have many Christian friends, they are very good friends to me."

I had to stop him here. For someone who'd written four volumes on comparative religion, he knew little about Christianity.

He shrugged all my explanations off as patently not worth troubling with. "It's obvious," he told me, "that Christ's resurrection was the revival of his spirit, his words, his teaching. That's the belief of the Muslims — what went up should be what came down." I'd never heard the Law of Gravity applied to the Resurrection before.

"The Bible of Christ is lost," Shalaby repeated. The statement seemed literal nonsense; I later discovered it wasn't. "I gave the Vatican this question" — his Resurrection theory again — "and they began to study it for a year before sending the reply." I pictured a cluster of cardinals huddled in a library racking their brains over Shalaby's question for an entire year, frightened they'd be out of business.

"Jews are not ready to cooperate with us," the premier scholar resumed. "They don't understand Islam. They may invite me to teach over there, but after a while they'll say, 'Thanks very much, don't come again.'" He was dead right about that — although, I thought, Dr. Shalaby could do more damage to Islam than the wildest schemes of any Israeli propagandists.

I asked him if he thought any state should be religiously governed. "Oh no," he replied, assuming I meant Egypt. "There should be a free state but full religion." What did this mean? "Political people should govern who understand religion," he elaborated. "You cannot be a man without religion. God gave us mind, but mind was not enough, so He gave us prophets."

"My friends and I love religion," he said, smiling beatifically, as if talking about gardening or art, "but we are quite happy. We live in beautiful places. We eat good. We go abroad from time to time, have wonderful clothes. I have four cars. Nothing we miss. And we can still follow religion and do our best to make our communities happy. Islam is a system of life — what to eat, how to marry. Alcohol is not good for the body or the mind, so Islam doesn't deprive us of anything. I enjoy everything; I have a good life. If there were Muslims in the United States, they would not help Israel against the Arabs." I was about to tell him that there *were* Muslims in the United States, but I realized he'd probably meant if everyone in the United States were Muslim. I said that if the Iranians were Jews, the balance of power in the Middle East would probably be different, too. He didn't understand this.

"Khomeini was not a good Muslim," he announced, as if I'd suggested Khomeini might have been Jewish. "Not a good Muslim at all. Shia is completely different to Islam" — this would certainly surprise the world's Shiites, I thought — "completely different. When people understand the real Islam, they respect it very much. We have many rich Arabs, but they are lazy. They don't understand Islam. Arabs rely one hundred percent on us, Egyptians, for teaching and books. Christian people understand us, but we feel unable to do anything with Jewish people. My books are taught in Israel," he told me, "but I write them scientifically." I presumed this meant that they didn't resemble his conversation. "The Israelis say about me 'good scholar,'" he boasted. "They asked me to go and make some discussion there — but I cannot go. According to the treaty, we are in peace — I *wish* they would support this peace. Every *day* they do something against the Arabs.

"We are not on good terms with Yassir Arafat," he said, "but then we are not on good terms with the leader of Israel." He smiled mischievously. "President Mubarak knows I'll be frank with you. The support of the United States, that's all: there's nothing else behind Israel.

"You know," he confided, in a final shattering non sequitur, "when I was in England, Christian ladies would not accept a Jewish student to live in their lodgings." What century was he in England? I wondered.

He sat looking at me expectantly, perhaps waiting for me to tell him things in England hadn't really changed. It took me a while to notice he'd stopped talking. I certainly wasn't going to ask another question, so I thanked him for the drink and cakes and left.

Outside, my head reeling, I sat on a fence post to recover. Christ, I thought, what a joke! The eminent professor had insulted two major religions, a large segment of European civilization, the United States, Jews in general, the head of the PLO, much of the Arab world, and, by virtue of saying what he'd said, his own faith. Since all such interviews are arranged through the Egyptian government's Information Ministry, I wondered if anybody there had ever looked at the results of such a meeting with Ahmad Shalaby. Could he really be an example of the best of Islamic scholarship?

Having read some of his many books, I can now say "I hope not" to that question. In the one I quote above, Dr. Shalaby trashes every religion in the world in the most superficial manner conceivable, upholding Islam as the one true faith, the goal of evolution itself. His work is riddled with contradictions, misconceptions, and grotesque oversimplifications. He does not appear to know the difference between Catholicism and Protestantism, Taoism and Buddhism, let alone the nature of the innumerable sects, heresies, and schisms in these religions. First Judaism and every other major religion are (with the exception of Islam, of course) dismissed as beyond salvation; then he concentrates on "proving" how Christianity was utterly corrupted by Western materialism, whereas Islam has remained pure and unsullied.

With his "four cars" and "wonderful clothes" and "trips abroad," Shalaby, one presumes, still views himself as immune from materialism. Similarly he overlooks or dismisses the divisions within Islam, and like the worst medieval pedant or money-grabbing Christian evangelist he can make the Koran support anything he wants it to.

For Dr. Shalaby, Islam's attraction seems to be its absolute control over every aspect of human life. You don't have to think — not a useful quality for a scholar. Orthodox Islam's extreme conservatism, its refusal to adapt, causes most of its conflicts with the Western world. A code laid down for nomadic tribes nearly a millennium and a half ago is bound to find life in the late twentieth century hard to handle. The original principles, as they exist in the Koran, were certainly an advance on existing religions when they were introduced. But the fundamentalists would like the clock to stop there.

The social advances Islam presented — particularly, equitable conditions for women — are no longer what they were. Muslim women are not viewed as the zenith of feminism anymore. The Prophet's wives were even judges and businesswomen. On paper Islam often reads like a perfect religion. In practice, very often, it appears far from that. And men like Ahmad Shalaby, professing to love their faith, are doing it irreparable damage. Tolerance is one of Islam's major tenets.

✦

Dr. Mamdouh Beltagi is the chairman of the State Information Service, besides being one of the most powerful men in Egypt and a close friend and confidant of President Mubarak. I'd also lay money on the likelihood of his becoming president himself one day.

The State Information Offices were set back from one of Cairo's main shopping streets past a gateway that led through the most crowded parking lot I've ever seen. Looking at the cars, you'd think they'd been picked up by a crane and placed side by side, one inch apart, filling every available space. They'd certainly have to be taken out that way. Parking anywhere in Cairo is ingenious, but this was art.

As with most government buildings, the interior of State Information was squalid and teeming. Some kind of reno job was being at least contemplated, to judge from the paint cans and fractured ladders strewn among rubble in various nooks and crannies. I wondered how many coats of paint it would take to make an impression on the grime these walls and ceilings had collected over the last few decades.

The kind of elevator you'd find in an old coal mine took me up to the top floor, where I was told to wait in the usual Third World bureaucrat's reception area: massive musty chairs, Koranic slogans in cheap frames, the ubiquitous portrait of Mubarak looking like Victor Mature.

Dr. Beltagi's office was therefore something of a shock. Enormous, clean, modern, with panoramic views over the city in three directions, it could have been in New York, Paris, or Milan. So could Dr. Beltagi. Ferociously handsome, he was wearing a sharp Italian suit tailored from grey mohair that was only slightly too shiny, an immaculate shirt and a pricy silk tie patterned just on the flamboyant side of conservative. His manner was brisk, worldly, and very Western — so Western that coffee was never mentioned or served. On his tidy desk, beside a sheaf of notes written in an elegant hand, and in English, not Arabic, were a bottle of mineral water and two packs of Merit Filters, which, judging by the half hour I spent with him, would last him till lunchtime.

He was in no mood for small talk. I felt my presence was an unwelcome but necessary intrusion, so I got straight to the point, outlining what I'd been hearing from the Islamic scholars. Dr. Beltagi watched me with unnerving concentration, his black eyes fierce as I spoke. When I'd finished, he replied in a cultured, concise voice devoid of any accent.

"We are a peace-making nation," he began, lighting another cigarette and leaning forward as if aiming his brain at me. "We're looking for peace in the region. We do try to get Arabs together. We are the only country in this area who can speak to everybody."

I asked him if there were really such a thing as Arab unity. He frowned, rattling off more short, sharp sentences. "If Arabs are now getting together, it's for the purpose of building peace in the area. The Israelis are refusing this."

I asked him whether the upcoming Arab summit in Baghdad was prompted by fears of Israeli expansionism sparked by the massive influx of Soviet Jews. Dr. Beltagi weighed me more than the question for a moment.

"We are not against the human rights of Soviet Jews," he eventually said, presumably deciding I might intend to raise the issue. This was more like chess than conversation.

"But," he continued, "these human rights must not be at the expense of Palestinian human rights. Their land is occupied. It *has* to be evacuated. This is law and justice. The Jews are perfectly free to emigrate from the Soviet Union if they want to, but they cannot settle in the occupied Arab territory."

I remarked that Dr. Shalaby had said Egypt didn't get along too well with Yassir Arafat. Dr. Beltagi narrowed his eyes. "We support the Palestinians," he answered. "They are struggling for a just cause. The most difficult country we have to deal with is the government of Shamir. Israel needs to establish a normal relationship with her neighbours. We certainly don't believe in pressure. The most important thing is dialogue."

I asked him if what he'd said was so, why was there such an image problem? "*That's* a problem of the Western press, not of the Arabs," he replied. "Arabs have clearly demonstrated that they are interested in peace, so why is the press against them?"

Did he believe the Western media were Zionist-controlled? "You said it there," he snapped. "Jews in the media want to show that Israel is in danger. That's *ridiculous*. Israel is the only nuclear power in the Middle East. *We're* the ones in danger! They've got nuclear, chemical, and biological weapons, and this will force Arab countries to develop them, too. The inevitable result of that will be war, catastrophe. We'd like to see an end to all weapons of mass destruction in this whole area. We believe in peace and moderation, but how can we be peaceful and moderate when this neighbour is armed to the teeth?

"Israel deals in threats; we'd like to deal in negotiation, discussion. The last thing we want is war. Egypt is working hard with the little she has to make something of this country, to develop industrially and economically, to raise the standard of living, eradicate poverty. We don't want to throw all that away in another war. We're working hard; we want only peace — for the whole region. We also want justice and order, but these are things that must be discussed reasonably. Israel is not willing to discuss reasonably, not willing to be a good neighbour."

I asked, somewhat presciently, whether he believed Saddam Hussein had, or was developing, a nuclear weapon, and whether Iraq could be viewed as a destabilizing element. He didn't confirm or deny the suggestions, only saying, "Israel has already attacked Iraq, you may recall."

Now, they are even. He expressed his hopes for Egypt's future, and as I left, I felt he was a decent and sincere man, though a pragmatic one. If his friend Mubarak surrounded himself with other such men, I thought, then Egypt was in good hands. Dr. Beltagi would probably make an exceptional president. I hoped he would have the chance.

Already, in the spring of 1990, something was afoot in Iraq. Arabs like Mubarak and Beltagi walk a very fine line between unity with their coreligionists and cooperation with Western interests. It was no coincidence the upcoming summit was to be held in Baghdad. I eventually attended it and decided the whole event was a last-ditch attempt to dissuade Saddam Hussein from the disastrous course he was about to embark on. Arab moderates wanted to see Mubarak assert himself now that Egypt was back in out of the cold where it had been banished after making peace with Israel. They wanted to see Egypt's president as the leader of the Arab world, the new Nasser. Instead, Saddam Hussein, the man with the biggest stick, was then emerging as that leader.

Yet again, everything came down to Israel. The man willing and capable of taking on the bad neighbour was still the man who could command the most respect from the followers of the Prophet.

Since the Great Pyramid had been built, it seemed to me, you couldn't tell where religion ended and politics began, or vice versa, in all the lands that had ever existed between the Nile and the Euphrates. The cradle of Western civilization had given up its baby to a battered childhood. No wonder it is now such a disturbed adult, confused and self-destructive.

I found this binge of religion and politics oppressive. I wanted to escape Cairo, the city to which all roads in Islam lead, and where at times the whole world seems to live. I needed room.

Packing little, I caught the last bus to Qena, two hundred miles south along the Nile road.

CHAPTER THIRTEEN

THE LAST FREE MEN

At night I often feel
The stars reaching through my flesh
Their soft fingers of light
Coiling around my heart
With a lover's embrace and the promise
That such love will outlast even
These endless sands that are my home …
Yet each morning I am once more alone
Hearing my camels proclaim their hunger
Feeling in myself just a thirst I cannot quench
From any well except the one hiding somewhere
    Somewhere deep inside my heavy heart …

                  —BEDOUIN POEM

A talented sunset had turned the river to burning mercury behind us. Now it was night, a coal-black night ensnaring the planet in its cage of brilliant starlight. At what looked like an abandoned military checkpoint, the taxi driver eased the gas pedal off the floor, where it had remained for twenty relentless and terrifying minutes, and rediscovered a brake. Outside the silence was thunderous. In air that managed, in its extreme dryness, to be cool and warm at the same time, I looked around in dismay at the handful of collapsed shacks scattered behind rusty remains of a barbed-wire enclosure.

"So this is *it*, is it, Mo?"

Mohammed and I had not been getting along too well, largely because he was invariably wrong about everything. The glittering heavens cast stark, jagged shadows over the rock-strewn sand. The place looked utterly forlorn and certainly deserted.

"No, Your Excellency" — he always called me that when I sounded annoyed — "now we look for *guide*."

"I thought that's what you're supposed to be?"

I expressed the doubt that we'd find a guide, or indeed anyone else, here. Our driver had started clambering over barbed wire and rocks, calling, "Raashid! Raashid!" as he roamed around wrecked huts in the compound. I was about to suggest we rethink this strategy when a figure emerged from the gloom, an old man in turban and *gelabia*, lean, wiry, skin like a relief map, teeth and eyes both seemingly stained by tobacco.

After a few muttered sentences, all four of us now climbed into the wretched vehicle and careered off down the narrow, twisting road, hitting as many potholes on the way as possible. Raashid, the old man, mumbled what I supposed were directions, although he peered through the windshield as uncertainly as everyone else did. Eventually we turned off the road and followed a set of tire tracks in the sand, weaving toward a space between two low black mountains. Veering right, we found ourselves in a small sheltered valley, skidding to a halt inches from an old pickup parked in the very tracks we'd been following. I could just make out the shapes of several small crude huts like garden sheds and the glowing embers of a dying fire.

Three men materialized, as if from the ground itself, and Raashid embarked on an elaborate round of cheek-kissing and hand-shaking while many voices kept repeating *"Salamaat"* — "Salutations."

Mohammed and I were then introduced, receiving warm handshakes but no kisses. The driver was paid and looked mightily relieved to head immediately back to Qena — where the word "Arab" is a perjorative, synonymous with "Bedouin" and meaning "dirty savage."

[The Ma'aza are] turbulent and dangerous; the men are professional robbers; and their treachery is uncontrolled by the Bedawi law of honour. They will eat bread and salt with the traveller whom they intend to murder.

—SIR RICHARD BURTON

The police in Qena had been reluctant to grant me a permit to travel into the desert, fearing the Bedouin would kill me. For the average Egyptian, these unpopulated expanses are a nightmare. Now poor Mohammed was sitting barefoot beside me on a square formed around a pit of camel-dung embers by narrow blood-red patterned rugs. Our Ma'aza hosts, members of the Khushmaan clan, Husseyn and Sa'ad, sat in the dignified and customary silence that always precedes traditional Bedouin offerings of hospitality. The tribe had come to this area from Arabia nearly two hundred years ago, and they still lived much as they had back then.

Husseyn's son, Alaa, a boy of twelve or so, soon arrived with a tray holding tiny cups and a slender-spouted copper teapot. With a politeness and deference to elders all but unknown in North America, he handed each of us mint tea, collected up a bunch of sticks, some balls of dried camel dung, and placed them on the fire, emptying about a half-gallon of kerosene over it. The resulting inferno lit up the entire valley and scorched my eyebrows. Boys will be boys.

Beyond and near where we sat was a collection of eight or so rectangular windowless shacks arranged in a rough semicircle around what I guessed was a crude well. The nearest one, I now saw clearly, had a crooked door of corrugated tin upon which childlike flowers and some clumsy Arabic letters had been painted.

"What does *that* say, Mo?"

"Says 'Oh God!'" he replied. For once he was right, but it's a phrase that doesn't quite translate literally into English anymore.

Mohammed kept looking uneasily behind him. Not far off, the sphinx-like silhouettes of squatting camels burped and snorted in their sleep. The desert terrified Mohammed. A shuffling close by, which proved to be the vague form of a veiled Ma'aza woman heading for the well like a small black mobile tent, sent him into a frenzy, brushing at the rug beneath him and banging his shoes against a fence made from old car fenders. Snakes, he informed me, were well known to hide in your shoes.

Husseyn and Sa'ad were clearly amused by this city-boy behaviour. I think they made up their minds to like me when they noticed I'd slipped a small twig into Mohammed's shoe when he wasn't looking.

Alaa, staggering under its weight, eventually returned with a plate the size of a coffee table, heaped with rice and hunks of lamb, capped by a dozen rounds of flatbread. We all ate from the vast dish with our fingers, the Bedouin encouraging me to take the rubbery wedges of liver, the best part, something I would have refused had I known more about their customs.

Bedouin hospitality dictates that a guest must *always* be offered the best portion of any meal; the guest's politeness, however, ensures that he in turn must *always* refuse this honour, ceding it to the oldest person at table. The Bedouin, though stock raisers, eat meat rarely, a major source of their income stemming from selling off the excess sheep, goats, and camels they breed. Most meals, except for occasions like weddings, circumcisions, or funeral rites, consist of little more than bread, beans, and rice. It's a diet that, while often bordering on starvation during lean periods, also keeps most of them alive and vigorous well into their seventies, eighties, and frequently beyond, if they manage to survive the rigours of nomadic childhood.

[The Prophet said:] Whoever kills a sparrow or anything bigger
than that without a just cause, Allah will hold him accountable
on the Day of Judgement. The listeners asked, O Messenger of
Allah, what is a just cause? He replied, That he kill it to eat, not
simply chop off its head and then throw it away.

—ISLAMIC LAW

Food is taken very seriously by the Ma'aza, as are all the necessities of their lives in a capricious environment, and this campfire meal was a solemn affair, almost a communion, eaten largely in silence. When Alaa had removed the giant dish, half of its twenty pounds of food was untouched. He returned with yet more tea, then, soon after, coffee, and endless cigarettes were passed around.

I lay back gazing at the flashing unfamiliar constellations emblazoned across the shimmering planetarium dome above. How real the night seemed out here, compared to the fierce illusions of day; forms merged into Form. The barely conceivable grandeur of the universe and man's minute but crucial place in it impressed their truths upon me. How many generations of Bedouin had been shaped by similar perceptions? This enormous peace had to account for the serene stillness that characterized almost every man I met during my ten days of crossing the Eastern Desert.

We were awaiting the imminent arrival of Sulimaan, I learned, shaykh of the Khushmaan Ma'aza and apparently on his way from Safaga, a small port on the Red Sea coast. The talk that night turned to Ma'aza perceptions of the outside world. They had a reciprocal disdain for the Nile Valley Egyptians, ridiculing their ignorance of and inability to function in the desert, although the term "desert" was never used to describe the Bedouin homelands; this was always "the countryside." Husseyn, the eldest of Shaykh Sulimaan's nine sons (the man had six daughters, too), continually referred to such Egyptians as "goats" or "mules": "They always need to be close to one another — like goats ..." The fellahin, or peasant labourers, he despised even more, regarding them as "like animals, except they can talk ... But even the life of animals is better since *they* don't have such big problems." Life in his "countryside" he considered freedom; the existence of those toiling in towns and cities was simply prison. The Bedouin cherish their freedom above all else. Compared to them, we are all prisoners.

Most surprisingly, my hosts were full of questions for me, many of them concerning geography. Where was China? for example. Some of them had seen Chinese engineers supervising construction projects in Luxor; Sa'ad thought they all looked the same. Where was Sweden? They knew that was where some trucks that frequently crossed the desert road carrying bauxite were made. Was Japan cold? This asked because Ma'aza, who owned Japanese vehicles, had to modify their carburetors to prevent overheating. On the same basis, Russia must be unimaginably cold then, they said, because you couldn't adjust Russian vehicles in the same way, and consequently they were always overheating. How large were these countries? Which way was America? And, most improbable of all, was it true Americans worshipped a goddess called Madonna who fornicated in public at vast concerts? This presumably arose from vague notions about Catholicism muddled with recent radio reports announcing that the rock star's records had been banned in certain Islamic countries.

Most startling for me was to discover that they not only refused point-blank to believe men had landed on the moon, although they were perfectly aware of and believed in the *Challenger* space-shuttle crash; they also firmly maintained the earth was flat and that the sun revolved around it. The argument presented was every bit as convincing, I found, as it must have once been in medieval Europe. The Koran clearly stated, Husseyn told me, that God had made the earth flat and placed great mountains at each corner to prevent it from tipping over. At the centre was Mecca, like a tent pole. Beyond were the Waq Waq lands and the "seas of darkness," an area Sa'ad referred to as "desolation" or "ruination." There was no end to this place, and no man there could tell the difference between up and down.

To questions I answered over the following days about time zones and the fact that the sun shone in my country when it was night in theirs, they would simply exclaim, *"Subhaan Allah!"* — "power or majesty of God!"

> *There are no people in the world so slovenly, so unpractical ...*
> *so footling, as the inhabitants of the Eastern Desert ... ragged*
> *weaklings, of low intelligence and little dignity ... of all stupid*
> *people these unwashed miseries are the stupidest.*
>
> —ARTHUR WEIGALL, 1909

Not wanting to sleep, that sky and the almost mystic tranquility being too rare and precious to waste, I found myself awaking as the predawn light was gradually drawn like an iridescent curtain of blue steel to hide night's secret splendours. Someone had covered me with a blanket that smelled of wet dog. Beneath my narrow rug I could feel the cool seeping up from pale soft sand. The sound of women's voices not far away amid a muffled clatter of pots and pans; the fire beside me now a low, cold mound of charcoal and ash.

Shaykh Sulimaan had not arrived, but, I was informed over the first of the day's innumerable cups of tea and Cleopatra cigarettes, we'd be riding out soon anyway and would meet him along the way. This struck me as a preposterously optimistic plan. Our camels were saddled and loaded up while we breakfasted on beans in oil with bread, and a fat red sun peered over the serrated desert peaks ahead.

Mohammed did not look happy perched unsteadily atop his camel. Whether it was the slights against city folk of the previous night, simply the notion of riding this beast, or encountering the "snake" placed in his shoe, I never discovered. I didn't care. But he remained sullen and uncommunicative throughout the next ten days, which, in his capacity as translator, proved a bit of a handicap for me. He even stopped calling me "Your Excellency."

While the saddle was painful, the going was painfully slow. Although we generally appeared to skirt the Qena–Safaga road, Husseyn and Sa'ad frequently embarked on long detours into boulder-strewn valleys where the odd clump of pitifully small green shrubs or the occasional lone acacia tree provided some meagre sustenance for our mounts and indicated the presence of precious water, usually tiny trickling springs concealed behind vast rocks. These people knew this wasteland the way we know our home cities. But, considering Ma'aza territory covers some 35,000 square miles, the skills involved are somewhat more impressive.

The scenery here is wild, desolate ... there was a feeling ... that one was travelling on the moon.

—ARTHUR WEIGALL, 1909

Weigall, given all his radiant ignorance about the Bedouin, might as well have *been* travelling on the moon. Yet the few who have ever journeyed in this region, whether sensitive to its inhabitants or not, have rarely failed to be deeply moved by the magnificent alien bleakness of the country they encountered. In 1931 André Von Dumreicher saw it as "Sublime ... a wonderful lunar landscape, a lifeless and ageless world." To the ancient Egyptians it was the "Land of Ghosts"; yet, being the only civilization to have ever drawn up a map of the next world, they respected this.

I, too, came to see that these seemingly inhospitable dead zones are full of riches to those who know them, who are finally indistinguishable from them. During the long journey from the Nile to the Red Sea, Husseyn would often point out various places, one called, for example, "Big Ears" after a man with extravagantly large ears who'd once lived there. The clan itself, the Khushmaan, derived its name from a word meaning "Big Nose," an epithet applied back in Arabia to its founding patriarch. To the Ma'aza, a man was much more than his body or his brief span of years. Far from seeing humankind as a species at war with nature, they believe devoutly that God gave man the burden of learning how to live responsibly with other living things. They also classify man, *Bani Aadam*, the "Sons of Adam," as a type of swine, on the same level as other nonruminating, unclean animals, like pigs, donkeys, monkeys, carnivores, and rodents, blessed only with the addition of a soul and a superior intellect.

> *I like to feel the stars turning over me, especially when the dew falls, ever so softly; making your garments soft, soft.*
> —KHUSHAYMI POEM

There were many star-filled nights spent reclining by a fire outside the "wool house" (tent). Husseyn and Sa'ad moved me deeply with their simple nobility, their lofty concepts of what a man should be. Honour and courage were the twin pillars of their lives, defining all actions and determining all responses. The population density in the Eastern Desert — roughly one person for every thirty square miles — is one of the lowest in the world, and it often struck me that this accounted for the extraordinary value the Ma'aza placed on human company and friendship, as well as for their anthropomorphic view of the land. Natural calamities were regarded as divine retribution for straying from the path of Allah. The land, humans, and God were inextricably linked.

"It is said the Palestinians ceased to believe in God," Husseyn once told me. "*Now* they have no homeland."

He was squatting by a circle of stones that marked the grave of a dear relative, placing ben-tree needles on the bare tomb as a mark of respect.

Guide us to the straight path,
The path of those whom You have favoured,
Not of those who have incurred Your wrath,
Nor of those who have gone astray.

—KORAN

We'd talked of Husseyn's father, Shaykh Sulimaan, of his wisdom and strength; we finally came across the head of the Khushmaan clan about halfway through the desert at Wadi Al-Markh. A group of three elaborately saddled camels were tied to large stones beside a black wool house.

"The shaykh!" Sa'ad exclaimed, pointing. As usual with the Bedouin, no one was in sight.

Husseyn nodded sagely, urging his camel into a trot. Mohammed complained that his legs were sore, his ass was sore, his … I told him to shut up. Circling back to ride alongside us, Husseyn explained his father was visiting one of his older sisters who now lived here a few thousand yards from the road.

Among his clan the approach of death from old age is not something to be feared. Pastoral nomads, like the Khushmaan, are really seminomadic, moving with their herds from site to site in search of grazing. When a person gets too old to keep up, he or she is moved to a location close to the Qena–Safaga road, where there is a well and a constant supply of fresh vegetables from passing trucks. The spot also means the old people will receive a steady flow of visitors journeying from the desert interior to the market towns along the Red Sea coast or Nile Valley. With the rigours of desert life over, they can pass their days in the comfort and constant company of family and friends.

Shaykh Sulimaan was clearly very old himself, a true desert patriarch with white beard, bright, piercing eyes, and an erect, imposing bearing that belied his deeply lined face and gnarled hands. Emerging from the tent, he grasped my arm with both hands and kissed my cheeks, saying, "*Salamaat,* you are the honoured guest of Allah."

Only Mohammed did not get kissed this time, but he still managed to look suitably respectful.

Khushmaan women are notoriously shy — "modest," they would say. They are generally seen as little more than distant black specks shooing sheep or goats between rocks and mountains. So it surprised me when the shaykh's ancient sister came out of her first and last permanent home and, uncovering a wizened, toothless face set with laughing, almost mischievous eyes, took my hand. The practice of veiling, as I now understand it, is optional and situational, and reflects the degree of comfort a woman feels with the company she's in.

This was no old folks' home, I thought, watching the sprightly woman laughing with two other men and some younger women as we rode off with the shaykh after a lunch of dates, fresh bread, and fruit.

Above a great plain there towers a mountain whose colour is like red ochre and dazzles the sight of those who look steadfastly upon it.

—DIODOURUS OF SICILY, FIRST CENTURY B.C.

The shaykh was clearly in charge now, and, apart from the perpetually whining Mohammed, all questions anyone had were deferred to his judgement. Mo certainly confirmed the very worst suspicions our hosts had of Egyptian city life.

About thirty camel miles from Safaga, Shaykh Sulimaan turned his mount north and took our little caravan well off the road, heading straight between the folds of massive lunar mountains deep toward the interior, the centre of the universe. I only learned much later that he wanted me to see the most revered mountain in all the Khushmaan lands, Jebel Shaayib, "Old Man Mountain." Known as Shaayib al-Banaat on maps, it is, at 7,150 feet, the highest mountain in Egypt outside the Sinai Peninsula. Diodourus was not the only visitor to find something profoundly impressive about this tremendous mass of rugged red granite.

George Murray, a Scottish cartographer and one of the few outsiders foolhardy enough to climb its treacherous and almost sheer face unshaded from a laser sun, described its formidable summit as "a monstrous webbed hand of seven smoothed fingers." Shaykh Sulimaan informed me that upon Shaayib grew one of the only two specimens known in the world of the "tree of light" (*dharamit an-nuur*). Its leaves, he said confidently, could cure blindness. Another reason for the tree's name was that, solely on one Thursday night a year, somewhere between April and May, it gave off a powerful luminescence visible for miles. I didn't question the shaykh. No one did.

Like his son, he had an extraordinary knowledge of this vast area. Not only was he intimately acquainted with the medicinal properties of various herbs and plants we encountered by desert springs, he also appeared to understand fully the delicate balance of interrelationships that sustain ecosystems.

"Man," the shaykh announced when we made camp at the foot of Jebel Shaayib, "is the king of Death." Carefully shifting pieces of charcoal around on the bowl of his *sheesha* pipe with a large pair of tweezers, he later elaborated on this. First he let the statement sink in. The rich Gulf Arabs' wanton overhunting of the wild Barbary sheep led to the animal's extinction. The Romans had reduced the once-plentiful forests of vital acacia to a few hundred scattered trees. The fact that he seemed to think the Romans had been in the area around 300,000 years ago in no way detracted from the force of his argument. Irresponsibility toward the environment that sustained human life was bad.

Sulimaan was perfectly aware of the limitations of the plants and animals that sustained his people. Cutting down a green branch, let alone a whole tree, was the ultimate taboo, the supreme folly. To feed camels, only the boughs could be shaken to detach leaves.

"A man who kills a tree to feed his camel once," went the saying, "is depriving the herds of his fellow men of food forever. He is a fool; he is not Khushmaan."

I wasn't foolhardy enough to contemplate tackling Jebel Shaayib's forbidding megalith; particularly after learning from Husseyn how many of its ravines and precipices were named after people who'd died plunging into them. As for the "tree of light," the last person known to have seen it, I discovered, was a Rashayda tribesman about four hundred years ago.

Men who dwell in the country are better than men who dwell in the city, for the former seek only the necessities of life from the soil, not the superfluities, and thus do not give their hearts to material things. Men who dwell on the land have a strong feeling for the common good and only those who have this feeling can dwell on the land.

—IBN KHALDUN, FOURTEENTH CENTURY

We set off down the Wadi Umm Dhalfa's desiccated trail. Its waters, in May, can be found only beneath the rocks and sand. We were heading for the Red Sea coast near Hurghada, not Safaga, in one of those frequent changes of plan typically Bedouin. Along the way we came across an acacia bearing Shaykh Sulimaan's *wasm*, or signature. Such marks proclaim ownership, or territorial right, and are accorded great respect among the nomads. *You are on my turf,* they point out, *use what you need with prudence, as any guest should do.* Belongings are frequently left tied up in such trees to protect them from wild animals. No one would dream of stealing them, thievery being one of the most cardinal of Ma'aza sins. Once, we even passed a tree in which a veiled woman sat, practically hidden behind leaves and branches.

On a planet where deserts are the only natural areas that are not rapidly dwindling — in fact, they are positively thriving — there is much we can learn from those who have over the millennia adapted to dwelling in such places and have even come to love them. It is perhaps too late, however, to think of relearning the meaning of words like "nobility" and "dignity" from these same people.

Shaykh Sulimaan was poignantly aware that the lifestyle of his people was just as threatened as the environment of which they were an intrinsic part. No one ever returned to "the countryside" after going to live in the towns or cities; the drift of pastoral nomads is one-way only. Still shunning radios and televisions, with the stars the only roof they want, the Khushmaan Ma'aza find the world is fast closing in on them, and with them one of our last links to a people who don't need a Green party to tell them how they should live in harmony with their planet. The Ma'aza were content, at one with their environment, in tune with the cycle of births, circumcisions, marriages, deaths, of moving on each day without necessarily having a destination in mind, of watching the great wheel of heaven slowly turn above their heads each night to signify the vast gyre on which they travel steadily through time. They were nature itself anthropomorphized.

"In thirty, forty years," the shaykh said with a sad, wise smile as we parted, "maybe there will be no one left who could guide you to Jebel Shaayib. But all is Allah's will, my friend." Husseyn told me the mountains themselves would mourn my absence.

Only Mohammed was glad to enter the raucous tourist village on the Red Sea coast where half-naked Germans drank beer beside turquoise waters stretching all the way back to Arabia, from whence the Khushmaan had come two centuries before.

CHAPTER FOURTEEN

BEHIND THE ZULU MASK

The LORD is a man of war:
The LORD is his name.
Pharaoh's chariots and his army hath he cast into the sea:
His chosen captains also are drowned in the Red Sea.
The depths have covered them:
They sank into the bottom as a stone.

—MOSES' SONG OF DELIVERANCE, EXODUS XV:2–5

In their way, the young Germans who ran most of El Giftun resort village were also in perfect harmony with their world. It was a large compound with small shuttered chalets backing away from a central reception-restaurant-bar structure all the way down to the beach. Finally free of Mohammed, I locked myself in my dark little room, showered away a pound of dust, and lay on the built-in bed. I felt claustrophobic. Everything seemed alien, unfamiliar, somehow too solid — as if matter were denser beyond the Ma'aza lands.

Finally readjusted somewhat, I put on swim shorts and a T-shirt — the garments undignified and comic — and went in search of some newspapers. Sitting in the spacious lobby, with its stucco walls, terra-cotta tiles, Bedouin rugs, and low, comfortable sofas, I began to leaf through those papers and magazines I'd managed to find. The world had been very busy while I'd been in the desert. There was a *Rashomon*-like quality to reading about the same event in *Time*, the *Egyptian Gazette*, the *International Herald-Tribune*, and the *Middle East Times*.

The intifada had been heating up in the Israeli-occupied Arab lands. Many Palestinians had been killed by Israel's army. Interviewed by a Lebanese magazine, Colonel Qaddafi had usefully predicted an "explosion of violence" around the world in reaction to this. King Hussein of Jordan's yacht had been fired on by an Israeli navy boat by mistake. The United States had "expressed concern" to Israel about the event. According to a Reuters report, a U.S. government spokesman, Richard Boucher, said, "The Israelis assured us that they have issued instructions to ensure that such an incident is not repeated." Every Arab paper expressed deep concern over the number of Soviet Jews immigrating to Israel. Columns that could all have been written by Dr. Shalaby cropped up everywhere.

In the *Egyptian Gazette*, Ambassador Muhammad Wafaa Hegazy announced that Arabs should be among the foremost countries supporting the American move aimed at revoking the United Nations resolution putting racism and Zionism on the same footing, because, he stated, Zionism was infinitely worse than racism:

> *It sounds rather funny that Zionists charge others of being anti-Semites, while they themselves are fanatic Semites, anti– all other races by conviction and practice. Zionism in the final account is to restore fully and completely what they call their Promised Land. To make it a homeland that is purely Jewish, inhabited by a society … purely Jewish, and ruled by a state … purely Jewish.*

Across the Arab world, old rifts were being repaired, new alliances formed.

A Swiss economic research institute called Pronos AG announced, in the *Egyptian Gazette*, that countries of black Africa were rapidly becoming a "Fourth World," dubbing the inhabitants of these countries "the problem children of the world." Arab papers eagerly printed any negative reaction from Western countries to Israel.

The African Development Bank announced that Africa's foreign debt now totalled $225.6 billion. Most countries were borrowing still more to pay off the interest on what they'd borrowed to pay off the interest. An Egyptian expert ventured to wonder whether, at this rate, it was conceivable that the African debt might never be repaid. Iran, for no discernible specific reason, called America "the epitome of state terrorism"; it must have been a slow day in Qom.

And everywhere in the Egyptian press, often featured in several separate stories spread throughout a single paper, was President Mubarak — signing treaties, making speeches, welcoming foreign dignitaries, announcing trade figures, hosting conferences, being *visible*. It was, I thought, not unlike the pharaonic concept of kingship; the king was the symbolic body of his country. Mubarak's little triumphs represented Egypt's importance and dignity in a world that was exploding, decaying, or collapsing around it. Surrounded by countries in various kinds of worse shape than any others in the world, it was vital for Egyptians to keep their spirits up. And Mubarak did just that; except that to maintain the respect of 55 million Egyptians, he'd have to succeed in some of the many tasks he'd set himself.

Just reading about these problems was giving me a headache. The oppressive nature of life's continual struggle in this part of the world — what I'd felt before leaving Cairo — descended once more. I walked down to the beach, and passing the line of thatched sunshades that stood between El Giftun's grounds and the sands, I stopped dead in my tracks.

On every side, tanned Western bodies, glistening with suntan oil, sprawled on deck chairs, chaise longues, and towels. Girls in spiderweb bikinis played volleyball with bronzed, muscular blond boys. Windsurfers leaned out from their huge multicoloured fins on a sea that was bluer than Paul Newman's eyes. I felt as if I'd wandered over the cliffs of hell and found Happy Valley on the other side. I'd forgotten people also came to the Middle East for fun. I'd virtually forgotten women went all but naked on the beach, too.

I walked over to a hut that served drinks and hamburgers, ordered a beer, and stretched out in the shade at the white sand's edge. The beach, I noticed, was enclosed at either end by a low wall. Behind the wall I could see a handful of Egyptian men and boys, in turbans and *gelabias;* the boys watching the antics of the windsurfers with rapt fascination; the men staring with a kind of hopeless yearning and wonderment at the women, at bouncing breasts, slim, shapely legs, flying blond curls, asses that rocked and rolled shamelessly, barely covered at all.

How odd it all was. Not a bow-shot from here, women hid their stout frames beneath shapeless shrouds, embarrassed to expose a mouth, an ankle. They also worked all day, expected little from their husbands, and would probably never travel farther than a dozen miles from where they lived. What thoughts went through their minds when they saw the way we Westerners lived? Envy? Pity? Disgust?

I think fascination is closest to an answer. The people of the Red Sea coast, where the desert meets the sea, are still unspoiled by tourist money; there hasn't been much to spoil them until very recently.

Seeing turquoise waters, vast blinding crescents of shimmering sand, I thought of all the resort paradises I'd visited. What was wrong with *this* picture, I realized, was *trees.* There weren't any. Beyond the sands of Hurghada's beaches there were only the steep reddish mountains that led back into the Ma'aza wilderness. Gradually trees are being brought in from the Nile Delta, but I liked the way it looked here without them. It resembled no other place I've seen, something stark and biblical about the miraculous respite of blue water after the parched deprivation of the desert. And such water, too, calm and utterly blue, stretching 125 miles to end at the even fiercer desert shores of Arabia. The sea promises so much more than just another desert on its far side. Did the original Arabian Khushmaan gaze across to the west, imagining it must be their promised land, just as Moses also promised his tribes better things beyond the eastern reaches of this same sea?

Mohammed, whose stay here with me was financed by his government, seemed just as out of place among the European tourists as he had been among the Ma'aza nomads. He walked toward me along the beach, wearing what he must have imagined was a quintessentially Western vacation outfit: Day-Glo-green baseball cap, lurid pink Bermuda shorts, baggy T-shirt emblazoned with a Caribbean motif that proclaimed something about surfing. He was no more comfortable surrounded by all this naked female flesh than the peasants in their *gelabias* were.

Seeing me talking with a couple of Californian girls — who, I soon deduced, were expensive "escorts" flown out by a Saudi prince who kept a villa nearby — he mistook the easy intimacy Westerners of opposite sexes are accustomed to sharing with each other as evidence of the legendary easy virtue of foreign women. In the case of these two girls — *if* he'd had a few thousand dollars to spare, that is — he was basically right. The fact that these girls had talked with me, and I with them, intrigued him; he kept urging me to ask them to join us for a meal, drinks, an outing.

But their evenings were occupied. An expensive four-wheel-drive vehicle, driven by a murderous-looking chauffeur in the classic Saudi white cotton *gelabia* and *kaffiyeh*, picked the girls up around five each afternoon, glaring at any other males in their vicinity with a proprietary air, returning his passengers just before dawn. Whatever they did during this period clearly tired them out, for they rarely appeared until after lunch, looking incongruously pale and worn, seeming to sport more and more jewellery as the days passed. I never asked them anything directly, but I sensed they knew I knew what they were, and it embarrassed them, spoiled the facade they wished to project of rich girls on vacation.

Since the peace treaty with Israel, Hurghada has become a favourite resort for wealthy Saudis, many of whom have built palatial houses all along the coastline. Although, I speculated, the coast here could hardly be much different from the Arabian shores 125 miles away on the other side of the Red Sea, Egypt is still a hedonistic paradise compared to Saudi Arabia. That was the difference. Just as I'd seen them do in Los Angeles, London, Paris, and even Bombay, these wealthy Saudi princes — they were always "princes" — lived by night, gambling through the small hours, drinking secretly in their rooms, where call girls were shipped in by the legion.

Cairo was no different, its hotel lobbies dotted with the personal servants of these "princes" waiting for their masters, with a rope of worry beads fashioned from semiprecious stones always dangling from their hands as they stared aimlessly into space, a fat roll of dollars, a pack of Marlboros, and a gold Cross pen invariably crammed behind the semitransparent material of their little breast pockets, the only sign of evolution I've ever perceived in classical Arab dress. They were prosperous servants, but servants all the same. In a feudal state there are only two classes in society.

In Hurghada, however, the "princes" had villas and were much less visible than they were in Western party zones; but their money was everywhere in evidence. It was helping finance the largest tourist development in Egypt, the brave new world of tourist Egypt, an attempt to lure those travellers who'd "done" the Nile trip back again, *and* an attempt to seize a piece of the lucrative business catering to those with no interest in ruins and history, but an annual need for sun and sand away from their dreary northern winters.

Judging by what I saw everywhere, this new promotional campaign had been waged successfully only in Germany. Arab countries are among the few foreign places where Germans feel free of the Nazi stigma and are least likely to run into Jews to make them experience that collective guilt they rarely admit to but that runs deep beneath the surface.

In such a setting I contemplated a story that, urged by his ally, the mufti of Jerusalem, Hitler had once apparently even contemplated converting to Islam. The *Egyptian Gazette* had reported, without comment: the Austrian president, Kurt Waldheim, apologized to Israel for what he still maintained he hadn't done during World War II. The writer did not question the contradiction in this.

The Red Sea, particularly between the straits of Gebal and Tīrān in the southern Sinai Peninsula, may contain the finest scuba diving in the world. Not sufficiently skilled — not sufficiently *trusted* is closer to the truth — to operate and maintain serious equipment upon which lives depend, the Egyptians have allowed Germans to run all the scuba facilities in the Red Sea hotels. With them came windsurfing and other diversions, including embarrassingly amateur nightly entertainments, which were inexplicably popular with Mohammed and other vacationing Cairenes. One could see the advantage of this arrangement; it guaranteed a German-speaking staff for a predominantly German clientele, and it also abrogated Egyptians of any responsibility for diving accidents and the concomitant shame that would be even harder to bear than the accidents themselves.

Two thousand years of foreign oppression obviously does little for a people's sense of responsibility. Now the Egyptians instinctively distance themselves from any situation with a potential for problems. The bureaucratic unwillingness to be the person who makes a decision — any decision — stems from the same root. An inferiority complex is one pernicious side effect of colonialism that has an exceedingly long — perhaps permanent — half-life.

I hadn't really seen Hurghada yet, so late that first afternoon, when the sun was content to bake instead of broil, Mo and I hired a car to take us north a few miles along the tidy, narrow coast road. Everywhere were buildings in a process of being built that implied it had gone on long and would possibly never end. The result was a gigantic construction site of small unfinished hotels, villas, inchoate restaurants — too much visible concrete, chaos, and mess. Even hotels already open were still being built, littered with workers' equipment and garbage — not in just one spot but in several areas that would one day be bars, diving "schools," swimming pools, more chalets. I asked Mohammed why those responsible didn't finish one project at a time so that guests wouldn't feel they'd been hoodwinked by brochures that frequently featured more "artists' impressions" than photographs. For all I knew, people arrived here at hotels that were still mere concrete skeletons, without walls, let alone beds, as had once often happened in Spain in the 1970s.

"Much development here," was Mo's enlightening reply.

Too much development was the truth. Since becoming Egypt's most profitable industry, tourism, under the guidance of its brilliant minister, Fouad Sultan, was the first major area of the public sector to encourage privatization. Allowed to deal in U.S. dollars — non-Egyptians cannot pay bills in local currency — foreign hotel chains, particularly German ones, have moved in to ensure cosseted Westerners will feel they've never left home, as has happened virtually all over the world. If you're paying five-star prices, you want five-star service. This has its advantages but its disadvantages, too. While the Hilton in Luxor is the Hilton anywhere, the Egyptian-owned (and disastrously named) Egotel, adjacent to the Winter Palace, is also excellent, at a fraction of the price. The Egotel group, a government enterprise like the Misr Travel organization, maintains a high standard in all its locations but fails to attract mistrustful foreigners, who book familiar names. PR and information are not the Egyptian Tourist Authority's strongest point. Again, this reflects on the Egyptians' low sense of self-esteem — the unquestioned assumption that foreign-managed establishments must be better. Hotel management colleges, as far as I know, teach the same information to all students, regardless of national origin.

But in Hurghada this sudden privatization has also brought with it what will become a major problem, I suspect. Wealthy Egyptians with no knowledge whatsoever of the hotel trade or the principles of commercial architecture are building small resorts and hotels on any remotely suitable land they can get hold of. Jerry-built, badly run, these hotels will do immeasurable damage to the Red Sea's image abroad if they start attracting Western guests — and Western travel writers. It has taken Spain twenty years to erase its tarnished tourist image.

Despite the pits and scaffolding and concrete slabs, the approach to Hurghada town is still extravagantly beautiful. Past a store called — for reasons best known to its owner — "Horse Foam," was a large billboard featuring a man in a denim shirt and the legend CONCRETE: THE MASCU-LINE LOOK. It advertised, I learned, a brand of shirt, but it also suggested something about the different response an Egyptian like Mohammed had to Hurghada's frenzied development. The concrete all around us symbolized progress, action, Egypt on the move, and that was pleasing, manly, *masculine.*

The centre of Hurghada is small and exceedingly charming. The bazaar is much cheaper than those in Cairo or Luxor and still features many tiny stores that sell "real" things: refrigerators, rope, ceramic toilets, fruits and vegetables. Locals still shop alongside tourists, who pay scarcely more than they do. Vendors are relaxed and genuinely friendly, proud of their wares and remarkably unconcerned about making a sale, quoting prices not far removed from what they actually expect. The bargainer hardened from Cairo and Luxor must adjust quickly or make a fool of himself here. An item for twenty Egyptian pounds cannot be had for ten piastres; seventeen or eighteen pounds, a 20 percent discount, seemed about the norm. It has, however, always struck me as incongruous that the same people who agonize at home about helping "the Third World" haggle over a two-dollar cab fare when they're in that world. An extra fifty cents is a great help to an Egyptian taxi driver.

Mohammed had a friend in Hurghada, it turned out, a man named Omar who had some official function connected with tourism. We met him in a shack resembling something in a cowboy ghost town, apparently the headquarters of the local tourist police. If all went as planned in this area, I thought, the tourist police would need to do some construction of their own pretty soon. Omar was a pudgy, likable man who vaguely reminded me of Rodney Dangerfield. His veined, exophthalmic eyes spoke of secret excesses, and a burgeoning paunch evinced more Islamically permissible vices. Like bureaucrats everywhere, he had nothing so pressing to do that he could not hang out with us for most of the next few days.

Discovering Omar's brand-new Peugeot Estate was not a surprise; half of Peugeot's net profit must come from Egypt since it's the only make of car you see in many places. We motored lazily into a newer part of town — half-finished, of course — past a stunningly beautiful mosque, gleaming white in the low, perfect sunlight. Remarkable in that it *was* finished. Mosques seem to have less trouble getting built than do other structures. Muslims also do not seem to have the misguided urge, rampant among Christians and Jews, to trash architectural traditions and construct places of worship that look like airports, warehouses, rockets, fast-food outlets, or prisons. The clean, simple lines, harmonic proportions, soaring minarets, shining domes, and restrained decorations of Islamic architecture have a timeless beauty, a look both daringly modern and resonantly ancient.

Omar wanted, however, to take us for refreshments, not prayers. We pulled up in one of the broader streets of the bazaar and sat outside a tiny shop drinking "Thumbs Up" cola. Next to us was a little souvenir store featuring a variety of exquisite shells and corals, as well as a vast selection of badly stuffed local fish, including a five-foot shark with a rather foolish, gummy expression on its grinning face.

Omar sat back, his paunch comfortably expanding, and watched a couple of Western girls in shorts and T-shirts walk by. He looked over at me, smirking. "Nice, no?" he said. "I think forty likes twenty."

Was he implying he was only forty? He looked older. I asked him, jokingly, if this was how he spent his days.

"No harm looking, dreaming," he replied.

His wife and family were in Cairo. The children had to be in school, and there were no good schools in Hurghada, so he lived alone. Sex was very much on his mind, but unlike other men I'd spoken with, he was open about it. The restrictions of Cairene Islam seemed to loosen up out here. They had to, with all the Westerners in their bikinis, drinking and dancing into the small hours. A dozen people walking by called out greetings to Omar. Clearly he was well known and well liked. I mentioned this, and he said, "Yes, I'm king here. King Omar of Hurghada." He laughed. There was a lazy affability about him and the town that seemed to go well together, were made for each other.

Yet he was lonely. Because of harsh economic realities, many men across the East are separated from their families the way Omar was. It had been a way of life. He'd worked in Kuwait alone before this, living in one air-conditioned box, working in another air-conditioned box.

"There's nothing to do there," he said. "Work and sleep, work and sleep. When the oil runs out, everyone will leave. And the first plane out will be the emir on his way to Switzerland." As things turned out, the emir had fled Saddam Hussein's forces by driving to Saudi Arabia, not flying to Switzerland.

There was a lot of resentment among the men I met who'd worked in Kuwait and Saudi for the rich, idle Arabs. In some ways Iraq's invasion of Kuwait was not unpopular across the Middle East. It was felt these cash-engorged feudal states should spread their wealth around a little more among their fellow Muslims rather than employing them as cheap labour, paying them a fraction of what their own citizens earned. Lowest in the pecking order of the labour force in these countries were the Muslims from India and Pakistan, who did the menial jobs. Next came the poorer Arabs, like Omar, who toiled in the administration or at technical posts. "Kuwaitis don't like to work," Omar told me. "But who does?"

He drove Mohammed and me out to see what he thought of as the best hotel in Hurghada, the Arabiya. A vast, grandiose structure, it looked more or less completed but far too large for its current needs. A Coptic woman, with an oddly lascivious manner and Western clothes a size too small, showed us around. A huge swimming pool had a circular bar in its centre, the stools under water, but it was not functioning, and its shelves were bare of bottles and glasses. The pristine white lines of spacious two-storey rooms stretched away on either side down to the sea, their arches demonstrating a pleasingly simple Islamic geometry.

The interior of the main building was not so free of excess. Unnecessarily lavish, it culminated in a monstrosity called the "Taboo Disco." As if the architect had been told to indulge his wildest fantasy, the place was so howlingly vulgar it had a weird charm about it. Every inch of the interior had been moulded out of concrete to look like a grotto, and sprayed with glittering gold paint that gave all the bumpy curves and stalactites a slimy, membranous appearance — like being in the belly of some wealthy alien beast. Omar tried a few clumsy dance steps on the glossy floor; the Coptic woman laughed, joining him to shake her heavy, prominent breasts from side to side, saying we should all come down to see the place in action that night; it would be fun.

Next she showed us a three-hundred-seat indoor theatre, its concrete floor slanting down steeply to a well-equipped stage. There was a bar here, too. Indeed, there were bars everywhere in this place — dozens of them, all empty. A handful of guests sat outside, served by waiters who fetched drinks and snacks.

Again we sat down, the woman asking us what we wanted to drink. I ordered an arak, but Omar and Mo stuck to tea. The king of Hurghada looked as if he were tempted to order something stronger, but he would never do so in public. He picked up a copy of the Arabic *Al-Akbar* newspaper.

On its cover was a photograph of King Farouk with a beautiful Western woman by his side. The late king looked prosperously fat, even compact in a bulky way, as fat rich people often do.

I asked Omar why Farouk was on the cover. He replied that the paper regularly featured racy articles about the monarch's decadent ways. After nearly forty years, Egyptians were still fascinated by their last foreign ruler, and this very Islamic newspaper still saw the need to spotlight his corrupt lifestyle, perhaps as a cautionary manoeuvre. King Farouk, Omar informed me, had the juice from ten roasted pigeons squeezed for him to drink each morning, "for *strength*!" A man with Farouk's busy sex life, it was implied, needed strength. Omar discussed all this rather mournfully, playing up to the Coptic woman and the odd Westerner in a swimsuit who passed, but conveying adequately enough that he needed no aphrodisiacs in his life.

I forced Mohammed to taste my arak which he did reluctantly, like someone puffing a joint of grass fully convinced it will enslave him, transform him into a Mr. Hyde incapable of self-control. "Now I'll go to hell," he commented, only half joking, wincing at the taste. Omar, in typical Egyptian fashion, tried to make me feel more comfortable about drinking alcohol, saying one or two were all right. After a while in Muslim countries you begin to feel like a hopeless reprobate, ordering a drink alone. Being drunk was the sin; you "lost your mind." And, Omar added, "mind is gift of God. It should not be lost." Islam's great emphasis on the mind, as Dr. Shalaby proved, meant anything that clouded it was evil. Thus, consciousness never got to change pace here; conversation never loosened up, no one relaxed. Indeed, as the day's formidable caffeine quotient built up, the reverse happened. By late evening, everyone was twanging with tension, babbling and chain-smoking like cocaine fiends.

The sun was low now, colours returning richly to the landscape as shadows slid across the yellow rocks and dust. Out on the sea, a large liner headed south out of the Gulf of Suez. We walked down to the spit of land reclaimed by the hotel to form an artificial bay. Named the *Maxim Gorky*, the vessel, Omar explained, was heading for the little port of Safaga about forty-five miles farther south. Soviet-registered, it would be carrying passengers on a world cruise.

"All old people," he said. "You know, they like to see it before they leave it." He chuckled.

The Soviets were apparently big in the world-cruise business, such voyages costing upward of $35,000 per head. When he mentioned the sum, Omar's voice had the tone of someone discussing the African foreign debt. Such amounts of money were impossible to conceive.

In the clear, golden light the *Maxim Gorky* looked shabby, badly in need of rust-proofing and paint. I said I wouldn't pay $35,000 to spend four months on board *that*, but Mohammed and Omar were not seeing what I saw. For them the ship symbolized something else. To sail away, around the whole world. *That* was the dream.

No place transforms itself as much as Egypt does when the evening comes. Back in Hurghada, lights were twinkling on in the bazaar, which now thronged with people, as cooling winds drifted in from the darkened sea. The three of us drank sugarcane juice squeezed by another of Omar's many business acquaintances.

We were watching tourists enter the "Santa Claus Bazaar," where a line of German-designed T-shirts with charming Jamaican-style emblems all over them were the hottest items. RED SEA: NO PROBLEM, they announced, or HURGHADA: SAND, SURF, FUN. Everyone I saw seemed to be wearing one.

Smells of spices and cooking came wafting from all sides; men sat smoking narghiles, chatting animatedly on stools in the street. The whole atmosphere of the town had changed; even its features had altered under a sky of pavonine blue riven with flaming red. It no longer looked dusty and bleached, its forms and colours now clear and vibrant, its inhabitants, like the other creatures of the desert, free to wander without that blinding inferno above their heads. The green neon lights on the new mosque blazed above busy streets, and the call of the muezzin began to sound from its loudspeakers, even this voice sounding milder and less reproving than its counterparts in Cairo. The word "alchemy" derives from *Al-Khem*, "of Egypt," and alchemy is all about transmutation, about changing the base into the transcendent.

The drive back to El Giftun was also transformed, the concrete of construction sites now no more than elegant shadows standing out against the flashing dark ripples of that subdued sea, its colour drained away up into a vast night.

Back in my room, I played with the television, finding only the God Spot, an unnaturally deep, rich voice intoning the Koran over beauty shots of sunsets behind mountains, of green valleys in early twilight, of lakes reflecting golden rays. Besides this "program" — a thrice-daily affair — I found only political discussions or football on the TV here. They were, after all, the two most popular forms of entertainment in Egypt.

Mohammed was excited over dinner — for which Omar joined us, eating two heaped plates from the extravagant buffet, not apparently having to pay for anything. Tonight, Mo said, the "Action Team" would be performing a cabaret starting at 9:00 P.M. The "Action Team" was what the young Germans who ran the scuba and windsurfing facilities called their performance troupe. It had an inappropriately paramilitary ring to it, I thought.

I left Omar and Mo, returning to my room through the outside patio where dozens of much older, and much fatter, Germans were drinking and making a lot of noise. Since my room was nearby, I hoped they didn't intend to stay there all evening — which, as it turned out, they did. A news program was now on the TV: many items concerning President Mubarak, many serious discussions taking place, much crudely shot footage of riots in the Israeli-occupied territories interspersed with these serious discussions. The program looked as if it would go on all evening, so at nine I wandered over the darkened grounds to the walled-off open amphitheatre, an essential feature of all hotels here, where this cabaret Mohammed seemed so captivated with was already in progress. I stood at the entrance, not far from the stage, unable and unwilling to find Mo among the throng of silhouettes seated in an elevated semicircle on concrete benches.

Immediately the attraction was obvious. It had nothing to do with the performance and everything to do with the performers. The bronzed German girls, whose bodies they'd built themselves with weights and the daily exercise they peddled on the beach, wore "naughty" outfits onstage, which were largely irrelevant to the skits they performed in. The older German tourists, of course, who brought on their vacations the kind of lowbrow general-interest magazines with nude girls on the cover found everywhere in Europe, would view all this as nothing out of the ordinary. But in a country where some foreign fashion magazines had their underwear ads censored, this was hot stuff indeed.

The sketch I watched seemed also to contain another message. To a prerecorded sound track of tribal drums, a flaxen-haired girl in a miniskirt and a kind of bush shirt unbuttoned to her navel was claiming to be lost in the jungle. From the wings sprang a stereotypical Zulu — a young German painted and dressed as one — wearing a demonic mask. He crept up behind the girl and roared frighteningly; but the girl merely turned, shooing him away, unafraid. The Zulu disappeared only to reemerge seconds later wearing an even more hideous mask. He repeated the same action a few times, until finally, exasperated, he removed his mask. Seeing his real face, the girl screamed in terror and ran offstage. The audience roared with laughter. I wondered who had dreamed up this "entertainment," what part of their subconscious had unwittingly led them to this stark truth disguised as a stupid joke. The realities of Africa — or Egypt — were what no tourist wished to look upon. Kenyan safaris were the Africa they'd come for; famine and violent anarchy in Somalia or the Sudan were not. A bleeding heart is often guilt for a turning stomach, for finding fear and revulsion where compassion should be.

Leaving the amphitheatre and its gales of laughter, I walked down to the deserted beach and sat in a deck chair listening to the sea splash beneath silver moonlight, looking up at the eternal constancy of stars. With them so close, pulsing so brightly, in such unfamiliar profusion, it was easy to see countless patterns assert themselves, then give way to others. At one point a gigantic pharaonic flail and crook appeared quite distinctly, composed of many stars all equal in magnitude. Distant and crude laughter sounded from the amphitheatre. How, I wondered, could people come to Egypt and watch such mindless bullshit when Karnak and Luxor lay a mere five hours' drive away through the desert? How could they remain untouched by what the country really offered? Even the warm silence of this night by the Red Sea seemed infinitely rich.

Unable to sleep, partly because of the Biergarten hullabaloo beyond my door, I walked back to the beach later on again. But its atmosphere had changed. The peace of sea and stars was now broken by the thud of music from El Giftun's disco, thoughtfully situated away from the chalets near the shore. I also realized the muffled grunts and groans I could hear sporadically were not produced by hectic dance-floor exertions but by a young couple making love behind me in the shadows of a beach hut. A pair of wobbling, disembodied buttocks gleamed in a pool of moonlight, covered and uncovered by a kneeling darkened form that thrust at them roughly to and fro with a wet, slapping sound.

I wandered over to the disco, intending to have a nightcap, something to aid sleep. I fully expected to find the place packed and was mildly surprised to find it completely deserted apart from a lone bartender who seemed relieved to have a customer. Although a change from Zamfir, the noise of Prince was deafening, alien, and unwelcome. I gulped down the brandy I'd had to scream for and left quickly, my head clanging.

Omar and Mo had had a great time that night, they wanted me to know. "Forty likes twenty," Omar said again, grinning his self-deprecating Rodney Dangerfield grin. We were sitting having coffee in a smaller and very pleasant hotel farther south the next day.

I mentioned I might like to go back into the desert for a while, that I liked it there, liked the people. Omar chuckled, mentioning what rascals the Bedouin were, what trouble they caused the police. Some tribes were apparently involved in the dope trade, bringing cocaine and hashish in from Israel. Israel was presented as the real culprit here, naturally.

Something else also obsessed Omar. There had been stories of locals finding car tires washed up on the shore full of drugs abandoned by Turkish or Israeli traffickers tackled by the Egyptian Coast Guard. These locals had sold the drugs and become rich men. The incident had stuck in Omar's mind; he fantasized about it, about sudden wealth. "Your life is made," he told me more than twice. "Made."

Wouldn't that make him no better than the Bedouin? I asked. He didn't seem to understand the parallel — as if *finding* the drugs and then selling them was far different from first buying them. The cost of living was rising in Hurghada, he said by way of answer, property prices nearly doubling in a year.

Wouldn't that make many poor locals rich? I inquired. Apparently not. The government somehow owned most of the land, so the government would get rich.

But, I thought, this was one government that needed to get rich. With the exception of Port Safaga, which was really no more than a grandiose dock surrounded by a handful of tattered dwellings, smaller than a village, the whole coast had been nearly unpopulated until quite recently. The "locals" were really retired nomads or people from elsewhere. Ownership of land was an alien concept to nomads, so no one had bothered to "own" any up to now. There was plenty of it, and there had been no demand for it until the Ministry of Tourism noticed what the Israelis had done with the shores of the Gulf of Aqaba when they'd occupied the Sinai. They decided the Red Sea coast would be similarly attractive to vacationing Westerners. And they were right. Omar returned to dreaming about dope wealth washing up in tires. "Your life is made," he repeated. His, I assumed, had been unmade — like his lonely bed, when I saw it.

Later that day Mohammed received some important communication from Cairo, instructing him to accompany me to the southern Sinai. I'd hoped to go alone, particularly since I was taking care of him and not vice versa, but I was learning to enjoy seeing the country through his eyes, albeit perversely. He was a big, spoiled child really, from a large middle-class family who doted on him. He had the fears of a child, and this job of his, easy as it was — a permanent vacation, in fact — seemed taxing. I wondered what he was expected to do when he returned, or while he was with me, for that matter. Would he write reports? Was he supposed to shield me from shameful sights? Or none of the above? Was he just another generous if misguided gesture by a government that was overly worried about its country's image abroad?

Omar had invited us to his house for tea that afternoon. It was a tiny concrete cube in a line of identical structures, all recently built, containing two minute and forlornly bare rooms, with a rudimentary kitchen. He seemed embarrassed by the place, pointedly calling it "King Omar's palace." We sat outside on a narrow porch. A herd of ugly brown-black Egyptian sheep was being driven past up a nearby alley by a young Bedouin girl. The animals store body fat in their tails, which gives them the appearance of huge shaggy beavers.

"She maybe wife for you, Mohammed," Omar remarked, indicating the slim black-shrouded figure with her smiling face. Both men laughed. Obviously a Bedouin wife was a joke in Cairo.

A donkey cart piled high with watermelons slowly clip-clopped up the steep hill leading out of town, scenting the air as it passed. A pickup truck pulled up opposite, and Omar dashed into his house, running out with a jug, which the truck driver filled from a large aluminum urn. "Fresh milk," Omar said, returning with it. The milkman waved at us, more customers appearing at his side. Two colossal women entirely concealed beneath black chadors waddled past, huge watermelons balanced on their heads, plastic baskets brimming with vegetables in both hands. It was a pleasant scene, peaceful and simple, apart from the odd evidence of technology. Like Omar, it was slow — slow and dreamy, yearning for something that was not really expected to arrive.

Deciding we'd had enough of his house, Omar drove us to the oldest hotel on the coast, the Sheraton. A fat, circular tower of several storeys, the building seemed architecturally inappropriate, part of a development that had never happened, had taken instead a different direction. It seemed no busier than the Arabiya except for a more Western feeling of order and control about it. Everything was in place, everything was ready, everything had been *finished*, long ago.

After dinner, Omar promised, we would go to another hotel where there would be "belly dancers." He rolled his bulging eyes, saying, "You like belly dancers?" I reassured him I did, knowing even this innocuous and traditional entertainment was a rare and risqué treat in Islamic Egypt or the Egypt that bent over backward to appease an orthodox minority.

This other hotel proved to be a discreetly lavish compound, with privately owned condominium-style houses, as well as villas, chalets, and rooms.

One entire block of these houses was owned by a Saudi prince who, along with his family and retinue, was occupying them right now. His block had its own private beach, roped off and patrolled by bodyguards. The entertainment was to be staged in a small, intimate area just outside the main building. The prince, a huge, imposing figure in white robes and *kaffiyeh*, was already seated in a segregated area, surrounded by many turbulent children, shy, silent women, and menacing-looking men. Omar and Mohammed clutched their Thumbs Ups, watching the little stage eagerly.

Soon the "Oriental orchestra" — something like Mantovani on opium or at the wrong speed — started up, and three men, two of them dressed in a pantomime horse, pranced out, performing a rather ludicrous dance that delighted the prince's children and had everyone else clapping along. This was followed by two plain-looking women in traditional, if overdone, Bedouin dress, performing a dance with walking sticks, which, I knew from experience, was a version of a traditional wedding dance. It wasn't particularly clever, and one of the women dropped her stick while trying to balance it on her head.

I asked where the belly dancer was. Omar looked around him, perhaps assessing the nature of the audience, saying, "Maybe not appearing tonight. I don't know." He and Mo became restless at this thought, looking less interested in a sort of nomadic clog dance two overweight men performed next.

"Maybe we leave?" Omar asked speculatively. I shrugged. Traditional Bedouin dancing was not what anyone had come to see.

"Perhaps Action Team is on at the Giftun?" Mo wondered.

We all left. It was just another of life's many disappointments, nothing serious. I said good night to them in the hotel lobby as they headed out toward the amphitheatre. We had a boat to catch early the next day, so I intended to make some earplugs and get an early night.

Coming in from the patio were the two Californian "escorts." It was an odd hour to find them in. I asked how things were. Things didn't seem to be very good, but they didn't explain. I told them I was off to the Sinai and wished them a pleasant trip.

"Maybe we could come along?" the blonder, bustier, tackier one asked. Her friend looked doubtful. I told them they'd have to get tickets for the boat, and I wasn't sure where this could be achieved at 10:00 P.M.

"Well," the girl said, slightly annoyed, pushing forward her chest as if its temptation were irresistible. "Couldn't you fix us up? We're bored here."

"Maybe he could show us around Cairo later," her friend suggested. The crudeness of their assumptions and the manner in which they stated them offended me after Arab restraint and courtesy. Nonetheless, I said it was possible, telling them to try me at the Rameses, knowing they'd have found another mark, another john, long before I returned to Cairo. In their chamois and silk and jewels and makeup, they looked faintly pathetic out here — like the Action Team and its tawdry pseudoeroticism. Go back to Santa Monica, I thought. All of you go back to where you belong. The only problem was that the Orient I loved wanted to go back *with* all of them, and the part of it that didn't would want *me* back where I belonged, too.

CHAPTER FIFTEEN

FROM PEACE TO PIZZA

Thou shalt neither vex a stranger nor oppress him: for ye were strangers in the land of Egypt.

—EXODUS XXIII:21

A cab driver who kept telling us we were going to the wrong place dropped us, on Mohammed's absolute insistence, at the barrier post to a deserted quay. We lugged our cases toward an enormous but somewhat ragged vessel called *Noor al-Hussein,* the "Light of Hussein" — the same name King Hussein of Jordan's American-born Lebanese wife, Lisa Halaby, had taken on becoming queen. Her yacht — even if the Israeli navy *had* blown it up — would probably look better than its namesake. In a smaller marina to our right, stout new cruisers were filling up with Westerners staggering under the weight of deep-sea diving equipment. A toothless old-timer, sweeping the quay with a bald broom, said the *Noor al-Hussein* was not going to the Sinai today — or in the foreseeable future. I sat watching Mohammed, fascinated with how he would handle his problem.

"Ticket agency told me this boat," he protested. "They told me come here and meet them." I nodded, not about to offer him any assistance. We sat on our cases. It was fifteen minutes before the boat we were supposed to take was due to leave. Mohammed grew nervous, looking around helplessly. Then he boarded the *Noor al-Hussein*, and emerged with a sinewy geriatric who'd clearly just woken up. No, the man said, his boat was definitely not sailing for the Sinai in fifteen minutes; if it were, he'd know about it, and it wasn't. Mohammed looked panic-stricken, no doubt realizing both the driver and the sweeper had been right — or, more terrible still, that *he'd* been wrong. He ran off back to the administrative building at the quayside entrance. I looked at my watch, reassuring myself that the boat we were supposed to be on would probably not depart anywhere near the appointed time. This was Hurghada, not Zurich. Ten minutes later a twenty-seater minibus screamed up the dock, Mohammed waving frantically through its open door.

Arrived at where our driver had wanted to drop us in the first place, we found a long line of people, mainly young Westerners, and their luggage waiting in a muddy alley by gates that led to another quay. Officials were being officious, not letting anyone near the vessel we could barely see beyond the gates, offering no explanations. Soldiers — boys really, in untidy, crumpled uniforms — stood laconic guard with prewar bolt-action Enfield rifles slung over their shoulders. One had a broken fly on his pants gaping; another had buttoned his jacket unevenly; still another had no laces on his filthy boots. No wonder the Israelis had won so many wars.

In the lineup of weary people, I recognized the huge-breasted German girl who'd caused such a disturbance in Aswan. She wore the same baggy tank top and squatted over a rucksack, one grimy breast bulging out beneath an arm. She looked as if she'd walked from Aswan — or done many strenuous favours for truck drivers while hitchhiking. Everyone seemed irritable, and no one more so than Mohammed, who kept complaining about his "ticket agents," asking me where they were. How would I know? He bothered numerous officials, flashing his government credentials, which seemed to impress no one.

Eventually, half an hour after the stated time of departure, everyone was allowed to approach the ship. As it came into view, the passengers began to groan. Facing us was the most decrepit old hulk imaginable — something like the one Robert Mitchum had captained in a forties' movie I recalled, where he'd played a hard-bitten old sea dog who'd transport anything or anyone anywhere for a price, no questions asked. It didn't look large enough, let alone sturdy enough, to hold all the passengers now showing their passports and tickets before being herded up a rickety wooden gang-plank onto it. We'd be entering international waters — indeed, the Gulf of Suez must constitute some of the most international waters on earth — before disembarking at Sharm al-Sheikh only fifty miles away, yet seven or eight hours by ship, across the northernmost boundary of the Red Sea.

Mohammed was still cursing under his breath and wondering above it about the ticket agents who were supposed to meet us. I gathered that something had gone disastrously wrong from his professional point of view. No one got fired from the Egyptian bureaucracy, I reminded him.

True, the boat was a bit of a disappointment — but then I hadn't known what to expect anyway, thus was not *that* disappointed. Mo was. Up to the moment we pulled away from the quayside, he argued with officials and peered into the distance with exaggerated gestures, looking for his ticket agents. He'd been conned — and if he'd been conned, the government had been conned. He acted as if the whole universe had been conned.

There were two areas where passengers could sit on the boat: an open upper deck littered with capstans, ropes, and tarpaulins, and an interior, lower room with bench seats, grimy tables, and a squalid galley, which served candy bars, tea, and coffee. Everyone quickly staked a claim to a spot, torn between getting a seat out of the sun and enjoying the sea air while facing the prospect of being roasted alive as the day progressed. There wasn't an inch of extra room. A young American couple with ruck-sacks stripped down to their swimsuits and promptly went to sleep. By the time we reached the Sinai, their skin looked as if someone had taken an oxyacetylene torch to it. Others crouched in whatever shadows were available, constantly obliged to move as the vessel turned.

We watched Hurghada's coastline slowly dissolve into the shimmering distance, plowing through azure waters past a series of deserted islands that were no more than barren platelets of rock and sand without a single sign of life on them. They looked like cartoon islands — without the palm trees.

After a couple of hours the deck looked like a scene from *The Ancient Mariner:* people throwing up over the rails, huddled beneath shirts and handkerchiefs, groaning and sweltering, gazing hopefully for any sign of land. On a map the distance seemed negligible, but, although the ancient turbines powering the vessel made an extraordinary amount of noise, the ship moved at an agonizing pace. Once in the open sea, with no landmarks, I couldn't even tell whether we were actually moving at all. A fresh, salty breeze deceived those in the open sun into thinking they weren't being fried alive.

Mohammed had found a bench in the restaurant, urging me to come down with him before someone else grabbed it. The galley crew occupied one whole table themselves, playing the noisiest game of *sheshbesh* conceivable, slamming the counters down with a continual clacking sound, shouting, and chain-smoking. If you really insisted, they'd boil up some dishwater and throw a tea bag into it for you, or even sell you chocolate bars filled with synthetic coconut tasting of Brylcreem.

Mo looked despondent. "What about *meal?*" he kept saying. "Ticket agent promised full meal on board." He was a man of regular habits; the thought of going without his lunch drove him into a tantrum bordering on lunacy. Perhaps he was hypoglycemic? I bought him a dozen candy bars and three bags of potato chips that tasted like something that had lived in the U-tube beneath a kitchen sink for several years, been beaten flat, fried in old hair oil, then coated completely with salt. They made you terminally thirsty, too — which, when the warm colas and dishwater ran out, proved something of a problem. Pale as a baker's apprentice, a woman who'd perhaps eaten a bag of these chips moaned and wailed, clutching her stomach, helped back and forth to the washroom by her friends — an odd collection of women who looked like middle-aged punk rockers, wore too many studs in their ears, and were accompanied by a fat, shifty man who resembled a debauched Turkish pirate.

This washroom, when I finally had need of it myself, was something else again. The door locked with part of a wire coat hanger — not that you wanted to lock yourself in *there*. The toilet bowl brimmed with a vast array

of shit, and the smell was stupendous; within a second I was retching, trying to breathe through my shirt, and eventually obliged to stop breathing.
As the ship rolled, the contents of the toilet bowl slopped over your feet.
If you weren't feeling sick before you entered the Washroom from Hell,
you were by the time you left it. Bladders and bowels were bursting, and
those who had savoured the Potato Chips from Hell were mad with thirst.
After four hours, only the passengers' physical conditions prevented a full-
scale mutiny.

I returned to the upper deck, now awash in sunscreen, which had
become worth its weight in gold, people trading bottles of mineral water
for a dab, mineral water being only marginally less valuable a commodity.
As the sun pulled itself up to its full height, human ingenuity blossomed,
sunshades fashioned from shirts were tied up with bras and belts to any
available object. Women stripped down to their underwear — much to the
delight of the crew.

An old Muslim couple — who, I overheard, now lived in New York —
gaped in awe, the man watching his daughter with barely concealed rage as
she was chatted up by our handsome captain. This girl wore the head scarf
and long skirt of the Westernized orthodox Muslim, but was clearly besot-
ted enough with the ship's dashing boss to loosen her scarf and laugh
freely. In her father's eyes I could see all the festering contempt of the old
for the ways of the young. At one point he dispatched his son, a garrulous
twenty-year-old with a heavy Brooklyn accent, to summon the daughter
back. But she soon returned to the open door near the bridge and the
attentive young captain, in his starched white uniform and even whiter
smile. At this rate, for all I knew, the ship could be going around in circles.

If Moses had led the Israelites out of Thebes, as seems possible, then this
was the route he would have taken across the Red Sea, or rather through it.
Even running, the journey would have taken as long as mine was taking. In
Cecil B. DeMille's *The Ten Commandments,* Charlton Heston is through in
minutes, the Red Sea there being narrower than the Gulf of Suez, which
would have made a logical place to cross … unless you had Pharaoh's army
in hot pursuit. It would have been a very *hot* pursuit, too, the only way of
reaching the sea from Thebes being through the Eastern Desert. The Red Sea,

turquoise not red, derives its name, many think, from the "Reed Sea." Since I never saw a single reed anywhere in it, this, too, is mystifying.

Lake Timsa, about forty-four miles north of Suez City at the southern end of the canal, seems the best possible route for the Exodus crossing, which would have meant Moses was leading his tribes from the treasure cities constructed by Middle Kingdom pharaohs in the eastern Delta region, and possibly constructed with Hebrew slave labour. Joseph's granaries were probably in this area, too, conveniently close to the fertile Delta plain where the grain would have been grown. The fact that no mention is made of such a vast mass emigration in any dynastic records is also puzzling. I've never read those books called something like *The Bible as History*, but my experience of the Bible as history has shown me that, as history, the Bible is about the most unreliable book ever published.

Some young American Jews were also on board, retracing Moses' steps, ultimately bound for Israel. One had strict instructions from his father back home to document his journey copiously with photographs. Since I was standing in the shade closest to the bridge and would be among the first to sight land — if we ever sighted land again — he urged me to tell him the moment I did.

～つ

After six hours the ship was a floating nightmare. Some Westerner had pissed over the side to avoid the Washroom from Hell, managing to piss off a crew member below. Other people were burning up badly, one German screaming a death yodel when his friend unwittingly slapped his skin. I went below to check on Mohammed. He was sick and thirsty, lying back on his bench clutching his stomach and staring up with helpless, imploring eyes. I suspect he wanted his mother. The roll of the vessel was more pronounced down here, people bouncing from seat to seat as they walked along in urgent search of sunscreen or water. I suggested to Mo that he'd be better off upstairs, and he meekly accompanied me, floundering like a drunk, his skin the colour of slate.

Tying my jacket over the railings, I made him a little spot of shade beneath which he curled up in the fetal position, all but sucking his thumb. Back in my lookout's spot, I finally saw the thin yellow line of land, shouting to the Jewish boy, who dashed over, camera at the ready. The land appeared to get no nearer for half an hour, then, passing a bleak, mountainous coastline, we again had some sense of our speed. The closer we drew, the more spectacular the scenery became: high pointed peaks, descending all the way down to vast rocky outcrops in the turquoise and cerulean waters, clear and deep on every side.

"That's Ras Muhammad," someone shouted.

Ras Muhammad is a spit of land at the southernmost tip of the Sinai Peninsula, renowned for what many divers consider the finest coral reef in the world. Spirits on board revived somewhat at this news, people staggering to their feet to get a glimpse of what they'd gone through the fires of hell to reach. By now they were downright angry people, all the more frustrated by having no idea whom to blame for this ship.

"Oh fuck, man!" I heard the German girl from Aswan saying. "My 'ead 'urt bad." She'd made a friend on board, a young Scandinavian boy. She lay in his lap, the breeze conveniently blowing her top open so he could gaze longingly down it while stroking her sun-frazzled head.

Although the passing coastline proved we were moving, we didn't *seem* to be moving. The distant curve where Sharm al-Sheikh's harbour was alleged to lie was getting no nearer as the minutes passed. The initial enthusiasm on board waned, most people sinking back beneath their makeshift shelters, aware once more of aching bodies, churning stomachs, pyrotechnic bowels, searing bladders, raging thirst.

The old Muslim man from New York rudely elbowed me aside so his son could photograph him: *Here's Dad just arriving at Sharm al-Sheikh in 1990.* If Dad, or any of us, ever *did* arrive, I thought.

Finally we did. I helped Mo up, almost losing him off the gangplank along with our luggage. By some miracle he'd arranged a car to meet us, another fancy Peugeot Estate, which was parked right on the quay. Soldiers checked my papers, for some reason saluting and carrying my bags to the car. The other passengers were clearly impressed; *they* had a long wait, then a long walk.

Seeing Muhammed, the driver, a tall, friendly young Egyptian with close-set eyes and a nose like a boomerang, rushed over and kissed him. Another friend. Abdel was his name, and he sped us to the Customs checkpoint before any of the other passengers had staggered within a hundred yards of it, dragging our luggage over to the most antiquated and dangerous-looking X-ray machine I've ever clapped eyes on. I yelled, managing to extract my camera and film canisters before my bag had been conveyed into the jaws of the Death Ray. This contraption would probably have every item you possessed glowing in the dark for months.

Back in the car, we pleaded for water first. Abdel produced a bottle that was not only sealed, and thus almost certainly still mineral water, but actually *cold*. No water has ever tasted so good. Waving good-bye to the ship of fools, we sped off along the coast road.

It seemed hotter here than in Hurghada, probably because it was also about as humid as anywhere in Egypt can get. What I could see of Sharm al-Sheikh looked as if it had recently been through a war. Then I remembered that it *had* recently been through a war. Low concrete structures with blast-proof shutters were scattered everywhere. So were soldiers, and they looked a good deal more serious, more *soldierly*, than the ones in Hurghada. They had to; if another war started, it would begin less than 125 miles north of here, where Egypt ended and Israel had constructed a border less than a year previously, having finally handed back the last patch of occupied Sinai. Admittedly Egypt had been obliged to get the International Court to make Israel do this, to honour the letter of the peace treaty Anwar Sadat and Menachim Begin had signed right here in Sharm al-Sheikh twelve years before. Israel was reluctant to part with the last few miles, mainly because the resort of Taba had been very popular with tourists — one of those tourists being Menachim Begin.

We turned up a dusty road heading along the edge of a stark and formidable mountain range. When Moses arrived here, this prelude to the Promised Land couldn't have looked too promising to his Israelites; little wonder they would be back worshipping the "Golden Calf," perhaps the Bull of Montu, before long.

Turning off this dead-straight barren road, we wound our way down to

the resort part of town, where a collection of attractive Nubian-style holiday villages had been recently built, and even more or less finished, along
a curving crescent of bay with a wide strip of eggshell sand framing a more
turbulent, azuline sea, its whitecaps sparkling in the fierce sunlight. Our
hotel, the Marina Sharm (which means "Marina Marina"), hadn't been
built as recently. In fact, it had been constructed by the Israelis during their
occupation, and not constructed very well, either. Doors wouldn't lock
(which, since they were only made of something like cardboard anyway,
didn't matter); the shower was like an Egyptian rainstorm; the balcony
window slid shut and locked you out on the balcony (but since this lock
didn't work, either, that didn't matter); the bed was made of quivering
matchwood, its mattress stuffed with what felt like tire rubber; coat-hanger
hooks uncurled when compelled to bear the weight of anything heavier
than a necktie; and you had to walk up three flights of nearly vertical exterior stone steps to reach the place. The beach seemed nearly deserted; in
fact, the whole resort seemed nearly deserted.

I recalled coming down here in 1974, driving from Jerusalem and passing no border. Then the place had been hopping, crowded with young
Israelis and American Jews on vacation. It was warm in the southern Sinai
when snow fell over Tel Aviv. The Israelis must miss owning it. Before they
turned it into a resort, virtually no one came here. The 1929 Baedeker only
refers to the whole Sinai in passing as a province of Egypt, capital Al-'Arish
— nothing more.

When the sun was lower, Abdel reappeared with his car, and Mohammed
said we would go "downtown." This proved to be a collection of forlorn
warehouses transformed into a halfhearted bazaar selling food and souvenirs, the vendors all seemingly too depressed to bother moving from
their stools, let alone hustling business. Mohammed kept gesturing at
shops, saying "shops." We arrived at a bleak little plaza surrounded by war
architecture — bullet-pocked concrete walls, no windows — and Mo,
indicating a drab and minuscule store, said, "Post office."

"So what?"

"Maybe you need stamp? ..."

I narrowed my eyes and just looked at him. Abdel suggested we leave.

On the way back he pulled off the road onto a dusty patch of land at the base of steep cliffs.

"Look," he said, pointing toward the end of this desolate area. "John Kennedy, American president, no?" I hardly expected to find the late John F. Kennedy roaming around the edge of the Sinai Desert, so I assumed I'd misheard. I had not. Abdel was pointing at a small mesalike outcrop that, in this light, did not slightly resemble President Kennedy in profile; it *exactly* resembled him, jutting forehead, square jaw, neat quiff, the lot. I assumed it was man-made, but it wasn't. As with the wind-eroded mesas of Arizona, Nature had arbitrarily decided to form this piece of rock into the profile of the former president whose assassination had ensured his status as the most popular in American history. It was an eerie sight.

Abdel looked very pleased with himself, his nose reaching his chin whenever he smiled. He then told me with some satisfaction that, under Israeli rule, this area had been enclosed and visitors charged a dollar to view the JFK Rock. Now it was liberated like the rest of the Sinai. Since Abdel couldn't possibly have been here during the Israeli occupation and I was never shown the rock when *I* was, I don't know whether the story is true or not.

Sitting over an excellent meal of sea bass on the terrace of the hotel restaurant, Mohammed and I watched the light fade over the Strait of Tīrān and the sea turn a dark, iridescent Prussian blue. Lamps all along the shoreline blinked on, and the circling mountains to the west were wreathed in a heliacal mist beneath which the sun was bleeding to death out of sight, stabbed by the sharp peaks onto which it had fallen.

Pointing to a squat white building some few hundred yards away, Muhammed said, "That is White House — like in Washington, no?" He laughed, and I began to think his experiences at sea had unhinged him. After all, this had been his first time on a boat, I had learned. Then he explained the building in question was where President Sadat and Prime Minister Begin had signed the peace accord. Both men had been fond of Sharm al-Sheikh; one hadn't seen it in over ten years, the other was unlikely ever to see it again. The building was known as "the White House" because it was white, although it wasn't a house. Now it was a pizza restaurant.

I strolled the boardwalk alone later on. The other hotels were quite busy: people sitting in open-air restaurants listening to live Gypsy bands or wandering like me past little souvenir stores with few souvenirs to sell. The Hilton seemed by far the most attractive place here, a sprawling village of elegantly designed chalets, chic stores, open-air bars. Everywhere there were uniformed members of the UN peace-keeping forces off duty, drinking and trying to pick up girls. No one seemed to have told them that they shouldn't try to pick up Egyptian girls. The presence of the UN troops also meant you could pick up the CNN cable news piped in from Europe, along with American movies made since 1968 — which was when the American movies you occasionally found on Cairo TV ceased to be made.

It was odd watching familiar programs while being down here at the mouth of the Red Sea. I wondered if what was designed to comfort the troops in fact made them more homesick. Jim Henson had died, I learned; so had Sammy Davis, Jr. It all seemed remote, like getting news from Mars.

I was getting bored with resorts, bored with being a tourist. Yet I'd vowed to see every inch of modern Egypt. The itinerary I'd planned would end when I entered the fourteen-hundred-year-old monastery of Saint Catherine's, built on the site where God spoke to Moses from the burning bush below Mount Sinai, in the heart of this southern end of the peninsula. That was some days away, however, and I had Mohammed to keep entertained in the meantime.

Late the following afternoon I hired some scuba equipment from a sullen German who looked like Conan the Octogenarian — hair from Hulk Hogan, face courtesy of W. H. Auden, body on loan from the Steroid Research Foundation. He charged me a scandalous sum of money — probably three months' salary for Mohammed — and did it with about as much charm as someone stomping you with jackboots, reminding me to bring the stuff back at 6:00 P.M. — sharp.

Abdel drove Mo and me the half hour or so around the coast road to Ras Muhammad. The trip was quicker by boat. As we entered the narrow spit leading down to the reef, the landscape transformed itself dramatically. There was something familiar about it, very familiar. If the NASA lunar footage were fabricated anywhere, it was done here. Circular craters, jagged, low mountainlike hills, huge lone boulders, everything pocked and pale and hauntingly desolate. Ras Muhammad has now been designated a national park, so it has a gate. Vast monoliths of sheer stone lean at each other at crazy angles, looking like the modern conceptual sculpture of pharaonic artists, forming an arch as you approach. This is the "gate," guarded by two old men in turbans who were sound asleep when we passed through.

Bouncing over corrugated road, we drove until there was no more road to bounce over. Only then did I notice the sheer cliffs leading down to turquoise waters. Abdel led us to a tiny cove. I put on the scuba equipment and, walking backward in flippers, headed into the sea. Instantly I hit huge, uneven lumps of coral and fell over. Hobbling gracelessly out to where the water was about one and a half feet deep, I lay flat, propelling myself along with my hands until I was able to swim.

Even here, looking down at the variegated coral, I could see many exotic fish, all so brilliantly coloured they could have been illuminated from within. Following one exceptionally beautiful creature of shimmering lacmoid with a broad marigold pinstripe across the rainbow corals, I suddenly saw the floor fall away beneath me countless fathoms into liquid turquoise. It was awesome and terrifying; I forgot I was in water and thought I'd fall down, down, down, to where the light turned cobalt, then indigo and black.

Turning, I saw the edge of the reef behind me, the paler light of day above, and, swimming down along the reef, I came across more and more fish of breathtaking beauty. Shoals of small green ones; big narrow ellipsoid ones with pouting mouths and feathery cadmium fins; medium-sized pale grey ones with faces like toy horses and manelike gamboge extremities. There were fat, puffy ones that resembled the floating heads of obese sheep wearing false eyelashes. There were thousands and thousands of these jewelled denizens of the deep everywhere I looked. Streaming in flashing blizzards in and out of clefts; lazily pondering this nook, that cranny — even pondering me. My presence seemed not to bother any of them. I felt like just another overweight fish, however, crude and ungainly. The splendour of it all was shocking. I lost all sense of time, dazzled continually by more and more of these living works of art, more exquisite than any Fabergé, than anything ever made by human hands. Only when my air ran out did I reluctantly surface, finding myself not even far from where I'd started, Mohammed and Abdel waving frantically from the shore. I waved back. They were trying to tell me the park had closed, and we might be locked in. Which meant it was after 6:00 P.M., and Conan did not have his equipment back.

Speechless, my head full of sights more splendid even than the treasures Howard Carter found in Tutankhamen's tomb, I sat back letting the warm wind dry me until I was frosted with Red Sea salt. The gatekeepers were still asleep, the gate still open. We hurtled back to the hotel, forced to swerve to a halt at one point by soldiers who scrutinized our papers, clearly having nothing else to do. Conan's diving store was closed. I banged on the windows and door. An irritable young blond-haired girl eventually slid open one window, wearing a T-shirt that read DIVERS DO IT DEEPER.

"Writers do it alone," I told her. She didn't even ask what I meant, telling me "Hans" had left and only Hans could take the equipment back, so I'd have to pay two days' rental on it tomorrow. No, *she* couldn't take the stuff back, *only* Hans could, she repeated when asked, and Hans had left. I bet he'd left mulling over what he'd do to me when he next saw me.

As it happened, he never saw me again. Instead of paying two days' rental, I paid no rental at all, leaving the equipment with the hotel at dawn, when Abdel collected Mohammed and me to drive us north.

Pausing at Dahab for coffee, we looked around a rather rudimentary resort with big plans to be a "PLM Village" one day. The manager showed us numerous Nubian-style chalets in various stages of construction. Something had gone disastrously wrong here, it struck me. It struck the manager, too. When showing me an interior that featured a shower large enough to park a bus in with its bed-sitting room barely wide enough to contain a pillow, he remarked, "It's a narrow room, no?" I reassured him that people came here to spend their time outside, not to worry. It was a little late for that. By this time he had about a hundred similar structures on his hands.

In the diving school the manager proudly introduced me to Eva, the woman who ran the diving operation. A good six-four, Eva was built like Chuck Norris, and you got the feeling that when she ran something, she *ran* it — and ran it her way. She looked me up and down, and clearly decided I was a pitiful specimen. This was the best diving anywhere in Egypt, she announced, and also the most dangerous. The famous "Blue Hole," an abyss over four hundred feet deep, had claimed many lives. "Zey go down zere," Eva said scornfully, "to see 'ow deep zey can go. *Und* zey often find out." This was apparently a diving joke, for she laughed. She had been here nearly ten years and was determined the place wouldn't be "ruined" as Hurghada had been. Anyone out to "ruin" Dahab had better come with an army if Eva's still around.

Next the manager showed me his beach and the sea. Politely I admired them both. "No pollution here," he explained, unnecessarily. "No factories, no car exhausting." This was all true. Only Abdel's "car exhausting" polluted the clean air as we drove up into the mountains. In gulleys on either side, I began to notice burned-out vehicles, mangled metal everywhere. We stopped to take a better look. Bullet casings littered the stony dust, too. This had been the scene of some of the worst fighting during the war with Israel.

> *He that killeth a man, he shall be put to death. Ye shall have one manner of law, as well for the stranger, as for one of your own country: for I am the lord your God.*
>
> —LEVITICUS XXIV:21–22

The Nuweiba Touristic Village was our destination. Surrounded by palm trees, it was also somehow a bleak, forlorn place that exhibited spacious villas and well-kept grounds. But no one was around. One elderly Western woman sat on the beach reading a book without ever turning the page she was on. After lunch I insisted on driving farther north forty-odd miles to the Israeli border. For some mysterious reason this excited Mo.

The coast road up the Gulf of Aqaba was empty. Steep dark mountains climbed to the west, empty beaches and a mere twelve miles of blue water spread between us and Arabia to the east. The odd Bedouin woman could be seen herding goats or sheep wherever there was a lone acacia tree or patch of scrub. Besides that, we could well have been hurtling down the same weaving ribbon of road endlessly.

Before reaching Taba, the end of the road, we swerved down a steep incline behind towering rocks to emerge near the strangely isolated citadel of Salah al-Din. When I went to school, he was called Saladin and presented as an archenemy of the heroic Crusaders. To Arabs, naturally, he is a noble figure who defended the honour of Islam against the infidels, ending the Third Crusade. There's more than one history of the world.

Why he built his severely elegant fort on this tiny island in the Gulf puzzled me. "So he could see enemies coming," Muhammed offered helpfully. He could have seen enemies coming more effectively if he'd built the place higher up. Its one advantage in being where it was had to be its defensibility; no one could get anywhere close to it, by land or sea. It was a sad, lonely line of walls and towers now. At low tide you can walk out to it over a causeway. There seemed to be no point, and it wasn't low tide.

Before the new border, we reached the old border. This consisted of a clapboard ghost town festooned with barbed wire, the signs on its drab little huts still reading TABA CUSTOMS AND IMMIGRATION, POLICE HEADQUARTERS, and even DUTY-FREE STORE. The area was still fenced off, an oil drum blocking the entrance to give the person who had to remove it when you drove past something to do.

The real strategic point was farther south behind us, where the coast road passed the highway leading west through the mountain tunnel toward Suez. This was the route the Israeli army had taken when it swooped over the Sinai, humiliating Nasser and massing ominously along the banks of the canal. Whoever controls Suez controls all maritime trade east of the Mediterranean. At the start of the Suez road there had been a formidable military outpost and checkpoint.

Taba, by comparison, was not a serious place. It wasn't even the real border. That lay a couple of miles along, just past the Taba Hilton. Many Jews still came to stay at this lavish, Israeli-built hotel where the signs were still in Hebrew, regardless of the new border. It is an exceptionally beautiful spot, the clear waters of the Gulf curving away from a stony beach past four countries, all visible — Egypt, Israel, Jordan, and Saudi Arabia. Gunboats now patrolled these dangerous waters, flying various flags. Over in Jordan the crucial port city of Aqaba, once "liberated" by Lawrence of Arabia and his Bedouin "army," teemed with activity. Not much later it was to be closed down by an international embargo, since it was one of Iraq's major supply lines. Now, however, oil tankers still slid in and out, transporting the wealth of the Middle East all over the planet.

Behind heavy wire-mesh fencing, the Israeli flag flew above the hell of its Customs inspection point. Cars were being stripped; tourists were shouting at officials; officials were shouting back. Just outside the fence a bearded Israeli boy with a rucksack sat despondently, looking up apprehensively as Abdel, Mo, and I approached. War, fear, boundaries, checkpoints, customs barriers, passports: all hideous and unnecessary inventions of human folly, I thought, turning back to where a huge new sign proudly proclaimed WELCOME TO THE ARAB REPUBLIC OF EGYPT. I was relieved not to have to go on into Israel. But Mohammed wanted to be photographed just inside no-man's-land, with the pale blue Israeli flag fluttering limply over his head. On a map, Israel is a wedge driven into Arab land, which is how it suddenly felt, standing there at its sharpest point.

A map I purchased in Cairo had clearly been adapted from an old German World War II cartographical study, roads still marked "suitable for armored vehicles" and place names in German. Israel was not identified at all. Beside Jordan, the purple wedge was identified as "Negev," all its place names in Arabic. Tel Aviv did not exist.

We drove back through the gathering darkness, the mountains growing red, then black, lights twinkling on across the vespertine gulf in Arabia. A low mist swirled above the hot basalt waters. Beyond those few lights on the far side I tried to imagine what vast expanses of burning sand were there, who lived in them, what those people did, what they thought. The lights are on in Arabia, I said to myself, over and over again, but darkness is descending across all the world.

CHAPTER SIXTEEN

A CAREFUL REHEARSAL OF DEATH

*Military victory in Sinai brought Israel not only direct gains —
freedom of navigation, cessation of terrorism — but, more important, a heightened prestige among friends and enemies alike.*

— MOSHE DAYAN, 1975

*I asked myself what madness had sent me to the place whither I
was going ... I verily believe that these four days were the most
perfectly happy and completely busy of my life ...*

— ALEXANDRE DUMAS THE ELDER,
OF HIS JOURNEY TO MOUNT SINAI, 1836

After reading the biblical accounts of Sinai's desert wilderness, I was ill prepared for its breathtaking beauty. The road from the Red Sea coast twists
up through steep gorges into the interior, then straight along roller-coaster
lines across vast, stark plains of rock and sand, the surrounding mountains

growing larger, many of them exotically shaped like sphinxes or bulls or camels.

By the roadside, Bedouin had spread out fossils, quartz crystals, chunks of raw turquoise for sale. All of these can be found in abundance by anyone willing to spend an hour wandering the desert. The great mines of the pharaohs were here, supplying the minerals that would be ground into pigment for temple murals, or polished and fashioned into amulets, sacred objects. It seemed almost strange to come across buildings in the heart of this untouched and wild landscape.

At the foot of Gebel Musa, Mount Sinai itself, sits the monastery of St. Catherine's, a few miles from the airstrip the Israelis built and the tiny town that has recently sprouted up to handle the tourist trade. From a distance the monastery is almost invisible. Sheer rock faces soar up on all sides of a little fertile patch of land at the end of a valley, dwarfing the massive square walls of the building itself.

The monastery is the oldest continuously inhabited convent in the Christian world. The site on which it stands is holy ground for three religions. The Jews believed it was here that God had supremely revealed Himself to Moses, according to the Book of Exodus. The emperor Justinian had it constructed in the sixth century A.D. to defend local monks from marauding Saracens when the area was under Christian rule. The monastery's defensive walls, at some points over one hundred feet high and ten feet thick, look substantial enough to last forever.

Three months after coming out of Egypt, the children of Israel arrived in this fiercely beautiful wilderness, pitching camp in the valley facing the mountain. On the morning of the third day there was thunder and lightning and a thick cloud on the mountaintop, and then a blast like a colossal trumpet, which made the Israelites tremble with fear. Climbing Sinai alone, Moses received the Decalogue, the ten great Commandments from God.

It was here, too, that Moses saw God for the first time, while he tended his father-in-law Jethro's sheep, before he returned to Egypt. In another Exodus tradition the angel of God reportedly appeared to him in the form of a flame of fire in the middle of a bush, which, though burning, was not consumed. God's voice called out from the flame, "Do not come near.

Take off your shoes from your feet, for the place on which you are standing is holy ground." Afraid to look on God, Moses hid his face.

But, according to the text, Moses did in fact see God. Returning down the mountain with the stone tablets upon which were carved the Ten Commandments, Moses frightened those who saw him, for the skin on his face shone. He veiled himself when he spoke to his people, removing the veil whenever he spoke with God. As the Bible says after his death, "there has never been such a prophet in Israel as Moses, the man who knew God face-to-face."

Scholars have since argued about the exact location of the mountain. Their quibbles are neatly cast outside by a Dominican, Father Louis Grollenberg, in his massive *Atlas of the Bible*, first published in 1954. Some have maintained that the mountain was clearly a volcano, which Gebel Musa is not, for example. Calling the quibblers "armchair scholars," Grollenberg adds, "A visit to the traditional Mount Sinai suffices to dispel all these doubts. The huge granite formations are an awe-inspiring spectacle. The atmosphere, the light and the colours, the incredible stillness, all conspire to make the scene an unforgettable setting for the meeting of God with man."

In the first book of Kings, Queen Jezebel decided to kill the prophet Elijah, who fled from her, taking refuge in a cave on the side of Mount Sinai. Sitting in his hideout, Elijah heard God's voice saying, "What are you doing here, Elijah?" Then, standing out on the steep rocky face, the prophet witnessed God himself pass by:

> *There came a mighty wind, which tore the mountain and shattered the rocks before God. But God was not in the wind. After the wind came an earthquake. But God was not in the earthquake. After the earthquake came a fire. But God was not in the fire. After the fire came the sound of a still small voice.*
>
> —1 KINGS XIX:11–12

The monks of Mount Sinai later built a chapel over Elijah's cave.

The original name of the monastery commemorated these appearances of God to men, as it was originally dedicated to the Transfiguration of Jesus Christ. The first three Gospels record that Jesus, too, went up a mountain — Mount Tabor — and that his face shone as Moses and Elijah appeared, talking with him.

To be transfigured, to see God. These were the goals of the monastic life. The whole monastic tradition of the Christian church developed in this desert wilderness.

Centuries before the building of the monastery, hermits lived in caves dotted around the mountainside. The emperor Constantine permitted Christianity in his empire in A.D. 313. Soon after, the hermits of Sinai, men and women, petitioned Constantine's mother, the empress Helena, for her protection. In 330 she built a small church dedicated to the Virgin Mary on the mountain, and had a tower constructed to protect the site of the burning bush.

Saint Anthony, scion of a wealthy family, who renounced his inheritance to seek God, was the first Christian ascetic to eventually withdraw to the solitude of the Egyptian desert. When the hermit died there at the age of one hundred and five in the year 356, Saint Athanasius wrote an account of his life that inspired many others to follow his example. Their lives were odd, even bizarre, by any standards.

An Egyptian monk called Paphnutus wrote the life of a hermit named Onophrius. According to the *Lives of the Desert Fathers*, when the two men first met, Onophrius claimed he had been living in the desert for over seventy years: "At first he had lived with a community of monks, but the example of Elijah and John the Baptist drove him into the wilderness. His clothing fell away. Hungry and thirsty, he had lived on dates. He had suffered extreme heat and extreme cold. He was spiritually at peace." Inviting Paphnutus into his hut, the hermit suddenly grew very pale. After asking his biographer to bury him, Onophrius promptly died. One hermit named Stephen had trained a leopard to protect his meagre supply of vegetables from other animals prowling for food. To escape rampaging Saracens, another was reported to have turned himself into a palm tree. A number of the most widely revered lived for decades on the tops of pillars.

But they also managed to transform their inner selves, living with each other as models of Christian charity. In 374 Rufinus of Aquilea noted:

> *I have seen among them many fathers that lived the life of heaven in the world ... I have seen some of them so purged of all thoughts of suspicion or malice that they no longer remembered that evil was still found on earth. They dwell dispersed throughout the desert and separate in their cells, but bound together by love. They are quiet and gentle. They have, it is true, one great rivalry amongst themselves: it is who shall be more merciful, kinder, humbler and more patient than his brother.*

Solitude and fasting were the cornerstones of this life. But, as Abbot Anthony pointed out, these practices only brought the hermits closer to their real struggle: "The one who sits in solitude and quiet has escaped from three wars: hearing evil, speaking evil and seeing evil ... [Yet] against one thing we still must constantly battle — against our own hearts."

Superhuman humility and utter denial of the self were the goals of these men and women. A well-known story defines the nature of such a state: "The devil appeared to a certain brother, disguised as an angel of light, and said to him, 'I am Gabriel and I am sent unto thee.' But he said, 'Look to it that thou wast not sent to some other: for I am not worthy that an angel be sent to me.' And the devil was no more seen."

But it was not reverence for these godly hermits that caused the monastery to be built. Marauding Saracens had no respect for the inhabitants of Mount Sinai. In the fourth century an Egyptian monk named Ammonius hid in a tower during a Saracen raid, finding thirty-eight others dead when he emerged. One more died of his wounds four days later, and news arrived that the marauders had killed another forty hermits, as well as some women and children, in nearby Raithou. And so the monks approached the emperor Justinian for protection, begging him to build a monastery where they would be safe. Justinian agreed, decreeing that the convent should be "fortified so that no better could be found."

The emperor's decision had much to do with the remarkable woman he married. In the *Secret History* written by Procopius, the court historian, we're told that the empress Theodoura had originally been a notorious actress and dancer. She was born around the year 500 in Cyprus or Syria, and travelled to Byzantium, heart of the empire, with her parents. Her father obtained a job guarding bears in the amphitheatre but died young, leaving his widow and two daughters to fend for themselves. The youngest, Theodoura, joined her sister on the stage, collecting a growing crowd of admirers for performances that appear to have resembled those found in modern strip clubs. The historian Edward Gibbon was clearly so embarrassed by Theodoura's act that he consigns his description of it to a footnote written in Greek. It's worth quoting the famous account:

> *The beauty of Theodoura was the subject of more flattering praise, and the source of more exquisite delight [than her acting talents]. Her features were delicate and regular; her complexion, though somewhat pale, was tinged with a natural colour; every sensation was instantly expressed by the veracity of her eyes; her easy motions displayed the graces of a small but elegant figure; and either love or adulation might proclaim, that painting and poetry were incapable of delineating the matchless excellence of her form. But this form was degraded by the facility with which it was exposed to the public eye, and prostituted to licentious desire. Her venal charms were abandoned to a promiscuous crowd of citizens and strangers, of every rank, and of every profession; the fortunate lover who had been promised a night of enjoyment, was often driven from her bed by a stronger and more wealthy favourite; and when she passed through the streets, her presence was avoided by all who wished to escape either the scandal or the temptation.*

When she finally left the stage, it was to live with one of her lovers, who became governor of Pentapolis in Africa.

The affair was short-lived. Falling from favour, she was thrown out by the governor and wandered destitute, often helped by the charity of holy men. Procopius suggests she entrapped Justinian, not yet emperor, with spells and love potions. But she was by now nearly forty and a more respectable figure. Justinian's aunt, the empress, certainly opposed the marriage, but she died in 523, and Justinian's uncle seems to have gone out of his way to facilitate his nephew's relationship, making Theodoura a patrician and abrogating the law forbidding senators like Justinian to marry actresses or courtesans. In April 527, Justinian became emperor, and Theodoura was crowned empress on Easter Day.

She reigned with her husband for twenty-one years, earning a reputation for piety and courage. As she had once been treated kindly by holy men, so she treated them kindly. Partly in her memory, Justinian built the monastery on Mount Sinai, somewhere between Theodoura's death in 548 and his own, seventeen years later. Procopius never visited Mount Sinai; "I count it a toilsome and perilous task to cross a great ocean in a crazy vessel," he once wrote. He was not aware that the church his emperor built and the fortress protecting it were part of the same structure. "At the foot of the mountain," he recorded, "our emperor also built a very strong fort, and placed inside it a considerable garrison of soldiers, in order that the barbarian Saracens might not from that point secretly invade Palestine."

Clearly there were also more secular reasons for constructing the fortress. Politics and religion are never far apart in this region. Yet the piety of Theodoura and her husband cannot be questioned. Two inscriptions on the roof beams of the monastery's church, translated, still read TO THE SALVATION OF OUR PIOUS EMPEROR, JUSTINIAN, and TO THE MEMORY AND THE REST OF THE SOUL OF OUR EMPRESS. Thus, continuing the austere traditions of their spiritual predecessors, in a safer environment, monks lived and prayed within the walls of Justinian's fortress — and do to this day.

Less than a century after the monastery was built, Islam swept through Egypt, leaving St. Catherine's an isolated outpost of Christian monasticism in a Muslim world. According to tradition, the monks sent a delegation to the Prophet Muhammad himself in A.D. 625, begging his protection. The Prophet supposedly even travelled to Mount Sinai to visit the monastery;

you can still see the imprint of his camel's hoof, divinely magnified, on a rock. The monks secured for themselves a document, purportedly signed by Muhammad, that promised them safety. It was carried away by a later sultan, who left an authenticated copy that is still on display in the monastery.

With this event began another development of St. Catherine's tradition — the monastery's uncanny ingenuity at surviving under non-Christian rulers. For example, an Islamic mosque stands within the walls of the Christian monastery, designed to serve the spiritual needs of its Muslim servants. It was constructed in the eleventh century. Kalif Hakim was looting and razing Christian foundations all over the region, and Archbishop John the Athenian was later murdered by hostile Muslims. One account tells that the mosque was built overnight, the monks certain that the sight of a minaret within their walls would turn away an approaching army.

Meanwhile, in the outside world, the monastery was gaining fame. Its reputation for sanctity grew in the ninth century when the monks allegedly discovered on the mountainside the body of Saint Catherine, miraculously transported there from Alexandria. Catherine had been the wealthy daughter of a king and is said to have openly criticized the emperor Maximian for being a pagan. Bringing in fifty learned men to convert her from Christianity, the emperor was dismayed to find *she* had converted *them*. It's said that Maximian had the hots for Catherine and that her refusal to commit adultery with him was as great an annoyance as her staunch Christianity. He decreed that she be put to death. The spikes on the wheel on which she was to be broken broke themselves instead; so he had her beheaded. It is recorded that after the execution milk rather than blood flowed from her veins. The bones of the body found by the monks, Saint Catherine's or not, oozed oil for many years.

The first record made of a pilgrimage to the area dates to the fifth century, when a Spanish noblewoman called Etheria wrote, "There were many cells of holy men there, and a church in the place where the bush is." In front of the church, she observed, there was "a pleasant garden with abundant water." Shown the spot where God told Moses to remove his shoes, she also noted that the burning bush was "alive to this day and throws out shoots."

In the fourteenth century Mount Sinai was visited by Philip of Artois, Duke Albert of Austria, some Augustinian monks from Verona, and a Florentine called Frescobaldi, who noted two hundred monks living in the fortress and in caves around it. A German named Baldensel managed to make the treacherous journey on horseback, though hiring camel drivers to carry his supplies. He noticed the absence of fleas, lice, and flies on the mountain, remarking on the vast number of lamps hanging in Justinian's chapel. To this day the lamps are still there. At that time the bones and head of Saint Catherine were seated upright in a marble chair, covered in a crimson, gold-embroidered cloth. Baldensel spent much of his time kneeling before the saintly relics, returning to write a bestselling account of his pilgrimage. Other pilgrims and other popular accounts followed.

With fame came wealth. The monastery acquired land and possessions as far away as France, Crete, Moldavia, and Romania over the centuries. It also acquired manuscripts in many languages from across Christendom, as well as the largest and most important collection of icons in the world.

As Christianity escaped its Jewish origins, the practice of the faith assumed more and more aspects of the Greek religion. By the fourth century A.D. Christian writers were mentioning that images of Jesus and His apostles, as well as the Virgin Mary, were appearing in churches quite regularly, despite the Second Commandment: "Thou shalt not make yourselves a carved image, or any likeness of any thing that is in heaven above, or that is in the earth beneath, or that is in the water under the earth: Thou shall not bow down to them, nor serve them."

A controversy developed within the church, which came to a head in 726, when the emperor Leo III banned all image worship. The iconoclast debate lasted nearly 120 years, during which time many synods were called. Patriarchs and monks were put to death or exiled. Since the great Council of Chalcedon in 451 had declared that Jesus possessed two natures, one human, one divine, it was argued, why should the icons, which only depicted the human form, be banned? John of Damascus, safe in Muslim Palestine during the seventh century, asked why, if the Son of Man appeared in human form, his human form could not be painted on wood. All this seemed to contradict the Second Commandment, which is still rigorously upheld by Islam, and to a lesser extent by Judaism, but these opposing arguments gradually prevailed.

Nonetheless, for over a century some of the greatest works of early Christian art were destroyed. But not at St. Catherine's, where, safely removed from the iconoclastic Christian world in their bastion within Islam, the monks continued to create and preserve icons. In a collection of more than two thousand, the monastery still owns the oldest icons known to exist.

The monastery continued under the aegis of various rulers through the Crusades, when King Baldwin of Jerusalem offered his special protection to the monks. They, however, discouraged him from visiting Mount Sinai so as not to offend the sultan. The instability of the Sinai was a constant threat to St. Catherine's. When the Mameluke Ali Bey staged his revolution against Turkish rule in 1769, remaining undefeated until 1773, the monks remained neutral. In 1798 they obtained a decree of protection from Napoleon during his brief adventure in Egypt, because, the French emperor explained, he was "filled with respect for Moses, the Jews and also the monks, who were learned men living in the barbarity of the desert." He even ordered his soldiers to rebuild some of the monastery walls.

Expelling the French from Egypt, the British restored the country and the Sinai to the Turkish viceroy, Muhammad Ali, in 1802. Ali and his son approved of the monastery. The monks survived his rule, and then the British protectorate, without harm. They went on, thirteen hundred years of survival skills serving them well, to endure Nasser's revolution and the Israeli occupation, and they are still there, surviving the resurgence of fundamentalist Islam in modern Egypt.

Because of its isolation and the various times of dangerous turbulence that made access impossible to outsiders, the monastery was able to retain and continue to amass a library of over three thousand manuscripts. That collection is matched only by that of the Vatican itself. The contents of many of these are a mystery, for reasons that will become apparent.

On May 26, 1975, the monks made a discovery the significance of which may equal that of the Dead Sea Scrolls and the Gnostic Gospels. They were clearing away the rubble from a fire that had gutted the little chapel of St. George in the monastery's north wall when they uncovered a cell that had probably caved in during an earthquake two hundred years earlier. Picking through the debris, they found many ancient manuscripts, at least a thousand previously unknown documents, written in Greek, Arabic, Syrian, Armenian, Ethiopian, Georgian, and Latin. Since the present monks do not read most of these languages, and are reluctant to allow much scholarly access to them, no one is yet sure what revelations are contained in this trove.

There is, however, one book that the monks preserved for centuries that they now no longer possess, the Codex Sinaiticus. Josef Stalin sold the oldest virtually complete Bible in the world, the Codex, to the British Museum. How this happened and why the monks are now so deeply suspicious of outsiders was something I wanted to learn inside the walls of St. Catherine's.

⁓

I had been warned the monks were not the easiest people to deal with. Once there had been over four hundred in the monastery, from many Orthodox churches; now there were fewer than a dozen — all from the Greek branch of the faith, with their long black robes, pillbox hats, huge beards, and waist-length plaited ponytails. The younger ones look almost fashionable these days, as they probably did back in the late sixties.

I suggested Mohammed — still wearing his absurd and lurid beach togs — find something more sober to wear, out of respect. Dropping him in a chalet at the lavish but painstakingly subtle tourist village the government recently opened about a half-mile from the monastery, I watched him reemerge twenty minutes later in a screaming-red tracksuit, matching baseball cap, and white running shoes.

"You'd wear this to your mosque, would you?" I said.

"Yes." He looked perplexed.

Abdel had returned from the nearby village of souvenir shops and more tourist lodgings with three armed policemen. I asked him and Mo if they thought it appropriate to show up at a religious institution with armed guards. Were the monks *that* difficult?

"Important for you to have government officials," Abdel explained.

"These men will tell imam you have high-level clearance," Mo added.

"Archbishop," I corrected.

I sensed the two Muslims were intrigued by the thought of entering a Christian church. Neither Abdel nor Mohammed, when the issue came up, could understand monastic life, particularly celibacy. Apart from some Sufi sects, there was no equivalent in Islam. To them it seemed an aberration. Their imams lived much like rabbis or Protestant clergy. It was a job.

We drove down the narrow road toward the green oasis nestled at the foot of Gebel Musa and its sister peaks as if in the cupped palm of a granite giant. Dotted around the towering, rock-strewn cliff faces on either side were tiny stone shrines, some Christian, some the tombs of Muslim holy men. Under a high white sun, the deeply fissured stone gleamed acid yellow.

You reach the treed monastery gardens quite suddenly. The monks grew most of their food here for centuries, particularly dates, and here, too, they tended the tiny cemetery where over fifteen generations of their brothers are buried. Because space was and is limited, the oldest corpse has to be disinterred to make room for the newest occupant, the bones piled up in the ossuary or charnel house. Appropriately, this is the first building you pass, curving around it up the dusty gravel track that brings you to the courtyard in front of the massive western wall.

Not long ago visitors were hauled up the wall in a basket seat by winch, there being no other entrance. Now there is a tiny doorway, made all the more minute by the awesome bulk of the ochre granite surrounding it. Squatting in this entrance was an ancient man with a brown, weather-lined face beneath his turban, and a dusty jacket over his *gelabia*.

The emperor Justinian presented his fortress-church with two hundred Egyptians and two hundred Wallachians to work as serfs for the monks. Descendants of these servants are still working for the inhabitants of St. Catherine's. Although they're not quite Bedouin themselves, they have frequently intermarried with women from Bedouin tribes. Known as "Dschebelijah," their history of service, to the monks and the monastery's visitors, goes back to the building's foundation — a fact of which they are very proud.

Looking up warily at the contingent of armed and uniformed men approaching him, the old Dschebelijah sitting in the entrance heaved himself to his feet. After a brief exchange with Abdel and Mohammed, he unlocked the heavy metal door behind him and showed us into a dark narrow passage leading through the ten-foot-thick wall.

Inside the grounds I found myself in a little Greek village of winding flagstoned lanes and whitewashed buildings hung with lamps in glass cases. Immaculately clean, this was another world, a piece of southern Europe transported to the heart of the southern Sinai wilderness. The monastery is an architectural palimpsest, building built upon building, the relatively new alongside the ancient, for fourteen hundred years. A pale umber stone bell tower, a gift of Czar Nicholas II, its open sides revealing many bells, stands beside the gleaming massicot of a crude minaret. Beyond them the imposing form of Justinian's sixth-century basilica dominates the monastery, slanting away to the northeast corner toward the traditional site of the burning bush. Built lower than almost any other part within the monastery walls, the basilica does not dominate the structure. Its architect, Stephanos, compensated for this by designing the two great walls at the west and east ends to project above the roof higher than was structurally necessary. Thus, from outside, the building, made of the local russet-coloured stone seen everywhere, is still impressive, without appearing either too large or abnormally sunken below ground.

The servant asked us to wait and shuffled off out of sight. One of the policemen beckoned me to a small covered area opposite the northwestern corner of the basilica. Inside it was an old metal hand pump installed above a wellhead. "Well of Moses," the policeman told me, urging, "Drink, drink — iss good drinking. Very clean water." I heaved the creaking wheel, and a trickle of cold water spurted into my palm. It tasted good — sweet with mineral salts, a tang of iron.

> But Moses fled from the face of Pharaoh, and dwelt in the land
> of Midian: and he sat down by a well.
>
> —EXODUS II:15

Whether this was that well beside which Moses first met his wife, Zipporah, is, again, open to speculation. But the well couldn't have been too far from Horeb, the mountain of God — thought to be Mount Sinai — where Moses saw the burning bush.

The old Dschebelijah reappeared, beckoning us to follow him. We walked up a flight of wooden steps to a door that led into an opulent room — much gilt-edged furniture, many flashy nineteenth-century icons, an elaborate thronelike chair on a raised platform, gold glinting everywhere. Spotlessly clean, its floors and mahogany surfaces shining like still brown pools, this room belonged somewhere else, not in the middle of a wilderness.

A gleaming inner door opened, and through it came Archbishop Damianos. At three hundred pounds and counting, he didn't strike me as an ascetic. Possibly in his seventies, with a greying beard as thick and tangled as a bramble bush, and oily hair tied back in an untidy bun, he was garbed in a threadbare black robe that bore traces of many meals and was strained to bursting over his cauldron of a stomach. Framed by the grandeur of this room, he looked even shabbier, almost a bum caught sleeping in a palace after visiting hours. He had clearly just woken up, rubbing his bloodshot eyes and yawning as he shuffled over to where I stood. I explained I'd come to stay in the monastery to research its history and talk with the monks. As I spoke, he ducked and puffed like an old woman, wincing as if my words were causing him pain. Even the monstrous crucifix dangling from his neck had what looked like dried egg caked over Christ's legs.

"Ohhh," he groaned, screwing up his face and avoiding my eyes. "Oh, you see I am so sick — and so many of my monks are also sick with some stomach ailment … I have so many troubles right now. I do not know if this is good time for you … Maybe you could come back another time."

"That would be a little difficult, Your Grace," I said politely.

"Ah, difficult. Yes. I have so many difficulties. And this sickness. I do not feel well, you see …"

I got the picture. One of the policemen rattled off a volley of Arabic, rather angrily, I thought, showing the archbishop my government papers. His Grace sighed, holding the papers in thick, grimy fingers and squinting at them. He smelled dreadful.

"Yes, yes. Oh dear, oh dear," he eventually told himself; then, looking up, he shouted in Greek to an old bearded man in civilian clothes who resembled Ezra Pound and was walking across an adjacent upper courtyard. The translation was something like, "Hey, Konstantini! Another visitor to bother you. Do me this kindness, would you?"

"My honour, Your Grace," Konstantini called back in a rasping voice.

"Go with that man," the archbishop told me. "He is a great scholar. He will take care of you." He groaned again. "I must go back to my bed. You know," he added, turning back, "the monastery does not need any more propaganda. You will find my monks are afraid to talk with writers. There has been too much trouble … too much." He shuffled away through the polished doors, huffing and tutting.

Mr. Konstantini proved to be a curious character. He welcomed me effusively and told my retinue they could leave now. Mohammed looked disappointed. I said I'd see him back in Cairo. When he tried to protest, I thanked him and assured him he'd done a fine job.

Following Konstantini through various alleys, up and down stairs, I was ushered into a whitewashed structure in the upper northwestern corner that resembled a little cottage and contained only one large oblong room. Lined with old worn couches, the walls displayed an unusual collection of pictures. Flanking the standard matinee-idol portrait of President Mubarak were photographs of the entire Greek royal dynasty from 1863, consorts included, even the wife of Constantine I, Kaiser Wilhelm II's sister. There was a huge photograph of Archbishop Makarios, signed in red ink when he apparently visited the monastery to celebrate its thirteen-hundredth anniversary. Apart from a number of framed icons that appeared to be reproductions, the rest of the wall space was taken up by large coloured engravings depicting, in the idealized sentimental style of Victorian England, the various exploits of Moses — crossing the Red Sea, coming down from Mount Sinai with the tablets of the law, and so on. Compared with the work of these artists, Cecil B. DeMille was shooting *cinema vérité*. In a glass case standing on a side table was housed an intricate model ship dating from the late nineteenth century.

The atmosphere was cozy, right down to a small coal-burning fireplace for the winter months. Indeed, the atmosphere was so cozy that two old women dressed in the black of Greek widows were stretched out asleep on two of the many couches.

"This is the monastery guest house," Mr. Konstantini informed me. He spoke in short, rapid, abrupt sentences, his breath reeking of alcohol. His jacket was frayed and stained, like his pants, which also seemed too large for him; his shoes were scuffed, cracked, dusty, and worn down so drastically that the soles were thicker than the heels in places. Telling me to make myself comfortable, he left to arrange coffee.

One of the old women suddenly awoke, looking over at me with a pale, haunted face. She hoisted herself upright. Then she roused her friend, muttering something in an inaudible rasp. The other woman, sitting now, crossed herself as well and barked at me in impenetrably rustic Greek.

Konstantini returned, stubbing a cigarette out on the flagstones before he came in. The old widow brayed at him, and whatever it was he replied in his own stertorous rasp made both women scramble for their few belongings and shuffle out the door.

A Dschebelijah, a gentle, courteous old man, entered bearing a tray of coffee and small pastries. I asked Konstantini about himself. His parents had come to Egypt from Crete in the 1890s; he had grown up in Luxor. I asked him what kind of scholar he was.

"An archaeologist."

"An archaeologist?"

"Yesofcourse," he replied, the phrase he employed whenever another person would have said merely "yes."

Was he working in the monastery? "Yesofcourse." He'd been searching the surrounding area for undiscovered hermit caves for seven years, he claimed, but had found none. Was he still looking? "Yesofcourse." I asked him about Akhenaten and Professor Redford's theories about the heretic pharaoh. "Anyone who stood up to the priests of Amon was bound to have troubles," he replied irrelevantly.

He was no archaeologist. But what he was I couldn't fathom. Like Archbishop Damianos, he looked like a bum, albeit an intellectual one. This was going to be an interesting stay.

After coffee Konstantini grew edgy — his alcohol level needed a top-up perhaps — and said he'd take me to my room. High in the southern wall, this room featured a narrow pallet covered by a thin mattress and blankets, a repro icon of the Virgin Mary framed above it on otherwise bare walls, a tiny desk, and a chair. There was something deeply pleasing about this simplicity and about the monastery's tranquil atmosphere. Alone, I lay back on the unyielding bed, reminding myself where I was, who had been here before me. These thoughts were finally too awesome to contemplate.

～๑

Of what did a monk's life here consist? I wondered. Procopius, Justinian's imperial court historian, had written of the monastery, "On this Mount Sinai live monks, whose life is a kind of careful rehearsal of death." In his Rule Saint Basil wrote that a monk "must first of all possess nothing. His lot must be physical solitude. He must be disciplined in dress, conversation and tone of voice. He must eat quietly and not be obsessed with food and drink." Saint Basil's Rule speaks of a stern existence, of work and obedience, culminating in the great paradox that a monk must be "adorned with shame."

Father George, a young Australian monk who was assigned to show me around, reiterated these essentials of the monastic life. It was a deeply spiritual existence, he told me, making no concessions to a worldly life. Every monk had to be skilled in some way and self-sufficient within the community. The monks owned only the clothes on their backs and saw no need for anything more. Much of each day was spent in prayer, and a day started at 4:00 A.M., often ending after 10:00 P.M. The life was a training for greater and greater humility, leading, through a greater and greater love for others, to the ultimate union of the soul with God.

Father George struck me as a pious man, the kind of lean, ascetic monk I'd imagined I'd find here. He could have been no more than forty, with a long auburn beard and ponytail. His face was prematurely aged, particularly by laugh lines around his eyes, and unnaturally pale for this climate. His skin was more translucent than pallid, almost illumined from within.

Yet his eyes were what I noticed first; they literally shone, holding a blissful secret that could never be expressed in words, deeply private, like the brief spark in a lover's eyes. I've only seen such eyes twice before, and both times in monasteries. If they were the windows of Father George's soul, then his soul was doing just fine in there. But his face also held a certain pain, as if, I fancied, lover and beloved were still apart, and the separation were almost unendurable.

I didn't ask how an Australian had come to be a Greek Orthodox monk living on Mount Sinai — he was still young enough to look like a hippie with his hair and robe. He preempted the question by telling me how tired he was of being asked about it. Voluntarily he ruled out questions two and three. The tourists, he announced, inevitably asked the same tedious questions: What was the difference between Greek Orthodox Christianity and Roman Catholicism? Would he stay here for the rest of his life?

So I asked him about tourists, clearly a sore topic. The monastery, at the request of the government-it-can't-afford-to-offend, opens its grounds between 10:00 A.M. and noon most days, when its tranquility is rudely disrupted by the raucous hordes, and the monks' chastity must be fiercely tested by miniskirts, tight shorts, and tank tops. For the monks, like Father George, are ordered by their archbishop to act as tour guides, striving to avert damage and thwart potential thefts as much as to spoonfeed history sweetened with anecdotes.

"This monastery was built," Father George said wryly, "to protect us from barbarian invasions ... but one asks oneself who are the barbarians now." He smiled uncomfortably. And the presence of tourists was causing other problems in the monastery.

"Would-be monks come to stay here," he explained, "so that they can see if they like the life, wish to remain. But when they find themselves living in a tourist attraction, let alone realize they'll be expected to lead the tours, they are put off. We're having great trouble getting new recruits these days. A monk comes here to lead a life of peaceful contemplation."

I asked why the monks didn't move to another location, leave St. Catherine's to be the museum it's becoming anyway. "We must keep this place," he replied emphatically. "I hate to think what it would become if the Egyptian government ran it. We've been here for one and a half millennia. It's our home. It belongs to our church." As the photographs of Greek royals in the guest house demonstrated, the monks here still regard themselves as an imperial foundation, guarding a shrine placed in their hands by a Holy Roman emperor fourteen hundred years ago.

I also realized Father George was beginning to view me as another kind of nuisance. As I drew him into conversations about the outside world, he began to talk naturally and even garrulously, then would suddenly stop himself. His pre-monk persona was being drawn out, and it disturbed his equilibrium to realize how close to that discarded self he still was.

He told me he occasionally travelled to other monasteries run by his order. This was the only time he handled money, given to him by the monastery for his trip. He would be like a child, I thought, with his ticket and a little pocket money for necessities. One of these rare excursions had taken him to Israel. I'd heard St. Catherine's had especially bitter memories of the Israeli occupation of the Sinai, finding the new influx of Jewish tourists during that period all but unbearable.

An essay by James H. Charlesworth, a professor at Princeton Theological Seminary, recounted a visit he made to the monastery at the time, complaining about the "state of siege" that forced him to communicate with the archbishop by telephone only, and complaining about the profusion of armed soldiers everywhere, as well as the tourists, whom he termed "noisy and disrespectful." If Father George were typical of the monastery's attitudes, the hostility of St. Catherine's to Israel, and even Jews, was still undiminished twelve years after the occupation. Perhaps there was also a good deal of medieval theology at work below the surface.

Father George had other complaints, too. The Jews to him were beyond redemption. "They have no need of God," he said angrily. "They think they need no help from anyone. They ruined our monastery near the Brook of Kidron by redirecting waste and increasing the noise level around it."

The world was closing in on those who sought to keep it at bay, to be in it but not of it. The one luxury the monks were not denying themselves was that of leading this tranquil, unworldly life.

Father George's spiritual state seemed fragile to me, and this environment protected him from a world he couldn't handle. The deprivations suffered by the Desert Fathers, the utter self-denial, the loneliness of the long-distance ascetic on his mountaintop or in his isolated cave: these had long since vanished from St. Catherine's. On the other hand, there was no real hardship here. After solitary prayer, Father George and his brother monks had their fellowship to look forward to and the support of their community. What worries did exist were really trivial things blown out of proportion in the way that those with much time on their hands magnify slight annoyances. The peace and serenity in his eyes were perhaps no more than the peace and serenity I'd find in my eyes if someone paid my rent, picked up all my bills, and left me free to pursue my greatest interest undisturbed in one of the most fascinating and beautiful places on earth. For Father George, the equivalent of those hardships and sacrifices made by his spiritual ancestors would be to find a job in New York City and still retain his faith, still pray, still love his fellow man.

All in all, it was a petty, shallow, hypocritical existence, I found myself thinking. And I had not come here to think such things. It disturbed me. I was also not sure my perceptions were accurate — but I was not the first to have a negative reaction to the monks of St. Catherine's.

CHAPTER SEVENTEEN

MOSES' LEGS AND LIARS IN VERY HIGH PLACES

Oh, these monks! If I had the military strength and power, I should be doing a good deed if I threw this rabble over the walls. It is sad to see how a man can carry his baseness and wretchedness into the lofty grandeur of this mountain world.

—CONSTANTIN TISCHENDORF,
LETTER FROM ST. CATHERINE'S, 1844

Who was Constantin Tischendorf? you may well ask. Sifting through some letters from him that I came across by accident while working in part of the library at St. Catherine's, I made the great mistake of asking Father George the same question. In the world of the Mount Sinai monks, Tischendorf is about as popular as Adolf Hitler in Israel. In fact, he was one of the greatest biblical scholars of all time. The introduction to the first English translation of one of his essays says of him:

*As a critic and decipherer of ancient manuscripts he was without
a rival, and to his other services in this important department of
sacred literature he added one which, alone, would reward the
labour of a lifetime, in the discovery of the Sinaitic Manuscript.*

Born in Leipzig in 1815, Tischendorf swiftly rose to academic promi-
nence in the city's famous university as a theological scholar. In the
early nineteenth century Germany, birthplace of the Reformation and
Protestantism, was still rocking the boat of Christianity. This time the issue
was the authenticity of texts, the most extreme elements casting doubt on
the validity of the entire New Testament. Tischendorf, a man of immense
determination, became obsessed with the need to defend his Protestant
faith by producing an indisputably authentic text. The academic issues
involved are unimaginably arcane and often stupefyingly trivial.

After years of poring over versions of the Bible in libraries all over
Europe, Tischendorf realized that what he needed to get his hands on was
the earliest possible text, one written as close to Christ's own time as he
could find. He became convinced that if such a manuscript still survived,
it would be in the early Christian monasteries of the Eastern Church. To
this end he visited the Vatican, which allowed him to view Codex
Vaticanus, the oldest known biblical text then extant — but only for six
hours. Long enough for even the most accomplished scholar to handle
barely four or five pages of fourth-century handwritten Greek.

So he set out for St. Catherine's. Even at the monastery's branch in Cairo
he was rewarded. He learned any manuscripts the monks possessed were
all in the Sinai monastery, but noticing a cupboard in the library, he asked
that it be opened. It took the monk in charge half an hour to locate a key,
and inside the cupboard Tischendorf found a stack of ancient manuscripts
that the monks had long forgotten. Embarrassed by personal debt and failure back home, Tischendorf had no choice but to continue on his quest.
He hired Bedouin to guide him on the perilous journey from Cairo deep
through the heart of the Sinai wilderness.

Like Alexandre Dumas, who'd made the same journey eight years before
him, Tischendorf found little pleasure in riding camels. "Every sharp trot

of the dromedary was like the blow of an invisible sword, inflicting acute torture," was the way Dumas put it. In 1877 Philip Schaff, an American professor of biblical literature, also made the trip, writing, "The journey is a weariness to the flesh from beginning to end."

And at the end of the difficult trek there were the monks. Schaff soon decided these pious men were superstitious fools, writing that "their surroundings are replete with silly legends which disturb the gravity of a Protestant traveller." Mrs. Lewis, a stereotypically indomitable Victorian English lady Schaff ran into on the top of Mount Sinai, tended to agree with him. "The gradual degeneracy of the occupants of the monastery," she wrote in a letter, "might almost be traced in their style of building, run up to suit temporary wants since the time of Justinian." Despite his opinion of the monks, Tischendorf had to deal with them for the next fifteen years.

Not only did the German scholar and other Christian visitors find a virtually foreign religion practised in the mountains of southern Sinai; Tischendorf made another shocking discovery. That first visit in 1844 convinced him he was looking in the right place. He returned with odds and ends of great rarity, though not the thing he was after. What he did have to show aroused considerable interest, particularly in czarist Russia, and he was able to obtain financing for more visits. It was not, however, until 1859 that the monks finally produced a dusty package wrapped in red cloth. It contained the entire Bible, Old and New Testaments, handwritten in Greek on 346 parchments, as well as material previously unknown and the complete texts of documents that had been known only in fragments until then.

This was what Tischendorf had been hoping for. He'd found eighty or so leaves from the manuscript fifteen years before, and he was convinced the rest of it was in the monastery. He knew he'd hit the jackpot. "It is the only manuscript of its kind in the world," he wrote to his wife.

Now his problem was getting this treasure out of St. Catherine's. The monks were jealous of their possessions. They saw themselves as guardians of a legacy thirteen centuries old, and they were not about to let anyone remove anything. Tischendorf had to content himself with laboriously copying the scrolls by hand, enduring discomfort, interruption … and those impossible monks.

The story gets convoluted from here on. The gist is that the noble German scholar managed to "borrow" Codex Sinaiticus, as it's now known, and promptly presented it as a gift to Czar Alexander II of Russia. By the time of the Russian Revolution and the introduction of an atheist state, the Codex was established as the oldest complete Bible in the world. By then, too, it was of little value to the Supreme Soviet — if not a potential liability. In 1933, after much negotiation, Josef Stalin sold it to the British Museum for a mere £100,000. Of course its real worth was inestimable, literally priceless. To this day the inscription in the case where the British Library displays Codex Sinaiticus reads, "The manuscript was discovered in 1859 by the German Biblical Scholar Constantine Tischendorf in the Greek Monastery of St. Katherine on Mount Sinai, and subsequently presented by the monks to the Emperor of Russia."

On this subject Father George got as angry telling the story as he probably ever got about anything, swearing the monks had never given the manuscript — it was *stolen* — and they still want it back.

For Tischendorf, however, the Codex, though written less than three centuries after the Crucifixion of Jesus, did not settle the religious squabbles it was supposed to settle. It opened up a whole new can of very wriggly worms, worms almost as troublesome to Christianity as the activities of Martin Luther had been four hundred years earlier.

The Gospel of Mark is generally agreed by biblical scholars to be the oldest section of the New Testament, the Gospels of Matthew and Luke seemingly copied from it, since neither contain anything that Mark's does not contain. The Gospel of John differs from all three in its account of Christ's life. Comfortably ensconced in St. Petersburg, rich now and famous, Tischendorf set about translating his "indisputably authentic" text. One of the first things he noticed while working on the Gospel of Mark was that it ended at chapter XVI, verse 8, with the three women approaching Jesus' tomb with oils to anoint his corpse, finding the stone blocking the entrance rolled away and seeing a youth in a white robe sitting on the right-hand side. The youth tells them not to be afraid, that Jesus has risen, and that they should give this message to the disciples: Christ will meet them in Galilee as he promised. Curiously the women don't pass on this momentous piece of news in Codex Sinaiticus; instead "they went out and ran away from the tomb, beside themselves with terror. They said nothing to anybody, for they were afraid." On this grim note the oldest known version of the Gospel according to Saint Mark ends.

In the Authorized Version of the English Bible, and in the received texts of every orthodox Christian church, Mark's Gospel includes another twelve verses. These contain the story of Christ's Resurrection — one of the principal tenets of the Christian faith! This was also why the Vatican had long restricted access to its Codex Vaticanus — no Resurrection in Saint Mark there, either.

What Tischendorf had brought back from Mount Sinai, intending to strengthen his religion, could potentially destroy its very basis. The assiduous scholar also discovered a multitude of other discrepancies, and even additions by later hands. For example, references to Christ as the "Son of God" or the "Son of Man" frequently seemed spurious. Even the eventual punishments for sinners were minimized. In orthodox texts Saint Mark describes hell as a place "where the worm dies not, and the fire is not quenched." The Codex Sinaiticus contains no such phrase. The only worms that weren't going to die were the ones in the can Tischendorf had opened.

No "Son of God," no Resurrection. A man of lesser faith than the great biblical scholar would have been as afraid as the women at the original ending of Saint Mark's Gospel. But Tischendorf still believed Matthew was the oldest of the Gospels; conclusive proof establishing Mark as the oldest of the four had not yet been found, although the argument existed. Thus, Tischendorf was not as disturbed as he should have been.

In countless other ways, in minute but significant details, Codex Sinaiticus, the most authentic version of the New Testament yet discovered, appears to present Christianity the way it has always been viewed by Jews and Muslims. Like Moses, like Muhammad, Christ was a teacher and a prophet — not a divinity. It seems likely that the thousands of other manuscripts still kept from scholars by the monks of St. Catherine's will reveal the same story. As will the many documents on the Forbidden Index in the Vatican library, numerous eminent scholars believe, and the countless ancient texts yet to be translated in archives around the globe.

It seems only fitting that this revelation should have come from the place where the one called "I AM" first revealed himself to a human being. Professor Shalaby had been essentially correct in his view of the Resurrection, though that was virtually the only thing he was correct about.

In this ancient land, where three great religions had arisen from the supreme spiritual science of the pyramid builders, it seemed to me entirely appropriate to discover that Judaism, Christianity, and Islam were variations and refinements of the same theme. All the religious disputes that had ravaged the Middle East and much of Western civilization century after century were merely political disputes in disguise. The baseness of man had been blamed on God.

～๑

I decided to climb to one of God's favourite spots, the summit of Mount Sinai, Horeb, Gebel Musa, or whatever its name was. At 2:00 A.M., I rose and walked through the sleeping monastery. Deserted, the place assumed an immense serenity. The wizened old Dschebelijah, starting from his sleep on a mat by the door, let me out.

The night air was cold, the fierce light of three thousand stars like tiny needles prodding my brain. Without the aid of a moon, they illumined the landscape almost as brightly as an English summer day. Picking my way along the rocky track beneath the north wall, I found a camp of sleeping Bedouin with their camels at the eastern end. As I passed, a voice called out, "Camel! You want camel, meester?"

I shouted back that I was going to climb the mountain.

"Yes," the voice replied. "Camel take you good right to top mountain. You like?"

I found it very hard to picture this. Had Moses used a camel? I told the Bedouin no thanks. He took it well, returning to his blanket.

Since people have been climbing Mount Sinai for over two thousand years, the route to the top is not difficult to spot, although it zigzags all over the place, presumably following the path of least resistance. Even the shortcuts — vertical climbs cutting out 650 feet of zigzag — are fairly obvious.

Constellations I could only recognize by standing on my head throbbed like strobe lights. I imagined they were chinks in the fabric of infinity, revealing the blazing opalescent paradise beyond. I certainly wasn't groping in the dark; I practically cast a shadow. Wrapped in a *kaffiyeh*, I was still cold, yet sweating. After half an hour I stopped to rest. Looking back, I was shocked to find I'd hardly climbed three hundred feet above the silent monastery.

I trudged on, leaning forty-five degrees at times, my feet complaining about all the small rocks. I won't wear Topsiders the next time I climb Mount Sinai.

Turning another hairpin bend, I stopped dead in my tracks. Three hundred feet or so away, in the shadows of an overhang, an enormous angel stood, wings outstretched, glowing with a pale yolky light. My heart raced.

So soon, I thought; maybe God had a lot on His mind. I squinted at the vaguely amorphous form. It was definitely white and illumined from within. After all, this was holy ground. Was I ready for this encounter after all? What did the angel want?

I edged closer, wanting to find this apparition had a more mundane explanation. But it was only when, shivering with fright, I'd got within twenty yards of this being that I saw the large tentlike sheet suspended from a tree with some kind of lamp burning inside it. Plodding closer, I found a kind of makeshift shop selling soft drinks, cigarettes, candy bars, with a turbaned Bedouin snoring robustly, slumped over a folding table.

Business is business, even on holy mountains. Disappointed, I marched on. By 4:00 A.M. I decided I had made some progress, looking down over mist-wreathed valleys and mountain peaks almost level with where I stood. But as I looked up, this mountain seemed to recede indefinitely, a colossal tower of smooth stone with folds like a Jell-O mould.

One hour later I was gasping for breath, my legs seemingly twice their normal size and throbbing as if they were being slowly pumped up with hot liquid. By now at least the mountain seemed narrower, even if the summit was still invisible. The path was narrower, too, and zigzagging as drastically as a Brooklyn fire escape. Walking this way, then that way, I had no idea where the summit was even located anymore. By five-thirty, I reached an open area beyond a narrow passage going straight through part of the mountain right to the other side. To my amazement, three camels were sleeping with their owners here, beside another unmanned variety store. It was like finding a McDonald's franchise a stone's throw from the North Pole.

Was this perhaps *the top*? No sign of God; and anyway, I'd heard there was a small chapel there. I peered around. The path forked to the right and to the left. I chose the left. This brought me quickly to what looked like a crude, uneven staircase hacked out of the bare rock. Far from making the ascent easier, as I'd first imagined it would, the path made the going tougher. And the tough got lung cramps and thigh spasms. Some of the "steps" were three feet high. They wove around a narrow funnel in the mountain's side, often looking as if they abruptly stopped at sheer rock face, but, on closer inspection, continuing around a perilously narrow hairpin bend with a very long drop an inch away. The odd rock crumbled, cascading down with a noise like a two-year-old let loose on a cheap drum kit.

Just as I began to despair of ever reaching the end, fondly recalling my light stroll up the Great Pyramid, I saw the form of a stone building silhouetted against the stars. I felt confident this was the chapel dedicated to Saint Catherine. I was pretty sure also that I'd reached the summit, despite the odd crag jutting up here and there.

I paused for a cough and to stop my heart from bruising itself against my rib cage. I proceeded up to the railings protecting the chapel (from what?). It was 6:20 A.M., and there was not even a hint of anything approaching dawn in the sky; and this sky, festooned with its strobe lights, join-the-dots grid patterns, and all the costume jewellery it possessed, poured down on all sides in smooth shimmering walls, as if I were suspended three feet below the centre of a vast planetarium dome.

Edging around the corner of the chapel toward a wide ledge overlooking the east, with its misty valleys and small jutting peaks all crumpled as softly as a discarded blanket a thousand miles square, I found I was not alone. Huddled in sleeping bags, rugs, coats, and scarves, at least a hundred people, horizontal, upright, or crouching, were scattered all around a smooth terrace extending from the south side of the darkened chapel. There was even another flourishing business up here. A rambunctious

Bedouin with an uncanny resemblance to Anthony Quinn was doing a
brisk trade in coffee and cookies by the light of a flaming kerosene taper.
I doubted Moses ever encountered this.

> *And the LORD called Moses up to the top of the mount; and*
> *Moses went up. And the LORD said unto Moses, Go down, charge*
> *the people, lest they break through unto the LORD to gaze, and*
> *many of them perish. And let the priests also, which come near to*
> *the LORD, sanctify themselves, lest the LORD break forth upon*
> *them. And Moses said unto the LORD, The people cannot come*
> *up to mount Sinai: for thou chargedst us, saying, Set bounds about*
> *the mount, and sanctify it. And the LORD said unto him, Away,*
> *get thee down, and thou shalt come up, thou, and Aaron with*
> *thee: but let not the priests and people break through to come up*
> *unto the LORD, lest he break forth upon them.*
>
> —EXODUS XIX:20–24.

Moses must have had great legs.

I wondered how God felt about the current situation, with its refresh-
ment franchise and its camera-toting horde. Some of them, I noticed, were
either priests or people wearing Italian designer shirts. Some were old —
church groups on tour, probably — some were young. There was also a
powerful smell of marijuana in the air. Clutching thermos flasks, munching food, most leaned toward the east expectantly. It was like looking at a
cinema audience with your back to the screen, everyone gazing intently at
something invisible.

I found a nook above the terrace and sat quaking with cold and fatigue.
God would have to find another way to arrange our chat. What time did
these people get up? I wondered.

Suddenly the massive sky seemed to shudder, a flood of indigo soaking
through its velvety-black walls, the tone lightening rapidly through purples
into smoky blues until day arrived. Only one element was missing — the sun.

Since a cloud in Egypt is a thing the size of a ragged Kleenex, this was not a question of overcast dawn. It was odd. The brilliance grew, and I stared toward where the sun had been every time I'd ever found myself up at this hour before, and it wasn't there. Not a trace.

A buzz of excitement in the crowd had me staring wildly all over the nearly starless sky. Even the remains of this month's moon had put in an appearance, looking like a forlorn banana dangling from the pocket of a blue silk coat. Then I saw it. Of course, it wasn't where I was used to finding it; the horizon from the top of Mount Sinai is nearly forty-five degrees below its normal position. And there was a huge blood-red dome like the mushroom of a ten-thousand-megaton hydrogen bomb. Protean and pulsing, it continued to swell above the trembling distant peaks until I thought it would explode. Which in a way it did, shooting ethereal arms of amaranth-pink flames around the eastern shoulders of the earth in a fierce and loving embrace. Like a huge blob in a lava lamp, it gradually detached itself from the burning ocean behind the mountains, hovering unsteadily, then rising imperceptibly higher, growing firmer, more confident. It was the most stupendous and dramatically beautiful sunrise I have ever seen.

Of course, these moments are never allowed to last for long. No sooner had I decided perhaps I *had* seen God face-to-face after all than a throng of jovial Lutherans burst into song, or rather hymn, conducted by a kind of Teutonic John Candy in a beige duffel coat. The noise was deafening, and the hymns sounded like Oktoberfest drinking songs.

I tried to clamber out of earshot, finding myself in a small lower recess that smelled like a Rastafarian rent party. There on the floor, still in her filthy sleeping bag and only half-awake, was the German girl from Aswan, with her zeppelin breasts and the Scandinavian from the boat. They were sharing a joint rolled in what appeared to be the flyleaf of a paperback book. The boy looked a decade older than when I'd last seen him.

"'ey, man," she said, looking up at me. "I zink I know you, ya?" I told her it was entirely possible. "You 'ave zigarette vor me, huh?" I gave her a couple, and she smiled, sitting up, her thick denim shirt (or his thick denim shirt) hanging open — presumably for my pleasure. "Sanks, man," she said, pocketing the cigarettes. "You 'ave anyvhere I could stay, ya?

Coss my boyfrenn, 'e iss leavink dis day, and I like to stay 'ere, you know?"

The monks would love her, I thought. I shook my head, and catching my eye, she whispered something, pouting her lips and wriggling her hips while rubbing her crotch briefly with a dirty hand. I smiled and walked away.

By now the mountaintop was littered with choirs, all singing the kind of hymns that sound either military in nature or like the songs sports fans chant in chartered coaches. Enough of *this*, I decided.

I started back down the mountain, rediscovering one thing all children learn the hard way: if you run down any steep incline, you may find yourself unable to stop running. In this case the consequences would have been irreversible. I slowed to a walk, assuming it would at least be quicker and easier than the ascent had been. It wasn't. Before long each step, each small rock that smashed under my battered feet, was pure torture. The added momentum meant added weight, too.

Three hours later, passing representatives of every known racial and religious group on the planet, from querulous Japanese schoolchildren to Nigerian nuns, I finally hobbled past the Bedouin camel camp near the monastery. The same man, I believe, again tried to sell me a camel ride — but I'm sure this was his idea of a joke.

Staggering into the monastery like a man three times my age, I ran into Mr. Konstantini — a man who was three times my age. It was nearly 10:00 A.M., so he had already made good progress toward being acceptably drunk. "Come!" he cried. "The archbishop has invited you to breakfast."

"The archbishop?"

"Yesofcourse."

"Breakfast?"

"Yesofcourse."

It seemed a little late for breakfast, considering all the monks had been up for six hours already. But it was, I recalled, Sunday; that had to mean something here. I'd been used to Friday's being Sunday. I followed Konstantini, listening to him rambling on about something Napoleon had done to St. Catherine's. It sounded like a recent event the way Konstantini told it, so perhaps he was talking about some other Napoleon. The cognac, probably.

Breakfast was being served in the guest house. The sofas were crammed with monks and the two old Greek widows. There wasn't much space, so I sat in a large chair beneath the portrait of Archbishop Makarios, which was adjacent to the coloured engraving of Moses returning with the Tablets of the Law. He looked nothing like as tired as I felt. Before I'd even sat down, all hell broke loose, monks and women jabbering at me in a multitude of alien tongues. Konstantini explained: I was sitting in the archbishop's chair, his throne. I hobbled over and wedged myself between Father George and one of the elder brethren who could well have been Jerry Garcia, still grateful, not quite dead.

This was the first time I'd seen all the monks together. They were odder than any random collection of people you'd see on, say, a train. Like children anticipating a treat, I thought. They giggled a lot, all speaking at once to no one in particular. Most of them had clear, sparkly eyes that tended to look inward, and there seemed to be an immense psychic distance between them. Saint Basil's Rule counsels silence, forbids too much laughter, urges monks to keep a seemly spiritual distance even from each other. Saint John Klimakos, who lived in St. Catherine's in the sixth century, wrote, "If the remembrance of Jesus is present with each breath, you will know the value of solitude." All of them together, I thought, each of them alone.

But this was Sunday, a special day even for people who prayed and worshipped for several hours every day. Collectively these monks exuded an air of intense piety. They were truly out of this world. Many no longer remembered its ways. And those who did were frightened of intruders who could awaken slumbering habits from lives they'd left behind. Father George refused to enter into conversation with me, instead speaking in fluent Greek with a monk whose sparse beard made him look like a Tibetan sage.

When Archbishop Damianos rolled in, huffing and puffing, everyone fell silent. Lowering his bulk into the chair reserved for it — which creaked in protest — he immediately reorganized the seating arrangements. Apparently it was an honour to be asked to sit beside him. The lucky monk, a shrivelled little mouse of a man, limped hastily across the room, kissed his archbishop's impressive ring, and inserted himself at the end of the closest sofa, next to a burly monk who seemed reluctant to move. The old Greek women acted as if God had just showed up, crossing themselves and gazing at the plump archbishop in mixed awe and grief.

I asked Damianos how he was feeling, but he ignored the question, turning to chat with a stern monk to his right. Soon a Dschebelijah arrived with the first of three breakfast trays, each containing precisely the same items: date brandy, made in the monastery, and brown things the size of tennis balls.

The monks all but fought to get at this food, chomping down the sticky balls and knocking back their brandy in ravenous silence. The "tennis balls" tasted like sugar and flour that had been soaked in honey, then deep-fried. If this meal was recommended in St. Basil's Rules somewhere I'd be surprised. Ninety percent sugar in one form or another and 10 percent carbohydrate must be a nutritionist's nightmare. Mr. Konstantini was handling a brandy a minute by my estimate, exercising more restraint, however, with the treacle balls. And these were truly vile — hideously sweet and coated in a substance with the tenacity of epoxy resin. I spent the rest of the day mining it out of my teeth with matchsticks and dental floss. The brandy, on the other hand, was like rocket fuel. Besides removing every drop of saliva and mucus from your mouth, it hit the stomach with the impact of a hand grenade. After that, of course, you were so drunk you really didn't mind it anymore. No wonder Damianos had claimed half the monastery was suffering from digestive ailments.

If the monks did this kind of power breakfast every day, I thought, it was hardly surprising they seemed out of this world. I watched Konstantini, well into his ninth glass, totter out for a smoke, wondering if he'd explode the moment he struck a match. By now the monks were … "merry," I suppose, is the right word. Merry monks. Somehow the scene was all quite innocent. After a third brandy I was quite fond of them. They really were like children — not free of sin, but getting there. The world was no place for them; it would eat them alive.

I asked Father George if he'd show me the basilica. For the first time I recognized that he was by decades the youngest person here, and almost as out of place as I was. The reality of his life hit me like a blow to the plexus. He really was isolated here. Just him and God, when God was available. How terrifying. And his faith must be great. I regretted my earlier feelings. The real problem so many have faced, and still face, in dealing with these monks is their unwillingness to communicate on any level an outsider can understand. They are enigmatic, remote, self-contained. You can't be a friend; they don't want friends. They don't want conversation. They want nothing the rest of us assume everyone wants. I often think of them, out in the ancient wilderness, carefully rehearsing for death. There is comfort in knowing such places still exist.

As if sensing my change in attitude, Father George said he'd be glad to show me the monastery's treasures as soon as His Grace had left. And he said the words with great warmth and tenderness. With love.

〜〜

The only reason so much from millennia ago has survived almost intact in Egypt is, of course, the climate. Fungus and rot are practically unknown in the dry heat. Stone survives, wood survives, parchment, papyrus, and even paper survive. Pollution is changing all this now, but the real culprit is the unnoticeable but devastating rise in humidity directly resulting from the Aswan Dam, the creation of Lake Nasser, and a rising water table.

Being far from the dam, the Nile, and pollution, St. Catherine's has much the same climatic conditions it had in Moses' time. When Father George led me into the sixth-century basilica, I was astonished to find a building that had scarcely changed in fifteen hundred years. The enormous cypress wood doors that guard the entrance to the narthex, themselves installed as recently as the twelfth century, are in almost perfect condition. Exquisitely carved with swirling flowers, trees, leaves, angels, and the Christ, in geometric patterns with a strong hint of the Islamic about them, they lead into an area rarely found in later churches, a kind of gallery screening off the church interior, which cannot be entered directly. This serves some symbolic function, Father George explained, without elaborating. Now the area contains many of the monastery's greatest treasures — most notably the world's earliest icons. Of astonishing beauty, and far from the gaudiness of later examples, many of these perfect little masterpieces are painted in styles and with techniques that seem to belong to another tradition altogether.

One of the most famous of all icons hangs here: the twelfth-century image of Saint John Klimakos, accompanied by twenty-four other hopefuls, climbing a ladder to heaven. The saint wrote a treatise using a ladder with thirty steps as a metaphor for the thirty perfections a man must achieve to enter paradise. Hence his name: "Klimakos" derives from the Greek word for "ladder." Dapper little black devils with spiky hair, bows and arrows, and long hooks lurk at the edges of the ladder seeking out those who haven't made the grade. Klimakos, only second from the top and dressed far better than anyone else, looks assured of making it through the top right-hand corner into the arms of Saint Peter. But six of the other twenty-four have already been hauled from their rungs — one of them apparently from the same rung as Klimakos — and another appears to have been thrust headfirst into the jaws of a dung-coloured monster at the ladder's foot by an especially wicked-looking devil. In the top left-hand corner, as far away as they can get, angels look on with intense but doubtful expressions. And below on the right a group of very serious men, four of whom appear to be identical quadruplets, look as if they're applauding the spectacle but are probably raising their hands to invoke grace for the anxious climbers. Most of these climbers, instead of looking up to heaven's gate, are watching in pure fright the fate of their colleagues who've been shot, hooked, and hauled off to hell.

The icon is poignant, beautiful, and, unintentionally, I'm sure, amusing. The expressions on the faces of the failed climbers are especially worth examining. The one who was nearest the top looks downright angry, holding out his hands, palms up, as if saying *Come on, guys, give me a break. What did I do so wrong?*

Father George did not seem to find the icon funny. He moved me on to a glass case protecting Codex Syriacus, identified in 1892 as a fifth-century translation of the Gospels, part of which was erased in the eighth or ninth centuries so that the parchment could be reused. Because the Codex is older than the monastery itself, its presence proves the monks were collecting ancient manuscripts from the foundation of St. Catherine's.

Father George showed me the saddest possession of all in another case, a copy of Codex Sinaiticus published by Tischendorf and presented by the czarist government to the monastery. It was an exceptionally beautiful facsimile, I observed, almost as good as the real thing. Father George took a different view. Given his feelings, I'm surprised the monks didn't return this insult or burn it publicly. But Father George was optimistic that the British would return the original one day. And trained sheep will pilot the Concorde, I thought.

Like all Orthodox churches I've seen, the interior of St. Catherine's basilica was crammed from floor to rafters with so much *stuff* that it was hard to decide what to look at first. Huge, dangling octopuslike chandeliers designed to hold candles shone like new gold, their curved gleaming arms giving an impression of movement. All around them hung giant silver censers, elegantly shaped in a plumply Oriental manner. Cloth-of-gold banners; gilded thrones and altars; man-sized brass candlesticks; a floor of several types of marble inlaid in complex, subtle geometric patterns; and, on either side, facing each other, not the altar, rows of pews like surreal chairs with arms at shoulder height, their wood worn to a rich patina by more than a millennium of use.

A thick smell of incense permeated the air, soaked into every stone, every piece of wood. And there was an aura of sanctity, a deep and resonant silence. I looked up to where massive gleaming eggshell-white pillars rose to ornate black capitals before soaring into pristine arches. We walked behind them, proceeding along the basilica's northwest wall. Father George noticed me looking at these almost pharaonic pillars, saying, "The *National Geographic* came here, you know. They chipped away the plaster on one of our columns to see if it was monolithic."

"And was it?"

"Yes."

I could tell the incident ranked on his list of indignities and injustices to the monastery. Above the dazzling wall of gold that is the church's apse, we gazed up at the mosaic stretching across the entire space. It depicts the

Transfiguration of Christ, who stands flanked by Moses and Elijah, with the apostles Peter, James, and John at his feet. Above, to the left and right, are scenes from Moses' life. As others have noted, in place of the stone tablets quite clearly identified in the Exodus account, Moses brings the Law down from Mount Sinai on scrolls here. I would rather have brought it down on scrolls, too. They're lighter.

This mosaic is a supreme achievement, equalled only by two others in Ravenna, Italy, dating from the same period and possibly created by the same artist. There's not much you can say when faced with such shattering beauty.

I followed Father George through a roped-off area — NO TOURISTS PAST THIS POINT — around the side of the altar screen. Altars are still concealed in the Eastern Orthodox Church, still accorded their mystery and holiness. The work of ancient master craftsmen everywhere was breathtaking, every inch a treasure. Near the back of the screen sat a huge chest that I guessed was made of solid silver. Its sides and lid were worked with religious scenes and complicated patterns by the hand of a genius. I asked Father George about it.

"It was a gift from Czar Nicholas of Russia," he replied. "He sent it to us so we could place Saint Catherine's bones inside."

"Are they still there?"

"No. We never did put them in it," he said.

"So what's in it now?"

"Oh." He scratched his beard thoughtfully. "Odds and ends, I expect. I doubt if anyone remembers now. I think we lost the key for it some years ago."

It probably contained the original Ten Commandments, Aaron's rod, and the Holy Grail, I thought. The monks were spiritual misers, hoarding items they'd never use, or often never even understand, just because they were *there*.

Proceeding through a small arch into some kind of antechamber before a curtained-off area, Father George asked me to remove my shoes.

Put off thy shoes from off thy feet, for the place whereon thou standest is holy ground. Moreover he said, I am the God of thy father, the God of Abraham, the God of Isaac, and the God of Jacob. And Moses hid his face; for he was afraid to look upon God.
—EXODUS III:5–6.

And behind that curtain Father George parted was where all this had taken place. A few yards away was the spot chosen by the Creator of the Universe, the Primordial One, the Ancient of Days, the Indivisible, Unknowable, and Nameless, to bring one age to an end and to usher in the succeeding age.

This holy of holy places had, for me, the feeling of being very special indeed. Too special. Walking barefoot to kneel before the tiny enclosure, much adorned in silver and gold and containing THE SPOT, I struggled to feel the appropriate emotions. But all I could think of was the long, shaggy orange fake fur of the carpet on the Burning Bush Chapel's floor, the kind of fabric Jamaican cabdrivers tend to glue across their dashboards. Did the monks, I wondered, find this carpet attractive, the way Hindus see nothing wrong with wrapping a thousand yards of flashing Christmas-tree lights around an eight-hundred-year-old Krishna shrine? I wanted to ask Father George, but I didn't dare. I tried to feel, tried to grasp, the awesome significance of this place. The heart was willing, but the mind was wilful.

I pretended to pray instead. Father George looked gratified, and I thanked him for taking the trouble to endure my company. He seemed more at ease now, and as we left through a side door emerging into the iris-crunching light, he said, "Would you ever think of leading this life?"

"It's hard, isn't it?" I replied.

"Yes. It's very hard."

"Do you have doubts, think of quitting?"

"Yes." His voice was soft, sad. "Often. All too often."

"How do you deal with that?"

"I pray. I seek guidance from His Grace."

I wasn't sure whether he meant the archbishop or the grace of God. "Does that work?" I asked.

"It passes, like everything. It comes and goes."

"I don't think you could be happy out in the world."

"Of course not," he told me pointedly. "No one else is."

"I can't reply to that, Father."

"I know," he said, a tiny smile on his lips. "I know you can't."

"I'm going to say good-bye now. Is there anything I can send you?"

"What I want *you* can't send me." He laughed and took my hand. "Good-bye, my brother. I hope your life will be fulfilling."

"Thanks. Thanks for everything."

He shook his head. "Please don't thank me. I think that your time here has not been wasted. Seeds grow."

"If the soil's good, no?" I wasn't entirely sure the metaphor went like that.

"The soil's okay." He turned and walked back toward his cell.

I returned to mine and cried on the little bed for about ten minutes. Then I packed.

CHAPTER EIGHTEEN

NOT ANOTHER BOOK ON EGYPT

*In my opinion and in the absence of a better estimation, Cairo
is twice as large as Paris and has four times the population; if I
give a larger figure, it would still be an understatement ...*

— SIMON SIMEONIS, A.D. 1332

Before leaving, I visited the ossuary in the monastery grounds. Piles of
skulls and bones, the seated and partially mummified skeleton of a sixth-
century monk named Stephen, dressed in the robes of a deacon, guarding
the entrance: it is a horrifying place for the outsider. I thought of Hamlet's
Yorick soliloquy. What minds had once inhabited these skulls?

Though a horrifying spectacle, these thousands of human skulls and
bones did not resonate with the horror of similar sights photographed
at Auschwitz, Buchenwald, or on the killing fields of Pol Pot's Cambodia,
which latter I once saw myself. This cavern of death was not the same
death meted out by the butchers of the earth. It was the one those
monks whose mortal remains were now stacked here had spent their

lives carefully rehearsing for; the one still being carefully rehearsed by those living behind Justinian's immense walls behind me. I wondered whether Father George's bones would one day also be piled in this dark silent room, tangled with those of the men in whose footsteps he was walking. I hoped they would.

～๑

I was booked on the 11:00 A.M. flight to Cairo with Air Sinai. An amiable old man at the lazy little airport told me I had plenty of time. The plane had arrived, but since the crew had never been to St. Catherine's before, the flight had been delayed an hour or so to allow them to visit the monastery and the town.

In an adjacent one-storey structure I found a lounge decorated incongruously in a quasi-Hawaiian theme — bamboo, plastic palm fronds. Sitting on a gigantic rattan sofa of Early Elvis Den style, I ordered tea. Two men dressed like airline pilots were sitting nearby seeing which of them could smoke the most Marlboros. One asked if I was on the Cairo flight, which was somewhat redundant since the Cairo flight was the only flight listed that day. He was Selim, he informed me, the captain of that flight. His friend, Ahmed, was the copilot. Yes, he confirmed, the crew was touring St. Catherine's, and we'd leave when they returned. We chatted about nothing in particular, and eventually I dozed off, having a curious dream about Yassir Arafat, in which the PLO leader asked whether he could borrow my best suit for a speaking engagement.

By 12:45 I was in my seat aboard the tiny plane. At 1:30 we were still sitting on the tarmac, the plane's door open, steps still locked into position. I asked a flight attendant when we might take off. "One passenger has still not arrived," she replied.

"But we're already two and a half hours late," I said. "Perhaps that passenger isn't coming?"

"He's booked on the flight," she said.

"But the flight was 11:00 A.M."

She seemed unwilling to believe the passenger wasn't on his way, although the plane he was on his way to catch had left, presumably, two and a half hours ago.

"How much longer shall we give him?" I inquired.

She shrugged. Anyone who'd bought a ticket deserved the benefit of the doubt — three hours of it, as things turned out. Just after 2:00 P.M. a man who would have made Orson Welles look trim waddled into the plane. Wearing a puce leisure suit so tight it must have taken two men to button it up and carrying the smallest attaché case I've ever seen — a sheet of onionskin paper and a postcard would have filled it — the man rolled to his seats. He'd purchased two, since, lifting the central armrest and sitting down, he occupied all the space between window and aisle, buckling the left-hand seat belt, after opening it to its full length, into the right-hand one. I wondered if this entitled him to two meals.

After takeoff, a flight attendant informed me the captain had invited me to visit the cockpit. From the cramped module between the captain and his copilot, I got a spectacular view of the mountainous wilderness below.

"Sit down," Captain Selim said. A flight attendant appeared, folded out a central seat I hadn't noticed, and bolted it into place for me. Shoulder to shoulder between Selim and Ahmed, I quickly learned that my seat did not include a seat belt. "Have a drink?" Selim offered, pressing his button. A coffee arrived. "Cigarette?" Selim thrust the remains of that day's fifth pack of Marlboros at me.

A thin plastic takeout coffee beaker was held in a ring fixed above the instrument panel. It contained the remains of some coffee. Selim and Ahmed used it as an ashtray. So did I. As butts hissed to death, it occurred to me that if one burned through the soft white plastic, the contents would cascade over the countless buttons and gauges and the wiring behind them.

"Let's take a look at Mount Sinai?" Selim asked me. "Want to?"

I said sure. More cigarettes were lit, and the plane tilted forty-five degrees and turned round, swooping down low. We were about fifteen feet above a mountaintop. Tilting his joystick, Selim took us up and around until we were level with the summit of Mount Sinai and a crowd of horrified tourists who were crouching behind rocks in case the aircraft either crashed on them or opened fire with machine guns. I looked behind me down the aisle, where several passengers, pale with fright, seemed to think I was responsible for this unexpected detour.

After circling the mountain, Selim veered away, evening out in a south-easterly direction.

"Isn't Cairo the other way?" I asked, trying to sound nonchalant.

"Yes," Selim replied, peering through his windshield. "It's sort of that way." He pointed behind us.

"Ah. So why do we have to reach it by flying in the opposite direction?" I expected some kind of technical explanation involving air corridors, winds.

"We thought we'd go to Hurghada first," Selim announced.

"*Hurghada!* Why?"

"See if there's any passengers who want to go to Cairo."

"Can't you do that by phone or radio?"

"No," he explained lazily. "Much easier to hop over and drop in there."

It was like a flying cab. I hoped the crew had seen Hurghada before, or we'd have another three-hour delay while the flight attendants went scuba diving.

"There," Ahmed announced, pointing. "Ras Muhammad."

Captain Selim disagreed. "No, it's not," he said. "Ras Muhammad's over there ... or *is* it? Yes, see, Ahmed, *that's* Ras Muhammad." Both men craned their necks, peering at the sparkling expanses of azure and turquoise water now stretching out below us.

"See," Selim continued. "You were looking at Sharm al-Sheikh."

"Was I?" Ahmed wondered. "Isn't *that* Sharm al-Sheikh over there?"

Captain Selim considered this. "No," he finally decided. "I think that's that other place. The one that looks a bit like Sharm al-Sheikh on the map."

Lighting more cigarettes. Ahmed reached for a map. "Oh, that place."

Selim looked, saying, "No, that's another place. I meant *that* place." He pointed with his cigarette.

"Oh," Ahmed replied. "*That* place. Yes, that does look a bit like Sharm al-Sheikh."

Was this the sort of conversation that went on in cockpits around the world? Below, an oil tanker slid out of the Gulf of Aqaba, a black predatory shape leaving a considerable quantity of its cargo on the parted waters of its wake.

"Go right by that island," Selim told Ahmed.

"This island?"

"No, *that* island." Selim turned to offer me yet another Marlboro, saying, "Want to have a turn at the wheel?"

"Oh, no thanks," I replied, somewhat unnerved. "You go ahead."

"President Mubarak always likes to pilot the plane *he's* on for a while," Selim informed me.

"Yeah," I said. "But that's probably because he used to be in the air force and knows how to fly planes, wouldn't you say?"

Selim shrugged. "Do you want to try landing?" he asked Ahmed.

"Okay," Ahmed answered.

It wouldn't have surprised me if Selim had asked over the intercom whether any of the other passengers wanted to take a shot at landing if Ahmed had declined.

"If you overshoot," Selim advised his copilot, "just head off left over the sea and try again. That runway's a bit short."

No wonder this duo went through twenty packs of Marlboros a day. Lung cancer was the least of their worries. Ahmed heaved his joystick up, and we quickly lost height. "That all the fuel we've got?" he asked Selim, squinting at the watchmaker's warehouse on his dashboard.

"No," the captain assured him. "That gauge isn't working. We should have a full tank. Didn't I refuel in St. Catherine's?"

"Wasn't it Cairo?"

"Was it?"

Both men shrugged.

At this point we had turned and were moments away from landing on the runway at Hurghada — or Elat if they'd been looking at their map upside down, or indeed anywhere with an airport between Jordan and Saudi Arabia. I wondered whether they'd forgotten to tell me to return to my seat. Since they weren't wearing their seat belts, either, I assumed this, too, was no big deal.

We began to rock from side to side alarmingly. On the instrument panel a red light started to flash above a small rectangle that contained the word "danger" in bold letters. Selim turned to me smiling and, gesturing at the light, said, "Don't worry, it always does that."

Both men frowned with concentration, the captain flipping various levers, Ahmed struggling with his control wheel like someone operating a heavy lawnmower. A thud, a silence, another thud, and we'd landed, swerving to a snaky halt not far from the terminal's bungalow. I thanked both of them profusely for letting me sit with them, promising myself I'd never go near a cockpit again.

Taking on some people I recognized from the Giftun Village, we were off again within fifteen minutes. I asked one of the people who'd joined the plane at Hurghada how this deviation had worked. He didn't know. He'd been booked on an EgyptAir flight due to leave forty-five minutes later, but someone had asked him whether he wanted to leave immediately on Air Sinai. That had suited him fine.

No one seemed sure how Air Sinai worked this out with EgyptAir. I recounted my experiences in the cockpit until a woman in front of me screamed that she didn't want to hear any more.

"That's nothing," an Englishman across the aisle said. "I was on an EgyptAir flight where the captain had his whole family in the cockpit. You kept hearing him shouting at the kids, telling them not to play with the buttons and levers."

Worldwide, airlines are not that dissimilar, I find.

Before long we were emerging from the desert, descending over the step pyramid at Saqqara and heading toward Giza, where we hung a right over the Great Pyramid and passed above the boulevard leading into Cairo. I imagined Selim and Ahmed arguing over which pyramid was which, then perusing a road map of Cairo to work out where the airport was. They certainly seemed to be lost a couple of times, circling over a complex of industrial buildings that resembled hangars but weren't, then heading off in another direction, turning back, zigzagging, circling again, descending so low I could see earthlings looking up at us dubiously. We would ascend again, zigzagging, until identifying either an enormous empty highway or part of the Cairo airport's runway system. We landed without incident, four hours late.

⁓

A thick gold-embossed envelope was waiting for me at the hotel, in it an invitation from the Canadian ambassador, Marc Brault, to a reception at his residence. Putting on my best suit (the one Yassir Arafat had wanted to borrow in my dream), I took a cab to Kamal Muhammad Street on Zamalek Island. Taxi drivers never seem to be able to locate any but the largest thoroughfares, partly because street names have, in some cases, changed several times over the last thirty years. So I was late.

Zamalek at night looks like one of the fancier arrondissements of Paris, and the Canadian ambassador's residence is one of the most lavish mansions in it: vast, gleaming white, colonial, with an acre of walled garden full of fruit trees in blossom, their petals floating on the blue surface of an illuminated swimming pool. Outside were many limousines, armed guards, and, standing at the shiny black double doors, servants dressed like Nubians.

Inside the marble entrance, at the foot of an extravagant staircase beneath a ton of chandelier, stood Ambassador Marc Brault, an untidy little man with a thick black moustache and a tuxedo that appeared too large for him. He looked out of place, and many guests mistook the menacing security guard at his side for "His Excellency." The reception was for a group of businessmen, many of them Egyptian Canadians touring the country in search of business opportunities. Everyone looked unusually large and conspicuously rich. Gazing around at the marble, the polished mahogany, the silver, the Group of Seven paintings, the Persian rugs, the legion of servants ferrying platters of food and drinks, one man remarked loudly, "So *this* is where my tax dollars are going!" They weren't going to Professor Redford down in East Karnak, that much was certain.

I circulated, astounded by the wood-panelled drawing rooms stacked with treasures, the cool of a balcony overlooking the floodlit gardens, with lawn sprinklers spurting diamonds over mango blossoms in a quiet, scented night. Quite a life these petty bureaucrats from Ottawa had themselves out here. Trying unsuccessfully to enter several conversations with cigar-chomping men discussing portfolios, I eventually figured out that an animated and elegantly beautiful woman at the centre of much attention was the ambassador's wife.

Madame Brault seemed relieved to talk with someone who was not a businessman. She also seemed to know a lot more about Egypt than did her husband, since she was engaged in much charitable work that took her out to the rural villages. I asked her about the growing discontent among the young that one read of daily in the newspapers.

"There's educational chaos in this country," she replied. "The standard is very low and too many Ph.D.s are turned out each year, finding no jobs waiting for them. But if, say, the health minister turns to the education minister and says, 'Stop turning out Ph.D.s,' the education minister is going to reply, 'I can't — or I'll lose my job.' And this creates discontent — too many overqualified youths with nothing to do."

Was this, I wondered, what lay behind the brutal Muslim-Christian riots that had just taken place in the Fayyoum Oasis?

"Oh," Madame Brault replied, "this sort of thing is continuous. People are stirred up by the fundamentalists for political purposes. But" — she looked grave and thoughtful, as if debating whether she should be saying such things — "the problem is the government officials in these country areas only get paid fifty pounds a month, so they do nothing. The fundamentalists in effect do what the government *should* be doing — practical stuff like making business loans and leasing out machinery at minimal rates or even for free. So they gain influence.

"What I see in the villages is a very entrenched class system — totally contrary to Islam. But Islam is very ambiguous. What you see on paper is not what you find on the street. Most of the official people I meet are a mass of contradictions, but you can't contradict them."

Looking across the lawns to where the pale turquoise of the pool glowed with light amid the black shadows of trees, she said, "Egypt is so different from other Islamic countries — much more Westernized. But they don't see it. They're so caught up in the problems of this part of the world, the problems of Islam, of Arab and Israeli, that they don't realize their situation is exacerbated by their very difference from those they try to reconcile with each other. Egyptians can adapt; the other Arabs find it so much harder.

I have a lot of faith in this country's future." She'd come to love the country, love its people and her work among them.

Seven months after that party in Cairo, I learned Marc Brault had been replaced as Canadian ambassador. Madame Brault would have been more disappointed to leave, I suspect, than her husband.

～つ

I had been invited by the Egyptian art historian Liliane Karnouk to the opening of a one-man show at a small gallery called La Part du Sable on rue Ahmed Hishmat. Since this, too, was in Zamalek, I left the embassy party early and walked the quiet streets of the island's wealthy ghetto: so very Parisian, with its chic boutiques, tiny bistros, and square, shuttered houses. I soon found the address. The gallery was upstairs in a rambling, fashionably decayed mansion. The spacious rooms were packed with an art crowd that could have been at any similar event from Manhattan to Sydney, drinking wine, which was poured as if it were hard liquor here, and talking in huddles, ignoring the paintings. These were large, mediocre abstract-expressionist canvases by a young artist called Joseph Limoud, a French-speaking Black who could have been from anywhere in North Africa. As with all such gatherings, this was not so much for the artist and his work as for the gallery owner's friends.

Liliane Karnouk, a small, intense woman with short greying hair, had been educated in Canada where she had also taught on and off for the last twenty years. An Egyptian Christian, she was currently teaching at the American University in Cairo, presumably on the strength of her 1988 book, *Modern Egyptian Art: The Emergence of a National Style*.

It's an excellent study and one of the very few that exist. In it she deals as much with the national psyche of Egypt as she does with its contemporary art. "The Egyptian artist," she writes in her introduction,

> *has had to resolve a double dilemma. The first is whether or not to become an artist in the European individualistic sense and*

thus risk losing a connection to the native soil and its traditions, or whether to revive the traditional ethnic arts and risk remaining marginal to the world of international high art. The second dilemma is the need to articulate the existence of several value systems historically coexisting within this nation on two levels: the Islamic and the Egyptian.

Besides being a statement only a Copt, or non-Muslim, could make, it does highlight a universal truth applicable to all areas of Egyptian endeavour. As she states elsewhere, the Egyptian identity is rooted in a single historical factor: 2,400 years of uninterrupted occupation, beginning with the Persians in 525 B.C. She writes of "a country without being a nation, a land where civilizations flourished and influenced other nations while the Egyptian people remained under the power of a succession of foreign invaders."

Liliane Karnouk seemed to know everyone at the opening, and her opinions were much in demand. Conversations were conducted in English, French, and Arabic — at times a mixture of all three — and, sitting out on the broad, long balcony overlooking the trees and calm streets of the island ("This is the reason one comes to Christine's gallery"), Liliane held court, introducing me to this person and that person, maintaining several conversations at once.

"Not *another* book on Egypt," one bejewelled sophisticate said with a groan, on discovering my purpose in Egypt. "Give up."

A general air of bored cynicism prevailed. To one hairy, chain-smoking rich bohemian, Liliane was saying, "I'm looking for a cottage to buy in the south of France — it's the thing to do. We can go there when the Fayyoum gets too dangerous." Everyone seemed to be off to New York or Paris.

I was introduced to Steven Alter, a talented young writer also teaching at the American University. The son of American missionaries, he was well known in India, where he'd been born and had lived for much of his life, marrying an Indian woman. I asked about the students at AUC. It was a curious place, half Californian campus, half Islamic institution. Orthodox Muslim girls mingled with Westernized Egyptians in tight jeans, who smoked cigarettes and chewed gum, and even laughed with boys. Alter said he'd once set his class an essay project on the historical personage they'd most like to have known. "Most of them picked Adolf Hitler," Alter said, sighing with disbelief. "Also," he went on, "the boys tend to have antifeminist views that would get them strung up in the States." Alter confirmed standards were shockingly low, much of his time spent on remedial writing skills. I wondered how students viewed someone like Qaddafi. "Oh," Alter replied, "Egyptians don't have much good to say about any of their neighbours. They never did. Even in the hieroglyphs you have these endless references to the 'vile Hurrians,' and so on. It's such an odd muddle of superiority and inferiority."

How did Alter find living in Cairo and India? I wanted to know. It was wearing, he said, particularly in terms of everyday life. "If you need a car repaired or have to deal with the bureaucracy, it takes up a whole day, drives you nuts." Yet both he and his wife enjoyed it all the same. How different from New Delhi could it have been, after all?

"Come," Liliane Karnouk said. "Let's get out of here and go somewhere we can talk." In her battered Fiat we drove back across the July 26 Bridge into the teeming heart of the city. The favourite haunt of intellectuals, she claimed, was the roof bar of the Odeon Hotel. Not far from Tahrir Square, the Odeon Hotel was opposite the Odeon Cinema, where something called *In the Line of Duty II — The Super Cops* was playing. It seemed like a neat and tiny place, a slow wood-panelled elevator taking us to the top floor, which housed a restaurant and bar extending out over a pleasant open-roof patio. At 1:30 A.M. the place was fairly packed.

Again Liliane knew everyone. Mainly, of course, men. There *were*, however, several Egyptian women here: intellectuals in hybrid outfits of Western and Arab clothes and jewellery that gave them the appearance of sixties hippies. A couple of them even smoked *sheesha* pipes; everyone else puffed cigarettes and poured glasses of Château Ptolemy or Omar Khayyam Red, talking loudly and intensely.

Liliane elaborated on her theories about Egyptian art. Style was imported from the West, she said. After thirty years of government-controlled art, an import from the Soviet Union, there was now a glut of abstract expressionism, another import. "Why are the artists working like this?" she asked. "What are their motives? Is it altruism or toadying?"

The problems of Egyptian art suddenly interested me less than the more general issues. Even in the relatively hedonistic atmosphere of the Odeon Hotel's bar, there seemed to be a gulf between men and women, although at least women were there. Did Muslims lead the chaste lives they appeared to lead?

"Yes, oh yes," Liliane replied. "You see those two men sitting together there?" I did. "That's a love affair — in every way but sexual. Their wives are at home, and they will be the ones who go out to dinner together. Probably for the rest of their lives. There are really two Egypts, you see. Divorced women, like those few over there, enjoy more tolerance, but not much more. I know divorced women who live with homosexuals so that each can pursue their lives without arousing the suspicion of neighbours."

Were there *bassassin* (spies) everywhere, ready to report unorthodox goings-on to the appropriate authorities, as I'd been told when visiting the Sufi gathering?

"Oh yes," Liliane replied. "It's a leftover from more repressive times, but the memory of those times is fresh. People don't trust their neighbours, each other. It's like Romania after Ceausescu; no one is sure who's an informer, an agent. But, corrupt as leadership in Egypt is," she added, "it's still very benevolent. They're willing to ruin the country to subsidize the poor. And people still do what they feel like doing, regardless of censorious attitudes. When you consider what Cairo is — the vastness, the population — it's still remarkably problem-free. But, you see, you have to break the system to get anything done, and that's corruption. If I want a paper signed for something, I have to pay to get it done this side of next year, and that's corruption."

It was not the kind of corruption we're used to in the West — the bigger kind. It had more to do with low salaries and the constant fear of rising food costs than it did with greed or the manipulation of power. It was an irritant, little more. An irritant in a society that expected much of itself, a society of lofty ideals, many of which were practised, I found, to a degree that shamed Western societies.

Egyptians are hard on themselves; their sense of superiority makes all failure intolerable and thus leads to a simultaneous sense of inferiority. But still many Cairenes I met reminded me of those people who warn you what a terrible mess their house is in before taking you into a place that looks far tidier than your own. It is fear that eats at their souls, though, fear things are deteriorating.

For the poor, rising food prices are the greatest of these fears. Everything is insidiously interconnected: farmers in the Nile Delta are switching from growing cotton, a major export, to growing food, because it's become more profitable. The result: a loss of jobs as the cotton-manufacturing plants are forced to close. Such chain reactions were common, and talking with Liliane's friends, I heard many others. Yet these people, all wealthy, were removed from such realities, free to theorize but strangely out of place. As Westernized as they all were, they would not be at home in the West, and they were not at home in Cairo beyond their little cliques. Arguing about where Egypt had come from artistically, politically, socially, and where it was going, they did not appear to be a part of the past or the future. Caught between worlds, like so many born during the twilight of colonialism, they now dwelt in a theoretical zone with only each other for company, waiting for someone else to invite them back to earth.

CHAPTER NINETEEN

AN INVISIBLE CITY

If a man make a pilgrimage round Alexandria in the morning,
God will make for him a golden crown, set with pearls, perfumed
with musk and camphor, and shining from the East to the West.

—IBN DUKMAK

The train out of Cairo's enormous Ramses Station was absurdly cheap and
as luxurious as a first-class airplane cabin. Because of the confusion between
Arabic numerals and English ones — what looks like a 0 is actually 5, and
the symbol for 6 looks exactly like an English 7 — I changed seats a couple
of times. Although I could read Arabic numerals, the conductor had a problem with English ones, insisting I sit in seat 65 when I knew I should be in
seat 70. You can learn Arabic numerals after a morning looking at car
licence plates, which are written in both English and Arabic, right to left, not
that numbers care so much as letters do which way you read them.

The crumbling sprawl that seems to line the rail exits of most cities soon
gave way to more pastoral scenes beyond Cairo as the train sped into the

heart of the Nile Delta. Camels and buffalo roamed by the train tracks, alongside women wearing what looked like big nightgowns and carrying huge baskets of vegetables on their heads. But it was the sudden expanse of green stretching as far as the eye could see that impressed me most. After months of dust, rocks, ochre sands, with the odd strip of cultivated land wedged in between, I'd almost forgotten what real arable land looked like, or that Egypt contained any. Here were lush farmlands, as rich and green as any spring landscape in northern Europe. Acres of orchards, rice paddies, wheat fields, and even vineyards. You move suddenly out of Africa and into the Mediterranean. And the difference between desert and fertile land is as great as the difference between Cairo and Alexandria.

According to the view from the window, I could well have been pulling into Nice or Naples, a mere two hours after leaving Cairo. Palm fronds waved beneath a Wedgwood-blue sky; broad boulevards were lined with pale yellow-plastered buildings in the imposing, chunky, European colonial style. The people looked different.

The cars looked different, too. Every city in Egypt seems to favour a certain make of car. If Peugeot was cleaning up in Aswan, Fiat was doing a brisk trade in Alexandria. My taxi driver wanted me to sit in the front seat next to him — so he wouldn't have to ply me with Cleopatra Milds over the headrest, presumably. I told him my destination was the Palestine Hotel, but although it's one of the two best-known hotels in Alexandria, I had to pronounce it "Falesteen Hotel" before we could set off. Hurtling along at a rate that would have been alarming even by Cairo standards, we narrowly avoided three major accidents before levelling off to a more reasonable speed. It reminded me of an airplane's takeoff.

The dashboard was covered in what could have been part of the Burning Bush Chapel's carpet and held a mounted photo of the Ka'aba surrounded by flashing fairy lights. Cars here were more personalized than they were in Cairo. Many bore bumper stickers. LOVE ME, LOVE MY CAR, read one, and another, LADY DRIVERS ARE STUPIED [sic], MEN ARE TOP, next to WARNING TO LADIES, DRIVER FROM UPPER EGYPT. Were Upper Egyptians considered sexist, I wondered, or sexy … or perhaps diabolical drivers?

The cabbie hammered a tape cassette into his dashboard, turning the volume up on a tempest of static and tape hiss. Instead of Zamfir or wailing quarter-tone pop, however, I was deafened for five minutes by the chronically tone-deaf bleating of someone reciting the Koran accompanied by a noise like babies being strangled. Then, suddenly the tape was extracted and the machine turned off. It was midday-prayer time, so I assumed this interlude comprised the driver's obligatory devotions.

Almost empty compared to Cairo, the city must have undergone a recent and major renovation. It was clean and spacious, full of parks. I'd assumed the railway station was fairly central, and also that the Palestine Hotel wouldn't be far from it, but this taxi ride seemed interminable. Heading through streets that looked like Nice badly disguised as Marrakech, we emerged onto a broad corniche, the Mediterranean a turbulent smoky blue in sharp bright sunlight. The air was much cooler, heavy with the salt tang of the ocean. This corniche also seemed interminable, a wall on one side, and rows of elegant houses mixed with smart modern hotels on the other. Eventually the cabbie zipped into the small drive of a place quite clearly labelled Galaxy Hotel, coming to an abrupt and shuddering halt.

"Uh-uh," I told him. "*Falesteen* Hotel. Not Galaxy Hotel."

He did his best to convince me first that this *was* the Palestine Hotel; then, changing strategy, he told me it was as good as the Palestine Hotel, and much cheaper. He could have been right.

The Palestine Hotel is in the grounds of King Farouk's Al-Montazah summer palace, entered through a forbidding stone arch. The grounds and their gardens are open to the public, but the public has to pay to get in. Officious armed guards stopped us at the entrance and seemed reluctant to believe I was going to the hotel and thus didn't have to pay the twenty-five cents or so to get into the grounds. The driver looked terrified but kept on arguing with the guards although I'd offered to pay the admittance fee anyway. He kept on arguing with me, too, after I'd given him 10 percent of the hundred U.S. dollars he'd demanded for this ride. He pursued me right up to the hotel door, almost convincing me I'd robbed him. As it turned out, I learned I'd paid him only twice as much as the fare was worth.

The Palestine was designed by someone intent on causing its guests as much inconvenience as possible. Everything inside was as far from everything else as space would allow, and all exterior doors were designed to make you walk around the entire building to reach the area they served. The staff appeared to be afflicted with narcolepsy, either asleep or catatonic. Nothing you ordered, from wake-up calls to meals, ever arrived. Although the place had about five thousand rooms, it seemed to have only five or so guests. Part of the problem could have been its location; it was so far from the city centre that it was practically outside Alexandria.

From my balcony I overlooked a miniature children's park — one slide and a seesaw — called "Mickey Mouse World," and King Farouk's old palace. In an odd sort of way, the palace was extremely beautiful. It looked as if it had been assembled from leftover parts scavenged from various mosques, Roman villas, and Bavarian castles. Apparently an Italian had designed it for the late king.

I turned on the TV to find *Alexander the Great* playing. *That*, I thought, is either an amazing coincidence or a permanent feature in the hotel. According to the TV guide card it was an amazing coincidence.

Alexander was twenty-five years old when he ordered the city built some 2,300-odd years ago. By the time he returned, some eight years later, having conquered the known world in between, the city was complete. Alexander was also dead. His corpse had originally been sent for burial to Memphis, but the high priest there wanted nothing to do with it. Take him to his own city, the priest said, "for wherever this body must lie, the city will be uneasy, disturbed with wars and battles." Wrapped in gold and enclosed in a glass coffin, Alexander the Great was shipped down the Nile again to be buried at the centre of Alexandria, by the city's great crossroads, becoming both civic hero and tutelary god. His tomb has never been discovered, and unless someone intends to bulldoze half the city, it probably never will be. On TV, Alexander was an impetuous fellow, prone to bad-tempered bursts of rhetoric and staggering megalomania, which none of his companions appeared to mind or even notice.

Alexander was nowhere close to building the city I was now in when the phone rang. Someone named Mr. Alaa, from the government, was in the lobby. Tall, stooped, he could have been Colonel Qaddafi's brother, which was perhaps why he looked so incredibly sad. In fact, I thought he was about to burst into tears. I asked him if he was all right. He seemed surprised and claimed he was fine. I didn't believe him. He'd come, he said, to take me to the meeting I'd arranged with the governor of Alexandria.

I hadn't arranged any such meeting but saw no reason not to take the opportunity since it had arisen. Mr. Alaa had a huge Mercedes with curtained windows waiting outside. Mournfully he climbed onto the back seat next to me.

"Don't worry," he told me, pointing at the chauffeur, "he's not a fundamentalist."

"What?" I asked, looking at the chauffeur, who smiled, as if to confirm this about himself.

"His beard," Mr. Alaa said.

"His beard?"

"I thought you might think he was a fundamentalist Muslim because he has a beard. Then you might not talk as freely as you might wish to me."

"Do all fundamentalists have beards?" I inquired.

"No," Mr. Alaa admitted.

"Are all people with beards fundamentalists?"

"Not all. But most."

"Did you think Salman Rushdie was a fundamentalist Muslim when he had a beard?"

"Who?" Mr. Alaa asked.

Assuming, perhaps, we were still debating his religious affiliations, the chauffeur picked up a tape cassette emblazoned with the Stars and Stripes and put on something called "Midnight Sax." It was quite good, creating the mood of a boozy jazz club in the wee small hours. Which didn't suit Alexandria in broad daylight.

The governor's office was in an impressive modern building that could have been the headquarters of a big insurance company. Mr. Alaa escorted me to a large crowded office run by an extremely pleasant woman who owned much jewellery. We sat down beside a number of prosperous-looking men holding large file folders and talking together in urgent whispers. They looked Greek or Italian but spoke in Arabic — a lazy, muted Alexandrian Arabic, far removed from the aural mugging of Cairene.

I hoped we weren't the last in a long lineup. These men, I imagined, wanted the governor to approve complex schemes that would make them richer and would take considerable time to explain.

A large telephone rang on the pleasant woman's desk; her rings clacked against the receiver's plastic limb as she listened to it. Then she came over, saying, "The governor will see you now. Follow me." I followed her, and Mr. Alaa followed me. She opened the door of a towering built-in wardrobe and motioned us to step inside it. There must be some mistake, I thought, reluctantly entering the pitch-black space, wondering what we would be doing in this wardrobe. But the back wall contained another set of doors, big polished mahogany ones with shiny brass handles, and the woman opened one of these while closing the wardrobe door behind us.

Beyond lay a room that Napoleon himself would not have been ashamed to call an office. Lavishly furnished with fine eighteenth-century European antiques and oil paintings in illuminated gilt frames, a silk Persian palace rug on the rich wood floor, the place could easily have housed ten families. It was also very dark, the heavy damask curtains drawn, numerous ornate electric desk lamps casting a mellow glow. Behind a vast desk strewn with the kind of expensive toys you find in stores specializing in gifts for the man who has everything sat Counselor Al-Gawasaki, the governor of Alexandria. A portly, aristocratic man with pale skin and a gentle, courteous manner, he rose to greet me warmly and kept calling me "Your Excellency."

Was there perhaps some mistake? Had Mr. Alaa been sent to meet an ambassador from some foreign country and fallen prey to the Palestine Hotel's laconic blundering? He'd never asked me my name, I realized. Oh well. What would a foreign ambassador be here for? Trade? Business opportunities?

The governor ushered me over to a couple of cozy wingbacks placed on either side of a low table. It was so dark in this corner of the room I could hardly see him until he flipped on another lamp.

"As Your Excellency may have observed," he said, ordering the pleasant woman to fetch coffee, "I keep my curtains drawn."

I confessed I had noticed this, to be told that sunlight was bad for the room's furnishings, rugs, and paintings. Wondering if I'd soon be arrested as an imposter, I asked some general questions about where the governor thought his city was heading in the near future.

He looked puzzled at first, as if I were implying Alexandria might soon be towed off to Greece or somewhere; then, in a slow, soft voice, he launched into a lengthy account of various ambitious projects under way, all of them preparing for an event that would take place in the year 2005. He never said what this event was, and I struggled with what I knew of the city's history for an appropriate anniversary, only coming up with the year A.D. 5 as a possible date for either the birth of Saint Mark or the child Jesus' visit to Alexandria with his mom and dad. Neither of these seemed much cause for a major celebration by an Islamic republic.

All the sewers had been repaired or replaced, the governor assured me, and the electricity and telephone system had been totally revamped. "Everything in Alexandria is brand-new," he announced.

This seemed a bit of an exaggeration. He talked about parks and green belts, terming them "lungs for the city." Apparently 40 percent of Egyptian industry was situated around Alexandria, so the city needed new lungs. What with the cool Mediterranean breezes, the air seemed clean enough to me as it was. Cairo needed new lungs if ever a city did; Cairo needed an oxygen tent as well.

The pleasant woman brought coffee and stood watching us drink it, her gold glinting in the lamplight. The governor looked at me expectantly. Now, perhaps, I was supposed to discuss the $100 million development project my government was contemplating. Instead, I asked about recent archaeological discoveries.

There is an island in the surging sea, which they call Pharos, lying off Egypt. It has a Harbour with good anchorage, and hence they put out to sea after drawing water.

—HOMER, *ODYSSEY*, BOOK IV

This is the shortest recorded visit by a well-known person to Alexandria. There wasn't much for Ulysses and his crew to do there at the time. Keit Bey Fort now stands on Pharos, but before that it housed the Pharos lighthouse, one of the ancient world's seven wonders. "Submerges" of this lighthouse, the governor informed me, had recently been found and would be exhibited in a projected maritime museum, along with the remains of the French fleet recently discovered at the bottom of Abukir Bay.

Off with his army to beat up the Mamelukes and spend a night in the Great Pyramid, Napoleon had told his admiral, Brueys, to look after the fleet in his absence. Not wanting to risk the reefs that then still existed in the entrance to the Western Harbour, Brueys thought he'd be better off in Abukir Bay. He was wrong. Nelson and his British fleet attacked at 6:00 P.M. on August 1, 1798. By seven o'clock Brueys was dead. At 9:30 the *Orient* blew up, resulting in, among other things, a dreadful poem about a boy standing on its burning deck; and by noon the following day all but four ships of the huge French fleet were on the bottom of Abukir Bay. Napoleon was not happy about this, returning to command a dazzling and ferocious land battle near the bay. Although he was victorious, something told him this was a temporary trend. Somewhat unheroically, he deserted his entire army and returned to Europe, where he created havoc for another seventeen years.

"Yes," the governor said, "all these submerges of this French fleet will be in our maritime museum." What shape would they be in after two hundred years? I wondered. And what was left of the Pharos lighthouse after more than two thousand years? I assumed this maritime museum would contain more than just rotten wood and eroded rock. "Wherever you dig here," the governor announced proudly, "you find something."

Under a department store just a few streets back from the corniche, Professor Redford had told me, the archaeologist Sami Chenouda had found fragments of limestone with the incipits of certain classical books; he'd probably stumbled across part of the stacks of the Great Library of Alexandria. When the other stores on the street fall down, someone else will presumably find more of antiquity's greatest library.

But what every archaeologist in the world is after is Alexander the Great's tomb. I asked the governor where he thought this might be. "It's down there somewhere," he replied confidently. "You see, Your Excellency, Alexandria was one of the few cities in the world ever planned before it was constructed. Some of the streets still have the same names as they did twenty-three hundred years ago." The pleasant woman whispered something in Arabic. "She says," the governor told me, "that the oldest Christian church in the world is here, too."

"San Marco," the pleasant woman added helpfully.

This proved to be the third "oldest Christian church in the world" I was shown in Egypt alone. I've seen others in England, Armenia, Turkey, and Israel. *One* of them must be the real "oldest Christian church in the world."

Christianity was introduced to Alexandria, as far as we know, by Saint Mark. In A.D. 45 he converted a Jewish cobbler named Annianus. Like all converts, Annianus was a little too zealous. Seventeen years after his conversion he was rewarded with martyrdom for publicly objecting to the worship of Serapis, a composite deity manufactured by the late Ptolemaic rulers of Osiris and Apis, the bull. The god was more Greek than Egyptian, and no one seems to have minded him until Annianus came along. The notion that one religion is right and others wrong is really a Christian innovation, and the Greeks and Egyptians fully accepted each other's deities. The Second Commandment doesn't say there *are* no other gods, rather "Thou shalt have no other gods before me."

But Saint Mark and his successors clearly didn't do a very good job of explaining the basics of their new religion to the citizens of Alexandria. At least, the emperor Trajan, visiting the city in the first century A.D. was not particularly impressed with its Christian community. In a letter ascribed to him, he writes,

> *Those who worship Serapis are Christians, and those who call themselves bishops of Christ are devoted to Serapis ... As a race of men they are seditious, vain, and spiteful; as a body, wealthy and prosperous, of whom nobody lives in idleness. Some blow glass, some make paper, and others linen. Their one God is nothing peculiar; Christians, Jews, and all nations worship him. I wish this body of men was better behaved.*

One wonders precisely what Saint Mark was preaching. It sounds more like a course in practical handicrafts than a religion. To Trajan, of course, bad behaviour meant refusal to worship the emperors. Although the Romans had a leniently eclectic attitude toward religion, they still held certain standards.

The "behaviour" of the Christians apparently didn't improve. By the time of Diocletian (whose memorial in the city is still wrongly referred to as "Pompey's Column"), a full-fledged persecution was under way.

This would have been when Saint Catherine died, although (with apologies to the monks of Mount Sinai) it seems unlikely she ever lived, probably being an invention of Western Catholicism, recognized by the Egyptians only out of politeness to the French. Many did die, however, if not as many as the 144,000 martyrs estimated by the Egyptian Church. Finally, however, the Egyptian Church emerged triumphant. It still dates its chronology from the Era of Martyrs in A.D. 284, not from the birth of Christ. As for Saint Mark, his corpse was stolen by some enterprising Venetian merchants who smuggled it home to give their city more prestige.

"Christianity began in Alexandria," the governor stated with absolute certainty. "The pope still lives here." I queried this, discovering he meant Pope Shenouda of the Coptic Church. "He calls himself pope," the governor added. "He calls himself pope of Alexandria. He's a nice man, very quiet." This was hardly surprising, I thought, since Pope Shenouda had apparently been under house arrest until very recently.

"Protection," the governor explained. "For his protection. There was some trouble once from the fundamentalists. But I believe he visited Canada last year, no?" This was true. "Yes," the governor said again, pleased to be right. "Yes, he's a very nice man. I've met him."

Possibly, I considered, the governor thinks I'm connected with the Human Rights Commission or something. He started looking at his watch.

Then he told me he'd been a student in Alexandria and felt he owed the city a debt. "Now," he said happily, "all my dreams are coming to be true. I have great love for this city, and I am doing the best I can for it."

The telephone rang. When he'd finished talking, I told him he seemed busy, thanked him for his time, and left, hoping I hadn't ruined a total stranger's diplomatic career. Although other Egyptians had called me "Your Excellency," I'd imagined I would call a governor that and not vice versa. Egyptians are so studiously polite, however, that you'd never know you'd offended one even if you had.

Back in Mr. Alaa's car with the chauffeur-who-wasn't-a-fundamentalist, I said, "What a nice man the governor is."

Mr. Alaa, once more on the verge of tears, replied, "He's ruining the city. He's not from Alexandria."

"Where is he from?"

A place about forty miles away turned out to be the answer, though I'd half expected Mr. Alaa to say, "Jupiter."

"How is he ruining the place?"

Mr. Alaa gestured vaguely around him. "Look," he muttered. "He's dug up half the city for his damn parks. Notice that's all he wanted to talk about, these parks. He doesn't care about anything but his parks. But he's not from here, that's why. He's from another place."

"He said he'd fixed the sewers," I pointed out.

"He fixed nothing," Mr. Alaa said despondently. "He just dug everything up. This city is finished. It's over." He continued on this theme for some minutes, until the car pulled into the drive of another smart high rise. "Now you'll meet Dr. Zahran," he announced.

"Who?" I wondered whether I should ask him who he thought I was.

"Director of the Bibliotheca," he explained. "*If* he's still in. We're late now, and he may be taking lunch."

It dawned on me that I *had* requested to meet someone connected with the rebuilding of the Great Library of Alexandria, about the only major project in Egypt not directly connected with the tourist industry.

The original library began with Ptolemy Soter around 300 B.C. He shipped over one of Aristotle's followers, Demetrius Phalerus, from Greece and told him to organize an institution of learning on the lines of the Athenian Museion, which contained Aristotle's library and was a sort of philosophers' clubhouse. But Phalerus had bigger ideas. Before long, the Alexandrian Museion had burgeoned into something far grander and infinitely richer than anything Athens contained. In essence a court institution controlled by the palace, it was not unlike a modern university, except the scholars, writers, and scientists it financed were not obliged to teach, only to continue with their studies and research to boost the prestige of the Ptolemies.

The most important section was the library; indeed the post of librarian was held by the Museion's chief official. This connection between palace and Museion, however, as many outsiders were quick to point out, was not the best arrangement in the academic world. The inhabitants of the palace, since they were footing the bill, used the Museion as an all-purpose repository of imagination and knowledge, often making demands on the learned that were almost insultingly absurd. For example, Queen Berenice, wife of Euergetes, lost her hair from the temple where she had dedicated it. So she ordered the court astronomer to scan the heavens until he'd detected the hair as a constellation, and then commanded the court poet to compose an elegy to commemorate the whole event. This created even more problems. Stratonice, another aristocratic matron, who was utterly bald, let it be known in the Museion that someone had better write an equally fine poem about her hair, too. Odes to celebrate victories, dirges for funerals, songs for marriages, good jokes, flattering genealogical trees, medical recipes, ingenious mechanical toys, all sorts of maps, diabolical engines of war: whatever the palace fancied, the Museion staff immediately went to work on. No one wanted to risk upsetting the royals and be kicked out of that privileged realm to look for another patron or starve.

Despite these awkward working conditions, the achievements of the Museion were nothing short of extraordinary. They also argue strongly that much of Western civilization was built on the science of ancient Egypt. Here Herophilus established the rules of anatomy and physiology, Euclid "invented" geometry, and Eratosthenes calculated the circumference of the earth. Aristarchus and Dionysius Thrax systematized the grammar of classical Greek; Hero the geometrician invented the diopter surveying instrument; and Claudius Ptolemaeus founded cartography and developed the principles of astronomy. In a mere four-hundred-year period, from the third century B.C. to the first century A.D., the foundations of modern scholarship and science were laid here, in Alexandria. It's no coincidence

that all the so-called discoveries made by the "fathers" of this and that science are thought by many to have been known and practised two thousand
years before the Museion of Alexandria by the pyramid builders of Memphis.

The original library in the Museion is known as the "Mother Library." It
was destroyed in the Caesarian civil war, to be replaced under Cleopatra's
reign by the "Daughter Library," an even grander affair with over 500,000
books and attached to the great temple of Serapis. The index alone occupied 120 volumes. This colossal library made Alexandria the most learned spot
on earth for four hundred years. In 391, when the patriarch Theophilus led
a mob of Christians to sack the temple of Serapis and smash the statue of
the god, the books, which were arranged in cloisters surrounding the
temple, were destroyed by the fires that left the Serapeum temple complex
a smouldering heap.

All that remains today are some smashed fragments of statuary, chunks
of friezes, gloomy, enigmatic subterranean chambers, and "Pompey's Pillar."
The column has nothing to do with Pompey, bearing an inverted figure
and the hieroglyph of Pharaoh Seti I and a Greek inscription to the emperor
Diocletian invisible from the ground. It is generally something of a mystery. The Arabs had tossed virtually everything standing into the ocean to
obstruct an invading fleet, so when the Crusaders visited Alexandria in the
fifteenth century, all they found was this one lonely column. Not famous
for their scholarship, the Crusaders had heard of Pompey, however, and
decided to name the pillar after him, even elaborating on their fabrication
by saying Pompey's head was enclosed in a ball on top of it.

Deliberate or not, this destruction of the Alexandrian library by
Christians started a tradition of enmity between the church and secular
scholarship. The conflict, especially regarding science, was still thriving a
thousand years later when Galileo found himself persecuted for proposing
what Aristarchus and Eratosthenes had put forward in the third century
B.C. at the Museion, the theory that the earth revolves around the sun. Since
Greek science was not based on any spiritual authority but grounded in
hard facts, it would have been interesting to know the details behind
Aristarchus' theory, but we never will; his writings perished with all the
other masterworks of the ancient world under the same burning roof.

The Crusaders, who were little more than Vatican-sanctioned thugs, pirates, mercenaries, and adventurous thieves, came to symbolize how Christianity had managed to paralyze the progress of Western civilization until the Renaissance and the Reformation.

Unfortunately the Arabs are popularly believed to have destroyed the Great Library, even by many Arabs. There's not a shred of firm evidence to support this theory, but the Egyptians, always willing to believe the worst of themselves, still suspect their ancestors were to blame. This is probably why they feel obliged to rebuild the library.

Dr. Mohsen Zahran is the executive director of the General Organization of the Library of Alexandria (GOAL). This was the man Mr. Alaa was now taking me to see. At least I probably was, after all, the person he thought me to be.

Dr. Zahran is a personable academic who has given up his post at the University of Alexandria to oversee this massive project. His office was like an operations centre with its charts, plans, artists' impressions, people working on phones and typewriters, and he seemed a brisk and efficient operator. He needed to be; as well as a lot of work ahead, there were many problems to be solved. The main problem was money. Already, estimates had placed the cost of building the library at $150 million — before, that is, any books were purchased for its shelves. In a country where the national debt had reached $55 billion (exactly one thousand dollars per inhabitant), this was not going to be easy. UNESCO had stepped in at an early stage, Dr. Zahran informed me, making the project an international venture, like the Aswan Dam.

A Norwegian company had won an open competition for the design, coming up with an extravagantly beautiful structure, half underground and half comprising a round, sloping wall covered with what looked like Egyptian hieroglyphs but were in fact examples of every language on earth, the roof capped by a dome that resembled the eye of Horus and the rising sun. The architect's model gave the impression that the materials employed would be solid gold and various precious stones, though this is not the case. It definitely looked like $150 million worth of building.

Dr. Zahran asked me if I'd like to view the other short-listed designs.

I wasn't surprised the Norwegians won. This collection of architectural monstrosities shocked me more than most. If this was the cream of the largest international competition ever staged — over one thousand four hundred entries from five hundred-odd countries — one dreaded to imagine the rest. Pinned on a mobile board were plans and detailed coloured sketches, or photographs of actual models that, thanks to Fate, would now *not* be the new Bibliotheca Alexandria. One was a Venusian spaceport with an incongruous pagodalike roof supported by what looked like glass rods and surrounded by many transparent tunnels whose function was obscure; another was simply a windowless box of grey steel around which ran many walkways and fire escapes. Many were obviously designed by people who knew little about the Egyptian climate. Only the Norwegians seemed to have recalled that they were designing a library, including spaces where books could be stored and even areas where people could read the books.

I asked Dr. Zahran if anyone had suggested trying to reconstruct the original Greco-Egyptian building, but I think he thought I meant including the temple to Serapis with it. That wouldn't have gone down too well with the mufti and his imams in Cairo.

Fundraising had got off to a great start, Dr. Zahran assured me, on February 12 that very year at a gathering in Aswan. It had been an impressive gathering, too. French president François Mitterrand attended, as did Princess Caroline of Monaco, Queen Sofia of Spain, Queen Noor of Jordan, Sheikh Zayed bin Sultan al-Nahayan of the United Arab Emirates, and Melina Mercouri — presumably in her capacity as the former Greek minister of culture. Guilt was clearly still weighing heavily on Arabian consciences; in twelve hours $64 million had been pledged, most of it from oil-rich Arab states. Christian consciences were obviously clear, the extremely minor and deposed royals presumably present as decoration. The government of Mauritius, Dr. Zahran informed me, had sent a cheque for one thousand dollars. So far the United States and Canada have contributed nothing, although some schoolchildren from perhaps Ohio donated a book.

"Books are pouring in," Dr. Zahran claimed, indicating the rows of bookshelves behind him, which contained possibly a hundred volumes and were otherwise empty.

I asked if the library intended to include rare manuscripts in its collection. This was when the subject of St. Catherine's monastery came up. Dr. Zahran said the University of Alexandria had helped the monks catalogue part of their library back in the sixties, so he knew precisely what sort of things it contained.

"They have a wonderful collection," he said. "Wonderful and priceless." Dr. Zahran certainly planned a rare-manuscript section, as well as facilities for the restoration of such manuscripts and other rare books. Would he take over the Mount Sinai library?

"We'll have to see," he replied.

As he outlined what the new library would comprise on its ten-acre site, I understood that what he was building here was more like the ancient Museion itself than just its library. A planetarium, a conference centre, research facilities: the list and the ambition were endless. Books, he emphasized, particularly textbooks relating to Mediterranean history, were the project's most urgent need. Anyone wishing to donate anything at all could send it care of any Egyptian embassy. He proceeded to sell me the Bibliotheca's elegant poster for twenty dollars, going to much trouble to provide me with a very official-looking receipt. I wished him luck and promised to spread the word.

Mr. Alaa looked less optimistic. "We'll probably never finish it," he said. "Things never get finished here."

President Mubarak was big on getting things finished. Hotels, libraries, whatever: they had to be finished. First they had to be started, however, and Dr. Zahran had been personally ordered by Mubarak to begin construction in 1991. Indeed, a large hole in the ground now exists. "Mubarak's always saying that," Mr. Alaa commented, staring vacantly out the car window at the crowded streets, adding suddenly, "This was where Cleopatra committed suicide."

"Where?" I looked around, seeing only sidewalks, shops, shoppers.

"You can't see anything," Mr. Alaa announced. "You can't see anything here anymore. It's an invisible city." He got as close to laughing as he probably could.

This turned out to be true about Alexandria. It's frustrating. You walk over ground that has seen more momentous historical events than almost any city on the planet, yet there's nothing to see, nothing left, or nothing left above ground. There wasn't much left when the Arabs invaded in 642, either, and after they built their new capital in Cairo, Alexandria all but lay fallow until the early nineteenth century, when French, English, and Turkish expeditions landed in the area at one time or another, drawing Egypt back into the sphere of European influence once more.

Turkish viceroy Muhammad Ali quickly saw that a maritime capital was essential to this new Egypt, and rather than enlarging the existing ports of Rosetta or Damietta, he decided to recreate Alexandria. If Alexander the Great's city had been one of the few planned before it was constructed, Muhammad Ali's was one of the many not planned at all. Alexander wouldn't even recognize Alexandria — not that he ever did get to see it anyway. Greeks, Turks, French, British, all had their sectors in Alex Mark II, and each sector revelled in its own character, regardless of the whole. There are still Greeks here, and the difference in the faces I first noticed is merely evidence of the great melting pot of races and cultures that Alexandria became in its second prime.

A crossroads of east and west, of north and south, Alex gained a reputation for wild living almost as notorious as its reputation for "bad behaviour" two millennia earlier. E. M. Forster, Constantine Cavafy, Lawrence Durrell, and others enjoyed the perfect climate as much as the liberty the city provided them to live as they wished, far from the petty morality and hypocrisy of Europe. In return, they immortalized the city in literature. But the Alexandria they recorded is also invisible now, crushed by what one foreign diplomat I met called "the dead hand of Islam."

Alexandrians, I soon learned, despise Cairenes the way Venetians despise Neapolitans, the way Chinese despise everyone, the way Beethoven would have despised Sid Vicious. In this, Mr. Alaa was the very soul of Alexandria. The staff at the Palestine Hotel weren't narcoleptics; they were terminally depressed. Half of Alexandria shared Mr. Alaa's temperament; it, too, was terminally depressed. Alexandria *should* be towed off to Greece or somewhere more congenial. The Alexandrians don't belong in modern Egypt.

I asked Mr. Alaa where he was taking me next. Nowhere, he answered.

If I wanted, he'd pick me up later and show me around the city. He made it sound as appealing as a tour of an embalmer's workshop, so I agreed. He shrugged.

"Maybe we can go to Pastroudi's," I suggested. "And the Cecil Hotel?" These places were hot spots in Durrell's novels and, I'd been told, still existed.

"Why?" Mr. Alaa inquired, without seeming at all interested in the answer.

"Fun?" I offered. "And Cavafy's room in the Greek consulate — is that still there?" I asked.

He nodded; then, having considered the question for some time, he said, "Why are you so interested in homosexual writers?"

"Goodness," I exclaimed, "was Cavafy a homosexual?"

Mr. Alaa nodded grimly. We reached the Palestine, and I told Mr. Happy I'd see him later.

Alexander the Great was still on TV — its third run that day, according to the chart — with the Great still trying to convince a group of dubious-looking men in cheap wigs that they should seriously think about conquering the known world with him. Since this improbable venture was better than listening to the Great deliver deafening hyperboles all day long, the men in cheap wigs all shrugged like Mr. Alaa and went off to tell their wives they were going to Persia and would be back in about eight years. The women were either very understanding or relieved to get rid of them.

CHAPTER TWENTY

UNKNOWN SOLDIERS
AND LAST RESORTS

*[Alexandria] suffered severely, however, during Arabi's rising in
1882, and a great part of the European quarter was laid in
ashes; but all traces of this misfortune have disappeared and the
town is again quite prosperous.*

—BAEDEKER'S *EGYPT*, 1929

That high priest in Memphis was certainly right about the fate of the city
that would house Alexander the Great's tomb. Sixty years after Baedeker's
1929 survey, "prosperous" is not a term most Alexandrians would employ
to describe themselves or their hometown.

Mr. Alaa arrived at sunset. We drove back into the city, which by now
had changed utterly, sparkling with lights, teeming with people strolling
the corniche, sitting in squares and parks with ice cream, pouring in and
out of stores with blazing yellow windows stacked with all manner of
goods. It looked so very European it was hard to believe I was still in Egypt.
Mr. Alaa showed me the major streets, all of them prosperous-looking,

crammed with prosperous-looking people, hardly a *gelabia* or turban in sight. I asked him why he seemed so down about everything we'd encountered.

"Look at these streets," he said, hunched, smiling weakly. "You wouldn't think this country was bankrupt, would you?"

The economy, the future, were what depressed him. "I look at my two sons," he said, "and I see no hope for them. No hope."

The Egyptian currency was losing value against the U.S. dollar, indeed had been since I'd arrived in the country; I was receiving more each time I changed money. This meant the Egyptians continually paid more for essential imported machinery or agricultural equipment, forcing up prices, particularly food prices. Mr. Alaa paid two Egyptian pounds a month rent, yet he paid eighteen pounds for two pounds of shrimp. There were two economies: the one the government could control and the one it couldn't. "My father told me he grew up in a European city," Mr. Alaa sighed, "but that's all gone now. All gone." And with it had gone many dreams.

We found Pastroudi's, an elegant restaurant, café, and bar situated on a quiet, tree-lined corner. Plump, wealthy Alexandrians sat at sidewalk tables with newspapers and drinks served by red-jacketed waiters. People were speaking English or French more than Arabic. The area reminded me very much of the main piazza in Trieste; even the people looked northern Italian. We sat down across from the most elegant shoeshine "boy" — he was a man of seventy — I've ever seen. His box of polishes and brushes was immaculate, its brass horns glowing in the pearly gaslight of streetlamps, which hissed faintly and burned like magnesium against a steely indigo sky. Coffees and fresh lemon juice arrived.

Mr. Alaa looked about him in despair. He seemed so terribly lonely in his gloom, yet he looked every bit as dapper and affluent as anyone around us. It was yet another good Egyptian facade.

He'd wanted to go to Canada or America when he was a young man, he informed me. Now, of course, few Egyptians could travel; they couldn't change their currency, except on the black market at a 10 or 15 percent premium. Instead, he, too, had worked in Kuwait for a few years at the Ministry of Education, moonlighting at the Sheraton Hotel by night.

Foreigners earned half as much as Kuwaitis, he also confirmed. Like King Omar in Hurghada, he'd lived in a box there, too, and worked in another. It was too hot to walk the streets much of the time. "After ten years of that," he said, "you get sick and die." He'd also been separated from his wife out there, so he came home to Alexandria and was now resigned to the fact that his life was over.

Under orthodox Islam the city and its people lacked any definition now, I felt. It was very different from when E. M. Forster and Cavafy had sat in this very café, and still very different when Lawrence Durrell and the characters in his *Quartet* had sat here. The listlessness and depression took the edge off even the most heated of subjects — Israel.

"Israelis are working here now," Mr. Alaa said — no one had mentioned *this* to me before — "helping with agricultural projects and the like. Yes, they're propped up by American money, but we're propped up by Arab money. It's all the same. America doesn't like to help us because there are too many military regimes in the Arab world — Iraq, Libya. Even Mubarak's really a military man. We've got to get rid of these regimes if we want things to improve. Tourism is our biggest business, but the slightest hint of trouble in the area and tourists stay away." This was true. During the buildup to the Gulf War and the war itself in late 1990 and 1991, hardly a single tourist visited Egypt.

In the course of his job Mr. Alaa met many Israelis arriving by boat for vacations. They were frightened, he said, worried about whether or not they'd be safe in Egypt. "You lived here before," he told them, "and you were safe then. Why should it be different now?" But, he added, Israel didn't want to believe that things had changed, or "they'd be forced to change."

But "economic catastrophe" was Mr. Alaa's favourite theme, and there was nothing anyone could do about it, he maintained. Nothing. Yet life was going on around us, and as we strolled back to Saad Zaghloul Square, I remarked on the brisk business all the stores seemed to be enjoying, the relative affluence compared to Cairo. It was a mistake to mention Cairo; Mr. Alaa informed me that Cairenes were to blame for the ills of Alexandria. It could have been a conversation taking place centuries ago. Alex was where those Cairenes who could afford it came to escape the summer heat; and in a way the whole city now existed to host them during those brief few months.

"I'll show you," Mr. Alaa offered. "Tomorrow if you like. We'll drive west, and I'll show you."

I'd wanted to visit Al-Alamein anyway. At the Cecil Hotel we parted, agreeing to meet early the next day. I watched Mr. Alaa walk slowly off with his loping stride, head down, shoulders at ear level.

The Cecil was another good facade. From outside it looked like the kind of small, elegant European hotel listed in the *Michelin Guide* that would contain a superb restaurant and a cozy, intimate bar furnished with antiques and comfortable wingback armchairs. Instead, I found a dreary lobby with the usual souvenir and blurred-postcard shop, and a large, over-lit, and Spartan bar full of Egyptian men drinking coffee, beating the devil's tattoo with their knees, looking around aimlessly as they chain-smoked and talked without interest. Nearby was a nightclub-casino that offered "entertainment," a board outside bearing a photograph of three men and a woman in ruffled shirts, straw hats, waistcoats, holding guitars and mara-cas. No thanks.

Outside, a cold wind was blowing in off the wine-dark Mediterranean. Shops were pulling their shutters down, lights were being switched off, the streets began to empty. Within fifteen minutes I was walking a ghost town, mad with shadows, otherwise empty, chilled, forlorn. Invisible. The place had simply turned itself off and vanished.

> *The beach at Abukir is in places still littered with the wreckage of ships. We saw a number of sharks that had been washed up, and our horses trod on shells at the edge of the sea. ... The weather was magnificent, sea and sky bluest blue, an immensity of space.*
> —GUSTAVE FLAUBERT, LETTER FROM EGYPT,
> NOVEMBER 23, 1849

Fifty-one years after Admiral Horatio Nelson's destruction of the French fleet, Flaubert could still see the future contents of Alexandria's maritime museum on the beach. When I took a look, the beach at Abukir was only littered with the wreckage of Egyptian bodies. Two enormously fat men wearing childlike woollen bathing trunks were attempting to jog up and down the sands. Their doctors had clearly just told them to shape up or be shipped out. Although they had mastered the posture of jogging, elbows bent and pumping, knees raised, weight on toes, I was *strolling* at twice their speed. Yet they were keeping their doctors and wives happy. How could it not be good to eat as much as possible of the richest imaginable foods in a country where most could not afford much more than beans and bread? It proved you were not poor, that you were in the successful minority. And Egyptian food *can* be irresistible.

Mr. Alaa arrived very late. It was the driver's fault. I asked if we could visit Cavafy's room, now transported intact to the Greek consulate. Mr. Alaa shrugged. Outside the consulate we found a long lineup of unruly Egyptians waving passports at a guard behind the tall wrought-iron gates. Presumably Cavafy's room was not *this* big an attraction? Making himself very unpopular with the unshaven mob, Mr. Alaa got the guard to let us in ahead of everyone. From the stares of these people I could tell they saw us as rich folks getting preferential treatment, as always.

A pretty, studious-looking Greek woman led us up a marble staircase lined with sketches and portraits of Cavafy, photographs of the house he once occupied, now a run-down pension. But through palatial double doors we were shown into an airy, spacious room where Cavafy's library, furniture, and many manuscripts and first editions are preserved much as he'd left them. Partly a little museum, it is also partly a faithful recreation of his own small apartment, with its uncomfortable settees and chairs in the tacky neo-Byzantine style that was the height of fashion in middle-class homes of the period. You can also sit at the modest desk where he wrote the poems that were to make him famous: "Ithaca," "The God Abandons Anthony," "The Barbarians," and his great tribute to Alexandria, "The City." Newspapers and magazines from the week he died still lie on the table as if he'd just read them. The only jarring element is an insipid white plaster bust, somewhat Vorticist in style and grievously out of place among Cavafy's Greek icons and baroque tastes. Mr. Alaa made it clear he was bored with this place, but I browsed through Cavafy's modest collection of books: the classics in Latin and Greek, leatherbound volumes of history, slim limited editions by long-forgotten contemporaries. It all spoke of an intense but restrained existence, a quiet, productive life. Apollonius, Theocritus, Callimachus … Constantine Cavafy was the last poet in a great Alexandrian tradition. I felt that his position would never be challenged — although perhaps I'd spent too much time with Mr. Alaa. Durrell, however, Cavafy's first major English translator, felt the same way when he last revisited the city in 1977.

"You can't catch AIDS from reading poetry," I told Mr. Alaa, who looked relieved to be back in the safety of the car. It was a mistake to mention AIDS; it was clearly something he hadn't considered adding to his multi-volumed list of Things to Be Depressed About. Now he did, and it kept him in brooding silence for some time.

> *Who art thou, shipwrecked stranger? Leontichus found thee here dead on the beach, and buried thee in this tomb, weeping for his own uncertain life; for he also rests not, but travels over the sea like a gull.*
>
> —CALLIMACHUS

Dodging through the city centre, we eventually reached an area with more of a seaside-resort feel to it, emerging by a far bluer version of the Mediterranean on a spit of land called Hannoville. It was coffee time, Mr. Alaa decided, and we'd stop at a hotel he knew so I could get some idea of the facilities offered by Alexandria's famed beaches.

Called the Hannoville Hotel, it sat on Harfal's Al-Agamy Beach. Perhaps I should leave the description of the place to the hotel's own brochure, unedited:

> *A the western top of ALEXANDRIA the pearl of the mediterranean, the hannoville with the white sandybeaches and clear waters.*

All quest rooms are beautefully appointed and comfortably
furnished, each its own private balcony overlooking the sea,
with te lephone (l ocal and international), certralmusic, private
bath with hot and cold water. 24 hours room service, there are
appartements consist with 2 double rooms, one reception one
bath room and a balcony overlooking the sea.

Oriental cafeteria dardacha. At the swimming pool you enjoyed
with the turkish coffee and drink the chicha with tobac. In the
evening the 2 bars sets the mood for a superb night, dining and
dancing with music Restaurants: RABAB, HARFAL'S,
CREVETTES. you will find our meals at its best offering the finest
french haute cuisihe with added international and specialify dishes.

A map proved the hotel was not far from the "Railluvay Station." The
manager greeted us like gods who'd arrived in answer to his prayers, his
effusiveness fading as he realized we were only here for coffee. It was a
miserable, tacky establishment and deserved its high vacancy rate. All it
possessed was the broad stretch of soft white sand beyond its gates, leading down to the gentle waves of a sparkling azure sea flecked with foam.
I couldn't wait to leave.

Back in the car, speeding west along the broad new coast road, I complained about the hotel, its fraudulent brochure, inept management,
peeling wallpaper.

"We are not professionals," said Mr. Alaa, agreeing defeatedly with every
word. "We just don't know how to do these things properly."

"What about learning?"

He shrugged dejectedly. Learning wouldn't work. Nothing would work.
It was hopeless. This car was beginning to feel like the Cave of Trophonius
on wheels. We stopped at various other resorts: some new, pleasant enough
apart from the areas still under construction; some older, and vast enough
to be towns of identical crumbling villas sprawling around bleak central
plazas with depressing two-thousand-seat cafeterias. One project, still very
much under construction, was absurdly immense. Its architect, whom we

met in his on-site hut, described it to us. Several miles long, it would eventually feature a giant marina capable of handling the trans-Mediterranean yacht business (if there was one), thousands of extremely luxurious two-storey villas, dozens of restaurants, sports facilities, health clubs, shopping centres, and more. The project was frightening.

"Why build more resorts when the existing ones are empty?" I asked Mr. Alaa.

He shook his head once more, repeating again, "We are not professionals. We don't know what we're doing ... but we have to do something."

He added that foreign tourists weren't coming to Alexandria these days. It just wasn't on most itineraries. And the Red Sea resorts had more to offer, so much more, Mr. Alaa claimed, that even the Cairenes were spending their summers there in increasing numbers. He had never seen them himself. The empty beaches we passed spread for mile after mile beside the sea, which transformed itself into a rippling expanse of glowing liquid turquoise the farther west as you went. The contrast of colours — sand, sea, sky — was breathtaking. At certain points all you could see were three broad bands of luminescent colour, white, turquoise, and an intensely clear azure, that became the whole world. Yet behind, south of the road, was the desert. Flat, bleak, its quivering mirages shimmered with something evil. And this merciless wilderness continued relentlessly for thousands of miles.

> *At the doors of Africa so many towns founded*
> *Upon a parting could become Alexandria, like*
> *The wife of Lot — a metaphor for tears*
>
> —LAWRENCE DURRELL

As we neared Al-Alamein, site of Field Marshal Montgomery's decisive victory over the "Desert Fox" Erwin Rommel and his German and Italian armies during World War II, the cemeteries and memorials materialized. "Which one do you want to see?" Mr. Alaa inquired.

Human suffering is human suffering, in English, German, or Italian, so I had no allegiances in this immense graveyard. I chose the Italian memorial, a graceful modernist structure at the end of a long, straight drive lined with flowering hedges. Gleaming white against the sky's extravagant blue, the monument exuded something faintly Islamic in its design.

I left Mr. Alaa with his nonfundamentalist driver and walked alone from the road toward the memorial. The place was unnaturally silent, only the desert winds ruffling hedgerows, and the sea faintly growling from somewhere behind the blinding walls I was approaching.

The memorial seemed locked and deserted until an aged fellah in turban and *gelabia* appeared from nowhere with a large key. Inside I found a vast circular hall of marble, its sharp, clean lines reaching up to a dome high above. Facing me stood a simple altar; behind it, through stained glass, the now-silent ocean. The walls were stacked with marble squares, stretching around into adjacent chambers. Riganini, Reisalvatore, Renna, Ricca, Riccardi, Riccini, Ricci, Riccevuto, Rizzini, Rizzo … it went on and on, the roll call of death. Sadder still were the rows of simple plaques marked *"Ignoto."* Wall after wall of them, wall after wall of bodies mutilated beyond recognition.

Retreating, the German army had pushed its Italian allies into the front lines. Over thirty thousand died in a single day, many fleeing into the desert to perish from thirst, their wounded bodies devoured by jackals. *"Ignoto."* I thought of the waste of so many young lives, of the madness and horror of war, all the platitudes, clichés that rained upon me in this quiet house where only death decorated the walls. I wrote my wife's Italian maiden name in the visitors' book, my son's middle name, hoping his young body would not rest in such a place as this one day, marked *"Ignoto"* for the rest of time.

Emerging, I paused in the savage light, staring south over the barren wastes. The wind was blowing in sand like snow. In the air still, hiding in time, were the rumble of tanks, the crack of guns, the thunder of explosions, the screams of the dying, all now enfolded in the silence of the dead. In the dust at the edge of well-tended lawns lay the shattered remains of a child's toy gun.

"The American government is giving us seven hundred tanks, I heard," Mr. Alaa said as I climbed back in the car. "And I asked myself, what do we need with seven hundred tanks?"

"Bring them here," I suggested. "You could drive tourists around in them and re-enact the Battle of Al-Alamein. It'd go down big. Boost business."

Nearby was the PLM Azur Hotel, by far the best on the whole coast. Compact, nestled around an exquisite little bay, it consists of large, well-equipped villas lining a broad and flawless beach. Yet it was also deserted. It had everything a resort hotel could ask for, except customers ... and a town not named after one of the most savage and destructive battles in history. Once the battle was named after the town and the area, but now all anybody knows about Al-Alamein is the battle. Every year, the survivors still come, in ever-diminishing numbers, to pay their respects to friends they never saw again, and to stand as I had done, listening to the wind, staring at the malevolent desert, wondering why they had been spared, why they weren't still here, between Riccini and Ricco, Roberts and Robertson, Kreis and Kreuz.

I asked if the survivors stayed on to holiday nearby, hardly surprised to find they generally leave the next day.

"See," Mr. Alaa resumed. "There's no planning. We don't think things out."

He also blamed Cairo for not promoting Alexandria, for not providing adequate information, for everything.

After being so close to death, one's thoughts often turn to Nature's antidote: sex. I asked Mr. Alaa about his wife.

"It's all over by the time you're forty," he replied, shaking his head. "I used to buy her flowers, and we'd go dancing, but that's all gone. The spark dies." Did his wife feel the same way? "Oh yes. She knows it's gone. There's no feeling anymore. We just have the children in common."

I tried to picture it, tried to imagine what it must be like for children growing up in the Slough of Despond. But I'd noticed Mr. Alaa was quite at ease with the other Alexandrians we spent time with. They all understood each other, shared in differing degrees the same malaise. Life went on. The whole city was something written by Ibsen or Strindberg or Ingmar Bergman. If the monks of St. Catherine's were carefully rehearsing for death, this was the performance itself. Mr. Alaa had sunk into despair as into a warm bath, soaking in the luxury of absolute pessimism, knowing he was immune to any disappointment.

The curiosities of Alexandria are few, and easily seen. We went into the bazaars, which have a much more Eastern look than the European quarter, with its Anglo-Gallic-Italian inhabitants, and Babel-like civilization. Here and there a large hotel, clumsy and white-washed, with Oriental trellised windows, and a couple of slouching sentinels at the doors, in the ugliest composite uniform that ever was seen, was pointed out as the residence of some great officer of the Pasha's court ...

We went the round of the coffee-houses in the evening, both the polite European places of resort, where you get ices and the French papers, and those in the town, where Greeks, Turks, and general company resort, to sit upon uncomfortable chairs, and drink wretched muddy coffee, and to listen to two or three miserable musicians, who keep up a variation of howling for hours together.

—WILLIAM MAKEPEACE THACKERAY,
NOTES OF A JOURNEY FROM CORNHILL TO CAIRO, 1844

Thackeray would find little had changed.

As we approached the outskirts of Alexandria, I noticed strange conical structures in many gardens, like giant anthills pierced by wooden rods, pocked with fist-sized holes. They turned out to be pigeon houses. Alexandrians are as fond of pigeons, and their aphrodisiac qualities, as are Cairenes or King Farouk. Mr. Alaa couldn't seem to understand how these odd charming structures, each one slightly different in design, gave me such pleasure. "I've never seen one before," I explained. He still didn't get it.

"Do you like Egyptian food?" he asked. Egyptians always assume foreigners don't. I said I did, and he then offered to take me to the finest restaurant for lunch the next day.

When we returned to the Palestine, he suggested we take a walk over to King Farouk's old summer palace. The grounds were exotically laid out with rock gardens and countless brilliant flowering plants, but the huge iron gates to the palace itself were locked, armed guards manning a sentry post nearby and looking edgy as we approached. "Mubarak loves this palace,"

Mr. Alaa informed me in his sinking monotone. "He's always bringing guests here. We don't like this. It belongs to the people, and it should be open to the public. It's wrong."

I do believe he brought me here just to convey this extra tidbit of depressing information.

"Don't you think it's good to impress foreign guests?" I asked.

"No," Mr. Alaa said firmly. "They should see how people really live here."

> *It occurs to those who would require God to be loving as well as powerful ... and it is the weakness and the strength of Alexandria to have solved it by the conception of a link. Her weakness: because she had always to be shifting the link up and down — if she got it too near God it was too far from man, and vice versa. Her strength: because she did cling to the idea of love, and much philosophical absurdity, much theological aridity, must be pardoned to those who maintain that the best thing on earth is likely to be the best in heaven.*
>
> —E. M. FORSTER

This questioning about how the human can be linked to the divine was, for Forster, *the* Alexandrian question. It may be the fact that the omnipotent Allah and Islam do not ask this question that makes the faith of the Prophet seem alien to the Alexandrian soul still. When the great seventh-century Arab general Amr lay on his death bed in Fustat, his inland city, he was asked how an intelligent man feels when faced with death. "I feel," he replied, "as if the heaven lay close upon the earth and I between the two breathing through the eye of a needle." The conversation, Forster pointed out, could never have taken place between two Alexandrians.

Before Islam, all other religions to reach the shores of Alexandria were moulded by the city, by an idea of love she clung to above all else. Forster, like Gibbon, like Gore Vidal, viewed the advent of Christianity as a monumental catastrophe for civilization, a kind of senseless and petty vengeance on the Greek ideal, barbarizing all it touched, epitomizing monomania, hypocrisy, and antihumanism. He ascribed its influence on the modern world to the money behind it rather than to any spiritual appeal it contained. But in its earliest stages in Alexandria, Christianity briefly acquired a philosophical turn that even Forster could approve of — although it was the Neoplatonism of Plotinus he credited for this. Had the city enjoyed a less turbulent history, the course of Christian civilization might have been very different indeed.

There are still many good reasons for going to Alexandria. I spent a morning looking around the Greco-Roman museum and was surprised by the richness and variety of the collection. E. M. Forster vaguely disapproved of the museum in 1922, finding its exhibits second-rate. This was probably true then, since the collection was not formed until 1891, by which time many of the best items available had fallen into private hands. But things have changed.

The museum now houses an impressive range of objects that arouse a genuine sense of life in Alexandria two thousand years ago. The most magnificent piece is a life-size bronze Apis bull, so realistically fashioned you expect it to bolt off its pedestal around the room. But I found myself more interested in displays of clothes and hairstyles, household items and everyday objects, the little details of ordinary lives. Fashions came and went as they do now, and those who could afford to follow them then were every bit as obsessed with the latest fads as we are. For grotesque ingenuity, what Greco-Roman women did to their hair is matched only by the razored, tie-dyed cockatoo plumes of London punks.

Mr. Alaa's wife worked in this museum, I discovered, wondering why he had wanted to meet me here. A shy, attractive woman, she made a brief appearance, shaking my hand nervously before returning to her vaults or archives.

Before lunch, Mr. Alaa and I took in the ruins of the amphitheatre. While it is small and well preserved, there was still much excavation going on in the surrounding area. The sight of these past glories seemed to upset Mr. Alaa — more evidence of what Alex had lost. He seemed anxious to know what I thought of his wife, relieved to find I liked what little I'd seen of her. I doubt if he bought flowers later that day, though.

Next we hit the Kom Es Chogafa catacombs. I've never liked catacombs, but these were different. As you descend a sickening metal spiral staircase, you discover three levels, all hollowed out of solid rock like the tombs of Thebes. There was even a party area where funeral guests and relatives could enjoy a lavish lunch after the rites were finished. Dating from the second century A.D., these chambers are decorated in the crude and eerie Romano-Egyptian style, with lifelike statues perched in recesses. As we stood at the gaping maw of a shrine of some sort, the lights cut out. Since the lower level is partly under water, traversed by tightrope-walking along a series of narrow planks, this posed problems. From somewhere in the depths we heard the hoots and giggles of what I assumed was a crocodile of children on a school outing. Our guide told us to wait where we were — there was no danger of me moving — while he ran back up 130 feet to get a flashlight. Any second now, I told myself, and the first schoolkid would be plunging into eighteen centuries of sewage, or whatever these murky tunnels contained. Hysterical chuckling and screams echoed through the pitch darkness.

"Very dark down here," the invisible Mr. Alaa observed usefully. "Too dark."

"That's because there's no light." I thought he should know.

"No light."

The guide reappeared with a battery-powered strip light; clearly power outs were not unknown in these catacombs. After temporarily blinding us, this bar of light, too, went out. The guide hammered it against a wall. It blinded us once more before again dying. The guide asked us to wait and dashed back up to the world. A heavy splash sounded from the depths, followed by floundering and panicked screams and more giggling. I thought I should perhaps use my cigarette lighter to see exactly who was drowning back there, but its light was too feeble, sucked away by the thick subterranean night.

When the guide made it back with a functioning light, we followed him across the slippery gangplanks, soon coming upon a large family of Egyptians — mother, father, four girls, two boys — all bunched together in a tomb recess. One girl was very wet, and all eight of them were laughing and smiling as if they'd never had such fun in their lives. Even Mr. Alaa seemed more amused by the incident than I'd imagined him capable of being.

The catacombs were discovered in 1900. I learned that no one was sure who the original occupants of the tomb had been. E. M. Forster passes on a theory claiming the place began as a family vault that was later taken over and enlarged by a burial syndicate. There was certainly room down here for many customers.

I didn't feel particularly hungry after emerging from this three-storey mausoleum and funerary complex — complete with wake-party room — but Mr. Alaa assured me we were going to the finest restaurant in the city. Perhaps death gave him an appetite, too. I think this restaurant was called the Al-Ekhlass. It certainly served the best Egyptian food I've ever tasted. They did something to hummus that made it taste like smoky cream, but the waiter refused to reveal how.

Over lunch I got the impression Mr. Alaa's real problem was that his talents were wasted in his government job. He needed something more taxing, and much better paid, to keep his mind off gloom and doom. Like so many in Egypt today, he'd been educated beyond the sort of employment available to him. He was highly intelligent, well read, and spoke several languages. His education made the waste harder to bear, I suspect.

The taxi driver who took me to the Cairo train at Ramleh Station confided that the governor had ruined the city with his damn park. He also revealed that he, too, had a Ph.D., in agriculture. In New York the cabbies tend to be nuclear physicists.

> *When at the hour of midnight*
> *an invisible choir is suddenly heard passing*
> *with exquisite music, with voices —*
> *Do not lament your fortune that at last subsides,*
> *your life's work that has failed, your schemes*
> *that have proved illusions.*

But like a man prepared, a brave man,
bid farewell to her, to Alexandria who is departing.
Above all, do not delude yourself, do not say that it is a dream,
that your ear was mistaken.
Do not condescend to such empty hopes.
Like a man long prepared, like a brave man,
like to the man who was worthy of such a city,
go to the window firmly,
and listen with emotion,
but not with the prayers and complaints of the coward (Ah! supreme
  rapture!)
listen to the notes, to the exquisite instruments of the mystic choir,
and bid farewell to her, to Alexandria whom you are losing.

—C. P. CAVAFY, "THE GOD ABANDONS ANTHONY"

CHAPTER TWENTY-ONE

INSIDE THE GATES OF EDEN

*And out of the ground the Lord God formed every beast of the
field and every fowl of the air; and brought them unto Adam to
see what he would call them: and whatsoever Adam called every
living thing, that was the name thereof.*

—*THE BABYLONIAN GENESIS*

*I create and I command for him who commands the good;
My lips are the Twin Companies,
I am the great Word,
I am a redeemer — so I shall be redeemed, and I
    shall be redeemed from all evil.*

*I am that space which came about in the waters,
I came into being in them, I grew in them,
but I was not consigned to the abode of darkness.*

I am Eternity, the creator of the millions …

—*THE PYRAMID TEXTS AND COFFIN TEXTS,*
CIRCA 2300 B.C.

Time was running out. Three hours after arriving in Cairo, I was waiting for the overnight bus to "the New Valley," the oases of Al-Khārga and Al-Dakhleh in the heart of the Western Desert. The bus-station yard was packed with fellahin who appeared to have picked up a year's supplies in Cairo to take back with them the five hundred miles south to their homes and farms in one of the remotest areas of Egypt. Everyone sat on vast sacks and bulging crates, surrounded by cardboard packages tied with string: car and tractor tires, lengths of rubber hosing, coils of electrical wiring; one even had what looked like an old telephone switchboard. The bus was there, but its driver wasn't, and the doors were locked. Fifteen minutes after departure time, everyone was still waiting. I went into a small, chaotic office to make inquiries. On the wall was a large hand-drawn map, coloured with crayon like a schoolroom project. It showed the route to Al-Khārga.

"The 7:00 P.M. bus?" a man who was attempting to look efficient asked. That was the one, I told him again. "It is on time," he announced. We both looked at the giant wall clock. It had only one hand, and that hour hand was nearly on seven. The minute hand lay bent at the bottom of the case. "See," the man said, "it is almost seven only. Bus will shortly depart." It was a perfect clock for Egypt.

Eventually a huge unshaven pirate of a man, his cauldron belly straining the fabric of a stained *gelabia,* began opening luggage flaps along the side of the bus. One hundred people rushed over at once, struggling to cram a whole bazaar of baggage into the long, narrow recess. A violent argument broke out, the fat pirate shouting in a voice so loud and grating that it had a physical effect on the passengers. Then he opened the doors, and I carried my one small bag in with me, intending to stash it in an overhead rack. These racks, however, were about three inches lower than the roof, capable of accommodating a couple of paperbacks or a wallet at most, not a hold-all. I put the bag on the floor beneath my seat. This left the rest of me little room. The seats were made for thin children, and this journey would take at least ten hours.

With everyone piled in, every inch of seating space was filled — the floors, the armrests, everything but the luggage racks … and people were eyeing those. The fat pirate was also the driver. When the front side door was closed, he folded down a seat that filled the step well and another that blocked the aisle. This front row was occupied by two men who could easily have been his twin brothers. Above them was fixed a prominent sign reading, in Arabic and English, DO NOT TALK TO THE DRIVER. These men, of course, did nothing *but* talk to the driver for the next eleven hours. And their voices were as loud as his — I imagined they'd evolved this way from years of talking above the clattering roar of the engine.

The bone-rattling hulk wove recklessly through rush-hour traffic; even Cairene motorists swerved over sidewalks to get out of its way. An accomplished sunset was dissolving the sky into a golden mist behind Muhammad Ali's skyline-dominating mosque. It was nearly June now, and the heat in Cairo was warning everyone it would soon be back in business, riding high again. From the Citadel, high on the slopes leading up to the Mukattam Hills, I could see the packed labyrinth of the shadowed medieval city wreathed in strato-cirrus smog and dust clouds. Did those living there realize it wasn't air they were breathing anymore?

Through the narrow lanes past the City of the Dead we hurtled, forcing pedestrians into doorways, scattering lone donkeys into yards and fields, braying with fear. The three fat pirates and their galleon on wheels were obviously the terror of the road, blasting a custom-amplified horn every few seconds like cannon fire. The conversation in the front of the bus continued unabated, interspersed with frequent fits of diabolical rasping laughter and hideous epic bouts of coughing. Its content appeared to be a continuous exchange of dirty jokes. All three were prodigious smokers, major patrons of the Cleopatra Mild Company.

Beyond the old outskirts lay the new outskirts of the City of May 15, a low-cost housing project from Sadat's time designed to handle a population growing by a million each year. Although complete, it was insufficient even before construction began; the living inhabitants in the City of the

Dead alone proved that. But the New Valley, where I was heading, had been President Nasser's attempt to deal with a burgeoning population back in the early sixties when the situation was still manageable. The Western Desert oases were the only areas in the country with sufficient arable land and a supply of water that did not depend on the Nile. Nasser embarked on an ambitious development scheme of housing, industry, irrigation, and land reclamation that abruptly halted with the 1967 war. There has never been money available since to restart the scheme, hence the Delta region and the "Old Valley" of the Nile are still shouldering the burden of 55 million, or perhaps 60 million by the time you read this sentence. Five percent of Egypt houses 95 percent of its population.

After half an hour of rocketing into night down a narrow strip of road following the Nile, past strolling camels and fellahin returning from fertile fields thick with palms, we swerved to a spine-snapping halt in a tiny town. "Ten-minute rest stop," the fattest pirate roared at us, heaving himself after his cronies into the dusty street. The town was little more than a double line of open-fronted stores, fluorescent with strip lights or smoky yellow from kerosene tapers. Hunched figures with infrared vision played *sheshbesh* in the dark or smoked *sheeshas* around plate-sized tables or sat munching pita sandwiches under the harsh glare in miniature restaurants. Woodsmoke filled the warm air, mingled with gasoline and oil from jacked-up trucks undergoing major repairs. Here and there, waving oxy-acetylene welders' torches burned and roared like jet-powered fireflies.

A roadside washroom the size of a warehouse seemed to be where my fellow passengers were most interested in heading. The place was perfectly acceptable, as long as you held your breath for the length of time your visit required.

Soon everyone was back in the bus — except the driver and his accomplices. Ten minutes became half an hour; the bus became a sauna. No one seemed to mind waiting for the driver — apart from me. After forty minutes I left the bus and searched the nearby cafés, soon finding the pirate trio among a mob of disreputable-looking men gathered in front of a black-and-white TV set in a dingy café. Everyone clutched outsize bottles of Stella beer and shouted at the TV. They were watching football. I tapped the driver on the shoulder. Droplets of beer glistened like dew on his moustache. Having practised the phrase, I asked in Arabic when he imagined he'd return to his job. He was watching the football, he replied. I showed him my government documents, festooned with official stamps, and said I was late for urgent business. I doubted he could read. For a man who could have crumpled my head like newspaper with one hand, he reacted in a remarkably docile and sheepish way, summoning his henchmen and following me back to the bus.

It was going to be a long, uncomfortable night. I chewed a couple of Xanax, hoping to sleep, but every rut, bump, and pothole in the road bounced my skull against the window like a squash ball. Peering into the mossy blackness outside, I counted within one hour the mangled remains of seven crunchy accidents jutting from ditches and fields. My neighbour, a portly, soft-spoken man, whose elbow warred with mine over the territory of our central armrest all night, informed me this particular road was famous for its frequent and gruesome accidents.

Truck drivers, I noticed, were the people most anxious to maintain the road's hard-won reputation. The secret of their success lay in driving with their lights off as fast as possible on the wrong side of the road. It was brilliantly effective. But it also gave rise to another problem. While puny cars, let alone donkey carts and cyclists, readily drove off into mango groves and rice fields to avoid ten tons of high-velocity metal coming their way, our bus driver considered *his* vehicle a match for any truck. Every fifteen minutes I'd see the silhouette of a ten-wheeled monster loom into our beam (only one headlight functioned), watching in fascinated horror as the fat pirate gripped his huge steering wheel and leaned toward the windshield with extra concentration, aiming straight at the challenger. At times the two vehicles got as close as thirty feet or less before one would swing aside, bouncing over the uneven mud and rock shoulder at a forty-five degree angle (potential impact velocity: 185 miles per hour). The score was about 60 to 40 in favour of our man. With each triumph he and his crew would roar and bray with wicked laughter, beating the dashboard with their fists, slapping one another's backs, their cigarettes bursting into red showers over the laps of passengers behind. Out of sheer fright I fell into a series of fitful slumbers, waking each time my neighbour's elbow annexed no-man's-land or during especially savage highway duels or when we skidded into packed and noisy truck stops.

There seemed to be a major break in Asyut, where we parted from the Nile road, heading off southwest into the desert, another fat front-row pirate now taking over the wheel. This road, mercifully, seemed more or less empty and almost dead straight. No more duelling trucks, no roller-coaster bends.

When I awoke, the air felt warmer and drier. On either side of a broad boulevard hunkered low concrete bungalows the colour of stale cream in the sodium light of tall streetlamps. Most places look like ghost towns at 5:30 A.M., but Al-Khārga resembled a town that had been deserted in the early sixties, the architectural blunders of that most styleless of periods still perfectly preserved by the bone-dry climate. Blasting his horn with unnec-essary enthusiasm — the spiteful glee in making noise that predawn work-ers around the world share — the driver tore into the heart of the town, stopping at a four-way junction extending from a small roundabout.

I asked my neighbour whether this was the only stop in Al-Khārga. It was. No one else got out, however.

As I watched the battered bus blast off hooting through the silent streets, I wondered if my neighbour had lied just so his elbow could finally reign supreme over armrest land. This did not look like the downtown core of a place where humans had been living for at least four thousand years. It looked more like a flat, cheap suburb where humans had lived for about twenty-five years — then left. There was a ghostly post-Apocalypse silence about the place. The concrete beneath my feet was lightly dusted with fine sand.

Then a voice called out, "Welcome to Wadi Guedid." That was Arabic for "New Valley." I peered around. From the shadows a cheerful young man in an immaculate *gelabia* emerged, pushing an ancient motorcycle. "You want guest house, yes?" he asked. He told me to hop on the back of his bike, kicked it into life, and drove me around the roundabout, stopping at a low concrete structure on the other side, no more than fifty feet from where we'd set out. "Guest house," he announced. The building had been designed by someone trained in a packing-case factory: square, no windows, not even doors, in monotone concrete.

Propping his motorcycle against a low wall, the man introduced himself as Haroun and led me around the side of this minimalist masterpiece until we reached a kind of courtyard surrounded by more boxes. These did have doors. Inside one, I found a sitting room with TV, small kitchen, washroom, and a bedroom filled by two double beds. "Call me when you like breakfasts," Haroun said, handing me a key.

I threw my bruised and buckled limbs onto a faded pink candlewick bedspread and fell into Xanax land. I awoke at 9:30 to find it was still dark outside. Eventually I realized that it was only dark *inside;* this is why windows are so useful.

Haroun was sitting in the courtyard. He'd meant "call" him *literally.* Throughout the next few days he acted like my personal butler and valet. Like every single person I encountered in the Wadi Guedid, he was untiringly kind, thoughtful, and happy. Alexandrians should be forced to spend one month every year being reprogrammed in the oases.

I obtained a formidable vehicle, a tanklike fifties American four-wheel-drive Estate wagon, owned by a gentle old man named Yussef, who could have been King Hussein's grandfather. We all drove into town. The real Al-Khārga. It was more what I'd expected to find, and it certainly predated the early sixties. In fact, much of it predated the early 1360s.

"This was big rest town on Route Forty," Haroun announced.

"Route Forty?"

"Camel route. It take forty day by camel to go from Asyut to Sudan. So, Route Forty."

As the pulsing yolk of a megawatt sun sailed up into high blue air, dissolving all forms into its blinding gaseous light, we cruised in the old Wagoneer. The vehicle was given to bizarre eccentricities, like one functioning door and an ignition key that could be pocketed after the engine had been started. But it was robust; you *knew* it wouldn't let you down.

The beauty of the area was the first thing I noticed. Although the low mountains of the desert around us were always visible, the oasis was exuberantly lush: newly irrigated rice paddies lying like gargantuan mirror tiles reflecting azure; fields of thick pale corn; orchards pullulating with a dozen or so kinds of fruit trees; palms and acacias acting as giants' umbrellas, providing, with the assistance of generous breezes, the kind of cool, shady roads you find in southern France. It certainly wasn't the archetypical oasis, a huddle of ragged palm trees circling an overgrown puddle, surrounded by scorching rocks and sands. *This* was an embarrassment of riches.

"It's like the Garden of Eden," I said.

"Not *like*," corrected Yussef, the driver. "It *is* Eden Gardens."

Maybe it was. The original must have been somewhere between here and Iraq. Man, too, I noticed, as if in appreciation of nature's generosity, had also been moved to create here works that studiously avoided grandiosity. They were all the more moving for their human scale. There was no Great Pyramid, no Karnak or Luxor, no Abu Simbel, but there were temples of major importance, towns and villages of astounding beauty.

The earliest signs of human habitation in this area date back fifty thousand years, and the first ancient Egyptian settlement was established before 2000 B.C. under the Sixth Dynasty pharaoh, Pepi II. Anyone who ever came across this paradise must have been captivated by it. But we still know little about the area. Pharaonic records scarcely mention it. It appears to have been regarded as only "a place of banishment" during the Twenty-Second Dynasty. People must have been *fighting* to be banished here; it would be like getting sentenced to twenty years on Bora Bora today.

Haroun wanted to show me the famous hot sulphur springs, so we drove a short way out of town, turning onto a dirt road by a sign that read NASSER T. GUEST HOUSE. I didn't like to ask about the "T." Nasser's name was still evident on all manner of buildings here — from the Gamal Abdel Nasser Mosque on Nasser Street to the Nasser Date Emporium.

The Nasser T. Guest House was a dilapidated hut with ambitions situated in the middle of an unruly garden crowded with lofty palm trees. It looked dark and dusty inside. Exchanging greetings with several old men who appeared to be living there, we walked through its garden and out a little gate at the far end. The desert's edge was close here, a few hundred yards off, and the dwindling clumps of long spiky grass seemed made of sterner stuff than did their colleagues farther back in the oasis.

A little way off were what Haroun termed "the Baths." Two circular pools made of very old concrete were joined by a three-foot-wide channel. They were filled with water the colour of month-old tea. A powerful smell of rotten eggs hung in the hot air.

"What's *that?*" I inquired.

"Hot-spring bath. You like?" Haroun was already stripping down to his underpants. After he'd plunged into this tannic trough without apparent ill effect, I followed suit. The water was the temperature of a fairly hot bath, and it ran over the end of the far pool into a narrow ditch, so it was obviously *coming* from somewhere. The rotten-egg smell could be accounted for by sulphur, but what was this colour about?

The concrete sides were coated with big moist flakes of brown scum that resembled — let's face it — shit. I felt like an ant in the Toilet from Hell I'd encountered on the boat from Hurghada. Iron oxide was the explanation; the rocks and soil were rich in iron, and the hot sulphur springs bubbled through them. On closer inspection, this pool was actually lined with zinc, which must have been what attracted this rusty robots' dandruff. I stretched out against the edge, watching my limbs grow pale as they collected millions of tiny bubbles like a human Alka-Seltzer. Hot water, hot air, hot sun: it was oddly refreshing and deeply relaxing. There were rumours about turning this region into a five-star health spa, but I couldn't picture the Palm Springs crowd sipping piña coladas in pools of shit and stewed tea, iron oxide or not. My underpants were still pale russet six months later.

A couple of locals came to watch us, offering cigarettes, telling me that these waters would cure all known diseases. The landscape shimmered like a soft glass curtain in the breeze. It was an odd vantage point, like being buried up to your neck in a field that succumbed to lone and level sands, which in turn became ochre hills, wobbling behind the dancing glass curtain. It was quiet, too, just the wind in palm fronds and the birds.

We stayed an hour and, dressed again, I felt invigorated, nourished, even cooled from within. Not far away was one of the rare examples of pharaonic architecture from the period of Persian domination, around 400 B.C. A fairly intact temple to Amon built by Cambyses, it stood on a low hill surrounded by the remains of a Coptic village built some seven hundred years later. The great Egyptian archaeologist Ahmed Fakri, who died shortly after I left the country, did some work at the temple, discovering a cartouche of Darius there in 1970. Besides this, few have visited the oases, and only recently has a Canadian team begun the first large-scale multi-disciplinary survey, concentrating on the sister oasis of Al-Dakhleh, sixty miles farther west through the desert.

The Copts lived in the Wadi Guedid for some four hundred years, from the second century A.D., and Al-Khārga contains their vast Al-Bagawat necropolis, in itself evidence of the size of their community. It was possibly the earliest Christian settlement on any scale in the world. No one is sure why the Copts chose this spot, though escape from the bloody Roman persecution in Alexandria seems a good bet.

The necropolis sprawls around the rocky slopes of another modest hill and contains the remains of 263 chapels, which in turn often contain the remains of extremely deep shaft tombs in their dim interiors. The remains of a chapel differ from the remains of a shaft tomb. What remains of a chapel is frequently just a pile of disintegrating mud bricks; what remains of a shaft tomb, however, is still a wide hole one hundred feet deep and cut out of solid rock — at the bottom of which you might easily find the remains of yourself.

Few sites offer such an immense range of Coptic brick architecture and early Christian painting. Compared to Karnak or Luxor, or the Theban necropolis, of course, the place is a mere shantytown with aspirations. But there is some charm to the brickwork patterns, the careful arches, the tiny cross-shaped windows, the modesty of scale. The hot, dry wind made eerie noises blowing through the clefts and fissures of these small domed chapels, and this, combined with the desolate silences inside their crumbling walls, made me think of Shakespeare's line, "Bare ruin'd choirs, where late the sweet birds sang." These humble ruins evoked a bittersweet sadness for the simple devotion of those lives that had ended so long ago.

Calling my attention to a larger, roofless structure, Haroun said, "This oldest Christian church in world. *Oldest.*" My second in less than a week.

The best-preserved chapel here is called the Chapel of Peace. It was built around the fifth century, and according to a hand-painted sign outside, MANY SUBJECTS FROM THE BIBLE ARE PAINTED ON ITS DOME SUCH AS ADOM

AND EVE, EBRAHAM AND HIS SON, THE SYMBOLS OF PEACE AND JUSTICE, ST POUL AND THE ARK OF NOAH. The sign spoke truth, but I kept wondering why whoever painted it hadn't learned to paint *before* he embarked on this project.

Many of the faces on these frescoes have been smashed. We're told conquering Muslims mindful of the Second Commandment are to blame, but the vandalism could well have been the work of a wandering aesthete who just couldn't tolerate bad art.

Almost plummeting to the bottom of an early tomb, I noticed there was also a good deal of graffiti in these chapels. Some of this was old, like an ancient Egyptian ankh cross alongside its Christian equivalent, some more recent. Alongside SAPPER J. F. THOMPSON, 1917, RULE BRITTANIA, was a spray-painted inverted pentagram, sign of satanists or heavy-metal fans. It was hard to imagine what either would be doing out here.

After early Christian mud brick it was a relief to move on to the Hibis Temple, a Twenty-Sixth Dynasty structure situated in a grove of waving palms on the edge of Al-Khārga. With reliefs as fine as those at Philae, the place resembled a miniature Karnak, imposing despite its size. Egyptologists from Brown University have been engaged in heavy restoration here, managing, because of the modest scale of the site, to produce a reasonable impression of the original structure. Unfortunately the stone used in rebuilding the walls and pylons was rich in iron-ore content, and with the new high water table — courtesy of the Aswan Dam — moisture has seeped up through capillary action and rusted the veins of iron, leaving the stone looking like very coarse cream-and-brown marble. The effect was not unpleasing, I thought, but the Egyptian Antiquities czar, Sayeed Tawfiq, apparently didn't agree. He planned to move the whole temple to drier land before he died prematurely while I was editing this book. What was another few million dollars the government didn't have for the preservation of its antiquities compared to the other few billions they already didn't have?

Even this little Hibis Temple, tucked away among palm fronds and verdant fields, hardly ever visited, lost for two thousand years, still exhibited vivid patches of original paintwork, the turquoise as bright as the day it was mined in the Sinai Desert before Christ's birth. On the pylons of Nectanebo's Gate, built around the time Alexander the Great was born,

I noticed the graffito of the great German scholar Carl Ottfried Müller (1797–1840). It must be only the conviction that no one else will ever reach whatever remote spot you're in that persuades an otherwise intelligent man to indulge in such a puerile activity. Flaubert seems to have been the only person of his era who found this popular pastime imbecilic. Did all nineteenth-century tourists pack a hammer and chisel in their steamer trunks?

∼◦

When the busy sun was through for the day, heading for its couch on the gilded horizon, I set off into the living part of town. The bazaars were bustling now. The sheer quantity and variety of the fruits and vegetables, arranged in neat rows and pyramids by conscientious men, bore witness to the fecundity of the dark oasis soil around Al-Khārga.

Beyond a wide square I followed a narrower dusty road lined with tailors, cloth merchants, candle-makers, vendors of string, of straw bags and mats: the whole panorama of a medieval world. Off this street were tunnel-like alleys, the houses built right around them, creating a labyrinth of walkways perpetually sheltered from the relentless midday sun. Wandering here, I passed smooth, worn mud-brick stairways leading up to heavy, ancient studded doors, or sometimes leading nowhere at all. Through passages, open windows, and doors I spied open courtyards, rooms, and hallways where the business of life went on in a thousand timeless ways. Milk was being churned into butter by giggling kohl-eyed girls; an old veiled woman was grinding corn into flour with a massive granite mortar and pestle; a young boy was studying by oil lamp at a little desk beneath a framed Koranic sura in elegant Arabic calligraphy; an old man with black eyebrows and a blazing red hennaed beard was reshoeing his mule; a group of huge women wearing earrings like huge fishing lures sang as they prepared vegetables for dinner. Nothing had changed here. And no one seemed to think my presence unusual. I was an invisible traveller through time. For the year here was 1590, at the most.

In the twisting alleys it was night, but back on the open streets a gentle gold-and-purple light still filled the immense sky, illuminating the muted greens and blues of window frames and doors. Pouring from a dozen rectangles, open storefronts lit by pressure lamps, was a light almost solid in its pulsing brilliance, yet still softened by those vast sheets of greater light above. A tingling tranquility filled the town. The forms, the faces, the colours: all were soft. No frowns, no hostile stares, no anger: just smiles, sweet as the spiced air and just as comforting. Were we all like this once?

For less than fifty cents I bought ten feet of fine Egyptian cotton — enough to make a shirt — without even attempting to bargain. Wrapping up my purchase carefully in brown paper and tying it with string, the merchant ordered his boy to fetch mint tea. It's so much more relaxing to have tea *after* business than before. Sitting in the street on stools, we shared a smouldering narghile packed with pungent tobacco, and the merchant told me countless strangers had come to live in Al-Khārga. Arriving with their camel caravans, he said, many had loved the town and even fallen in love in the town. The Sindadia family had built much of the area in which we sat, he claimed proudly. They were traders "from the West," he informed me, back in the sixteenth century. What was the West then? I wondered. Libya? Or merely perhaps Al-Dakhleh, half a week's ride away by camel in those distant days.

I asked about the economy, the wars, the troubles of contemporary Egypt. He merely smiled, saying, "*Here* we know only peace."

Leaving, I thanked him.

"*Ahlan was'ahlan,*" he replied — "With all my heart."

With all *my* heart, too, I told myself.

CHAPTER TWENTY-TWO

BULL'S HEAD SOUP

Over the early history of Egypt there hangs a mystery greater
than that which shrouds the origin and home of the Egyptian;
of the period which preceded Menes, the first historical king of
Egypt, nothing is known.

—SIR E. A. WALLIS BUDGE, *THE MUMMY*

A man smelling strongly of something unpleasant had recently been performing a task that involved much brown greasy liquid. He wanted to show
me something; that much I understood. And it was quite important to him
that I see it. "*Meshy,*" I told him, "Okay." Whatever it was I had to see so
urgently was not nearby. After ten minutes and many streets, we arrived
outside a tawdry, untidy house on a street of well-kept, neat little homes.
The man motioned for me to wait, hastening into the house through a
door that looked as if it had been chopped up and nailed back together in
no particular order. Part of it dropped to the ground when he closed it
behind him. From a side passage a woman and some children appeared to

have a look at me. They were undoubtedly the man's family. They, too, had been dealing recently with the same greasy brown liquid. The children were not just dirty, they were indescribably, staggeringly, and impossibly *filthy*. The woman's *abaya* and whatever lay beneath looked as if they had been used to mop up a few gallons of stew from a dirty gutter. ·

Above me an expressionist masterpiece in burning coral, gold leaf, and molten lapis was being painted somewhere high over the Libyan Desert. A few faces had appeared from nearby doorways and in thick-walled windows. They vanished as soon as I noticed them, reappearing as surreptitiously as possible. I wondered if this man, his family, and his house were the neighbourhood embarrassment. He was probably always bringing strangers back like this and shaming the whole street.

Fighting his way through the hopeless door, the man finally emerged carrying a large and heavy object wrapped in cloth even filthier than his wife's veil. Wheezing with the effort and looking disturbingly enthusiastic, he placed the bundle at my feet and proceeded to peel away its covering. Inside was the head of a very big bull that had only recently been separated from the rest of its body. Its open eyes were the size of snooker balls, and one of them stared up at me angrily through a milky film. It had extremely long, thick horns, slightly dark blue in parts. The inside of its neck was the colour of the sky at that moment, apart from slimy knobs of white bone and a number of yellow tubelike tendrils.

The man made a sort of theatrical *Voilà* gesture with one arm, looking up at me and beaming with pride. I wasn't sure quite how to react. I nodded appreciatively, like a connoisseur of such things. Near the house, the whole family, too, were smiling, indicating the head, which had also begun to attract the interest of many flies by now.

Why was he showing me this? Were foreigners notorious in Al-Khārga for their insatiable passion for severed bulls' heads?

"That's great," I finally said. "That's really a great ... bull's head you've got there. It really is. You must be very proud ... I know *I* would be ..."

The man went into a paroxysm of delight, shaking my hand and coating it in greasy gore, shouting joyfully at his family, who clapped and shrieked.

Oh no, I realized, I've just bought a dead bull's head. How much do they go for these days?

At ten Egyptian pounds it seemed a bargain, although doubtless I could have got it for half that. I handed over the money, which the man received as if it were millions. Then he invited me into his house for coffee. I pictured wading through congealed blood and offal to recline on the rest of the bull.

I was in a real hurry, I tried to convey. Because I was late, very late, for an urgent appointment. The man seemed disappointed, but shrugged, shook my hand warmly and slimily once more, stooping to rewrap the bull's head, then presenting it to me with the flourish of a master salesman.

The thing weighed a ton. As I staggered off down the street, the man's family waved fondly, and on all sides eyes watched from the shadows, presumably muttering to other eyes that he'd done it again. That man had done it again. The shame, oh, the shame.

Back in the main bazaar, where the light was better, I saw that I was beginning to look like the bull's executioner myself. Greasy brownish gore had oozed through the cloth over my shirt and pants. A galaxy of flies hovered around me. I thought of just dumping the thing in a gutter but wasn't sure what Islamic protocol might have to say about such matters.

Passing the Date Centre, a fastidiously tidy glass-fronted store run by the orthodox Muslim equivalent of *Vogue* models, I noticed, among the many kinds of dates on sale, ones that were stuffed with almonds. I had a sudden and unnatural craving for them. I thought, I'll put the head down, walk in, buy the dates, walk out ... and forget the head.

All this worked out as planned. As I walked off enjoying the dates — but not the rank smell on my fingers — voices behind me yelled out, "Hey, Mr. American!" Two men came running up holding the head between them. "You forget eet," one said. I thanked them, shoved the dates in my pocket, and staggered all the way back to the guest house with my package and its ever-growing blizzard of flies.

"Good for soup," Haroun said as I threw the head down on the courtyard outside my room. "And stew. I make for you, yes?"

"No, Haroun. You have it."

"You buy for me?" He seemed overwhelmed.

"It's yours, Haroun. Go in peace. *Salaam Aleikum.*"

"*Aleikum was'ahlan,*" he replied.

I wondered what the Western equivalent of this gift would be. Presenting an assistant manager in the Park Plaza with several pounds of fresh filet mignon, perhaps? Haroun must own an enormous soup pot, I decided.

Instead of bull's-head stew, I had salad, beans, hummus, and bread that night as a guest of some official in a building not far away that turned out to be the Presidential Guest House. The size of a small hotel, it contained only two bedrooms — one the size of a small hotel, the other the size of a small bedroom.

Sadat had ordered the guest house built, staying there only one night himself. President Mubarak had not yet had cause to stay, so the large bedroom was pretty much as Sadat had left it. It was like a shabby suite in one of the more run-down Las Vegas honeymoon hotels. Acrylic long-haired polar-bearskin carpeting, ornate bed, tassels the size of heads holding back curtains so crisp with decades of dry dust and heat that they'd disintegrate if drawn. Downstairs was one more gigantic room, furnished as if it were a modest sitting room — a teeny settee in black plastic flanked by matching armchairs with matchsticklike legs was placed at one end, a Formica coffee table in the middle, and an early colour TV at the far end. Seated in the chairs or settee, you needed a telescope to watch the TV, which was never turned off, and arms thirty feet long to place your coffee on the coffee table.

The government official never spoke a word throughout dinner, besides urging me to eat everything in sight. I found myself unable to muster the energy to soliloquize for more than fifteen minutes, and thus shut up, too. The cook stood beside me, wringing his hands all evening — as if much could go wrong with bread and raw vegetables. Even when I thanked him profusely before leaving, I had the impression he thought I was lying. Possibly he hadn't cooked a meal since Sadat's visit and wondered whether he had lost his touch.

Strolling back through perfumed air and night-cooled streets, I wondered why on earth this "official" had invited me to dinner in the first place. Maybe it was merely that charming but inexplicable Arab hospitality.

The evening had, however, yielded up one intriguing treasure. Being nosy, I'd found a dusty, dried-out Koran with one of its pages turned down in a drawer by the presidential bedside. Noting the suras marked, I discovered months later they concerned the attempted murder of Isaac by his father, Abraham. The event is, of course, termed "sacrifice," not "murder." But one wonders which of the two was really the victim.

～o

Yussef, Haroun, and I set off in the wolf hour, driving through the deserted night streets of Al-Khārga and off west on the narrow hardtop highway toward Al-Dakhleh, the L-shaped sister oasis 50 miles long and 15 miles wide that lies about 185 miles west of the Nile, on the edge of the Libyan Desert. The air was still cool, and on the outskirts blown sand as fine as talcum powder slid across the roads like liquid, swept into gutters by the wind's invisible broom.

The desert appeared abruptly, terrifying in its vastness. To the south, the towering skeletons of hydro pylons shouldered their burdens of cables carrying Aswan's electricity and the technology it made possible out into the wilderness.

To the north of this snaking road the scalloped humps of smooth dunes had buried telephone poles up to their necks and frequently blocked the road entirely, forcing our faithful Wagoneer into four-wheel drive, bumping around them over rocks and sand. These dunes are on the move, travelling at over three miles a year, depending on the winds, and unstoppable. Whole towns and villages have been lost beneath them, something that the archaeologists working out here are just beginning to realize is of incalculable importance to science. Their spines rippling in the wind, the dunes looked alive, rousing themselves lugubriously for another day's slow trek.

We stopped by the roadside, and I walked out a few hundred yards into the silence to watch the sun rise. No sooner was the copper-red disk visible than shadows began to flow out like ink from the ochre rocks around me, and every dune acquired waving bands of sandy gills.

A few miles later we entered a landscape of confounding and eerie beauty. Stretching as far south as I could see were small reddish-black mountains shaped exactly like pyramids, the low cadmium light revealing on many of them four distinct sides as sheer and faultlessly straight as anything at Giza. It was hard at first to believe they were not man-made, even the angles perfectly matched and harmonious. "Yardangs" is the technical term. There were hundreds of them, all approximately the same size. Surely the Old Kingdom architects had found their original inspiration here. Only walking closer to these "pyramids" finally convinced me they were natural formations. Alongside them were other monolithic sculptures carved by Nature's hand, many, as in Sinai, resembling animals — camels, bulls, and sphinxes — from certain angles. Only in the high desert of California's Joshua Tree National Park have I seen anything similar. One feels the place *must* be the ruins of a city constructed by giants.

Carved into the rock face close to some of the most spectacular formations I found a vast frieze of hunting scenes and runic lettering that dates from the Old Stone Age fifty thousand years ago. These petroglyphs are the most ancient works of art in Egypt, evidence that the Wadi Guedid has been continuously inhabited by humans as far back as we can conceive. The stone here was shot through with bright bands of colour from metallic ores, which gave these antediluvian carvings an extraordinary vibrancy and life. Many of the animals depicted were recognizable, especially the giraffes, which outnumbered any of the other creatures. It's presumed these are hunting scenes, but no men are represented, and it's possible the images served some other function. But the style is unmistakable and ubiquitous in sites from this period around the globe. Looking at this communication from our most distant ancestors, I considered these animals that were more akin to patterns or pictograms. Perhaps here were the beginnings of writing, with the same symbolic and phonetic values of the Egyptian hieroglyphs. But there will be no Rosetta Stone, no Champollion here. What this rock face had to say will remain a secret forever.

The wind rushing through our car was heating up now like the blast of a monster hair-dryer as we hurtled on toward Al-Dakhleh. We didn't hurtle for long, however. Turning a sharp bend past a steep wall of rock, the road ahead disappeared, heading straight into a sixty-foot-high mound of sand. Dunes on the move again. This was clearly a king dune, too, a great whale of sand taking its time to cross the road. It's probably just about made it as I write.

"Where are they going, these dunes?" I asked Haroun.

"Taking vacation," he replied. "Heading to Red Sea coast."

This was basically true. The dunes move until they either meet an obstacle they can't roll over, like a mountain, or water. Presumably, these dunes will have to settle for the Nile, not the Red Sea. I asked what happens if one is heading toward your house.

"You move," said Yussef. "Come back after six month."

Soon the oasis appeared in the distance. After three hours of desert the sight of green fields, water, trees, is miraculous. Sir Archibald Edmonstone, the first European to visit Dakhleh, took three days to cross from Khārga by camel in 1819 — and found the sight even more miraculous. Only those who have travelled for days through deserts can truly appreciate water. As many have noted, the image of the Muslim heaven — flowing crystal streams, shady trees, attentive virgins — is the paradise of desert nomads. The Prophet Muhammad, being a desert trader before becoming God's Messenger, would naturally have pictured heaven this way.

If Al-Khārga was the Garden of Eden, Al-Dakhleh might as well have been heaven itself. Few places on earth can match the unspoiled beauty and charm of this area. Protected by a range of umber mountains to the west, behind which lies the Libyan Desert, the oasis is impossibly lush, hills and plains all green with crops and trees, water everywhere. It is also the only place in Egypt and the whole Middle East and North Africa where men wear broad straw hats instead of the traditional *kaffiyeh*. This and the landscape made me feel I'd entered the Provence of Van Gogh. Egypt is full of surprises, of hidden treasures, and Dakhleh is almost a microcosm of the country, containing in an area of eight hundred square miles more variety than seems logically possible.

Our first stop, at Haroun's insistence, was Bashandi Village. It is the Egyptian equivalent of St. Tropez or Santorini before the tourists moved in. Built like the Nubian villages in sculpted mud brick, Bashandi was clearly Hassan Fathy's real source of inspiration. It was a work of art in which people lived.

Spotlessly clean, the narrow streets were covered in fine, rich yellow sand; and there was not a straight line in sight. Every wall, step, passage, flowed organically, as if rising from the earth itself. Thick, ancient studded wood doors, all painted muted pastel greens and blues, were framed by thick curving mud walls and arches. Some walls were painted in a pristine blue so pale that it was virtually white; others were left natural ochre, pouring into and out of the sand. Although obviously centuries old, every building was so immaculately clean that the village looked brand-new. Many walls bore delightful murals depicting their owners' pilgrimage to Mecca, the hajj that every good Muslim must try to make at least once. Various modes of transport were shown — camel, bus, airplane — and every stage of the journey was documented, from family farewells to the kissing of the Ka'aba stone.

"Why's the place so incredibly tidy?" I asked Haroun.

"They like this way. It is tradition here."

Each building was distinctive, blending harmoniously into the whole. The architects of the world should be shipped here before they're let loose on our cities. Bashandi looked as if one man had designed the entire place, yet it had been built — was indeed *still* being built — by thousands of individuals over many centuries, each house added onto or modified as the needs of its occupants changed. I found it hard to imagine a more idyllic place to live.

It's believed that this is probably the kind of town ancient Egyptians lived in, stone being reserved for tombs and temples, and there is in fact still a small Ptolemaic temple incorporated into the curving walls of one of Bashandi's little streets, its carved reliefs and meticulous mason's art not looking remotely out of place alongside the plasticity of mud brick. Elsewhere, a seventeenth-century Islamic tomb exists in equal harmony.

The people of Bashandi were also themselves works of art, the women wearing elaborate veils and magnificent silver jewellery, the men sporting luxuriant beards and moustaches, as dignified as kings in their manners and bearing. They reminded me of the Ma'aza nomads, and it's possible these villagers may be descended from Bedouin who stumbled across this oasis and finally saw no reason to move on. Many villagers are artists or craftsmen, producing pottery and tapestries unlike those found anywhere else in Egypt.

For an embarrassingly low price I bought an unusual handwoven abstract tapestry good enough to hang in any museum of modern art. The man responsible for it explained he was trying to portray the desert area I'd just travelled through, pointing out the road, the pyramid mountains, the dunes, and the oases at either end. I asked him how he'd arrived at this modernist style, and he replied that it seemed the best way to adequately convey such a vast and strange landscape. He worked straight on the loom, with no sketch or pattern to guide him, using wool dyed with local vegetable colours and as subtle as those in the landscape itself. It hangs on the wall behind my bed now, and each time I look at it, I see more to admire. The only problem is the powerful smell of wet beast it emits in humid weather.

What Haroun had particularly wanted to show me in Bashandi, however, were the Canadian scientists working on the first survey of this region ever attempted, and currently headquartered in the village. Unfortunately they had left for the season just one week before.

Headed by Anthony J. Mills, a research associate of the Royal Ontario Museum's Egyptian Department, the Dakhleh Oasis Project is an enormous multidisciplinary survey of all periods, from the Neolithic Old Stone Age through the New Stone Age, Ancient Egyptian period, and the Romano-Byzantine era, up to the Islamic age. That's about 100,000 years of history. No wonder the project's funding was cut off by the Canadian Social Sciences and Humanities Research Council in 1988 for being "insufficiently focused."

Just as Professor Redford had lost his funding after making the international front pages with his discovery of Akhenaten's Geena-paten temple, so Mills lost his the year after he'd interested world media with the discovery of two ancient wooden-paged books in Dakhleh. Under the sands that had buried the abandoned post-Hellenic city of Ismant, he found what was widely reported as a previously unknown work by Aristotle written in Greek on eight wooden pages bound with string. However, it turned out to be three essays on monarchy by Isocrates, a fourth-century B.C. philosopher who had taught Aristotle. Although the writings were not unknown, the book was six hundred years older than the earliest known texts.

More exciting to Mills, though, was the other volume discovered under the sands of Ismant. A farm records book belonging to a certain Faustianos, it details the accounts of his tenant farmers, as well as listing the crops grown two thousand years ago in Dakhleh. Cotton, wheat, alfalfa, barley, olives, grapes: they're still grown in the area, and show that agriculture was well established in the oasis since the earliest times. Recent evidence currently being analyzed suggests there were experiments in cultivation being carried out on the edge of the Libyan Desert over twenty thousand years ago by people we know absolutely nothing about.

Anthony Mills, defending his project against the charge of insufficient focus — which strikes me as grossly unfair — has often said that since nothing is known about the western oases, the various teams under his supervision were "starting from scratch," without the benefit of any previous work, and with such a vast area to survey they were forced to select specific foci at random. The books at Ismant were just lying beneath the sand where they'd been thrown by their owner as he hastily fled his home just before the city was attacked by an unknown enemy. Soon the desert had closed in over everything, preserving it perfectly. The books made news, although Isocrates proved less newsworthy than Aristotle, but the most interesting discoveries of the project have been made by physical anthropologists examining Neolithic butchering sites and graves. The media, of course, aren't interested in Neolithic butchering sites or graves.

Analyzing bone samples from men who may have been responsible for the desert petroglyphs, scientists have found high levels of tetracycline present, along with a remarkable lack of disease. Alan Hollett, one of Mills' technical assistants, assured me this didn't mean Neolithic man had pioneered the pharmaceutical industry. Tetracycline is naturally produced by a fungus that grows on wheat. Yet, just as the ancient Egyptians were perfectly aware of and used organic antibiotics, it could be reasonable to think the prehistoric inhabitants of Dakhleh were also conscious of the disease-fighting properties of mouldy wheat. After all, one assumes no one would eat it for fun.

Mills had regained his funding for the 1989–90 season, for a price, but was constantly travelling the world to lecture and urge other organizations and individuals to help offset the enormous cost of his project. He was much pressured to publish something of substance, too. Although he'd discovered a sizable Ptolemaic temple under the sand, initially mistaking its roof for the floor, excavation was going to be slow, expensive, and complex. Perhaps completely intact, the stone is nonetheless very fragile, and only the surrounding sand is supporting the structure at present. Restoration and preservation will have to be simultaneous with excavation, and the operation could well prove prohibitively costly and time-consuming.

When I met Professor Redford at the University of Toronto's Faculty Club after my return from Egypt, in November, he looked a decade younger out of the Theban inferno. He, too, had an interest in Dakhleh, he told me. And in archaeology, I've learned, the term "interest" has personal, almost proprietary connotations.

"He's giving the best bloody sites away," Redford said through his sandwich, about Tony Mills. "The French have got *my* temple ... and they're excavating it. They're not supposed to be excavating — it's a bloody *survey*."

This was true. Mills' project only had permits for a survey, not any excavation. So why were the French excavating? Since I already knew Redford's views on French archaeological practices as "just a bloody treasure hunt," I could see this doubly irked him. The most amiably benign curmudgeon I've ever encountered — his grievances made him roar with laughter — Redford brooded over how he could liberate "his" Dakhleh temple from the tyranny of French ineptitude, while also continuing to work at Geena-paten. The season in East Karnak had been somewhat disappointing, I gathered, and he'd never managed to spend any time at the Delta sites, where major discoveries were showing up daily and history was being rewritten. His interest in Dakhleh confirmed my own suspicions that the area was still wide open; anything might show up.

But Mills had been forced to give prime concessions to French, Australians, and others who could bring in financing. The French had got the most promising temple site; the Australians had got the two wooden books — although I wasn't sure whether Redford was implying they'd discovered them or been accorded the discovery, the books themselves perhaps destined for a museum in Sydney. Mills had even once, apparently, contemplated taking the entire project out of Canada to an American university with the cash necessary for continuing it.

In the meantime, Haroun informed me that Yussef, our driver, was feeling hungry, and we should move on. When I asked Yussef where he wanted to eat, he told me he wasn't hungry yet, so I assumed Haroun was hungry. In any event, we didn't eat for some time, heading from Bashandi into the verdant heart of the oasis. Date palms, eucalyptus trees, acacias, fluttered in a warm, kind breeze; fields were full of rustling wheat, countless other crops. Everywhere water flashed like scattered diamonds. Even the air seemed scented. For Shaykh Sulimaan and his Khushmaan, this place would literally be heaven, I thought. They'd crossed the deserts of Arabia, the Sinai, and the Red Sea, but they'd never crossed the Nile.

We next stopped at the village of Al-Kasr, as different from Bashandi as Gauguin is from Goya. Constructed in the early Islamic style, Al-Kasr is now largely uninhabited but in remarkably good repair, the exquisite calligraphic carvings on huge wooden door lintels still fresh. Everywhere I noticed the arches and oddly vegetative columns, all patterned with forms both geometrical and organic, that inspired the great cathedral builders of Europe. Indeed, the sources of the Renaissance and Europe's golden age lie in the glorious zenith of Islamic civilization. The forms were still fairly basic here, yet their potency must have had a profound effect on any European who ever saw them in their original state, returning to the clunky, graceless fortified bunkers that then passed for architecture back home. Beauty and pragmatism had not yet wed in Europe a millennium ago. They weren't even dating.

Above the roof of a distant ruin I noticed what looked like a simple Christian cross. "Christian mosque" was how Haroun answered my query. He meant "church," but for a moment I wondered if there had been a fusion of faith no one was aware of. It was odd to realize that, even during the golden age of Islam, Christians and Muslims had lived side by side here peaceably. The church still stood, and there are no records of persecution. Perhaps the merchant in Al-Khārga had been right: Here, they *did* know only peace.

Al-Kasr also contains the shrine of a Sufi saint called Nasruddin. His body lies in its dusty, draped sarcophagus, with dried flowers scattered by the faithful who, contrary to Islamic law, believe that the saint can intercede for them, even perform miracles. Once a year the believers gather here, around Nasruddin's corpse, celebrating his birth.

I asked Haroun about Sufism. He looked uneasy, stressing that only a few believed in it, implying they were probably wrong to do so. He didn't like the extremist fundamentalists, mainly because the strictness of their beliefs aimed at removing all of life's innocent little pleasures; and he wasn't talking about sex or alcohol. In parts of Saudi Arabia to this day music is banned, and only a fool would smoke a cigarette in public.

"You like another sulphur bath?" he asked to change the subject.

We drove down a long, shady road a short distance from Al-Kasr, drawing up to a large white-walled enclosure. It reminded me of a fifties open-air swimming pool with its changing chalets, veranda, concrete patio, and kidney-shaped pool. But this pool, instead of being the usual Paul Newman-iris blue, was filled with gravy that poured in a steady torrent from a large drainpipe protruding over the far edge. Again the bad-egg stink of sulphur, the bitter tang of iron oxide. This water was hotter, however, and attempting to swim in it was exhausting. A group of prosperous and Westernized Egyptian men sat in rust-coloured underpants beneath the shade of a doum tree, occasionally throwing one another into the vat of gravy. An attendant brought out glasses of cold water while Haroun and I leaned at the pool's rim. Only after downing two glasses did I learn I'd been drinking what we were swimming in. The water was clear and had been refrigerated, but the taste of sulphur and iron was still powerful.

"Very good for health," Haroun announced, ordering more. After eight glasses I did feel invigorated and cleansed — or needed to convince myself I did.

We dressed and wandered out into the tree-lined lane. Approaching us slowly was a boy wearing the local straw hat and riding a sleepy old mule that also carried two large round sacks. *"As-salam aleikum,"* he called out.

"Aleikum salam," we chorused, and, my Arabic improving, I added, *"Ismak eh?"* ("What's your name?")

"Ismi Badr," the boy said proudly. Nice name: it meant "Full Moon."

The incident was one of those memories you take to the grave, recalling many times in many places: the boy, his hat, the mule, the white dusty road, the brilliant flash of bird's wings, the sporadic twitter of song, the breeze rustling in the quiet fields, the shafts of strong light piercing down through the leaves like luminous crystal bars. These fragments shored against my ruin …

When we arrived at an elegant colonial bungalow set in a rich garden back from the road, Haroun announced this was the guest house where we'd take lunch. He was a master of organization, this Haroun. How or when he'd organized this particular treat I don't know, but we were greeted by three men and an elegant woman who appeared to be expecting us, then led us through the hot and murky interior of the bungalow and out onto a broad veranda where a table had been elaborately prepared with fruits and appetizers, cold juices and mineral water.

"How did you manage *this*?" I asked Haroun as we were seated where a cooling breeze came in off the fields. He merely smiled in self-deprecating fashion and encouraged me to eat.

Beyond the garden were orchards and wheat fields where peasants from Van Gogh landscapes toiled languidly, their straw hats, faded blue work clothes, and archaic hoes composing a vision from a lost time. I had an eerie sense of *déjà vu*.

The other men and the woman joined us, followed by servants carrying dish after dish of painstakingly prepared food: salads, roast pigeon, shish kebabs, hummus, babaganoug, barbecued chicken, minted potatoes.

The only drawback to this feast in paradise was the uninvited guests. Flies — not a few but countless thousands of them — descended. And these flies were skilled at their work, skipping aside to avoid death yet back on your pigeon breast or potato in under a second. Servants stood behind us with whisks of dried grass, but the flies knew this trick. The scene became amusing, both guests and servants armed now with whisks, the whole table a mass of waving arms like some arcane sit-down martial-arts ritual. It was a losing battle, so I decided to eat them, too, if it came to that.

Our hosts were government officials with functions involved — using Salman Rushdie's term — in P2C2E — processes too complicated to explain. All bureaucracies involve processes that substitute for work, for action. But they were courteous, considerate, gentle people — products of this oasis and its tranquil beauty. To my horror I heard over the meal that big plans were under way here. I listened to descriptions of resort complexes, casinos, health spas, arts-and-crafts emporiums. We've wrecked virtually every other paradise on earth, including the original one, so it's inevitable that Dakhleh's days are numbered, too. The 1929 Baedeker has less to say about the western oases than it does about the Sinai; the writer clearly never visited the area, aware only that the drive by car from Khārga took nine hours. But now, I told myself, the place is still all mine.

My hosts didn't know what to make of my enthusiasm — thinking perhaps I'd picked up too much Egyptian politeness during my stay — unwilling to believe I found their simple shabby guest house (rooms: one dollar per night) not only adequate but preferable to any resort complex. No piped-in Zamfir, for instance.

After lunch, we drove into Mout, the capital of Dakhleh, named after the ancient Egyptian goddess of night, of the heavens. A sleepy little town, its newer areas resembled Khārga. But forty-two centuries ago, during the Sixth Dynasty, a small but significant necropolis was built here. None of the Old Kingdom pharaoh's tombs have ever been found — or rather found with a mummy inside them; the Mout necropolis, however, housed governors and generals and other high-ranking officials, indicating that the oasis was a significant centre of the pharaonic empire over four millennia ago.

By now time was running very short. I had a meeting with the governor back in Al-Khārga, which I *had* requested. Haroun took me out to see one area where a health spa was already under construction. Driving down a narrow bumpy dirt road, we found ourselves stuck behind three monstrous trucks carrying gravel, the dust from their wake enveloping us in a choking cloud. Beyond, steep white mountains rose, the natural wall separating Egypt from Libya. Their whiteness gave the illusion of snow. To the far right, higher than the others, stood Gebel Edmonstone, the mountain named after Sir Archibald, who'd been deeply moved by all he'd seen here 170 years before me.

The trucks veered off at the edge of the oasis, heading for quarries in the foothills, and we turned into a small grove of palms, the very last vegetation before the mighty desert began. At the end of a narrow mud path, we came to the perfect stereotype of an oasis: a circular pool fifteen feet or so in diameter shaded on all sides by towering palms. Bubbles rose steadily up from its centre, but besides some fairly disgusting brown scum at the edges the waters were clear. We stripped and waded in. The sides were steep, the bottom stony, and at the middle I was up to my chest in water that was almost perfectly warm and only faintly perfumed by sulphur. Just by the point from which the hot spring bubbled up from the depths was a large, smooth rock, where one could sit and let bubbles tickle across the skin.

Leaning back to watch palm fronds dance in the light, I tried to imagine how many weary travellers had tied their camels to these trees after emerging from weeks crossing the trackless sands, stripped off their dust-caked robes, and plunged into these relaxing waters while their dehydrated mounts knelt to drink and to munch leaves. For hundreds of generations this spot must have been all that kept people going through the biting sandstorms and the incendiary heat. Egrets, hoopoes, larks, wagtails, and swallows fluttered and swooped through the branches and among the waving grasses. High in the blue air a pair of kestrels rode the currents motionlessly, one of them suddenly falling like a meteor on some small creature trapped in open ground.

Some distance away, a low line of concrete structures was in a rudimentary stage of being built. "Health spa," Haroun announced proudly. The plan was to divert this natural spring into the spa pool. Soon this idyllic little spot, which had served numberless parched caravans since the beginning of time, would be gone. I asked why it couldn't be left, as a novelty, perhaps, for spa customers. But Haroun couldn't believe people would prefer to sit on rocks and mud when they could have the latest amenities right next door.

⁓

By 10:30 P.M. we were back in Khārga, the night desert floodlit by a fierce crescent moon that gleamed like a giant Arab dagger stuck in the wall of infinity. That astounding landscape, reduced to stark silhouettes, had looked even more alien, more powerfully enigmatic.

I had a minute to scrape away the bodysuit of dust I'd collected on the drive, Haroun anxious not to keep the governor waiting. It seemed rather late for an official appointment, but I assumed Haroun knew what he was doing. The gubernatorial office turned out to be not far from the guest house, past a sleek white mosque bathed in green neon, along the broad, tree-lined boulevard. The structure had been designed to be grand and imposing and had ended up merely stout and clunky. Outside, a string of Mercedes sedans dating to the late seventies waited with their chauffeurs. A sleek black one bore a licence plate numbered simply "1." It was, presumably, the governor's vehicle, the rest belonging to ministers attending a late-night cabinet meeting?

The interior of the building reminded me of a small provincial hospital constructed in the early sixties: odd partitions, irregular, windowless rooms, frosted-glass doors, half-walls, boring posters about health and safety.

An aide appeared after Haroun and I had waited in a stifling little room for five minutes to usher us through many flimsy doors and down a long brown corridor over squeaking floors covered with more polish than linoleum. He reached a pair of doors made of concertinaed plastic and concealed by a large brown curtain. Throwing the musty curtain aside, he struggled with the doors, sliding them apart to reveal an enormous office containing about thirty men seated in chairs and sofas against either side, all of them facing a man seated behind a desk the size of a pool table in the centre of the far wall.

This man was big. Very big. He rose and offered a limp, chubby hand, indicating a chair to the right of his monster desk.

"*Parlez-vous anglais?*" he asked me.

"*Mais oui, monsieur.*"

He then proceeded to speak in English for the entire meeting, first proffering me a business card. "My business cards were printed in Canada," he announced grandly. I told him mine were, too. At least mine spelled my name correctly, though.

"My name, you see," the governor told me, "is Eltallawy. Man in Canada made a mis-spell, so … I have five thousand of this cards and must make correction each time I am giving one." I couldn't picture the governor of California doing this, but it made me like the man.

His card read: Dr. FAROUK ELTALWY, Ph.D., GOVERNOR OF THE NEW VALLEY GOVERNATE EGYPT, brown lettering on cream. Above the "L" and "W" in his surname an "LA" had been clumsily inserted in ballpoint.

Physically, with his thin, greased hair, wobbling jowls, and pencil-thin moustache, he resembled a sinister character, a fixer or white slave trader, a regular customer huddled beneath a fez in some corner table at Rick's Café in *Casablanca*. But he was actually a gentle, polite, and highly intelligent man, who clearly worked very hard and believed in his job, in his governate, and passionately.

Obviously some kind of political/business confab was taking place, but no one seemed to mind my presence, talking among themselves after I'd been introduced, which wasn't so easy since half the room was sixty feet away from the other half. Just as Governor Eltallawy began to answer my questions about the oases, a phone rang. Within the reach of both his arms were several different phones, some of them remote, at least one radio. It took a couple of tries before he located the right one.

I looked around the room. Many toys. Maxi-TV with video and numerous accessories; short-wave radio (to warn Cairo of revolutions?); electric cigarette lighter the size of a beer bottle, operated by merely picking it up (it didn't work); a combination electronic clock-calendar-calculator-computer-diary like the dashboard of a small starship, flashing a series of numbers and letters on its liquid-crystal screen. Many plaques and awards, too, as well as a vast array of local handicrafts, including the superb tableaux of clay figurines depicting village life by the sculptor Mabruk, whose skill at detailed satirical characterization was more art than craft, often imitated in Egypt but never matched.

Coffee arrived, and the governor apologized for his phone call, offering me a soft-pack Marlboro Light, which proved he'd travelled abroad recently. Banging around with the hefty desk lighter in vain, he ended up handing me a book of matches from a restaurant in Rome. What did I think of the New Valley? he wanted to know.

When I told him, he seemed genuinely moved, truly pleased. Hearing I would happily live in Dakhleh, he made a startling gesture: he offered me ten acres of land near the hot springs if I'd build a house on it. Since about thirty people witnessed the offer, I assume he meant it; and since you can build a Nubian-style palace in the Wadi Guedid for around five thousand dollars, I'm taking up his kind offer. It was then that I realized I was in the presence of a latter-day tribal chieftain, complete with his retinue of advisers and hangers-on, as well as the power to grant large favours, confer generous sinecures, present extravagant gifts.

He wanted the best for the oases, wanted to bring their people economic prosperity — wanted *tourism*. Yes, he confessed, he'd dearly like to make the New Valley into Europe's Palm Springs. Only outsiders hoped the place would never change; its inhabitants wanted better lives, schools, businesses, improved agricultural practices, technology … and tourist dollars. His only hope, he admitted, was to attract foreign investors, but these had little interest unless they could take their profits out of the country, in a currency that had value beyond Egypt. The minister of tourism, Fouad Sultan, the governor said, was working on this problem, but the process of gaining the confidence of foreign businessmen was going to be slow.

The Egyptian Tourist Authority would be the one to develop Wadi Guedid, not that that was necessarily bad. Minister Sultan told me that the health-giving properties of the hot springs were practically miracle cures for countless ailments and that the oases were high on his target list, just below the Red Sea resorts. Every Middle East "crisis," however, sets back Egyptian tourism a couple of years. Plans will be shelved, as they've been before, as they no doubt will be again. I thought of Naguib Mahfouz's image of Egypt as a group of drowning men struggling to reach the surface, seeing them thrust fathoms down again and again by the brutal hand of … what?

Governor Eltallawy enthused over his hot springs, asking whether I'd like to see a medical analysis of the waters' mineral salts. Why not? He asked a bookish-looking fellow in a grey Lycra leisure suit if a copy of this report were available. It was, oh, it was indeed, the man assured us, promising to get me a copy first thing the next day. I never saw the man again. Haroun promised he'd get the report posted to me. Of course it has never arrived.

Not wanting to hold up government business, I thanked the governor for my free land and for the beauty of his governate. With classical Arab courtesy, he tried to insist I stay, offered me more coffee, implored me to return soon, told me I would always be his honoured guest, and gave the impression I could have his house, his daughters, all his money, merely by asking for them. Such manners seem alien to us now, unnecessary and irritating; yet we in the West practised them ourselves not so long ago, in a slower world, a more humane time. An hour in New York always convinces me they should be brought back.

⌇

I was up before dawn, savouring the ancient stillness of Al-Khārga, walking its medieval lanes alone, basking in it. Mules snored in their sleep, leaning against the walls near the empty bazaar; camels slept in a large huddle nearby, burping occasionally, their front legs folded daintily and impossibly beneath their chests, their necks still upright, long-eyelashed eyes closed, like small furry sphinxes.

Strange animals, I thought, haughty, aloof, ugly, and graceful; their relationship with man more symbiotic than that of most domesticated beasts: able to take their owners across that parched wilderness no man could survive alone, yet able to do so only because their owners knew where water holes could be dug, wells could be found, humps could be gassed up. The relationship was more equal than most farmyard deals; hence the haughtiness, the self-possessed manner.

The muezzin called, and the eastern sky blushed at his exhortations, at his reminder that the barque of the sun had sailed around the whole world, returning with the light from which no man could hide. Roosters crowed; a camel cart with great creaking wood wheels carried a tiny old man in a clean white turban off for a morning in his fields. A group of girls with head scarves walked past with the same stately aplomb as the camels; and close behind them well-upholstered women slid out from alleys like royal barges. Al-Wadi Guedid was another hard place to leave.

At the guest house, Yussef and Haroun were waiting in the trusty Wagoneer, ready to go. First, I insisted, we must visit Mabruk's pottery. I was in no hurry, no hurry at all to head east of Eden.

Besides being a folk-art genius, Mabruk was no fool. Every member of his staff was not merely young, attractive, and female; they were probably the best-looking women in the whole New Valley. The place looked like a rustic modelling academy.

A wry, lethargic character, Mabruk showed me his work: dozens of clay figurines about a foot or so high arranged in groups. He had created a world in microcosm here, his consummate skill making clay into flesh, embedding tiny nuances of character in the twist of a smile, the angle of a finger. Nor was he shy about suggesting flaws of personality, subtle streaks of nastiness cloaked in piety or power.

A sly old mullah with many missing teeth and the expression of an arch pedant was waving a bony finger above an open Koran he held, expounding an especially severe sura to a semicircle of seated schoolchildren, who looked both terrified and bored; three old men shared a *sheesha* pipe and obviously spouted spurious and highly embellished anecdotes at each other; a young veiled woman held her newborn baby, her face expressing the deepest tenderness and maternal love; two young men, full of macho pride and bursting egotism, played *sheshbesh;* a plump woman, her manner radiant, prepared food for three impish and expectant children. The characters went on.

I wanted to buy this whole world so I could recreate a small Al-Khārga wherever I found myself. But the thought of opening a package of shattered fragments put me off.

"You choose one piece," Mabruk said.

"I couldn't break up a set." Each piece was an original; there were no moulds. "It'd be like breaking up a family, Mabruk."

"So which family you think should be broken up here?"

"Huh?"

"How about old mullah?" Mabruk said, pointing out the sly old cleric and his captive audience of bored kids. "You think those boys miss him?"

"Doubt it," I agreed. "I'd be doing them a favour. How much?"

Mabruk tutted, picking the sermonizing old pedant out of his classroom and handing him to me. "You give to your wife as present from Mabruk."

I was touched, although the governor had probably been behind this gesture in some way.

"*Mabruk!*" said Haroun. The sculptor's name also means "Congratulations" in Arabic.

And so I left Al-Khārga, heading to the airport, where the diligent Haroun had somehow contrived to get me bumped to first class for the flight to Cairo. Ushering me into the VIP lounge, an opulent but tacky sitting room, Haroun pointed out Governor Eltallawy and an entourage. He, too, was bound for Cairo, receiving a full military send-off by a few dozen armed troops lined up on the runway. Even crowds of locals gathered to cheer him up the steps to the airplane. He was indeed a potentate here, and a popular one.

We sat together, treated like deities by the crew, though at least no one suggested he or I take a shot at piloting the thing. Away from his retinue, his court, he became shyer, more reticent. Flying scared him, I realized. I liked him even more by the time we reached Cairo. His responsibility to his impossible job seemed almost a sacred obligation to him; and he clearly worked very hard indeed. Too hard, I thought, able to observe the toll these hours, this labour, was taking on his health. He slumped in his padded seat, unfailingly polite to any flight attendant or copilot who came up to say hello, but looking tired and overburdened when left alone.

By the baggage carousel in Cairo, met by another entourage, he resumed his amiably positive public persona, offering me a lift into town and, when I declined, again wishing me well, insisting I return to his kingdom soon. He had a new black Mercedes waiting outside — licence plate "2" — and he waved as he disappeared behind its smoked glass.

For some reason I felt his days were numbered. Perhaps, though, it was *my* days that were numbered. In fact, they were.

～っ

One day left before I returned to *my* kingdom. Did I understand the country I'd been in for three months now any better than I had when I'd arrived?

Heading into the eternal metal river of traffic back into the City of the Caliphs for the last time, I felt as if I'd merely expanded the range of my ignorance. Yet I also felt close to the Egyptian soul for the first time, able to refract my information through its prism.

I thought about the book I would write, its contradictions, unities, perplexities, certainties, beauties, and ugliness: all beads strung on the thread of my journey. In many ways it is the story of a love affair. Let me count the ways ...

CHAPTER TWENTY-THREE

ISLANDS IN THE SAND

The 1919 Revolution failed ... The nation reaped nothing but a crop of self-suspicion, egoism and hatred, between individuals and classes alike. The hopes which the 1919 Revolution was expected to realise faded. The fact that they faded only and did not die out is due to the natural resistance of those hopes which our nation had always entertained. This resistance was still alive then and preparing for another trial.

—GAMAL ABDEL NASSER,
THE PHILOSOPHY OF THE REVOLUTION, 1955

A farewell gift awaited me at the hotel. I'd been trying to meet the most widely respected man in Egyptian politics for some time, but, what with President Mubarak's lightning world tour and the upcoming Arab summit in Baghdad, he'd been even busier than usual, and he was usually busy. But suddenly here was an appointment with Boutros Boutros-Ghali, the minister of state for foreign affairs. Along with Mamdouh Beltagi, he was one of the most important men in Mubarak's life. (Just as I'd completed this book, he was elected secretary-general of the United Nations.)

The Ministry of Foreign Affairs was literally a palace, although it was soon to move into new headquarters resembling a five-star hotel on the banks of the Nile. The Arab League — by coincidence, not symbolic intent, one assumes — was set to move into the old palace. In a heavily guarded compound, it looked like a scaled-down Versailles: grand staircases, marble pillars, faded gilding, mighty doors. Unlike the other government offices I'd encountered, this one had an atmosphere of deadly seriousness and brisk efficiency. An aide who'd probably graduated top of his class at Harvard or somewhere informed me crisply that anything I wrote about my interview would be subject to security clearance. Did I understand that? The minister could spare me no more than twenty minutes.

Surrounded by about a million dollars' worth of eighteenth-century French antiques in an office that was tastefully grand yet cozy, Boutros Boutros-Ghali could have been the president of France or Italy. Elegant and courteous, he exuded an air of fierce concentration, forbidding intellect. Coffee was served, but small talk was minimal. I switched on my tape recorder; the aide switched on his.

"Let us go," the minister said, crossing his legs, knitting his brows. His black shoes were unnaturally shiny.

What *was* going on in the Arab world these days? I asked. What was this urgent call for unity about? And why was Egypt suddenly attempting to reassert its traditional role of Arab leadership?

Boutros-Ghali's answers were succinct. Egypt's role was due to geopolitical factors. Between the Arab countries of Asia and those of Africa, it was the only Afro-Asian country. There was also the demographic weight; one in three Arabs was an Egyptian. The country also enjoyed considerable technical and cultural advantages. Having had independence since 1922, Egypt got a head start on other Arab states, its sixteen universities attracting students from the entire Muslim world — 22,000 from Africa alone — as well as dispatching over two million Egyptian technicians to work in these foreign countries. This cultural weight was indisputable and operated independently of any crisis between Egypt and the other Arabs.

He meant, of course, the rift that had occurred after Sadat signed the peace treaty with Israel in March 1979. But, he was swift to point out, such disputes were common. The same thing had happened in September 1961 when Egypt ended its union with Syria. There were many ups and downs between Arab states outside Egypt — Iraq and Syria, Morocco and Algeria. "In fact," he told me, "in 1975 I wrote a book about inter-Arab disputes and found something like twenty-two of them." They would continue, too, until a system was found to settle them: an Arab International Court, for instance, or a permanent commission of arbitration.

I questioned his notion of an Afro-Asian country, saying I felt Egyptians were more Westernized than they realized. Yes, he agreed, again referring to cultural weight. Under Muhammad Ali, Egypt had been as important as any Mediterranean power, her armies reaching Constantinople, or fighting in Uganda.

I tried to get him to admit the real incentive to Arab unity was really Israel and the growing nuclear threat the Jewish state posed to the region. Mubarak, I said, was trying desperately to have weapons of mass destruction banned from the entire region, adding that no one I'd met believed for a moment this would happen. Boutros-Ghali's wife, I learned, was in fact Jewish, adding to the anomaly of his elevated rank in an Islamic state.

The minister agreed that the Arab League had been formed in 1945 to contain Israeli expansionism, but there were other reasons for Arab unity, he insisted. He cited the economic union of Europe then less than two years away. Already, plans had been discussed for an inter-Arab Common Market, with Egypt, Jordan, Iraq, and Yemen in the process of creating a trial economic association. Only Yemen now remains, thanks to the Kuwait crisis, Egypt barely on speaking terms with Iraq and Jordan over positions taken during the 1991 war. But the spectre of European unity still looms and worries Egypt. How can any developing nation compete with an economic bloc that scares even the Americans?

Did he picture an inter-Arab Common Market ever really happening? He suddenly looked sad, and I could tell I was treading over the broken fragments of youthful dreams. "I don't know," he replied gravely. "I don't want to make predictions." He paused, feeling he owed me an explanation.

"When I was a very young man, a student and militant in Paris after the war, I was in contact with many of the different Arab movements — '46, '47 — before the independence of the Magreb countries. In those days we were all under the impression that the United States of the Arab World would come about within ten or twenty years ... Now I am less optimistic."

I asked him who he thought this union would most benefit. It was more difficult, he admitted, to create economic unity among developing countries than it was among countries with an established tradition of economic development and political maturity. Another important factor in this kind of economic integration, he pointed out, was that the Arab countries with the smallest populations were the richest, the ones with the largest populations the poorest. There were two other contradictions standing in the road to integration. After disparity in wealth, there was disparity in size. Third, he went on, the Arab world was really like an archipelago, a group of islands separated by desert.

"You can drive," he explained, "from Paris to Moscow through unbroken civilization. But with Egypt, you have Cairo and Alexandria, then a vast desert after which you'll find Bengazi; then another huge desert and you'll find Tripoli. So you simply don't have the kind of infrastructure that will aid integration of the countries. Look at Syria and Iraq. Between Baghdad and Syria all you have is desert; there just isn't the geographical contiguity necessary for the possibility of integration."

There is now something far worse than desert between Syria and Iraq. I suspect Boutros-Ghali knew back in May 1990 that Saddam Hussein was about to shatter the dream of Arab integration, or at least postpone it for another decade — why else was the Arab summit going to be held in Baghdad? But his insights were devastatingly acute. I've never heard this geographical angle used by anyone else to explain the solitudes of the Arab world, obvious as it is.

I asked if he thought cultural differences were also a roadblock. The Egyptians, I said, sat on top of five thousand years of continuous civilization, whereas the Saudis had about five minutes' worth behind them.

Boutros-Ghali accepted this, but pointed out that the Arabs shared a common language, which, as the history of Europe has shown, counts for much more in the question of unity. "We have," he stated, "established a common market of the brain. An Egyptian doctor can work in a hospital anywhere in Saudi Arabia or in Yemen. An Iraqi professor can also work anywhere; a newspaperman … So at least we have this common background — the same language, the same religion. It's not so easy for a German doctor to work in Paris, but the same is not true for a Tunisian doctor working in Baghdad. At certain times we have over two million Egyptians working in Iraq."

Now, presumably, there are two million more unemployed Egyptians. His examples were unfortunate. Those Iraqi professors have had their academic horizons somewhat reduced, too, sending off résumés to Yemen, Sudan, and Jordan now.

On the subject of Israel he was more guarded. I suggested that Mubarak's campaign for making the Middle East a nuclear-free zone was simply not going to happen, and that Arabs and Israelis would only be able to negotiate on an equal basis when there was an Arab bomb — just as the United States and Russia could only achieve a meaningful peace treaty when they were equally strong.

"I totally disagree," the minister stated emphatically. "First of all nobody is sure an Israeli bomb exists, and secondly you have so many different weapons now that are comparable to the atomic bomb — the chemical warheads, the germ bombs — that equality exists. But I believe that if there is the political will, then it will be possible to find a solution. When we started the peace process in '78, everyone said *what!* — but obstacles were overcome, the treaty was concluded."

I said the treaty didn't appear to mean much in Israel's Knesset these days, but Boutros-Ghali was a formidable optimist. "Today maybe," he conceded. "But it does not mean it will not again be possible tomorrow. Or the day after."

I asked how he dealt with a government as volatile as Israel's, which that particular week didn't even appear to exist at all.

"We wait," he said. "That's all we can do. There'll be a new government one day, and then we'll try a new peace process."

Did he find it distressful to see the United States constantly supporting Israel?

"Certainly," he replied, but added calmly, "We, however, must share the responsibility for this. Ask yourself why the Arabs haven't been able to build up over the last twenty-eight years a lobby in the U.S. administration as strong as Israel's."

I asked him instead. The answer was rather pathetic. Out of the million or so Arabs living in the United States it was virtually impossible to find anyone willing to get involved in that kind of work. Even if an institution were established, Boutros-Ghali speculated, it would close within a couple of years because of apathy. The lack of continuity in Arab affairs resulted in a lack of credibility in Western political circles.

"I believe," he continued, "that the Arab world is just a newcomer in the field of international affairs. They don't have the sophistication yet. We've tried, but we've just not been successful. It's like asking someone in the middle of Africa to produce a Swiss watch. You need infrastructure, tradition, political imagination ..."

I cited Libyan support for Louis Farrakhan, the radical U.S. Black Muslim activist, and Saudi funding for notorious American neo-Nazis. "That proves the point, doesn't it?" he answered. "We've made mistakes. We did once have an arrangement with Mr. Fulbright, but we weren't able to use him." He didn't elaborate on this mysterious "arrangement." The Saudi lobby, however, had outmanoeuvred the Jewish lobby in 1981 over the AWACS sale.

We continued talking about the future, although neither of us then presumably knew the drastic turn events were soon to take. Egypt's concerns, Boutros-Ghali emphasized more than once, were with the growing north-south gulf, the conditions in those countries that contained the sources of the Nile, controlled the lifeblood of his country. He was deeply worried by the increasing marginalization of Africa. Egypt needed extra sources of water for the developments on the Red Sea coast and the projected new desert cities. And that water could only come from Ethiopia, Kenya, Uganda, Tanzania, Burundi, Zawanda, Zaire, and the Sudan — places that certainly weren't exactly famous for their skill at constructing elaborate storage lakes and pipeline systems. Egypt would have to help, but more than that she had to maintain special relationships with these countries to get such projects approved and carried out. That meant aid, technical assistance ... money. Being $55 billion in debt, Egypt still had an obligation to help those in even worse shape. There was a nobility in this attitude, even if a somewhat self-serving nobility.

But I sensed the minister could see the old order rapidly changing. The days of Chinese or Russian aid were over. Those countries had their own internal problems now, and the West was suddenly more concerned with rebuilding Eastern Europe than with helping the developing nations. "Even certain European countries belonging to the south, like Portugal, are being marginalized," he said. "The political will needed to deal with problems of the south is vanishing. We're on our own, and we will have to do the best we can."

The new Iron Curtain was closing — closing out the horrors of the South from an increasingly self-centred North.

My footsteps resounding loudly on the marble floors, I left the Ministry of Foreign Affairs a wiser man. The country that Muhammad Ali wanted to make part of Europe was now resigned to making itself part of Africa, determined to construct a Rolex factory in the heart of darkness. But with men like Boutros-Ghali in control, Egypt had a fighting chance to make itself once more the dominating force on the continent, I felt. Raped and then abandoned by the West, she was just now regaining her pride and self-respect. What doesn't kill you makes you stronger. I could feel Egypt getting stronger, tougher — preparing for the greatest battle she has ever faced and determined to win.

It was curious that the most optimistic Egyptian I encountered was not only minister of state for foreign affairs but also a Christian married to a Jew. Curious, and yet somehow so typically Egyptian. He will prove to be one of the most effective secretary-generals in the checkered history of the United Nations, I suspect. Egypt's loss will be the world's gain.

CRY ME A RIVER

*Monday, 1 July [1850] ... Farewells ... My sadness at leaving
makes me realize what elation I must have felt on arrival ...
Our last night ... Up until three in the morning ... Dawn.
Cocks crow, my two candles are lit. I am sweating, my eyes are
burning. I have early morning chills. How many nights behind
me! In four hours I leave Cairo. Farewell, Egypt! Allah! as the
Arabs say.*

—GUSTAVE FLAUBERT, TRAVEL NOTES, 1850

My last night in Cairo. From the A-1 Stables in Giza I rented a white Arab
stallion an hour before sunset, galloping far out into the desert until the
pyramids were on my horizon, the only sign of human existence visible.
I was in better shape than Flaubert. The horse was a magnificent creature,
rippling with power and eager to run with me forever into the night,
beyond the bounds of earth and time, back to the gods of ancient Egypt.
We paused in a silent wilderness of jagged stones and sprouting shadows

to watch the body of Re touch the earth somewhere over Qattara, near the Sand Dune Sea. I recalled a translation I'd read of one of the Old Kingdom Pyramid Texts:

I know his name, Eternity is his name,
"Eternity, the master of years" is his name,
exalted over the vault of the sky,
bringing the sun to life every day.

And then another fragment came unbidden, a comment made by the supreme Lord of Creation in a magical text called *The Book of the Two Ways* written over four thousand years ago: "The gods I created from my sweat, but mankind is from the tears of mine eye."

Re's blood now streaming in the firmament, staining even the sleek white coat of my restless stallion a raw, fleshy pink. I felt myself outside creation, a lone speck of consciousness in an empty void. What secret did those pyramid builders know? Why *did* God create man? I tied my *kaffiyeh* back to stop the crazy wind troubling it, and as I did, the answer arrived, so obvious: because man is more moral than God.

Kicking the stirrups, lashing out with the crop, I galloped with my mount like a quarter of the Apocalypse toward the gathering gloom rising like smoke above Cairo. I've never ridden so fast and so urgently in my life, part of me terrified that I would find another desert beyond the pyramids, that I would be alone upon a deserted planet forever.

Thundering up to the sandy ridge on the western side of the Giza complex, I finally reined in the supernatural beast, slowing to a canter, then a walk. Flecks of foam around his mouth twinkled, his massive body heaved, and I could feel his animal heat in my legs.

Sitting on a folded chair just back from the ridge was a very old Western woman with a large sketch pad on her lap. Her moon-white hair was tied back in a clumsy bun, and the withered folds of her pale jaw quivered as she replaced paintbrushes and watercolour tubes in a stained wooden carrying case. I stopped, standing in the stirrups, stroking the horse's mane. On the old woman's sketch pad I could see part of an exquisitely detailed painting of the two main pyramids. Suddenly the woman turned around, staring at me with a look of puzzled yet pleasurable shock.

"James," she said in a quavering, very British accent. "You're back."

"Pardon?" I replied.

"They killed poor Richard, you know?"

"Who did?"

"I told him it was time to get out. He wouldn't listen, you know. We should let them all kill each other, don't you think?"

"Let who …?"

"Go back to the barracks, James," she urged me. "A good bath and a scotch; you'll feel much better."

It did seem like a good idea, so I told her so.

"Have you heard anything from Aqaba?" she inquired.

"Not recently. I was there a few weeks ago, though."

"Oh dear," she sighed, shaking her head. "There are rumours running rife. One fears the worst."

"What sort of rumours?"

"The tribes revolted, took everything, and deserted the bally place. I never thought we should have trusted those savages, did you?"

I shrugged.

"There you are," she said. "There you are. Now you run along and have a nice bath and a good stiff drink. Toodle-ooh."

"Toodle-ooh," I told her, turning my horse south along the track back to the stables, in the awesome shadow of the booming black mountain men had placed there at the beginning, knowing it would still be there at the end.

❧

After dinner I walked along the Nile Corniche. By October 6 Bridge crowds were gathered, buying fresh-roasted corn from ash-covered men with little braziers and sitting to eat them on benches or on the sloping grass verges. The night was hot and swarming, yet the slow, ancient river still managed to dispatch cooling breezes. Passing by the Nile Hilton and under Tahrir Bridge, I found benches packed with shy lovers enjoying an illicit moment of freedom from the strict glare of their families. Many people stared across the chaotic teeming road with mournful longing at the lights of the glitzy new Semiramis Hotel, where chauffeured limousines were dropping off rich Cairenes in evening dress for a wedding party.

Past Shepheard's Hotel, the Corniche darkened, and the twisted roots of banyan trees drooped like tentacles. On a bench beneath them an old turbaned man slumped, dozing; in his lap a monkey dressed in a red jacket decorated with little bells lay asleep, too. I'd seen the pair before, the monkey performing cartwheels and dances while the man collected piastres from passersby. They were a team. Beyond the Nile Long-Distance Swimming Association — which seemed dark and deserted because, I liked to think, all its members had died from dysentery or cholera or any of the encyclopedic range of malicious organisms encountered on their long-distance swims — beyond this club of suicidal fools, the throbbing mass of the city itself seemed to grow darker. A few lights glimmered in the American embassy, safe behind its massive wall, half-obscured by the old choking trees of Garden City.

Nearby, two old Gulf Arabs in pristine white *gelabias* and neatly folded *kaffiyehs* leaned on a low white wall, staring in rapt silence at the play of lights from Gezira Island's rich homes and hotels on the black waters below. I'd often seen a similar sight along the Corniche. For these desert Arabs the river held endless fascination; many vacationed in Cairo just to spend their days staring at this vision from their nomads' paradise. They were motionless except for the steady rattle of worry beads revolving in their fingers — keeping count, I thought facetiously, of the millions being pumped from the sand into their bank accounts while they stood there.

Reaching the tree-lined compound of the Meridien Hotel, I crossed over to Roda Island, taking a narrow, dingy path past the hotel's garbage bins and kitchen waste, emerging into a small, shadowy street at the end of which huddles of people stood beneath streetlamps or by roast-corn braziers. Drawing nearer, I could see they were all waiting outside the gates of a run-down hospital, many purchasing food to take to relatives within, some with faces riven by anxiety or sorrow, expecting to hear at any moment news that would, whether good or bad, change their lives utterly.

It was a tragic street, and I was happy to emerge at Al-Gamaa Bridge, crossing over to the west bank and the blazing shoe-store windows on Nasser Avenue. Although it was nearly midnight, a ragged old man was still fishing from the bridge, his sorrowful lined face implying he'd had no luck and might have to return home to a hungry family empty-handed. The streets leading north back toward Gezira were dim and yawning, flanked by fortified mansions watched by armed security guards in gloomy little sentry boxes. The people who lived here constantly feared that the Muslim Brotherhood might at any minute stage the fundamentalist revolution it ceaselessly threatened. The rich are right to fear the poor, both conditions inextricably interlinked, mutually reproachful.

Returning to October 6 Bridge, I was almost relieved to cross the island and see the countless lights of Cairo's hectic heart sparkling over on the east bank once more. At the centre of the long, broad bridge several cars were parked, all festooned with flowers and streamers. Without warning, a thunder of drums erupted, and a throng of smartly dressed Cairenes began shouting and singing. By the time I had reached this wild, incongruous group, I noticed, standing twenty or so yards from each other, two brides in unimaginably ornate and frothy white wedding dresses. Layered and puffed out in the traditional Western style, these dresses had been made even more complicated by added frills and veils. Both brides leaned over the stone wall throwing objects into the Nile, their bridegrooms at their sides. Behind them, wedding guests thumped drums and sang, occasionally blasting car horns, too.

It was a custom. On your wedding night you made an offering to the river that had given Egypt life since the dawn of time. The river that, flowing through the desert, tamed its inhospitable nature, making life possible, making civilization possible. Passing the second bride, her dress billowing in the river's breeze, glowing in the moonlight, I saw she was crying as she gazed at the man with whom she was going to spend the rest of her life.

Perhaps, I thought, this eternal river in the desert flows from the tears of God's eye. For those tears made humans, and only humans were able to create the incomparable splendour of Egypt, a land where God has been glorified by His creation throughout the span of human history, and a land where God first revealed Himself to the being He had created from His tears, setting the creature free to build a world of its own.

The bride wiped at her tears, smudging half a pound of mascara. Then she turned, laughing and sobbing, to throw a red rose down into the rippling basalt waters.

We sail across dominions barely seen, washed by the swells of time. We plow through fields of magnetism. Past and future come together on thunderheads and our dead hearts live with lightning in the wounds of the Gods.

—NORMAN MAILER, *ANCIENT EVENINGS*

Cairo–London–Toronto, 1990–1992.

SUGGESTED SELECTED
READING LIST

Al-Ghitani, Gamal. *Zayni Barakat*. Penguin International, 1990.

Bentley, James. *The Secrets of Mount Sinai*. New York: Doubleday, 1986.

Budge, E. A. Wallis. *The Gods of the Egyptians*. 2 vols. New York: Dover, 1969.

— . *The Egyptian Book of the Dead*. New York: Dover, 1967.

Carter, Howard. *The Tomb of Tutankhamon*. New York: Dutton, reissued 1972.

Desroches-Noblecourt, Christiane. *Tutankhamen: Life and Death of a Pharaoh*. New York: Penguin, 1976.

Durrell, Lawrence. *The Alexandria Quartet (Justine; Balthazar; Mountolive; Clea)*. New York: Penguin, 1982.

Edwards, Amelia B. *A Thousand Miles up the Nile*. London: J. P. Tarcher, 1983.

Fathy, Hassan. *Architecture for the Poor*. Chicago: University of Chicago Press, 1973.

Forster, E. M. *Alexandria: A History and a Guide*. Intro. Lawrence Durrell. London: Michael Haag, reprint, 1982.

Giles, F. J. *Ikhnaton: Legend and History*. Rutherford, NJ: Fairleigh Dickinson University Press, 1972.

Herodotus. *The Histories* Trans. A. de Sellincourt. New York: Penguin, 1954.

Hoffman, Michael A. *Egypt Before the Pharaohs.* New York: Alfred A. Knopf, 1979.

Hoving, Thomas. *Tutankhamun: The Untold Story.* New York: Simon and Schuster, 1978.

Karnouk, Liliane. *Modern Egyptian Art: The Emergence of a National Style.* Cairo, Egypt: The American University in Cairo Press, 1988.

Lamy, Lucie. *Egyptian Mysteries.* London: Crossroad/Thames and Hudson, 1981.

Lawrence, T. E. *Seven Pillars of Wisdom: A Triumph.* New York: Doubleday, 1991.

Lemesurier, Peter. *The Great Pyramid Decoded.* London: Element Books/Tempest Brookline, 1985.

Lurker, Manfred. *The Gods and Symbols of Ancient Egypt.* London: Thames and Hudson, 1980.

McPherson, Bimbashi. *The Man Who Loved Egypt.* London: Ariel Books/BBC, 1983.

Mahfouz, Naguib. *The Cairo Trilogy (Palace Walk; Palace of Desire; Sugar Street).* New York: Doubleday, 1990; 1991.

Mitchell, Timothy. *Colonizing Egypt.* Cairo, Egypt: American University in Cairo Press, 1988.

Montet, Pierre. *Eternal Egypt.* Trans. Doreen Weightman. New York: New American Library, 1964.

Murray, Margaret. *The Splendor That Was Egypt.* New York: Praeger, 1972.

Pellegrino, Charles. *Unearthing Atlantis.* New York: Random House, 1991.

Piankoff, Alexandre. *The Shrines of Tut-Ankh-Amon.* Princeton, NJ: Princeton University Press, 1955.

——. *The Tomb of Ramesses VI.* Princeton, NJ: Princeton University Press, 1954.

Posener, G., ed. *Dictionary of Egyptian Civilization.* London: Methuen, 1962.

Redford, Donald B. *Akhenaten: The Heretic King.* Princeton, N.J.: Princeton University Press, 1984.

Robichon, J., and Alexandre Varille. *Le Temple du Scribe royal Amenhotep fils de Hapou.* Paris: Sorbonne Press, 1936.

Schwaller de Lubicz, Isha. *Her-Bak.* London: Inner Traditions, 1955.

——. *Her-Bak, Egyptian Initiate.* London: Inner Traditions, 1955.

— . *The Temple in Man.* Trans. Robert and Deborah Lawlor. London: Inner Traditions, 1977.

— . *Sacred Science.* Trans. André and Goldian Vandenbroeck. London: Inner Traditions, 1982.

— . *Nature Word.* Trans. Deborah Lawlor. London: Lindisfarne Press, 1982.

Said, Edward W. *Covering Islam.* New York: Pantheon, 1981.

Steegmuller, Francis, ed. and trans. *Flaubert in Egypt: A Sensibility on Tour.* Boston: Little, Brown, 1972.

West, John Anthony. *Serpent in the Sky: The High Wisdom of Ancient Egypt.* New York: Harper and Row, 1979.

— . *The Traveler's Key to Ancient Egypt: A Guide to the Sacred Places of Ancient Egypt.* New York: Alfred A. Knopf, 1985.

— . *The Case for Astrology.* New York: Viking, 1992.

INDEX